ELECTIONEERING AND PROPAGANDA IN IRELAND,
1917–21

Electioneering and Propaganda in Ireland, 1917–21

Votes, Violence and Victory

ELAINE CALLINAN

FOUR COURTS PRESS

Set in 10.5 pt on 12.5 pt Ehrhardt MT for
FOUR COURTS PRESS LTD
7 Malpas Street, Dublin 8, Ireland
www.fourcourtspress.ie
and in North America for
FOUR COURTS PRESS
c/o IPG, 814 N Franklin St, Chicago, IL 60610

A catalogue record for this title is available
from the British Library.

ISBN 978-1-84682-870-6

Printed in England
by CPI Antony Rowe Ltd, Chippenham, Wilts.

For Cli

Contents

Acknowledgments

It is a great pleasure to be able at last to acknowledge all those who have contributed and helped in the production of this book. Many scholarly and personal debts were accrued and this is the moment where my heartfelt appreciation can be expressed to those who shared generously of their time and knowledge. This book had its origin as a PhD thesis in Trinity College Dublin and I am deeply grateful to my supervisor, the late Professor David Fitzpatrick, whose profound knowledge of contemporary Irish history and scholarly talent were awe-inspiring. He kindly imparted it with generosity and with his inimitable leadership style he encouraged students to strive for the best possible work that they could produce. In the latter years, my co-supervisor Dr Anne Dolan shared hours discussing the project and the critique she gladly gave to enhance the narrative contributed enormously, and for that I am truly thankful. I would also like to extend thank-yous to Professor Eunan O'Halpin of TCD and Dr Marie Coleman of Queen's University Belfast for their insightful comments and suggestions, and to Dr Fionnuala Walsh for her kind assistance and practical support. I thank also Martin Fanning and Sam Tranum of Four Courts Press who made the publication of this work possible.

The motivation and encouragement to follow a path in history came from a fellow colleague and good friend in Carlow College, St Patrick's. The knowledge and generosity of the late Fr Fintan Morris and his love of history deserves special mention. He was an inspiration, and he is sadly and deeply missed. I extend heartfelt gratitude to President Conn O'Maoldomhnaigh, Dr Thomas McGrath, Dr Margaret Murphy and all the other lecturers in Carlow College for imparting their wisdom and for their continued support and patience. Carlow College kindly provided a grant towards the publication of this book.

Motivation for the topic of this book also came from my many years of employment in the marketing, advertising and public-relations sector and for that I need to thank Wilson Hartnell Public Relations and all those I worked with there for many years, particularly its chairman Roddy Guiney, who was a great boss and colleague. The practical and theoretical knowledge gleaned from my history studies and past work experience in PR led to a desire to combine both fields into a specific history study.

I am deeply indebted to the librarians and archivists of the many repositories I visited to conduct this research, particularly the National Library of Ireland, Trinity College Dublin Library and Archives, the Public Record Office of Northern Ireland, the University College Dublin Archives, the National Archives of Ireland, the Military Archives in Rathmines, Dublin, and the many county libraries that I visited during the course of my research. All went above and beyond the call of duty to locate material, and responded to my many requests with great patience and efficiency. I also thank the American Irish Historical Society for accommodating my very pleasant visit to their archive.

To Maureen Egerton for all her practical help, and to all my personal friends who have given encouragement and gone the extra mile to be of assistance, and oftentimes carried out life's mundane chores on my behalf, my sincere thanks. I am in the very fortunate position of there being too many to mention by name.

My family have been a tremendous help over the past number of years both practically and emotionally. They have suffered through being ignored and forgotten, and they have proved wonderfully resilient and have continued to achieve excellence in everything they do. So, to my husband Caimin Keenan and two wonderful children Niamh and Matthew Callinan Keenan, I thank you from the bottom of my heart. I would also like to thank my brother John and his wife Rachel for their kindness and help.

I pay tribute also to my late parents John and Eileen (neé Doyle) Callinan who gave me so much in life, and to my Aunt Carmel, who cared for my children in many ways when she was here, which enabled me to continue with my studies. Last, but most certainly not least, I thank my late younger sister Cliodhna Callinan. This work could not have happened without her kindness and benevolence in funding all my studies. For that and for much much more, I dedicate this book to her memory with love.

Tables and plates

TABLES

PLATES

Appearing between pages 160 and 161

List of abbreviations

AC	*Anglo-Celt*
AFIL	All-for-Ireland-League
AIHS	American Irish Historical Society
AOH	Ancient Order of Hibernians
BMH	Bureau of Military History
BNL	*Belfast News-Letter*
CC	*Clare Champion*
CE	*Cork Examiner*
CT	*Connacht Tribune*
DÉD	Dáil Éireann Debates
DORA	Defence of the Realm Act
FH	*Fermanagh Herald*
FJ	*Freeman's Journal*
FOIF	Friends of Irish Freedom
GAA	Gaelic Athletic Association
HC	house of commons
HL	house of lords
II	*Irish Independent*
ILPU	Irish Loyal and Patriotic Union
ILP&TUC	Irish Labour Party and Trade Union Congress
IPP	Irish Parliamentary Party
IRA	Irish Republican Army
IRB	Irish Republican Brotherhood
IRC	Irish Recruiting Council
IT	*Irish Times*
ITGWU	Irish Transport and General Workers' Union
ITUC	Irish Trade Union Congress
ITUC&LP	Irish Trade Union Congress and Labour Party
IUA	Irish Unionist Alliance
IWFL	Irish Women's Franchise League
JD	John Dillon
JR	John Redmond
KP	*Kilkenny People*
LGB	local-government board
LkL	*Limerick Leader*
LL	*Longford Leader*
MP	member of parliament
NA	National Archives, Kew, London
NAI	National Archives of Ireland

NLI	National Library of Ireland
NLT	*Nationalist and Leinster Times*
NW	*Northern Whig*
PB	Piaras Béaslaí
PD	Parliamentary Debates
PR-STV	proportional representation–single transferrable vote
PRONI	Public Record Office of Northern Ireland
RDC	rural district council
RH	*Roscommon Herald*
RIC	Royal Irish Constabulary
SC	*Sligo Champion*
SCh	*Strabane Chronicle*
SFSCM	Sinn Féin Standing Committee Meeting
SIPTU	Services, Industrial, Professional and Technical Union
TCD	Trinity College Dublin
TD	teachta dála (member of parliament)
UCDA	University College Dublin Archives
UH	*Ulster Herald*
UIL	United Irish League
UUC	Ulster Unionist Council
UULA	Ulster Unionist Labour Association
UVF	Ulster Volunteer Force
UWUC	Ulster Women's Unionist Council
WS	witness statement

Author's note

A short note on nomenclature is necessary in a work of this kind and I begin with place names because Londonderry was also referred to as Derry. When referring to both city and county I have used Londonderry for convenience, without implying any political preference, and because this was mainly (but not exclusively) how the county was referred to in newspapers of the era. The *Cork Examiner* is the name given for this newspaper because it was used during the era under study as the newspaper initially covered the Munster region. It changed its title to the *Examiner* in 1996 and changed again in 2000 to become the *Irish Examiner*.

Unionists in Ireland belonged to a number of parties or movements, such as the Unionist Party, Irish Unionist Alliance, Municipal Reform, Ratepayers and so on. Unionists are often discussed in the generic sense to cover all with general sympathies towards maintaining the 1801 Acts of Union. I have also referred to Sinn Féin as 'separatists' and this was to distinguish them from their constitutional-nationalist rivals. Some have preferred 'advanced nationalists', but I see neither as more advanced than the other so have opted for the term 'separatist' to describe the desire for a complete separation from the Westminster parliament. Irish Volunteers and Cumann na mBan Volunteers receive a capital V to differentiate them from general volunteers or voluntary work.

The Labour Party began as the Irish Trades Union Congress and Labour Party and it was not until 1919 that the words 'Labour Party' featured before rather than after 'Trade(s) Union Congress'. For ease of understanding this work will refer to the party as the Labour Party throughout unless the specific party title or its abbreviation is used.

The use of the *síneadh fada* (acute or long accent) in the Irish language was irregular in this era, particularly in newspaper editorials and often in Sinn Féin's own propaganda. Because the word '*féin*' (self) means nothing without its *fada* it will always be used in this work even when directly quoting from material that did not use it. The *fada* will also be retained for the sake of consistency for the slang term Sinn 'Féiners' even though there is no such word or translation. Translations are provided in this work, but it is important to note that translations from Irish to English are sometimes approximate because often there is no satisfactory literal translation.

The electoral contests in this book take place before partition and cover the entire island of Ireland. Therefore, any references to Ulster comprise all nine counties of the province, although some analysis is included on election results in the six counties that go on to form Northern Ireland after partition.

Introduction

'I am in for a fierce struggle in East Mayo. Result uncertain … [T]he organized intimidation is terrific, and it is quite possible that I may be heavily beaten owing to the terror of the people,' John Dillon, leader of the Irish Parliamentary Party, exclaimed in December 1918.[1]

Election campaigns and their consequences can be turning points in history. The 1918 general election was the first modern election in the British Isles with its mass-media propaganda campaigns, systemization of electoral practice and democratization of the electorate. Politicians, propagandists and their voluntary supporters instigated forceful campaigns to promote ideologies that aimed to alter or imbed their established principles in the mindset of ordinary individuals, and the goal was victory at the ballot box. The 1917–18 by-elections, the 1918 general election, the 1920 local elections and the 1921 'partition' election motivated and inspired the majority of people to engage in decisions that went on to alter the course of Irish history. Running contemporaneously with war and revolution in this era were the political struggles, and they equalled any of the military upheavals that transformed politics in Ireland.

Sinn Féin evolved during 1917 to form into a cohesive party and their arrival challenged the constitutional narrative of the Irish Parliamentary Party's (IPP's) nationalist politics. Unionists were galvanized to defend the union and demonstrate their loyalty to the crown, and they systematically organized to secure electoral majorities in their Ulster strongholds. The upward curve of trade-union membership inspired confidence within the Labour Party to aspire to political representation in elections. Compelling propaganda that was fraught with controversy was unleashed by all political interests on the voting public, aiming to alter attitudes and reinforce entrenched beliefs. The 1918 general election was perceived by many as a plebiscite to decide on a favoured form of self-governance for the imminent arrival of independence – the Labour Party proffered this as the main reason for abstaining from this year's contest. Unionists, nationalists, separatists and Labour (until their withdrawal in the 1918 electoral contest) competed for votes in eighty constituencies to win electoral favour. The local-government elections two years later saw political interests, which now included the Labour Party, battle to secure constituencies at the local level, and the 1921 elections set the stage for clashes over partition, primarily in Ulster. These election campaigns and their results led to the establishment of Dáil Éireann, triggered the War of Independence and fuelled partition. Military insurgency and counter-insurgency during Ireland's revolutionary struggles has received extensive analysis, but the transformative political upheavals in this period remain neglected, and this is the void that this book aims to fill.

---

1 TCD Archives, JD, MSS 6742/567: John Dillon to T.P. O'Connor, 6 Dec. 1918.

The use of propaganda throughout election campaigns allowed political parties or movements to gain or hold onto power, oppose entrenched ideas or advocate for a cause.[2] An examination of the electioneering and propaganda campaigns reveals the extant divergent political ideologies in Ireland in this era because they were embedded within the dialogue, debates and conflicts that were presented in word, text, image and theme. The pursuit of obtaining votes and winning favour with the electorate was, and is, essentially a marketing or propaganda function.[3] It involved not only devising clever and creative ideas to promote policies, but also adroit strategies to convince and convert. By honing in specifically on how each party executed their propaganda campaigns, a multifaceted assessment of the electioneering strategies can be provided. The 1918 general election was extraordinary because within a period of eight years the IPP, which since its foundation had dominated politics on the home rule issue, went from political success to a cataclysmic fall, and a new order seized power. It is perhaps helpful to provide some background briefly, to give historical context.

In 1870 Isaac Butt, a Protestant lawyer, coined the term 'home rule' when he established the Home Government Association to seek a new Irish parliament. In 1873 the association was re-formed into the Home Rule League and Charles Stewart Parnell took over. Parnell swiftly exerted influence and with his New Departure in 1879 he convinced Fenians and home rulers to follow a constitutional path to establish an Irish parliament. In the 1880 general election the League won 62 of the 103 Irish parliamentary seats (2 later defected to the Liberals). The IPP did not drop below this number of seats until the 1918 general election. Parnell's success saw him elected chairman of the party in 1880 after the death of Butt and in 1882 he changed the name to the Irish Parliamentary Party.

Parnell's aggressive rhetoric on land reform and education, along with obstructionist tactics at Westminster, led Liberal Prime Minister William E. Gladstone to introduce the first home rule bill in April 1886, but the union or 'orange' card was played and as will be seen in chapter 2 the bill was defeated. The home rule crisis of 1885 and 1886 was marked by two climactic general elections and these transformed the IPP into a truly effective and disciplined political force at Westminster, but Gladstone was routed (see chapter 4).[4] He returned as prime minister after the 1892 general election, and attempted a second government of Ireland (home rule) bill in February 1893. After much debate, the bill passed in the house of commons but was rejected by the house of lords, and Gladstone left office in March 1894.[5]

---

2 Stephen A. Seidman, *Posters, propaganda and persuasion in election campaigns around the world and through history* (NY, 2008), p. 2.   **3** Patrick Butler and Neil Collins, 'Political marketing: structure and process' in Paul R. Baines (ed.), *Political marketing: concepts and theories* (LA, 2011), i, p. 2.   **4** See K. Theodore Hoppen, *Elections, politics and society in Ireland, 1832–1885* (Oxford, 1984) and Brian Walker, 'Parliamentary representation in Ulster, 1868–86' (TCD, PhD, 1976) for more on elections in the 1800s.   **5** Richard Shannon, 'Peel, Gladstone and party', *Parliamentary History*, 18:3 (1999), 317–52; Mary E. Daly and K. Theodore Hoppen (eds), *Gladstone, Ireland and beyond* (Dublin, 2011).

Constitutional nationalists challenged rivals in these electoral contests and those of the 1890s were often adversarial and marred with violence (although there were uncontested constituencies too). After the fall of Parnell, pro- and anti-Parnellites contested in heated by-elections in Kilkenny North in December 1890, Sligo North in April 1891 and Carlow in July that same year.[6] In 1892 and 1895 bitter electoral contests were fought between these two opposing factions, and while both laid claim to home rule, there were deep divergences of opinion on party policy, particularly in regard to whether to ally themselves with the Liberal Party.[7] While on a par with 1918 in terms of antagonistic electoral rhetoric, they were not fought on political principles but were fraught with acrimonious and personalized clashes that resemble more the contests of the early 1920s between pro- and anti-treatyites.

Following the 1895 general election, the Conservatives were in power for ten years. During this time the significant Local Government (Ireland) Act 1898 (following the English act of 1888) was introduced, providing for the first time the enfranchisement of local electors, and this initiated a system of localized home rule in many areas. In 1900, under the unanimously agreed leadership of John Redmond MP, the IPP merged with the United Irish League (UIL), and the UIL became accepted as the main support organization of parliamentary nationalists. The Liberals were returned in the 1906 general election with an overall majority, so Irish home rule was not on their agenda. However, after the 1910 general elections the IPP held the balance of power – in December they secured 74 seats in Westminster (plus ten more nationalist seats were won). In 1910 most IPP MPs had been returned unopposed, but again repeated hostile clashes broke out between IPP-UIL supporters and those of William O'Brien's All-For-Ireland-League (AFIL) in Cork, and against Timothy Healy in Louth. Weightier contests against unionists had taken place in Dublin and areas of Ulster, and volatile resistance to home rule had necessitated painstaking IPP negotiation tactics.[8]

After the 1910 electoral victories Redmond made strident demands for home rule by agreeing to support the Liberals and their 1909 'people's budget'. The irony was that the budget also created a weapon for Redmond to bring down the power of the house of lords, captured comprehensively in the slogan 'no veto no budget'.[9] The Liberals wanted their budget and Redmond wanted home rule and this led to the passing of the Parliament Act in 1911 by a narrow 131–114 vote.[10] This act abolished the veto of the Lords over legislation and replaced it with a

6 For further information, see Tom Garvin, 'Nationalist elites, Irish voters and Irish political development: a comparative perspective', *Economic and Social Review*, 8:3 (1977), 166   7 F.S.L. Lyons, 'The machinery of the Irish Parliamentary Party in the general election of 1895', *Irish Historical Studies*, 8:30 (Sept. 1952), 115–39; James McConnel, *The Irish Parliamentary Party and the third home rule crisis* (Dublin, 2013).   8 *Times*, 21 Mar. and 4 Apr.; 29 and 30 June and 2, 3 and 6 July 1891; *IT*, 2 Feb. 1910.   9 Michael Wheatley, *Nationalism and the Irish Party, provincial Ireland, 1910–1916* (Oxford, 2005), p. 158.   10 Hansard, HL Debates, vol. 9, cc 1075–7 (1911).

mere suspensory power.[11] This paved the way for the introduction of the third home rule bill in 1912.

Without the protection of the house of lords' veto, militant opposition by unionists was led by Edward Carson and James Craig and the anti-home rule campaign was launched on 25 September 1911. The organization of mass demonstrations, the creation of the Solemn League and Covenant and the formation of the Ulster Volunteer Force (UVF) were the armaments to defeat home rule, along with a propaganda campaign to undermine and destabilize Redmond's plan (see chapter 4).[12] In the southern provinces inspiration to form a retaliatory militia force led to the creation of the Irish National Volunteers (Óglaigh na hÉireann). Subsequently, a number of women formed their own organization called Cumann na mBan to work in conjunction with the recently formed Irish Volunteers.[13] In similar fashion to the electoral support given by the Ancient Order of Hibernians to the IPP in the 1800s, members of these Volunteer movements ran as candidates and campaigned for their favoured side in the elections of 1917 to 1921 (see chapters 2 and 3). Back in 1914 both the Irish and Ulster Volunteers successfully imported arms, placing Ireland on the brink of civil war.

The establishment of the Irish Volunteers posed a threat to both Herbert Asquith's Liberal government and Redmond's party. By June 1914 Redmond decided it was time to assert his authority over the Volunteers, so he negotiated with Eoin MacNeill to have twenty-five IPP members included on the provisional committee. MacNeill, despite the opposition of Bulmer Hobson and other members of the Irish Republican Brotherhood (IRB), accepted the demand. The Buckingham Palace Conference attempted to appease all sides but after three days the conference broke up without agreement on Ulster. The unfolding Great War in Europe eclipsed the internal domestic tensions.

At the outbreak of the war most county councils across Ireland voiced unconditional support for Redmond when he pledged at Westminster that the Volunteers would defend the coastlines of Ireland.[14] However, after he broadened this later to 'wherever the firing lines extends', the mood began to subtly alter.[15] A split developed in the Irish Volunteer movement, but the majority remained on the side of Redmond. Prior to the split the numbers enrolled in the Volunteer movement totalled approximately 188,000, and of this only 13,000 adhered to the original provisional committee, opposing Redmond (there are variations in these figures, however the overall ratios are similar).[16] Meanwhile, home rule was

---

11 Alvin Jackson, *Ireland, 1798–1998: war, peace and beyond* (Oxford, 2010), p. 161; Elaine Callinan, 'Discourse and discord: the rhetoric and rationale of John Redmond in the pursuit of home rule for Ireland, 1910–1914' (TCD, MPhil, 2011).   12 A.T.Q. Stewart, *The Ulster crisis: resistance to home rule, 1912–14* (London, 1967).   13 Cal McCarthy, *Cumann na mBan and the Irish Revolution* (Dublin, 2007).   14 See for example, *Nationalist and Leinster Times (NLT)*, 8 Aug. 1914; *Drogheda Independent*, 8 Aug. 1914; *Clare Champion (CC)*, 8 Aug. 1914; and *Cork Examiner (CE)*, 4 and 5 Aug. 1914.   15 See *Weekly IT*, 22 Aug. 1914; F.X. Martin, *The Irish Volunteers, 1913–1915: recollections and documents* (Newbridge, Co. Kildare, 1963), p. 148.   16 *Westmeath Independent* and *Sligo Champion (SC)*, 26 Sept. 1914; Wheatley, *Nationalism and the Irish Party*, pp 208–12; J.J. Lee, *Ireland, 1912–1986* (Cambridge, 1989), p. 22.

enacted with an amending bill for Ulster, and subsequently frozen for the war's duration.[17]

In 1912 the formation of a home rule parliament in Dublin seemed almost tangible, but by 1918 all had changed. Unionists, in their belief that the union was 'the constitutional form best designed to protect Irish Protestants from subjugation to a Catholic majority', had refused to accept a Dublin parliament.[18] The Volunteer split, the aftermath of the Easter Rising, the breakdown of home rule negotiations in 1916 and 1917 and the arrests in relation to the 'German Plot' – a spurious conspiracy alleged in May 1918 by the Dublin Castle administration to exist between the Sinn Féin movement and the German empire to start an armed insurrection in Ireland during the war – all instigated a drive for complete independence which became politicized through the Sinn Féin party during the 1917 by-elections.

Laffan correctly points out that 'the by-elections alone did not cause the emergence of the new Sinn Féin party', but they were pivotal in creating the political compulsion that transformed the opinion of many.[19] According to O'Leary, the 1917 and 1918 by-elections were unusual because they occurred at a time when revolutionary nationalism was replacing constitutional nationalism.[20] In effect, the content of an all-encompassing electioneering and propaganda campaign and the methods used to propagate Sinn Féin ideals during these by-elections changed many voters' perspectives from conciliatory politics towards more radical tactics and attitudes to gain self-government. This book intends to examine the methods, tactics and themes used to affect the popular change.

At the age of 66 John Dillon became leader of the IPP at a time when the destructive rhythm of the Great War had reached its height due largely to the German spring offensive. His forthright counsel to potential voters was that Sinn Féin's pursuit of a republic would lead to bloodshed and defeat, and he characterized their policy of abstentionism as 'a policy of lunatics'.[21] Nationalism assumed a dual approach to independence – constitutionalism versus separatism. Laffan rightly remarked that the 1918 results caused an upheaval in Irish politics comparable to that of the Parnellite landslide in 1885.[22] Irish politics transformed during and after 1918 turning from competitive personality-driven contests and bitter democratic affairs about the Liberal alliance, into hardened battles between discernibly opposing ideals on the future governance of Ireland.

In this era many candidates owed their selection to the roles they played in the struggle for independence, although, as will be seen in chapter 2, there were

17 Alvin Jackson, *Home rule: an Irish history, 1800–2000* (Oxford, 2003). 18 David Fitzpatrick, *The two Irelands, 1912–1939* (Oxford, 1998), p. 24. 19 Michael Laffan, *The resurrection of Ireland: the Sinn Féin Party, 1916–1923* (Cambridge, 2005), p. 115. 20 Cornelius O'Leary, *Irish elections, 1918– 1977* (Dublin, 1979), p. 7. 21 F.S.L. Lyons, *John Dillon: a biography* (London, 1968), pp 373, 381, and 439. See also Conor Cruise O'Brien, *Parnell and his party, 1880–90* (Oxford, 1957); F.S.L. Lyons, *The Irish Parliamentary Party, 1890–1910* (Westport, CT, 1975); McConnel, *The Irish Parliamentary Party*; Frank Callanan, *The Parnell split* (Syracuse, NY, 1992) and Maurice Manning, *James Dillon: a biography* (Dublin, 1999). 22 Laffan, *The resurrection*, p. 164.

constituencies, such as Waterford city, where the local candidate or a known candidate was preferred. After the formation of the Free State parties began to select candidates based on their having addresses in the constituencies in which they hoped to be elected.[23] With the use of the proportional-representation voting system in the 1920 local elections voters now had the option to express preferences freely between candidates regardless of party, and the urban election results in the next chapter show that there was a wide selection of representation. For the most part, in the elections of this era localism or issues of local concern were overtaken by the loftier ideals of competing parties, e.g. home rule, union or abstention from Westminster. Concerns were, however, also raised about the everyday issues of housing, pensions and taxation, which are investigated in chapter 5.

The 1918 election was unique by any measure as now there was a competitive party system instead of the 'undemocratic and single-issue character' of past Irish politics, and in the fray also were unionism and labour.[24] Until 1918 the home-rule-versus-unionism debate had dominated Irish politics, but with the emergence of a formidable challenger in Sinn Féin many nationalists abdicated in their favour, while unionists remained steadfast in their Ulster strongholds. The efforts made to raise funds for election campaigns are investigated in chapter 3, which provides insights into the importance that parties placed on electioneering and propaganda, and can give us some understanding of how the electorate identified with a political party. By investigating fundraising efforts it can be queried if the party that raised and subsequently spent the most money had greater success than others.

In identifying the methods and central themes of electioneering and propaganda in chapters 4 and 5 an examination on how content may have influenced voters can be undertaken. Dominant political actors introduced diametrically opposed opinions on common themes to uphold, condemn or highlight discordant stances. Propaganda content and themes provide a good indication on voter attitudes about the policies of political parties and candidates, although other external variables had influence too, for example the Great War. A new pattern of support emerged among voters in 1918 that persisted in subsequent elections, making this general election the real foundation of contemporary Irish politics. The victors went on to dominate government across the island for the next fifty years, and it is from this election that we can trace the true beginnings of Dáil Éireann, the Northern Ireland parliament and the development of the modern political landscape, north and south.

ELECTORAL REFORM

A novel characteristic of the 1918 general election was that it was the first occasion on which a general election was carried out on one day throughout the whole of

---

23 Michael Marsh, 'Localism, candidate selection and electoral preferences in Ireland: the general election of 1977', *Economic and Social Review*, 12:4 (1981), 267–86.   **24** Tom Garvin, 'Nationalist elites', 161–86.

the three kingdoms, and there was a new arrangement for a number of constituencies. It was also the apogee of a series of parliamentary reforms dating back to the reform bill of 1832 that culminated with the Representation of the People Act 1918.[25] In the closing years of the nineteenth century some of those excluded from politics became eligible to stand for elections and to vote. Propertied women were entitled to be elected as poor law guardians in 1896. In 1898 the Local Government (Ireland) Act provided a major step towards voting reform, granting all men over the age of 21 the right to vote in local elections, as well as women over the age of 30 if they were householders or lodgers occupying a portion of a house. Women could also stand for election to urban and rural district councils, but were disqualified from serving on borough and county councils until 1911.[26]

The Fourth Reform Act or Representation of the People Act passed through the Commons on 19 June 1917 with an overwhelming majority of 385 for to 55 against, receiving the royal assent on 6 February 1918.[27] This act increased the electorate substantially by granting the vote in parliamentary elections to all men over the age of 21 and removing practically all their property requirements. Servicemen who had turned 19 during the Great War could also vote.[28] Voting in general elections was also extended to women over the age of 30 years, but there were still some property restrictions.[29] The age and limited property qualifications for women appeased objectors to their suffrage and ensured that women did not become the majority because of the male death toll in the Great War. The effect of these changes was to triple the electorate in Ireland from 700,000 to nearly two million (see table 0.1).[30] Even though all adult women did not have the vote, 1918 nonetheless was a defining moment for democracy based on near universal suffrage in Ireland (and Britain).[31] As will be seen in chapters 4 and 5, some political parties now aimed specific propaganda messages directly at women.

Table 0.1 Growth in Irish electorate 1884–1918[32]

1884	1885	1892	1895	1900	1906	1910	1918
225,999	737,965	740,536	732,046	757,849	686,661	683,767	1,926,274

25 D.E. Butler, *The electoral system in Britain since 1918* (Oxford, 1963), p. 1. **26** Electorate figures for 1884 from Hoppen, *Elections, politics and society*, pp 87–8; for 1918 from F.S.L. Lyons, *Ireland since the Famine* (London, 1973), p. 399. Population figures from W.E. Vaughan and A.J. Fitzpatrick, *Irish historical statistics* (Dublin, 1978). **27** HC, PD, vol. 94, c. 1751: Division on Representation of the People Act, 19 June 1917; HL, vol. 27, c. 527, 10 Jan. 1918. **28** Eric J. Evans, *Parliamentary reform in Britain, c.1770–1918* (London, 2013), p. 135. **29** UK Parliamentary Archives, HL/PO/PU/1/1918/7&8G5c64: Representation of the People Act 1918. See also Evans, *Parliamentary reform*, p. 135. **30** Ibid. **31** S.M. Lipset and S. Rokkan, 'Cleavage structures, party systems and voter alignments: an introduction' in Lipset and Rokkan, *Party systems and voter alignments* (NY, 1967), pp 1–64. **32** F.W.S. Craig, *British electoral facts, 1832–1987* (Aldershot, 1989).

The first-past-the-post (FPTP) or single-member-plurality (SMP) voting system was used for all the by-elections of 1917–18 in Ireland, and for the 1918 general
election. FPTP voting required electors to place a cross in the box next to their
favoured candidate's name. The candidate with the most votes in the constituency
won. The advantages of this system were that it was easy to understand, it did not
cost much to administer, counting of votes was quick and a winner declared easily.
However, the votes cast for candidates not elected did not count, and MPs could
be elected on small proportions of the vote if they simply won the most votes in
a fragmented field.[33] The end result tended to favour large party control, with
smaller parties finding it harder to win seats.

Provision had been made in the 1914 Home Rule Act for the election of a
number of Irish MPs to Westminster under the system of proportional represen-
tation-single transferable vote (PR-STV) to safeguard unionist interests in the
three southern provinces and nationalist interests in Ulster. The act, however, was
not immediately implemented. PR-STV was, in fact, tried out for the first time in
the Sligo Borough election of January 1919. The reason for the by-election was the
poor financial condition of Sligo Corporation and to address this the ratepayers
formed the Sligo Ratepayers' Association (SRA). The SRA received 823 first-
preference votes in the election, gaining eight seats for the party (five Protestants
and three Catholics). The remaining seats went to Sinn Féin (7), Labour Party
(5) and independents (4).[34] The *Irish Independent* reported that the system proved
'quite successful, worked smoothly, and resulted in the election of a municipal
council fairly representative of all parties and sections of the people'.[35] The use
of proportional representation in Sligo was a pioneering experiment for democracy in Ireland. The 1919 Act made the system of proportional representation
universal.

The first island-wide use of the new PR-STV electoral system was in the local-
government elections in January and June 1920. The advantages and disadvantages
are evident in chapter 1, which demonstrates the variety of minority and independents elected, and the tendency for parties with a high number of candidates to
win a high number of seats. At the poll voters now had to place the number '1' in
the square opposite the name of their preferred candidate, then '2', '3' and so on
in order of preference. If the elector's first choice obtained more votes than were
needed to be elected (the quota) the surplus votes were transferred in proportion
to the next choices marked. The process continued until all surplus votes were
transferred. The introduction of proportional representation not only altered how
parties promoted candidates, it eliminated the sharp line of demarcation which
formerly existed in the FPTP system and blunted the personal element of voting

33 Michael Gallagher and Paul Mitchell (eds), *The politics of electoral systems* (Oxford, 2008); John
Coakley and Michael Gallagher, *Politics in the Republic of Ireland*, particularly ch. 4; and, David
M. Farrell, *Electoral systems: a comparative introduction*, 2nd ed. (Hampshire, 2011). 34 *Freeman's
Journal (FJ)*, 18 Jan. 1919; O'Leary, *Irish elections*, pp 6–7, 155–6; Gallagher and Mitchell, *The politics
of electoral systems*, pp 512–14. 35 *Irish Independent (II)*, 6 Jan. 1920; *FJ*, 18 Jan. 1919.

on the basis of past services. PR-STV was subsequently written into the 1937 constitution, and it is still in use throughout the Republic of Ireland.[36]

Local government in 1920 was largely a product of nineteenth-century statutes of the British parliament, but reform was instigated with the passing of the 1898 Local Government (Ireland) Act and the Local Government (Ireland) Act 1919, and both directly affected the 1920 elections. The primary purpose of the former was to put county government on a representative basis so, for instance, the business of grand juries transferred to elected councils. Elections were increased to be held triennially (although the 1917 local elections were cancelled because of the Great War). Administrative counties with county councils were created, and six of the larger cities – Dublin, Cork, Galway, Limerick, Waterford and Belfast – were made county boroughs where corporations carried out similar functions to county councils alongside the functions of a borough corporation. In Tipperary two administrative counties were formed, but elsewhere each county was one administrative area. The administrative county was divided into county districts – rural and urban (although in some only rural districts existed). Local government had (and continues to have) the power to make rates, borrow money, make, amend or revoke by-laws, elect a person to any other local body, supervise elections and bestow the freedom of the city on worthy persons.[37] The study of the 1920 local elections and their results, therefore, is crucial in understanding how voters at the very parochial level perceived and reacted to their political environment.

The final novel feature of elections in this era was the regrouping of former wards into electoral areas under the 1885 Redistribution Act and the 1918 Redistribution of Seats (Ireland) Act. Both Acts introduced the concept of equally populated constituencies to align representation across Great Britain and Ireland, and in 1918 the number of seats was increased from 103 to 105 (with the enfranchisement of two additional universities). Thirty-two electoral districts were altered in Ireland either by an increase in the number of divisions or in the number of MPs to be elected. Dublin provides a good example (see table 0.2).[38] The total membership of Dublin Corporation remained at eighty, but the new grouping altered the representation of the county and borough electoral areas, which increased from six to eleven divisions.

The 1921 elections, north and south, were called because the government of Ireland bill was introduced into the commons on 25 February 1920. It became law on 23 December and came into force on 3 May 1921. This act created two bicameral home rule parliaments: a southern parliament (which ultimately legitimized Dáil Éireann) and a northern parliament for the six counties of Ulster.

36 Michael Laver, 'A new electoral system for Ireland?', *Studies in Public Policy*, 2: The Policy Institute, TCD (1998).   **37** Richard Haslam, 'The origins of local government' in Mark Callanan and Justin F. Keogan, *Local government in Ireland, inside out* (Dublin, 2003), p. 26; Desmond Roche, *Local government in Ireland* (Dublin, 1982), pp 32–49; Basil Chubb, *Government and politics of Ireland*, 3rd ed. (London, 1992), p. 271.   **38** HC, PD, vol. 295, cc 679–751, 10 Mar. 1885; and Robert Henry Mair (ed.), *Debrett's house of commons and the judicial bench* (London, 1886), pp 165–244.

Table 0.2 Dublin electoral districts pre- and post-1918

Before 1918	After 1918
County	
County Dublin, North Division (1 MP)	North Dublin Division (1 MP)
County Dublin, South Division (1 MP)	Pembroke Division (1MP)
	Rathmines Division (1 MP)
	Dublin South (1 MP)
Borough	
College Green Division (1 MP)	College Green Division (1 MP)
Harbour Division (1 MP)	Harbour Division (1MP)
St Patrick's Division (1 MP)	St Patrick's Division (1 MP)
St Stephen's Green Division (1 MP)	St Stephen's Green Division (1 MP)
	Clontarf Division (1 MP)
	St James' Division (1 MP)
	St Michan's Division (1 MP)

Representation in all the provinces increased for these parliaments as the act provided for 128 MPs from 28 constituencies for the southern parliament and 52 MPs from 11 constituencies for the northern parliament. Representation from Ireland to Westminster reduced from 105 to 46 MPs and of these 33 had to be elected from southern Ireland and 13 from Northern Ireland. Each six-, seven- and eight-member constituency became a two-member constituency for Westminster, and every three, four and five-member constituency became a one-member constituency for Westminster (except for Dublin University which continued to elect two MPs), and Donegal remained a one-member constituency.

To form the two parliaments two sets of general elections were held using the single transferable vote system – one for the southern parliament on 19 May and one for the northern parliament on 22 May. These were the first general elections since 1918, but in the southern provinces the Labour Party, nationalists of the defeated IPP and southern unionists all decided not to contest, so 124 Sinn Féin candidates (and 4 independents from Trinity College) were elected unopposed. For the northern parliament Sinn Féin and other nationalists ran on a combined anti-partition ticket, with the former investing substantial resources in their campaign. This work will analyse the 1921 election in the first two chapters, in the section on partition in chapter 5 and intermittently throughout when relevant.

Propaganda and electioneering altered the nature of elections and accelerated the development of opposition parties as agents of change. This book will address how organized electioneering and propaganda was propagated by all parties in Ireland to win favour with the voting public. The main objective of propaganda was to affect the election results in a party's favour, with the fruits being electoral victory.

SOURCES AND HISTORIOGRAPHY

To comprehend the electioneering and propaganda of the past an enormous array of sources and opinion were vital. The primary sources essential to this study existed in a number of archives and repositories and many were within special or private collections. Material on Sinn Féin was easier to come by but sourcing IPP and unionist propaganda required intuitive detective work because it was rarely labelled 'propaganda'. A comprehensive bibliography is provided with this work detailing the archival sources used, but certain primary sources were indispensable and require special mention. The papers of John Dillon in the Trinity College Dublin Manuscripts and Archives Research Library were crucial to obtaining an understanding of IPP motives and plans (or the lack thereof) particularly for the 1918 general election. The Redmond Papers in the National Library of Ireland proved informative for United Irish League meetings and the early by-elections. To glean insight into the agenda and strategies of Sinn Féin the papers of Éamon de Valera and Richard Mulcahy in the University College Dublin Archives proved hugely beneficial and for detailed reports on the department of propaganda Desmond FitzGerald's papers were vital. Another valuable source was the vast collection of witness statements in the Bureau of Military History, which contain over 1,700 first-person accounts describing military and electoral deeds. It is important to note, as Fearghal McGarry points out, that these statements were made long after the revolutionary actions and individually they are inconclusive, contradictory and fragmentary. Collectively, however, they provide powerful insight into the separatist nationalist perspective to give a 'valuable, if necessarily subjective, guide to mentalities'.[39]

Unionist viewpoints and propaganda ephemera was available in the Ulster Unionist Council (UUC) Papers and Edward Carson's papers held in the Public Record Office of Northern Ireland. There was also political ephemera relating to unionists and Sinn Féin in this archive and in the Ulster Museum, Belfast. The main sources used to ascertain the Labour Party's electoral positions were the papers of Thomas Johnson in the National Library of Ireland and the reports of the annual meetings of the Irish Labour Party and Trade Union Congress.

National and provincial contemporary newspapers and foreign and special-interest publications were crucial sources for evaluating opinions. All newspapers in this era were notoriously biased and partial to a particular movement and party (see chapter 4). Nonetheless, diligent searching yielded journalistic perspectives on elections, candidates and parties. For other methods of propaganda, such as posters, pamphlets, handbills, ballads and symbols, the ephemera collections of the National Library of Ireland, particularly the William O'Brien Papers, the personal papers of all politicians, and sales at auction surrendered valuable examples – some of which have been depicted in this work.

---

39 Fearghal McGarry, *The Rising, Ireland: Easter 1916* (Oxford, 2010), pp 5–7.

Some key secondary sources are worth mentioning, but they are by no means the only valuable books available on parties, political systems or political leaders, and others are referenced in footnotes throughout this work. Constantly referred to, and an indispensable work for the 1918 and 1921 general election results, was Brian Walker's *Parliamentary election results*, which calculates electorate size and total votes in contested constituencies, with candidates' names and their party affiliation provided also.[40] Michael Laffan's *The resurrection of Ireland: the Sinn Féin Party, 1916–1923* is a significant work in the field and provides unique research and analysis on election propaganda from the Sinn Féin perspective, as well as party organizational structure and key political players. Without rejecting Laffan's findings, this book aims to build a more inclusive picture by incorporating the propaganda battles of those who were determined to defeat Sinn Féin.

For analysis and research into the IPP in the 1800s, K. Theodore Hoppen's *Elections, politics and society in Ireland* is a well-documented and empirical study that covers voting preferences, ownership of land and patterns of violence (to name just a few topics). Paul Bew, F.S.L. Lyons and Joseph Finnan have also delved into the politics of constitutional nationalism to assess the political performance of John Redmond. A more recent work by James McConnel provides an intricate analysis of the IPP and the third home rule crisis to reveal their adroit negotiating tactics and politicking in Westminster and battles against their domestic critics.[41] A number of interesting studies on unionism also provided context for this work. A.T.Q. Stewart's *The Ulster crisis* remains a significant force in the field and Patrick Buckland's *Ulster unionism and the origins of Northern Ireland* provides a detailed documentary history and politics of unionism.[42] Alan F. Parkinson's unique research on unionist propaganda in *Friends in high places* explores the erudite propaganda techniques that were implemented from 1912 to 1914 to defeat home rule. Other valuable works on unionism included Alvin Jackson's 'Unionism, and the future of the union' in *Ireland and the new century: politics and culture*, Graham Walker's *A history of the Ulster Unionist Party* and John F. Harbinson's analysis of the structures and composition of the Ulster Unionist Party.[43]

County studies elaborate on the military and political happenings at the local level and David Fitzpatrick's comprehensive research in *Politics and Irish life* hones in on the minutiae of military and political happenings in Co. Clare. His meticulous research uncovers the distribution of radical, partisan and cultural organizations in the villages

---

40 Brian Walker, *Parliamentary election results in Ireland, 1918–92* (Dublin, 1992), particularly pp 4–9.   41 Hoppen, *Elections, politics and society*; Paul Bew, *Ideology and the Irish question: Ulster unionism and Irish nationalism, 1912–1916* (Oxford, 1994); *Ireland: the politics of enmity, 1789–2006* (Oxford, 2007); *John Redmond: life and times* (Dundalk, 1996); Lyons, *The Irish Parliamentary Party*; and McConnel, *The Irish Parliamentary Party*.   42 Stewart, *The Ulster crisis*; Patrick Buckland, *Ulster unionism and the origins of Northern Ireland, 1886 to 1922*, vol. 2 (Dublin, 1973).   43 Alan F. Parkinson, *Friends in high places: Ulster's resistance to Irish home rule, 1912–14* (Belfast, 2012); Alvin Jackson, 'Unionism, and the future of the union' in Robert Savage (ed.), *Ireland and the new century: politics and culture* (Dublin, 2003); Graham Walker, *A history of the Ulster Unionist Party: protest, pragmatism and pessimism* (Manchester, 2004); John F. Harbinson, *The Ulster Unionist Party, 1882–1973* (Belfast, 1973).

and parishes to demonstrate that 'politics was an integral part of social life'.[44] Marie Coleman's methodical research on Co. Longford was another valuable local study, particularly the investigation into Sinn Féin's 1917 by-election victory there.[45]

Political scientists have also contributed enormously to the field of study on the foundation of statehood, electoral systems, parties and voters. Mention must be given to John Coakley and Michael Gallagher's *Politics in the Republic of Ireland*, Cornelius O'Leary's *Irish elections, 1918–1977*, Basil Chubb's *The government and politics of Ireland*, Bill Kissane's *Explaining Irish democracy* and James D. O'Donnell's *How Ireland is governed*. All identify the influences of Ireland's geographic location, religious divides, various forms of nationalism, the British influence and the 1922 Free State constitution. Other political scientists, such as Mair and Moss, have investigated Irish electoral politics in comparative perspectives, and voting patterns have been explored by Carty, O'Leary and Gallagher but mainly for elections in the 1920s.[46] The study of the micro-political of local-government elections and its effect on the national political process was crucial because local politics has and continues to play a key role in Ireland in policy decisions and party formation. To gain insight into the history and essence of government at the local level, and to provide context, structure and an understanding of the function of local councils this work relied on studies by Mary E. Daly, Virginia Crossman and Desmond Roche, and the selection of essays edited by Mark Callanan and Justin F. Keogan.[47]

Keiko Inoue, Ian Kenneally and Maurice Walsh have picked up the story of journalism and the media in Ireland's revolutionary years to trace how the confusing events of the era were defined and interpreted in print. Hugh Oram's account of newspapers in Ireland and Niall Ó Ciosáin's interdisciplinary approach in *Print and popular culture in Ireland* provided essential background for analysing the content and outlook of contemporary newspapers.[48] A study of the anti-war propaganda

---

44 David Fitzpatrick, *Politics and Irish life, 1913–1921: provincial experience of war and revolution* (Cork, 1998), p. 94 for quote.   **45** Marie Coleman, *County Longford and the Irish Revolution, 1910–1923* (Newbridge, Co. Kildare, 2003).   **46** See footnotes 20 and 23; Bill Kissane, *Explaining Irish democracy* (Dublin, 2002); James D. O'Donnell, *How Ireland is governed* (Dublin, 1965); Peter Mair, 'The autonomy of the political: the development of the Irish party system', *Comparative Politics*, 11 (1979), 445–65; Warner Moss, *Political parties in the Irish Free State* (NY, 1933); R.K. Carty, 'Social cleavages and party systems: a reconsideration of the Irish case', *Journal of Political Research*, 4 (1976), 195–203; idem, *Party and parish pump: electoral politics in Ireland* (Waterloo, ON, 1981); Michael Gallagher, *Electoral support for Irish political parties* (London, 1976); and idem, 'The pact general election of 1922', *Irish Historical Studies*, 22:84 (Sept. 1979), 404–21.   **47** Mary E. Daly (ed.), *County and town: 100 years of local government in Ireland* (Dublin, 2001); Virginia Crossman, *Local government in nineteenth-century Ireland* (Belfast, 1994); Roche, *Local government in Ireland*; Callanan and Keogan, *Local government*.   **48** Keiko Inoue, 'Propaganda II: propaganda of Dáil Éireann, 1919–21' in Joost Augusteijn (ed.), *The Irish Revolution, 1913–1923* (Basingstoke, 2002); idem, 'Sinn Féin propaganda and the "partition election", 1921', *Studia Hibernica*, 30 (1989–99); idem, 'Propaganda of Dáil Éireann: from truce to treaty', *Éire-Ireland*, 32:2–3 (1997); Ian Kenneally, *The paper wall: newspapers and propaganda in Ireland, 1919–1921* (Cork, 2008); Maurice Walsh, *The news from Ireland: foreign correspondents and the Irish Revolution* (NY, 2001), particularly pp 21–56; Hugh Oram, *The newspaper book: a history of newspapers in Ireland, 1649–1983* (Dublin, 1983); Niall Ó Ciosáin, *Print and popular culture in Ireland, 1750–1850* (Dublin, 2010).

of separatist nationalism was carried out by Ben Novick in *Conceiving revolution* through a thematic examination of how Sinn Féin used the war to undermine the recruitment drive of constitutional nationalists and oppose British rule in Ireland.[49] Kevin Hora's recent and fascinatingly detailed work *Propaganda and nation building: selling the Irish Free State* explores the history of propaganda in the Free State to assess how public relations and propaganda were used to construct identity.[50] One intention of this book is to fill the temporal gap between Novick and Hora by assessing the electoral propaganda war in Ireland instigated by the post-war elections. Many more historical scholars, such as Roy Foster, Tom Garvin, Charles Townshend, Anne Dolan, Brian Walker, Ronan Fanning and Diarmaid Ferriter, have also produced studies that were invaluable to the research for this work.[51]

Political communication and political propaganda forms part of an overall marketing and advertising skill, and contemporary and modern works that analysed visual and verbal persuasion, propaganda principles and practices, discourse theory and rhetorical analysis were central. Some examples include the contemporary work simply titled *Propaganda* by Edward L. Bernays, an Australian-American pioneer in the field of public relations and propaganda.[52] In Ireland an article by the National Council of Sinn Féin titled 'The advertising problem' offered consumer advice on existing propaganda methods.[53] Works such as *Political marketing: concepts and theories* edited by Paul R. Baines proved useful for definitions and concepts on the marketing of political ideas and opinions, as well as Guy Cook's *The discourse of advertising*, which explores the language of modern advertising.[54] While modern, they are valuable for exploring whether contemporary politicians were applying practices that later formed theory.

Despite extensive relevant scholarship, there is as yet no consensus on the definition of the term propaganda.[55] No modern theorist uses the term 'propaganda'

---

49 Ben Novick, *Conceiving revolution: Irish nationalist propaganda during the First World War* (Dublin, 2001), p. 55 for quote. **50** Kevin Hora, *Propaganda and nation building: selling the Irish Free State* (London, 2017). **51** Roy Foster, *Modern Ireland, 1600–1972* (London, 1989); Tom Garvin, *The evolution of Irish nationalist politics* (Dublin, 1981); Charles Townshend, *The Republic: the fight for Irish independence* (London, 2013); Anne Dolan, *Commemorating the Irish Civil War: history and memory, 1923–2000* (Cambridge, 2006); Brian Walker, *Ulster politics: the formative years, 1868–86* (Belfast, 1988); Ronan Fanning, *Fatal path: British government and Irish Revolution, 1910–1922* (London, 2013); and Diarmaid Ferriter, *The transformation of Ireland, 1900–2000* (London, 2004); and idem, *A nation and not a rabble: the Irish Revolution, 1913–23* (London, 2015). **52** Edward L. Bernays, *Propaganda* (NY, 1928). **53** Sinn Féin, *Leabhar na hÉireann: the Irish year book* (Dublin, 1910): National Library of Ireland, Ir 94109/i/8. **54** Guy Cook, *The discourse of advertising* (NY, 2001); Baines, *Political marketing*, particularly Patrick Butler and Neil Collins, 'Political marketing: structure and process', pp 2–12; John Egan, 'Political marketing: lessons from the mainstream', pp 17–25; Philip Kotler, 'Overview of political candidate marketing', pp 27–32; and Andrew Lock and Phil Harris, 'Political marketing – vive la différence', pp 35–6. **55** Jacques Ellul, *Propaganda: the formation of men's attitudes* (NY, 1968); Leonard W. Doob, 'Propaganda' in Erik Barnouw (ed.), *International Encyclopaedia of Communications*, vol. 3 (NY, 1989); Garth S. Jowett and Victoria O'Donnell, *Propaganda and persuasion*, 5th ed. (LA, 2012), p. 7.

unless it is with disapproval. However, in the early 1900s propaganda was a respectable term, and therefore it will be used throughout. It will be understood to encompass all communication activities regardless of whether the information is true or false, honest or deceptive, and regardless of the political affiliation of the communicant and the recipient. The word 'propaganda' comprises the attempt to persuade, convince or motivate, and encompasses the communication itself, the process by which the message was transmitted to a receiver and the themes employed.

AIMS

A key aim of this book is to provide a comparative study of the electioneering and propaganda of all the major parties in Ireland from 1917 to 1921 because it has long remained a missing link in Irish revolutionary history. Tom Garvin called the December 1918 general election 'a critical election'.[56] Certainly far more people were engaged in and affected by these political events than the military actions. While we can never know exactly how individuals cast their votes in these elections, it is possible to examine the issues that persuaded to give insight into many of the reasons as to why the IPP failed to impress and ultimately collapsed as a political force, how Sinn Féin altered the mindset of the Irish electorate, particularly in 1918, how unionists held on to their strongholds in Ulster and why the Labour Party withdrew from the contest.

Before a political propaganda contest could begin an election had to arise. By-elections ensued usually because of the death or retirement of an incumbent; general elections had a given time frame which was usually every four years in the British Isles. The Great War had ended on 11 November 1918 and no general election had taken place since 1910 and there had been a six-year gap in local elections. Lloyd George's 'war party' took advantage of their victory, and before the disruptions of demobilization could be felt, the general election date was set for 14 December and parliament was dissolved on 25 November, allowing for an intensive three-week propaganda campaign.[57] The electoral outcomes from 1917 to 1921 – particularly 1918 – were, by any measure, transformative moments in Irish history, so this book begins with their examination and analysis.

---

56 Garvin, *The evolution*, p. 131. 57 Martin Farr, 'Waging democracy: the British general election of 1918 reconsidered', *Cercles*, 21 (2011), 65–94.

The results

To begin by knowing the outcomes of elections in this era will give context to the propaganda created and disseminated by political parties in election campaigns from 1917 to 1921. In imagining the end goal of electoral victory, political movements, parties and candidates were spurred to develop stimulating and impassioned electioneering and propaganda campaigns to win voter approval. Electoral results also provide some insight into voter attitudes towards party propaganda communiqués because voting – or abstaining – was the practical demonstration of believing in or being swayed by electoral pledges and ideologies.

Aside from votes cast, a number of other issues need to be considered, such as voter turnout, to assess the effects of emigration, and absent voters primarily because of the Great War. Intimidation and aggression, which is covered in greater detail in chapter 4, impacted on results. The Spanish flu, spoiled votes, a candidate's age and occupation, the youth vote and women's votes all held bearing on election outcomes. However, as will be seen later in this book, the party messages and policies in election propaganda, and the speeches, canvassing and novel tactics to bring voters to the polling booths primarily influenced how votes were cast. Gallagher correctly points out that there are no official records of election results pre-1948 in Ireland, so those provided here come from a number of sources, particularly Walker's *Parliamentary election results* for 1918 and 1921, and provincial and national newspapers.[1]

THE 1917 AND 1918 BY-ELECTIONS

Electioneering and propagandizing knowledge was gleaned during the by-elections by nationalists (as no unionists participated), and particularly by separatist nationalists, who learned from IPP successes and failures – something that continued after their 1918 electoral success. Fitzpatrick rightly observed that 'old wine was decanted into new bottles', but in this era there was pioneering preparation and a freshness to electioneering battles with the arrival of separatist nationalists onto the political scene, even if later political formations emulated age-old British methods and past IPP principles. The outcome of the by-elections was heavily influenced by wartime happenings such as conscription and British cabinet decisions. All the

---

1 Michael Gallagher, *Irish elections, 1922–44: results and analysis* (Limerick, 1993), p. viii; Walker, *Parliamentary election results*, pp 4–9 for 1918 general election and pp 45–6 for 1921 election in Northern Ireland.

by-elections examined in this book occurred post-Easter Rising, including one in Cork West held in November 1916 where Daniel O'Leary (IPP) won by 116 votes. This did not reflect the IPP's strength in the constituency but rather the All for Ireland League's (AFIL's) growing disarray. AFIL candidates Frank J. Healy and Dr Michael Shipsey attained 1,750 and 370 votes respectively, with O'Leary reaching 1,806 votes, so O'Leary's win was less than the combined votes of the two League candidates. This seat fell uncontested to Sinn Féin nearly two years later in the general election.

On Christmas Eve 1916 internees involved in or connected with the Easter Rising were released and, among the 130 arriving at Westland Row on the early morning train from Kingstown, having come across by the 'mail packet from Holyhead', were Arthur Griffith and Michael Collins.[2] Their arrival enhanced political momentum, and the Roscommon North by-election in February 1917 galvanized them to action. The victorious candidate, Count George Noble Plunkett, was vociferously supported by Sinn Féin's Fr Michael O'Flanagan and Laurence Ginnell, and an entourage of cars carrying Collins and Griffith led the canvass. Plunkett's clear majority over the IPP candidate, Thomas Devine, who was a well-regarded county councillor, revealed there was a threat now facing the party that jeopardized their political predominance and wartime recruitment drive.

The sustained anti-war and anti-recruitment rhetoric added energy to Plunkett's campaign as disillusioned nationalists turned to what seemed like a viable alternative to IPP supplications at Westminster. Plunkett reiterated Griffith's abstention from Westminster idea and suggested an appeal to the post-war peace conference for Ireland's independence. As will be seen in chapters 4 and 5, these messages and methods shaped support for Sinn Féin as the by-elections progressed and particularly during the 1918 general election. In the early by-election of Roscommon North, however, a real vote catcher was Plunkett's ability to garner empathy from people for his sons' connection with the Easter Rising, particularly for his executed son Joseph.[3] As the *Irish Times* put it, 'Mr Redmond's formidable election machine was powerless against impassioned appeals like this.'[4] As will be seen in chapter 2, Plunkett was not exclusively a Sinn Féin candidate, but the ideals propagated in this by-election were picked up by Sinn Féin and promulgated in all future by-elections and in the 1918 general election.

After Roscommon North, IPP gloom was evident in a memorandum written by Redmond where he remarked on 'the remarkable and unexpected results of the election'. His 'fatalistic despair', as Lyons termed it, was evident (and only the protests of senior colleagues prevented publication of this memorandum).[5] Genuine trepidation over the IPP's future and an awakening to the mounting threat of Sinn Féin was expressed, but there was still an element of denial. Redmond wrongly

---

2 *IT*, 26 Dec. 1916.   3 See chapter 4, section on Easter Rising.   4 *IT*, 8 Feb. 1917.   5 F.S.L. Lyons, 'The new nationalism, 1916–1918' in W.E. Vaughan (ed.), *A new history of Ireland: Ireland under the union, 1870–1921* (Oxford, 1976; 1989), p. 226.

believed that people would not repudiate home rule in favour of 'the alternative principle ... which Ireland's enemies to-day assert'.[6] Unionists did not field a candidate in Roscommon North (or in any of the by-elections), but they denigrated the election result in the pages of their newspapers. The *Belfast News-Letter* in February 1917 maintained that Roscommon North was 'glorying in its treason' and that the 'rebel poll of North Roscommon' demonstrated 'what lies at the bottom of home rule'.

One contested by-election was insufficient evidence that the IPP was facing defeat by separatist-style nationalism – particularly given that Plunkett was not specifically a Sinn Féin candidate. What it demonstrated was that Plunkett's methods of propaganda and his novel themes had attracted voter attention.

Longford South's bitterly fought contest three months later between the interned Joseph McGuinness and the IPP's Patrick McKenna culminated in an expectant 'huge crowd' that gathered outside the courthouse. According to the *Longford Leader*, '300 Sinn Féiners and about 500 supporters of McKenna wearing their green colours' anxiously awaited the results.[7] An initial pronouncement gave a twelve-vote victory to McKenna. But it was promptly discovered that fifty votes had gone uncounted, and when these were added victory fell by a majority of a mere thirty-seven votes to McGuinness.[8] Determination had narrowly won the day for Sinn Féin in a constituency that had heretofore been ardent in its IPP advocacy. Frank Gallagher had acknowledged that Longford was 'strong it its support of the Parliamentary Party' and Griffith saw Longford South as a 'hotbed of the Irish Party'.[9] In this by-election Redmond had been attacked for suspending home rule and agreeing to partition by Sinn Féin, in an attempt to nourish the idea that partition was avoidable. They won over the younger clergy and some parish priests, who spoke out openly in their favour regardless of the politics of their bishops. Sinn Féin's majority was slim, but for a new party with novel policies contesting against the established regime they proved that their often wily and resourceful propaganda paid off.

Constituency disorganization and lack of intelligence on the political ambitions of Sinn Féin lost the IPP this by-election. McKenna's crude insults, evident in the 'Political Dustbin' poster (see plate 5), inadvertently gave credence to his opponent. While he had led in the polling districts of Newtownforbes, Longford and Kenagh, with an even vote in the townland of Caltrabeg (where out of 301 votes he attained 150), he was outvoted in Ballymahon and Carrikboy, and held a 'hopeless minority' in Lanesborough.[10]

---

6 TCD, JD, MSS 6749/649: letter from Redmond to Dillon with an enclosed statement for the press, 21 Feb. 1917. 7 *Limerick Leader (LkL)*, 12 May 1917. 8 BMH WS 907: Laurence Nugent; WS 722: Dan McCarthy. 9 UCDA, Ernie O'Malley Papers P17b/153: draft biography of Seán Connolly by Ernie O'Malley; P.S. O'Hegarty, *The victory of Sinn Féin* (Dublin, 1925), p. 28; Frank Gallagher, *The four glorious years*, 2nd ed. (Dublin, 2005), p. 8; Piaras Béaslaí, *Michael Collins and the making of a new Ireland*, vol. 1 (London, 1926), p. 151; William O'Brien, *Forth the banners go* (Dublin, 1969), p. 145. 10 *LL*, 12 May 1917.

In Clare East the IPP could have forecast a heated contest against a surviving commandant of the Easter Rising, Éamon de Valera, but not their annihilation in a constituency where Redmond's brother William had been MP since 1892. All was not calm within Sinn Féin either, as there were divisions over whether to take a physical-force approach to gaining independence, or a passive-resistance approach. Prior to de Valera's release from Pentonville Prison in June 1917 Cathal Brugha and Griffith 'had been at daggers drawn ... so much so that Brugha had threatened that if Griffith stumped the country for Sinn Féin, he would get the Volunteers to stop him'. Robert Brennan, Sinn Féin director of propaganda, claimed that in the immediacy of de Valera's release he 'was working night and day to get Brugha and Griffith in step'.[11] Concerns over de Valera's moderate political approach were voiced by some within the Irish Volunteers, who disapprovingly perceived him as similar to the constitutionalists. De Valera's skill during the election campaigns lay in pulling these dissonant elements together to present a united front (albeit only a temporary one, which crumbled under the weight of the Anglo-Irish treaty in 1921).

Many nationalist voters were overwhelmingly swept up by the promises of abstention from Westminster and a speculative appeal to the post-war peace conference in 1917. De Valera defeated the IPP candidate Patrick Lynch by 5,010 votes to 2,035, and his triumph heralded him in as the new Sinn Féin leader. The defeat set the IPP in a tailspin. Lynch wrote to Redmond on behalf of six MPs pleading for 'a review of our own policy and methods', suggesting a constitutional policy in pursuit of self-government on the model of South Africa or Australia.[12] John Dillon was utterly disheartened and proclaimed accurately that 'at this moment they [Sinn Féin] could sweep the greater part of the three southern provinces'.[13]

Kilkenny city proved that it was not all high idealism that secured victory for Sinn Féin as the focus in this constituency was on the everyday matters of taxation and industry (see chapter 5). This was a small city with a population of 10,514 and a register of electors of 1,676.[14] Torrents of rain fell for four hours on the evening of polling and candidates' agents went out to rescue voters from doorways, windows and the outer areas of the town and brought them to the polling booths to cast their votes – demonstrating political enthusiasm.[15] The end result was a win for Sinn Féin's William T. Cosgrave by 380 votes against the IPP's John Magennis.

Two by-elections were held in Ulster constituencies in Catholic-dominated areas. The first was in Armagh South, which was considered 'so irremediably nationalist as to make intricate local organization superfluous', but Walker suggests that this judgement was unduly pessimistic.[16] A variation of nationalist, unionist

---

11 BMH WS 779 (section ii): Robert Brennan. 12 NLI, JR, MS 5742/MS 15,202: Lynch to Redmond, 9 May and 31 July 1917. 13 TCD, JD, MSS 6840: Dillon to Hooper, 14 July 1917. 14 *Thom's Directory*, 1915. 15 *Freeman's Journal (FJ)*, 11 Aug. 1917. 16 Alvin Jackson, 'Unionist politics and Protestant society in Edwardian Ireland', *Historical Journal*, 33:4 (Dec. 1990), 839–66; NAI, 1911 census online; Walker, 'Parliamentary representation in Ulster, 1868–86', pp 390–1.

and independent candidates had held the seat over the years. If the history of the constituency was anything to go by, the field lay open for robust competition. According to the *Ulster Gazette*, the 1918 by-election 'created ... intense interest ... and the rivalry between the Irish Party and Sinn Féin supporters' was 'extraordinarily keen'.[17]

Armagh South was Sinn Féin's first election contest in Ulster. Their propaganda campaign fell mainly to Countess Constance Markievicz because their candidate, Patrick McCartan, was in an American jail. Volunteers were ushered in from Armagh city and neighbouring counties and a Sinn Féin committee arrived to run the election.[18] Visiting Volunteers distributed leaflets and posters across Armagh South, and marched to different areas to protect Sinn Féin meetings. Their efforts were in vain as the seat went to the IPP's Patrick Donnelly by a strong margin with 1,016 votes more than McCartan. Armagh South witnessed a number of bitter disturbances between the Hibernians and Volunteers, and often fisticuffs were considered by some as more effective than political arguments (see chapter 4).[19] The Tyrone East constituency had been created by the Redistribution Act in 1885 and usually returned nationalist members, as did Tyrone Mid. Tyrone North and South were traditionally unionist, although the former was captured by a Liberal with nationalist support in 1885. While Tyrone East was predominately Catholic it held a substantial Protestant and unionist minority. Unionists did not field a candidate for this by-election and many Sinn Féin Volunteers argued that this was due to an 'unofficial truce between them and the nationalists whilst the Convention was in existence', and that their votes favoured the IPP.[20] Contradicting this, the *Cork Examiner* reported that 'unionists of that constituency refrained as a body from voting for the nationalist ... although it is shrewdly suspected that in isolated cases any unionist votes recorded were given for Sinn Féin on the principle of "Divide et impera" [divide and rule]'.[21] Again, Sinn Féin's prominent Dublin leaders and the Irish Volunteers and IRB conducted election work.[22] Both Armagh South and Tyrone East were IPP victories, although Sinn Féin claimed that the energetic canvass had resulted in the establishment of networks with Volunteer, Sinn Féin and Cumann na mBan clubs being created.[23] Yet, Sinn Féin suffered heavy defeats in the 1918 general election in Armagh South and Tyrone East, although nationalist pacts make comparisons problematic.

Waterford city provided another IPP victory in a contested by-election. The final result was an anticipated victory for the party, but as the *Irish Times* correctly highlighted it was due to the 'attachment of the people to the Redmond family', which 'seems to outweigh all political considerations'.[24] The Redmond family had never lived in Waterford city, and John Redmond was an irregular visitor, but when

17 *Ulster Gazette*, 19 Jan. 1918. 18 BMH WS 658: John Grant. 19 Ibid. 20 See for example BMH WS 1770: Kevin O'Sheil. They were referring to the Irish Convention. 21 *CE*, 5 Apr. 1918. 22 BMH WS 893: William J. Kelly. 23 Ibid. 24 *IT*, 23 Mar. 1918.

he arrived he was usually 'received with enthusiasm'.[25] His son Captain William Archer Redmond won the city against a local doctor, Vincent White, by a comfortable 478 votes.

In 1918 Cavan East was the final contested by-election and before the battle began nationalists wrangled over format. Indignant debate ensued as to whether a contest or plebiscite should take place because of the imminent threat of conscription (the military service bill having being passed two days before the death of Samuel Young, the IPP MP). Sinn Féin suggested that an informal ballot could be held after Sunday mass and that the result of this would dictate the winner. As Laffan points out, this was a meaningless concession.[26] Sinn Féin had previously attained a seat in Tullamore in an uncontested by-election because the IPP candidate had stepped down. Dillon expected Sinn Féin to return the favour and saw their refusal to do so as indicative of the lack of a united 'spirit' being exhibited 'by the leaders of Sinn Féin' in 'making this indecent attempt to capture the seat'.[27] The subsequent 'German Plot' arrests and the internment of Griffith facilitated a re-run of the *Put him in to get him out* poster campaign (see chapter 4 and plate 6) and gave the Sinn Féin campaign platform to O'Flanagan. He took Griffith to victory with a massive 1,204 margin.

By-elections as predictors of general election results are by no means reliable indicators, and without the context of political ideologies there are limitations to interpreting these results at this stage. Furthermore, not all areas of the country voted in the eight contested by-elections in 1917 and 1918, and all contested elections were held in nationalist areas. By-elections are powerful at constituency level and they can forecast the fate of a government in that area in an impending general election, but generally speaking they may simply reflect the fact that all or most of the by-elections occurred in areas where support for a particular party was weak or strong, such as in the Waterford city by-election. Moreover, some parties – unionists and labour – did not run candidates in these by-elections so their totals are non-existent, but their support may have been stronger had they been an option.[28] There were also no contested by-elections in any counties on the eastern seaboard, although one might have taken place in Dublin South County in June 1917 following the death of Alderman William Cotton MP. The IPP candidate Michael Hearne obtained the majority of UIL votes and with the good fortune of having no competitor he was declared elected on 6 July.[29]

By-elections in general really only give an indication of voter mood in specific constituencies. However the geographic locations of the 1917 and 1918 by-elections strongly hinted at significant political transformation in many areas on the eve of the last all-island contested election in 1918 (see tables 1.1, 1.2).

---

25 Ibid., for example, see 7 Oct. 1916. **26** *Nationality*, 11 May 1918. **27** *Anglo-Celt (AC)*, 4 May 1918. **28** Richard Sinnott, *Irish voters decide: voting behaviour in elections and referendums since 1918* (Manchester, 1995), p. 251. **29** *Weekly IT*, 30 June 1917; *IT*, 7 July 1917.

Table 1.1 Results of the 1917–18 contested by-elections

By-Election	Date	Candidate	Party	Registered electors	Results	Total valid votes	Majority	% Valid Votes	% Win
Cork West	Nov. 1916	**Daniel O'Leary**	**IPP**	3,926	**1,806**	3,926	56*	**46.0**	1.4
		Frank J. Healy	AFIL		1,750			44.6	
		Dr Michael Shipsey	AFIL		370			9.4	
Roscommon North	Feb. 1917	Thomas J. Devine	IPP	8,449	1,708			31.5	
		Count George Noble Plunkett	**Independent**		**3,022**	5,417	627	**55.8**	11.6
		Jasper Tully	Independent		687			12.7	
Longford South	May 1917	Patrick McKenna	IPP	3,763	1,461			49.4	
		Joseph McGuinness	**Sinn Féin**		**1,498**	2,959	37	**50.6**	1.2
Clare East	July 1917	Patrick Lynch	IPP	9,117	2,035			28.9	
		Éamon de Valera	**Sinn Féin**		**5,010**	7,045	2,975	**71.1**	42.2
Kilkenny (city)	Aug. 1917	John Magennis	IPP	1,676	392			33.4	
		William T. Cosgrave	**Sinn Féin**		**772**	1,175	369	**65.7**	31.4
			Spoiled votes		11			0.9	
Armagh South	Feb. 1918	**Patrick Donnelly**	**IPP**	6,400	**2,321**		941	**62.7**	25.4
		Patrick McCartan	Sinn Féin		1,305	3,701		35.3	
		Thomas Richardson	Independent Unionist		40			1.1	
			Spoiled votes		35			0.9	
Waterford (city)	Mar. 1918	**Captain William Redmond**	**IPP**	4,170	**1,242**	2,006	478	**61.9**	23.8
		Dr Vincent White	Sinn Féin		764			38.1	
Tyrone East	Apr. 1918	**Thomas Harbison**	**IPP**	3,039**	**1,802**	3,039	580	**59.3**	19.1
		Sean Milroy	Sinn Féin		1,222			40.2	
			Spoiled Votes		15			0.5	
Cavan East	June 1918	J.F. O'Hanlon	IPP	8,851	2,581			40.5	
		Arthur Griffith	**Sinn Féin**		**3,785**	6,366	1,204	**59.5**	18.9

* over nearest competitor ** total number of votes recorded, according to newspapers, e.g. *Cork Examiner*, 5 Apr. 1918

Table 1.2 Results of the 1917–18 uncontested by-elections

By-election	Dates	Party	Candidate	Registered electors	Results	Majority	% Votes	% Win
South County Dublin	July 1917	Irish Party	Michael Hearne					
Offaly	Apr 1918	Sinn Féin	Dr Patrick McCartan					

THE 1918 GENERAL ELECTION

The general election was held on 14 December 1918, and a fortnight elapsed between polling and the declaration of results on 28 December. The number of contests renders it impossible to cover each individually so a broad analysis will be provided. The aim is to explore just how successful Sinn Féin was in the southern provinces and whether unionists held Ulster. The future partitioning of the island makes it worthwhile to examine Ulster separately.[30] The overall outcome in 1918 was a political upheaval in Leinster, Munster and Connacht that was reminiscent of the Parnell split of the late 1800s. Parnell's downfall, however, did not convulse the various sections of Irish nationalism to anything like the degree that accompanied the rout of IPP MPs across many constituencies by Sinn Féin candidates. Before the dissolution of parliament, Ireland returned 68 MPs from the IPP, 18 unionists, 7 AFIL, 7 Sinn Féin, 2 Liberals and 1 independent nationalist to Westminster. The political contests in 1918 resulted in 73 seats for Sinn Féin, 25 for unionists 1 independent unionist, and 6 IPP MPs (7 if T.P. O'Connor's Liverpool seat is taken into account). Driven and aggravated by a ruthless Sinn Féin electioneering and propaganda campaign the IPP was outwitted and overcome in most constituencies in Ireland.

There were twenty-five seats that were not contested by IPP candidates, which meant advantage fell to Sinn Féin, particularly in Munster (see table 1.3). The large number of uncontested seats makes it challenging to gauge voter rationale. Carlow perhaps illustrates the reason why these constituencies failed to put forward an IPP candidate, or any other candidate, in the 1918 general election, leaving the seats free for Sinn Féin. The Carlow Nationalist Election Committee at a meeting in December 1918 proposed and unanimously passed a resolution stating it was 'inadvisable to continue the electoral contest'. Reporting on the reasons for this decision the *Freeman's Journal* remarked that 'there was no mistaking the conviction under which the young men and the workers of Carlow were going to vote. They believed in the reality of the Republican policy, and they were going to vote straight for the republic.'[31] This was a constituency that had previously held

30 See appendix 1 and Walker's *Parliamentary election results*, pp 4–9 for full 1918 election results. 31 *FJ*, 5 Dec. 1918.

Table 1.3 Number of uncontested seats in the 1918 general election

Province	Seats
Munster	17
Connacht	3
Leinster	3
Ulster	2

strong Redmond supporters, even at the outset of the Great War and after the Easter Rising.[32] Effective Sinn Féin electoral propaganda had not only convinced Carlow, it had swayed many voters in these twenty-five constituencies, and had ousted potential challengers from the field. Dillon blamed 'stupid blunders on the part of our men' for two of these, and the 'hopeless lack of organization in the country' and 'sheer cowardice', which was an obvious reference to the retiring MPs (see chapter 2).[33]

The total electorate in contested constituencies in 1918 was 1,462,895.[34] The total number of electors on the register for the counties and boroughs, including uncontested seats and excluding universities, was 1,921,601. The total valid poll for the eighty (including universities) county and borough constituencies across the provinces was 1,039,145 (see table 1.4).[35]

In fifty-two constituencies there were direct two-way contests by Sinn Féin against another party or independent candidate, as can be seen in table 1.5. This clearly demonstrates that outside Ulster the contests were mainly between opposing nationalist candidates.[36]

There were twenty-one triangular contests in the general election: seven in Leinster and fourteen in Ulster, where the battle was usually between Sinn Féin, IPP and unionist candidates. These contests provided sixty-nine candidates in total. Triangular contests in four of the eleven Dublin constituencies saw unionists contend against nationalists, and in St Patrick's the three-way battle was between an IPP candidate, an independent and Sinn Féin's Countess Markievicz – the latter of whom won, becoming the first female MP in the British Isles. She did not take her seat at Westminster but did become minister for labour in the first dáil, making her the second female cabinet minister in Europe.[37] In all the other Dublin constituencies the battle was fought by IPP and Sinn Féin candidates, except for College Green, where a Sinn Féin candidate contested against a Town Tenants' League candidate.

32 *NLT*, 15 and 22 Aug. 1914, 19 Sept. 1914 and 6 May 1916.   **33** TCD, JD, MSS 6742/567: Dillon to O'Connor, 6 Dec. 1918.   **34** Walker, *Parliament election results*, pp 4–9.   **35** *II*, 30 Dec. 1918.   **36** Ibid.   **37** Margaret Ward, *Unmanageable revolutionaries: women and Irish nationalism* (London, 1983).

Table 1.4 Total valid poll for all contested county and borough constituencies in 1918 by province (excluding universities)

Party	Leinster	Ulster	Munster	Connacht	Total
Sinn Féin	193,346	109,446	87,609	104,409	494,810
Unionist	21,247	242,044	4,773	0	268,064
IPP	89,868	70,849	34,877	30,627	226,221
Labour Unionist	0	21,149	0	0	21,149
Labour (Ulster)	0	9,149	0	0	9,149
Independent	0	8,549	0	0	8,549
Independent Nationalist	3,768	2,602	0	0	6,370
Independent Unionist	0	4,833	0	0	4,833
Total	308,229	468,621	127,259	135,036	1,039,145

Table 1.5 Direct two-way electoral contests by Sinn Féin in 1918

Province	Sinn Féin vs Irish Party	Sinn Féin vs Unionists	Sinn Féin vs independents
Munster	5	0	0
Connacht	10	0	0
Leinster*	16	0	2
Ulster**	6	13	0
Total	37	13	2

* Including National University **Including Queen's University

In total there were 103 constituencies, with 105 seats. Eight Sinn Féin candidates stood for more than one seat, with de Valera nominated for four seats including Clare East (unopposed), Mayo East, Belfast Falls and Down South. De Valera was regarded as their strongest candidate, who could defeat Dillon in his home constituency of Mayo East, and naively Devlin in the Belfast Falls constituency, and generally make Sinn Féin gains in Ulster. He was successful in Mayo East, but was routed by Devlin and attained only a paltry thirty-three votes in Down South, revealing that the nationalist mood in Ulster was very different to that of Clare East. Five Sinn Féin candidates were elected to two constituencies, so subsequently they had to select the one they intended to represent. Therefore, after the final count Sinn Féin had sixty-eight elected candidates with seventy-three seats. Their victory was comprehensive in Dublin and in Dublin Co. South Gavan Duffy won by a margin of 779 votes over the unionist candidate, Thomas

Robinson, and by 1,314 over the IPP's Thomas Clarke. In all other constituencies Sinn Féin's margin was in excess of 2,000 votes, and Constance Markievicz attained 4,083 more votes than her nearest rival, the nationalist William Field. In Dublin county Sinn Féin made a clean sweep, except in Rathmines, where the southern unionist Maurice Dockrell recaptured the constituency by beating the combined vote of Sinn Féin and the IPP by fifty-four.

Ulster's results (as will be seen later) were weighted strongly in favour of unionists in the counties that later formed Northern Ireland. While this was not the sole cause for the later partitioning of the island, these results created a decisive power base that allowed the followers of Carson to 'leave Ulster immune from the horrible deeds of the sister provinces'.[38] In Dublin unionists also contested in the Pembroke and Dublin South Divisions, but the results were surprising victories for Sinn Féin. John Good was defeated by Desmond FitzGerald in Pembroke by a strong 1,976 majority, with the IPP candidate Charles O'Neill attaining only 2,629 votes out of a total poll of 12,881. Dublin South and Pembroke had previously been held by unionists (although Dublin South wins had alternated between unionist and IPP candidates in earlier elections of the 1900s).

Across many constituencies in the rest of the three southern provinces Sinn Féin secured immense victories. They had strong majorities in Cork city, Galway Connemara, Leitrim, Limerick East, Longford, Mayo North and West, Queen's County, Roscommon South, Sligo North and South, Tipperary South, Westmeath and Wicklow West. The IPP again prevailed in Waterford city, but they lost Waterford county to Sinn Féin's Cathal Brugha by an overwhelming majority. However, there were some very tight contests between Sinn Féin and the IPP. In Louth John O'Kelly only marginally defeated the IPP's Richard Hazleton by 255 votes; and in Wexford South Sinn Féin's James Ryan narrowly won over Peter Ffrench. Wicklow East could have been another tight contest had the IPP vote not been split with a unionist candidate in the field. Their combination total was 5,066 which still gave the Sinn Féin candidate Seán Etchingham a majority of 850. He polled 3,316 more votes than the nearest IPP rival.

A heated contest took place in Mayo East – the home constituency of Dillon – between the constitutional leader and de Valera, now the president of Sinn Féin. The Press Association referred to this as 'probably the stiffest contest in Ireland'. Dillon blamed 'organized intimidation', which resulted in 'the terror of the people', for IPP losses (see chapter 4). Dillon's defeat was catastrophic, with de Valera attaining a majority of 4,461 votes – a two to one decision. Daunted and perhaps frustrated by violence and intimidation from both sides of the nationalist divide, 8,146 potential voters abstained from the poll.

Cork city and county were previous strongholds of the AFIL, which withdrew to make way for Sinn Féin, even though in the December 1910 elections it had

---

38 PRONI, UUC Papers, D1327/20/4/142: *Where hand of murder rules.*   39 Joseph V. O'Brien, *William O'Brien and the course of Irish politics, 1881–1918* (Berkeley, CA, 1976), pp 201–2.

won eight seats.[39] AFIL leader William O'Brien's final address to the electors of Cork encouraged the AFIL to support 'the spirit of Sinn Féin, as distinct from its abstract programme', and he advocated for the 'full and sympathetic trial for enforcing the Irish nation's right of self-determination'.[40] The 'self-determination' axiom and republicanism of Sinn Féin was easy enough to understand, but the nebulous 'abstention from Westminster' offered no distinct or solid parliamentary alternative. Dáil Éireann, at this stage, did not feature in the imaginings of Sinn Féin. In the face of past losses against the AFIL and O'Brien's endorsement of Sinn Féin, the IPP made no attempt to secure the seven county divisions of Cork, giving victory to Sinn Féin. In Cork city two seats polled over 20,500 votes each for Sinn Féin, crushing the IPP candidates, who mustered a mere 14,642 votes between them. Two unionist candidates also contested in this constituency – Daniel Williams and Thomas Farrington – but their combined votes did not even come near the lowest nationalist vote.[41] In neighbouring Kerry, the four seats went uncontested to Sinn Féin.

An expected re-organization of the IPP had increased optimism within the rank and file for a return in 1918 'by a minority of votes'.[42] However, these hoped-for votes did not emerge, and Dillon's despondency indefinitely postponed party rejuvenation.[43] Their general election total was less than half that of Sinn Féin but they had attained nearly 200,000 votes; and in the municipal elections of January 1920 constitutional nationalists retained representation on the larger corporations. Structured leadership with an articulate and consistent strategy could have drawn future support from Great War absent voters and those who abstained out of fear of violence or intimidation. Furthermore, this election was contested using the FPTP method of voting providing a winner-takes-all scenario, whereas a couple of years later the PR-STV method of voting allowed for a greater array of political representation (see introduction, p. 24). A comparison could be made with the modern election of 2011, where Fianna Fáil suffered the worst defeat in the history of the Irish state. After six or seven years of propagandizing and strident opposition, public opinion oscillated back towards Fianna Fáil. By 2017 they had climbed to a 29 per cent approval rating as against Fine Gael's 28 per cent and Sinn Féin's 21 per cent (with Labour at 4 per cent and independents at 18 per cent).[44] The IPP's defeat in 1918 was severe but it need not have been fatal.

Across the nine Ulster counties candidates battled for thirty-eight seats, with fifteen nationalists and twenty-three unionists winning their contests. Four IPP seats were secured in Down South, Donegal East, Tyrone North-East and Armagh South – the party had succeeded in holding Tyrone East and Armagh South twice

---

40 Quote in Michael MacDonagh, *The life of William O'Brien, the Irish nationalist* (London, 1928), p. 234. 41 Walker, *Parliamentary election results*, p. 5. 42 Ibid., 25 Nov. 1918. 43 See Stephen Gwynn, *John Redmond's last years* (NY, 1919), pp 191–3. 44 *IT*, 2 Mar. 1917; Michael Gallagher and Michael Marsh, *How Ireland voted in 2011: the full story of Ireland's earthquake election* (Basingstoke, 2011).

during 1918 contests. Devlin topped the poll in the Belfast Falls Division. His only opponent was de Valera, who had secured the Clare East constituency without contest. Despite the violence, heckling and interruptions in this constituency (or perhaps because of it) Devlin overpowered de Valera by a majority of 5,243 votes. This attests to the fact that IPP candidates in Ulster were more organized and, unlike their southern brethren, were accustomed to fighting battles against those with opposing political viewpoints. It also suggests that nationalist voters in areas of Ulster were unnerved about partition and so they elected to remain with the status quo rather than risk voting for a more radical and unfamiliar Sinn Féin candidate.

Nationalists in Ulster eventually arrived at a pact through the intervention of Cardinal Michael Logue and the Roman Catholic bishops in a determined effort to defeat unionists, and four seats went to each side. The temperaments of Dillon and Eoin MacNeill at the original meeting to discuss Ulster candidates were fractious, with each stubbornly refusing to capitulate to the other. Dillon described the 'three hours tête-à-tête' as 'an absolutely sickening experience'.[45] While the principle of agreement over the eight seats considered in danger to unionism was accepted, no agreement on the allocation could be arrived at. Dillon came under pressure from Devlin that the proposal on Ulster 'ought to be accepted' in order to secure the representation of 'practically all the men of our loyal supporters ... who at present represent northern constituencies'. He stated that if the proposal was rejected 'Harbinson's and Donnelly's seats will be lost, and that Tyrone North-West will either go to the Sinn Féiners or the Tories', that there were no guarantees that the IPP would win any seat, except his own and that 'the proposal will strengthen us'.[46] Despite further protests from Devlin about clerical interference, the decision on seat allocation was eventually made by Cardinal Logue.[47]

Regardless of the attempted pact, Sinn Féin fielded a candidate in every contested election of Ulster except Down North and Belfast Shankill. In the counties that later formed Northern Ireland they lost out hugely to unionists, who won 58 per cent of the total, nationalists, who took 32.7 per cent and labour and others, with 9.1 per cent. Sinn Féin secured only five seats in the six counties (of the later Northern Ireland) and this was chiefly because of the nationalist pact. Unionists won Antrim (Sinn Féin only obtained 8,643 out of a total valid poll of 57,451, while unionists secured 48,808 votes), Armagh (except for Armagh South, where the nationalist candidate won), Belfast, Down (although with a tighter contest in Down East), Fermanagh North (but they lost Fermanagh South), Londonderry (except for the city, where MacNeill took a tight victory) and Tyrone South (with Sinn Féin securing Tyrone North-West and the nationalist candidate Tyrone North-East).[48]

45 TCD, JD, MSS 6742/561: Dillon to O'Connor, 3 Dec. 1918. 46 Ibid., 6730/201: Devlin to Dillon, 28 Nov. 1918. 47 Ibid., 6742/561: Dillon to O'Connor, 3 Dec. 1918. 48 Walker, *Parliamentary election results*, pp 4–9; appendix 1.

Table 1.6 Seats won in Ulster in 1918

Political Party	Seats won	Percentage win
Unionist*	23	60.5
IPP	5	13.2
Sinn Féin	10	26.3

* Including Labour Unionist and independent

The pact did not hold up, particularly in two Down constituencies, and in Down East the three-way contest gave victory to the unionist candidate David Reid. The combined votes of Sinn Féin and the IPP totalled 8,188 which could have defeated Reid by a margin of over 2,000. Down South was similar, but this time it was a four-way contest and the nationalist candidate, Jeremiah McVeigh, prevailed by a margin of 3,183 to his nearest rival, the unionist, John Weir Johnston.

Unionists had hoped to win thirty seats in total across the island, but did not do as well as expected. Twenty-six seats were secured, which did exceed previous parliamentary representation by eight (including labour unionists and universities). In total across Ulster, unionists won 23 seats, Sinn Féin captured 10, the IPP took 5 (see table 1.6).

The total electorate for contested constituencies in Ulster (nine counties) was 656,409, and the total votes cast in contested constituencies were 468,621 (there was no contest in either of the two Cavan constituencies so the seats went to Sinn Féin). Percentage turnout in Ulster (including Queen's University) was 71.4 per cent, so, unlike large areas of the other provinces, voter turnout in Ulster was high. Polling was also high because in Ulster, particularly in the six counties, there was more at risk. The threat of partition sent nationalists and unionists to the ballot box, and the more moderate approach of the IPP's home rule policy generally secured the votes, rather than Sinn Féin.

The unionist vote across the nine counties was 242,044 out of the 468,621, which gave them over 50 per cent of the province. They captured Antrim (excluding Belfast) with 84.9 per cent of the votes, winning all four seats. In Armagh Mid and North they heavily defeated the Sinn Féin candidates to secure 59 per cent. In Down Mid (Craig's constituency), North, West (nationalist pact) and East, unionists received 73.9 per cent of the votes (65.6 per cent if Down South is included). Fermanagh North was a difficult contest, but the unionist, Edward Archdale, defeated Sinn Féin's Kevin O'Shiel by 532 votes. The reverse occurred in Fermanagh South with Sinn Féin's majority of 2,149 giving them a comfortable win over the unionist and nationalist candidates. Londonderry South saw a three-way contest between unionists and nationalists where 'unionist workers left nothing undone'.[49] The unionist candidate overpowered their Sinn Féin

49 *IT*, 16 Dec. 1918.

rival in Londonderry North to attain a 72.7 per cent majority. A heated contest in Londonderry city gave Eoin MacNeill a slim majority over the unionist Sir Robert Anderson, and both wiped out the home ruler Major William Davey who attained a meagre 120 votes.

In Monaghan constitutional nationalists gained 27.4 per cent of the vote, and in Fermanagh South they attained only 1.2 per cent (Sinn Féin attained 58.9 percent), and in Donegal nationalists (constitutional and separatist) captured all the seats – three constituencies selected the Sinn Féin candidates and in one, Donegal East, the nationalist Edward Kelly secured the majority. There were no unionist candidates in Armagh South, Belfast Falls, Donegal North, South, West and Monaghan South.

The determination to hold Ulster invigorated an abrasive unionist propaganda campaign. Carson's Belfast Duncairn Division contest showcases unionist determination. This was a three-way battle between Carson, Major William Davey, a liberal home ruler, and Dr Russell McNabb of Sinn Féin. Carson mounted a continuous, challenging and bellicose election campaign. He and Lady Carson toured the constituency on polling day, and unionists ferried voters and supporters using 'numerous motor cars and perfect organization'.[50] Davey was unable to compete against Carson's ability to fund the use of motor vehicles, so he issued literature to instruct electors not to 'wait for motor cars! Major Davey had to foot it in France. Follow his example and walk to the poll.' Using similar warlike analogies to those of unionists in an attempt to appeal in a constituency that supported the war effort, he 'plastered' the district 'with bills and the request to "Go over the top behind the Major"'. He also promoted his educational achievements and his military accomplishments.[51] Defeating the leader of unionism, regardless of nationalist propaganda, was unachievable. But, while Davey lost out heavily to Carson, who received 11,637 votes, his 2,449 votes were better than McNabb's paltry 271. This indicates that Davey's nationalism and his strong publicity campaign won out against the Sinn Féin candidate, but it also shows that in this constituency any candidate was better than an unknown and perhaps even untrusted Sinn Féiner. But, in this strong unionist constituency, those who did not want Carsonism (perhaps because of the threat of partition) had no labour alternative. For instance, in Belfast's St Anne's, Shankill and Victoria wards Labour Unionists polled strongly, defeating their official unionist opponents and wiping out Sinn Féin (although Sinn Féin did marginally better in the St Anne's Division).

In Ulster nationalists had to compete against unionists even in constituencies where the pact held up. The IPP was more successful here than in the southern provinces, but Sinn Féin still secured more overall votes, with its total reaching 109,446. It had bravely contested seats in parts of Ulster where the IPP had never ventured, and only the unionist stronghold of Down North (and Trinity

---

50 Ibid., 23 Dec. 1918.   **51** Ibid., 16 Dec. 1918; NLI, ILB 300, p. 4 (item 2): election poster for Londonderry city.

College Dublin) was to be left unchallenged. The IPP attained only 70,849 votes across the nine counties, but their votes in Belfast exceeded those of Sinn Féin by 2,032.

THE 1920 URBAN AND RURAL ELECTIONS

The municipal elections took place in January 1920 amid escalating violence and labour agitation in some areas of Ireland. There were also elections to local boards, such as the board of guardians, but the emphasis in this section is on the urban and rural elections. The national issue remained to the forefront of electoral propaganda, but there was growing ire among agricultural labourers over low wages and post-war inflation, and among town businesses over increased rates. Volunteers were attacking British government property and carrying out raids for arms and funds in areas of the country. In early April many abandoned Royal Irish Constabulary (RIC) barracks were burned to the ground to prevent their being used again and income tax offices were also attacked.[52]

Strikes organized by workers to oppose the British presence in Ireland began in Limerick in April 1919 to protest against the county being declared a 'special military area' under the Defence of the Realm Act (DORA). By now special permits issued by the RIC were necessary to enter the city. In May 1920 Dublin dockers refused to handle any British military material, and they were soon joined by the Irish Transport and General Workers' Union (ITGWU), which banned railway drivers from carrying British forces. The situation was brought under control by the threat to withhold grants from railway companies, which meant railway workers would not get paid.[53]

This suggests that the local government elections should have been acrimonious and hostile, yet this backdrop of unease was rarely mentioned in electoral propaganda or electoral newspaper reports. Commentary across all newspapers stated that the municipal and rural elections were 'fought with good feeling'. Rivalry between candidates was keen in contested constituencies, but there were only very few instances of violence, with minor skirmishes.[54] Corporation contests excited the most interest, but most observations in newspapers remarked that there was an 'atmosphere of apathy' among the voting public. Concerns were raised that 'lamentable apathy was found among those who should have had the greatest interest in municipal affairs'.[55] Local elections are less exciting than national elections (but not less important at local level) and turnout tends to be lower, but given that

52 Michael Hopkinson, *The Irish War of Independence* (Dublin, 2004), pp 25–30; Richard Abbott, *Police casualties in Ireland, 1919–1922* (Cork, 2000); see also BMH WS 1440: Daniel Byrne. **53** *FJ*, 23 Apr. 1919 and *II*, 23 Apr. 1919. See also ILP&TUC, Report of the Twenty-Fifth Annual Meeting, Aug. 1919 and Report of the Twenty-Sixth Annual Meeting, Aug. 1920; and Liam Cahill, *Forgotten revolution: Limerick Soviet 1919: a threat to British Power in Ireland* (Dublin, 1990), p. 74. **54** *IT*, 19 Jan. 1920; *FJ*, 13 Jan. 1920. **55** *IT*, 3 Jan. 1920.

no elections had taken place for six years, interest should have been livelier. The *Connacht Tribune* classified the electoral mood as 'utter apathy' in the Galway and Connemara areas. In three of their five districts there were no contests, and many of the existing councillors withdrew.[56] While no reason was given for their withdrawal, the newspaper commented that 'more of the "old" men retire'; and it was also reported that they were asked to 'stand down' by the president of the local Sinn Féin Club.

The outcome of these elections can inform on whether Sinn Féin's 1918 election victory was an anomaly or if their policies had become embedded at the local level by 1920, particularly with the introduction of proportional representation. It is unfeasible to examine every contest, so the focus will be on the larger constituencies, where more enthusiastic campaigns resulted in interesting results. These provided data and returns from the large cities and towns and therefore afford a broader indication of voter behaviour. There were 1,847 vacant seats contested by over 2,300 candidates in the municipal elections, and of these 1,300 were Sinn Féin or Labour and 1,000 were constitutional nationalists, unionists or independents. Constitutional nationalists did not run under the banner of the IPP – or at least newspaper reports on results referred to them only as 'nationalists' – even though pleas were made to Dillon to reorganize the party.

Rank-and-file nationalists were not prepared to go down without a fight in January 1920 and at local level there were still some success stories, but despair had set in at leadership level. The Blackrock Urban District Council passed a resolution at their bimonthly meeting that deplored the 'present condition of the country' and requested that Dillon and Devlin 'take steps to re-organize the nationalist forces in Ireland'. Dillon's pessimistic reply was that no remedy was possible because the determination of Sinn Féin and the 'military Government' made 'any constitutional movement in Ireland impossible'. The solution proffered was postponement and deliberation until there was 'some general evidence' that the Irish people were 'growing dissatisfied with their present leaders'. He advised nationalists to 'get together, organize and discuss the situation' with those who voted Sinn Féin at the last election and with those who stayed away from the polls. This, he maintained, was the only way that in the future 'there may be some machinery in existence' to 'lay a programme of action before the people'.[57]

Nationalists rarely topped the poll, except in Dundalk where they headed in each of the four wards, but they won fourteen seats in Dublin Corporation and had a number of successes in the Dublin townships.[58] The nationalist John Harkin in the Victoria Division of Belfast became the youngest senior alderman at only 21 years of age.[59] And, as will be discussed later, nationalists held onto a number of other Belfast seats. Only a small number of unionists outside the north-east of Ulster survived the elections – sixty-six in the three southern provinces – but it is

---

56 *Connacht Tribune (CT)*, 15 May 1920.   57 Appendix 2; *IT*, 2 Jan. 1920.   58 *IT*, 24 Jan. 1920.   59 *FJ*, 19 Jan. 1920.

important to note that the Ratepayers' and Municipal Reform parties, as well as independents, included unionists.

In terms of campaigning, Sinn Féin and Labour Party candidates were 'extremely active' and the *Irish Times* warned readers that 'none of us wants to see our municipal affairs directed by a Sinn Féin-Labour bloc'.[60] Sinn Féin and ITGWU had fused in some constituencies to gain the republican and working-class votes, such as in Cork where the former obtained forty-two nominations and the latter fourteen. The Cork District Trades and Labour Council ran thirteen candidates to frustrate the attempt of the Sinn Féin-ITGWU coalition, indicating that not all in labour supported Sinn Féin. But, a majority of Cork's voters selected the Sinn Féin and ITGWU combination. The new composition was: Sinn Féin and ITGWU, 24 seats; nationalists, 14; commercial, 2; independents, 3; labour, 4; and Demobilized Sailors and Soldiers, 3.[61] Protestants still played a pivotal role in Cork's economy and local representation was important, and despite their low numbers unionists could still exert influence. While no unionists directly won in January 1920, three ex-soldiers (one each in three divisions of the seven) and two commercial candidates were successful across the seven divisions of Cork.[62]

In the municipal elections Sinn Féin captured 561 seats (30.1 per cent), unionists won 368 seats (19.9 per cent), Labour Party 400 (21.7 per cent) and nationalists 236 (12.8 per cent) with the rest going to Ratepayers, Municipal Reform and independents (15.3 per cent). The total number of councillors elected was 1,847. Across the country 650 Labour Party candidates were nominated and they made great strides. Next to Sinn Féin they gained control of the largest share of municipal government in Ireland. There was a strong Labour Party vote in Wexford town where fifteen candidates contested for twenty-four seats and secured ten.[63] This suggests that had they ran candidates in 1918 they may have captured votes in cities and towns from nationalists, particularly from those who did not turn out on election day.

Sinn Féin gains were made in Ulster, but (similar to 1918) a Sinn Féin-nationalist pact in many areas makes it difficult to assess overall strength. For example, in the Strabane, Cookstown and Dungannon Rural District Councils the Sinn Féin-nationalist combination won – in the latter two for the first time. Omagh Rural District Council was also retained by nationalists. Throughout their election campaign they suffered from raids, resulting in the seizure of literature on a number of occasions. Sinn Féin claimed that the purpose was to 'prevent voters giving free expression to their opinion'.[64] Griffith ranted against the injustices committed against Sinn Féin during the municipal elections, asserting that it had to face the election with its political organization suppressed by the English government, its election literature interdicted, its transit arrangements deliberately obstructed by the Motor Permits Order, its secretary, Alderman Kelly, seized and imprisoned without charge and its press stifled.[65]

60 *IT*, 3 Jan. 1920. 61 Ibid., 24 Jan. 1920. 62 Ibid. 63 Ibid., 20 Jan. 1920 64 *FJ*, 24 Jan. 1920. 65 *Donegal News*, 24 Jan. 1920.

Despite this, Sinn Féin secured predominance on municipal councils in Ulster outside the five counties of Armagh, Antrim, Down, Fermanagh and Londonderry. They were particularly dominant on the urban councils in Leinster and Munster.[66] Three-fourths of Dublin Corporation councillors were Sinn Féin and, according to Griffith, they polled 'almost man for man in Rathmines, the English garrison's one stronghold outside Belfast'. He pointed out that Sinn Féin had 'forced its way' into Belfast Corporation and in the south, east and west, and in most of the north 'it has planted its standard'.[67]

In Ulster approximately 142,000 votes were recorded and more than half of them were unionist, with the Labour vote at 25,000 and nationalists at 20,000. Londonderry city was one of the keenest contests, where nationalists bid for twenty-two seats and unionists for twenty-one. To gain a majority of two on the Council all unionist candidates had to be successful. Unionists issued two private circulars to their supporters warning that failure at the polls would result in 'the election of a Roman Catholic Mayor and a Sinn Féin Corporation'. Unionists were also warned that

> all hope of obtaining equality for the Unionists in the new Corporation, and the power of deciding the question of mayoralty depends upon every voter voting in alphabetical order and for all the Unionist candidates. To leave any one Unionist out would be fatal.[68]

These passionate pleas inspired, but they also bolstered nationalists who rallied supporters to 'relieve the Derry Corporation from the domination of the Unionists'.[69]

Londonderry city had 3,844 valid votes and the total unionist first preference vote was 2,035, with nationalists at 1,809. Of the valid votes it was estimated that 40 per cent were women.[70] Accusations of personation and gerrymandering of electoral borders abounded and the South East ward became the subject of a high court action. The end result in January 1920 was a bitterly disappointing nineteen seats for unionists, with constitutional nationalists gaining eleven seats, and Sinn Féin ten seats. Nationalists held a majority for the first time in the history of Londonderry Corporation, having a total of twenty-one seats. Scenes of 'great nationalist jubilation' took place, with 'bonfires blazing in the streets'. The *Freeman's Journal* reported that 'for the first time since the Siege [of Derry] a Catholic and Nationalist has been returned as the Chief Magistrate of the Maiden City'.[71] Chas Bradley of Sinn Féin in his address to the inaugural meeting of the corporation spoke in 'Gaelic', and 'it was the first time that the Irish language had been used in the Guildhall at a municipal gathering'.[72] Londonderry, however, did not hold its nationalist advantage when the Government of Ireland Act was introduced and after the border was eventually drawn to establish Northern Ireland. The abolition of proportional representation

66 Ibid. 67 Ibid. 68 *FJ*, 15 Jan. 1920. 69 Ibid.; *Strabane Chronicle (SCh)*, 24 Jan. 1920. 70 Ibid. 71 *FJ*, 31 Jan. 1920. 72 Ibid.

for the Northern Ireland elections in 1929, and the altering of electoral boundaries, returned unionists to local-authority power.[73] Disputes over electoral gerrymandering and voting rights continued, leading to the formation of the Northern Ireland Civil Rights Association in the 1960s.[74]

In 1920 Limavady was another devastating loss for unionists in Ulster as the constituency previously had been in their control. The contest returned 3 nationalists, 4 unionists, 1 Labour and 1 Comrade of the Great War. In Portstewart, another previous unionist stronghold, the unionist vote held, but one nationalist was elected in the West Ward and two Comrades in the East Ward out of a total of twelve seats. In Lisburn, where unionists held nearly all the seats, surprise came in the success of the Sinn Féin candidate W.F. Shaw. The *Fermanagh Herald* reported that 'the return of a Sinn Féiner at the head of the poll in one ward is an extraordinary result in so loyal a town'.[75]

In Belfast, unionists or labour unionists consistently remained dominant. Independent nationalist labour had posed a threat to Sinn Féin so (in similar fashion to Cork) they combined with labour to 'plant the flag of progress and toleration'.[76] Official unionists had nominated 55 candidates for 60 seats, but only 35 were elected (plus 2 independents). Belfast's new corporation comprised 37 unionists (including 3 independents and 5 Labour unionists), 13 Labour, 5 Nationalist and 5 Sinn Féin (see table 1.7).[77]

Table 1.7 Belfast Corporation, January 1920

Division	Register	Valid votes	Spoiled votes	Unionist	Labour	Nationalist	Sinn Féin
Cromac	17,014	10,635	209	5	1	1	0
Duncairn	15,259	9,945	248	5	1	1	0
Falls	13,193	9,811	764	1	1	2	2
Ormeau	13,264	8,328	160	4	2	0	0
Pottinger	13,474	8,379	267	4	1	0	1
Shankill	17,629	12,057	289	5	2	0	1
St Anne's	14,275	9,356	342	4	2	0	0
Victoria	15,917	9,275	300	4	1	1	1
Woodvale	15,523	11,245	212	5	2	0	0
Total	135,548	89,013	2,791 (3.1%)[78]	37 (61.7%)	13 (21.7)	5 (8.3%)	5 (8.3%)

73 A.C. Hepburn, *The conflict of nationality in modern Ireland: documents of modern history* (London, 1980), p. 152. 74 Walker, *A history of the Ulster Unionist Party*, p. 162. 75 *Fermanagh Herald (FH)*, 24 Jan. 1920. 76 *FJ*, 19 Jan. 1920. 77 See also *Belfast News-Letter (BNL)*, 19 Jan. 1920 for a comprehensive account of results. 78 See section on voter turnout for discussion on reasons for spoiled votes.

Unionists lost fifteen seats previously held and nationalists lost three, whereas Labour gained thirteen seats and Sinn Féin five. The retention of five IPP seats indicates the enduring strength of Devlinites and this can be attributed to a number of factors. Devlin's long-standing relationship with the AOH had heightened the electorate's perception of him as protector and defender of Catholic interests. Insecurity among Catholics, particularly because Ulster unionist propaganda regularly demanded their supporters to 'Keep Ulster in the empire by voting unionist', heightened anxiety about partition.[79] The more radical policies of Sinn Féin were taking some hold, but the conciliatory approach still appealed to many.[80] Labour's social policies were associated with benevolent societies and the skilled-craft trade-union workers, and their gains reflected cross-class support in Belfast city.

In Dublin the outgoing Corporation had been comprised of IPP members, with a sprinkling of Sinn Féin and Labour Party councillors. After January 1920 Dublin Corporation was divided between Sinn Féin, Labour Party, Municipal Reform, independents and independent nationalists, with one solitary unionist. Sinn Féin gained forty-one of the eighty seats to become the largest party in the corporation with a majority against all other parties put together.[81] Women fared best in the Dublin townships, where nine were returned, with Rathmines electing six, or nearly one-third of the whole council of twenty-one members. Six women represented Sinn Féin, one was a nationalist, one unionist and one Ratepayer. In all there were thirty female candidates in Dublin city (five elected onto the Corporation) and the townships, and fourteen were elected in total. In the provinces women were successful in Cork (1), Limerick (1), Coleraine (1), Carlow (3), Macroom (1) and Castlebay (2).[82] Dublin elected Kathleen Clarke as an 'alderman'. (Belfast was the only other area where a woman, the unionist Julia McMordie, was elected alderman.) In the Dublin townships Sinn Féin candidates fared badly, and Municipal Reform candidates did well in the more affluent areas of Dalkey, Kingstown, Blackrock and Howth.

Limerick had a big turnout for the municipal elections, with the *Limerick Leader* reporting that the corporation elections 'were fought out in a quiet, good humoured spirit, and nothing of an untoward nature, happily, occurred'.[83] Limerick borough was divided into five divisions (instead of the previous eight) and seventy-eight candidates vied for the forty seats. Of these, forty were Sinn Féin, nine Labour, twenty-nine independents (of whom some were nationalists) and Ratepayers' candidates.[84] The result gave twenty-six seats to Sinn Féin, five to Labour, four to independents and five to Ratepayers' candidates. Voter concerns in Limerick were 'abnormal rates, the wretched housing of the working classes, and

---

79 PRONI, UUC Papers, D1327/20/4/142: election poster titled *Ulster's claim on Britain, a proud record*. 80 Anthony C. Hepburn, *A past apart: studies in the history of Catholic Belfast, 1850–1950* (Belfast, 1996), p. 161; Conor Mulvagh, *The Irish Parliamentary Party at Westminster, 1900–1918* (Manchester, 2016), p. 53. 81 *Limerick Leader (LkL)*, 19 Jan. 1920 82 Ibid., 7 Jan. 1920. 83 Ibid., 19 Jan. 1920. 84 Ibid., 7 Jan. 1920.

the "scourge of profiteering"' – which hints at some of the other difficulties that caused strikes. Another 'scourge' was 'excessive drinking, bad picture houses, and the cursed system we Irishmen have of supporting everyone and anyone except our own'.[85] This indicates that members of the old nationalist council were out of favour and unlikely to be re-elected.

In the municipal elections in Galway city nine nationalist outgoing members were returned for ten seats alongside two outgoing independents, three new Labour and ten Sinn Féin candidates; however, in the rural district council elections all the Sinn Féin candidates were returned (except in Clifden, where an independent headed the poll). The return of nationalist candidates was measured on their past performance as the majority were incumbents. For example, Magennis in Kilkenny had lost out to Cosgrave in the by-election of 1917, but he topped the poll in January 1920 and, along with de Loughry of Sinn Féin and another nationalist, Edward Healy, he became alderman of the city.[86] The *Kilkenny People* believed that voters had cast in favour of constitutional nationalists because they saw them as 'a sort of breakwater against the rising tide of expenditure that threatens to plunge the city hopelessly into debt'.[87] In Ulster constituencies nationalists won seats in Londonderry city, Omagh, Belfast, Downpatrick in Co. Down, and Strabane Urban District Council. In Lisburn – which was described as 'a hotbed of Orangeism' by the *Strabane Chronicle* – voters returned 1 Sinn Féin candidate, 2 nationalists, 3 Labour candidates and 1 independent, with 8 unionists giving them a majority.[88]

In June 1920 four of the six future Northern Ireland counties retained large unionist majorities, but both Tyrone and Fermanagh were won by non-unionists. In the Falls Division in Belfast (contrary to the 1918 election results) two-thirds of Devlin's nationalists were swept out – no doubt because of Sinn Féin's 1918 electoral success, which instilled more confidence in the party.[89] In the southern provinces Mayo County Council became exclusively Sinn Féin, as did every

Table 1.8 Number of party seats in Ulster in 1920 municipal elections

Party	Seats	% of total
Unionists	302	46.7
Labour	109	16.9
Sinn Féin	103	15.9
Nationalist	94	14.5
Independents	33	5.1
Municipal Reform/ Ratepayers	5	0.8

85 Ibid., 16 Jan. 1920: letter to the editor by J.J. Hobbens of the W&IF Training School in Limerick.   86 *Kilkenny People (KP)*, 24 Jan. 1920.   87 Ibid.   88 *SCh*, 24 Jan. 1920; *FH*, 24 Jan. 1920. For a full list of urban election results see appendix 2.   89 Appendix 3; *BNL*, 16 June 1920.

district council in the county. Roscommon elected a complete Sinn Féin council; Tipperary North Riding was composed of nineteen Sinn Féin members and one Labour Party representative, with all independents being defeated; in Meath Sinn Féin won twenty out of the twenty-one seats, and in Louth Sinn Féin won eighteen out of twenty-eight seats. In Wexford there were contests in five areas, and with nineteen candidates, all the seats went to Sinn Féin and the Labour Party. In Dublin North out of a register of 3,642, 1,986 polled and two Labour and three Sinn Féin were returned. Kingstown saw two unionist candidates returned – Lady Dockrell, who received 1,383 votes from a total poll of 7,935 (15,519 on the register), and the official unionist, Patrick Merrin, who received 602 votes and was elected after the fifteenth count. He had been elected in the municipal elections in January 1920 with 249 first preferences from a valid poll of 1,064:[90]

Ratepayers fared well in some districts also, for instance in Donegal five Ratepayers were returned in the municipal elections, and in Ballina's Ardnaree ward two of the four seats went to Ratepayer candidates, with the other two going to the Labour Party in the RDC elections. They had previously fared well in the 1919 Sligo elections.[91] Municipal Reform candidates, on the other hand, were disappointed as they secured only a few seats in the local elections and most were in Dublin or areas of Munster.[92]

Outside Ulster, Sinn Féin and the Sinn Féin-Labour coalition often gained seats without contest. For instance, in Carlow thirteen Sinn Féin candidates and seven Labour Party candidates were returned unopposed, and similarly Clare had no contests with twenty Sinn Féin councillors selected. Whether this was because Sinn Féin was strong in rural areas or whether other parties decided not to enter the contests because of the expense, dearth of candidates or simply lack of interest is unknown. In areas of Ulster, separatists and nationalists again formed coalitions or pacts. The all island results are available in appendix three, and percentage vote is in table 1.9.

Sinn Féin took exclusive control of the councils in Tipperary South, Cork, Limerick, Kerry, Clare, Longford, Galway, Mayo, Roscommon and Leitrim. And took control with Labour in Carlow (7 Labour), King's County (2 Labour),

Table 1.9 Percentage vote by party or coalition in the 1920 rural district council elections

Party(s)	Seats	% votes
Sinn Féin	523	74.7
Sinn Féin and labour	567	81.0
Sinn Féin and nationalists (Ulster)	103	14.7
Unionists	85	12.2

90 *FJ*, 9 June 1920; *IT*, 19 Jan. 1920.   91 See introduction.   92 *FJ*, 19 Jan. 1920.

Tipperary North (1 Labour), Waterford (3 Labour); and in Cavan with 1 nationalist. The percentage gain in other counties was: Donegal (75), Londonderry (21), Armagh (21.7), Down, (20), Tyrone (30.8), Fermanagh (30), Monaghan (80), Dublin (63.1), Meath (95.2), Kildare (71.4), Queen's County (81.8), Louth (64.3), Westmeath (65.2), Wicklow (68.4) and Kilkenny (84.2).[93]

Sinn Féin's success in 1920 allowed them to progressively usurp authority from the imperial parliament by refusing to recognize the control of the Local Government Board (LGB) and encouraging councils to make declarations of allegiance to Dáil Éireann.[94] Local allegiance transferred in many counties outside the north-east region of Ulster from the LGB in the Custom House to the Local Government Department under William Cosgrave, although they did so at differing times, and some held out until agreed past and profitable deals were realized. In Dundalk, for example, the council chose not to pledge allegiance until the sale of Dundalk Demesne had been finalized because they needed the LGB to put up the money to purchase Lord Roden's interest in the property.[95] Once allegiance was pledged, copies of minutes and routine returns had to be sent to the Local Government Department of Dáil Éireann rather than to Dublin Castle.

By the end of 1920, however, Sinn Féin had established its constituent assembly and was in control of most urban and rural councils. By obtaining the adherence of councils, establishing the use of the Irish language (even minimally) and seizing the administration they had waged a symbolic battle in an unclear political environment. The British administration quickly notified local councils that no loans or grants would be made to any local authority unless accounts were submitted, routine audits allowed and the rules set out by the LGB followed. Belief in Dáil Éireann roused angry protests from some councillors such as those in Kilkenny, who acerbically asked 'are we going to sell ourselves for a few pounds?' According to the minutes of the council an order was given for the LGB letter to be destroyed. This was done, but when a second letter arrived two months later the council sent in their returns – financing the local area evidently took precedence.[96] This was more a matter of form than recognition or approval, and many councils humoured the authority that best served their needs. However, some municipalities faced bankruptcy because of the lack of funds from the LGB, particularly Dublin Corporation. Many property owners were reluctant to pay rates to these councils, diminishing funds further. Cosgrave, assisted by Kevin O'Higgins, instructed local bodies to carefully conceal their finances and use hidden bank accounts to avoid seizure of their funds.

Dealings with Dáil Éireann resembled and followed the practices of the LGB. According to the clerk of Kilkenny Rural District Council, Dáil Éireann was 'strictly adhering' to the LGB regulations and they added that 'in fact they are a little more strict that the LGB'.[97] The dual administration did not last as

93 *Ulster Herald (UH)*, 19 June 1920; see also *Irish Bulletin*, June 1920.   **94** See *KP*, 19 June 1920 for an example.   **95** BMH WS 353: James McGuill.   **96** *KP*, 7 Aug. 1920.   **97** Ibid.

councils moved progressively under the authority of Dáil Éireann, and eventually in November 1920 an order was issued to sever relations with the LGB.

Sinn Féin's 75 per cent success rate in the rural district councils does not necessarily indicate orthodoxy of voter belief. It was the result of a number of factors. They put forward candidates where other parties did not, and voters who turned up at the polls in contested constituencies were already Sinn Féin adherents or had been persuaded by their propaganda. Variances of opinion in larger urban centres resulted in a wider party spread in the councils. Sinn Féin's organization, discipline and Volunteer contributions at the rural level facilitated voters receiving propaganda messages and accessing the polling booths.

Their success in Ulster in January did not raise widespread concern among unionists. Richard Dawson Bates commented to Carson that 'at first glance the Elections, so far as regards Belfast, look worse than they really are'. He pointed out that Sinn Féin topped the poll in the St Anne's Division yet they were 'a negligible quality in that Division'. He apportioned blame to proportional representation, but also to the 'general apathy on the part of the public … which is frequently the case in municipal matters'.[98] In an earlier letter he remarked that 'the bulk of the rank and file would be quite prepared to accept a parliament for the six counties in preference to nine counties', and anticipation of this outcome may have resulted in voter apathy for local elections. A new parliament for areas of Ulster would, and did, allow for new laws on local government elections.[99]

In 1919 Major Bryan Cooper, acting Press Censor for Ireland, attributed Sinn Féin's increasing success to the fact that the government had 'turned a blind eye to the doings of Dáil Éireann' and was unable to 'bring the murderers to justice'. Fault lay with the 'already overburdened police force'.[100] For Sinn Féin, gaining success at the local level received equal attention to general election aspirations. A temporary transfer of available staff into the elections department to oversee the local elections provided experience and personnel.[101] And, a clear and resolute programme was adopted for the municipal elections, which aimed:

> to secure the expenditure of the rates raised in Ireland inside Ireland, to secure efficiency and purity of administration, to establish the principle of free and open competition for public appointments, and, to carry into effect the democratic programme approved by the elected representatives of Ireland.[102]

The content may not have been all that electrifying, but it set out to address the issue of rates, which was a focal concern for town businesses and local industry, and it set out to remedy the widespread perception of corruption and jobbery in local

98 PRONI, Carson Papers, D1507/A/33/20: Dawson Bates to Carson, 23 Jan. 1920.   99 Ibid., 33/1: 3 Jan. 1920.   100 *KP*, 29 Dec. 1919.   101 Sinn Féin Standing Committee meeting (SFSCM), 4 Dec. 1919.   102 Ibid., 26 Nov. 1919.

councils that had lain under the control of unionists and constitutional nationalists in the past. The Labour Party's mandate for the local elections had absorbed the ideals of the democratic programme. Sinn Féin's reference to this allowed for both the assimilation of similar ideals in the promotion of working-class values which facilitated alliances, and the targeting of the Labour Party or trade-union vote.

The 1920 local-government elections were pivotal in embedding Sinn Féin authority during the interim and politically transformative years from 1917 to the formation of the Free State. These elections demonstrated a diversity of electoral opinion, which was enabled by the introduction of proportional representation. As will be seen in chapters 4 and 5, industrious campaigning by candidates secured classified advertising in local and national newspapers that persuaded voters to cast for Sinn Féin.

THE 1921 GENERAL ELECTION

There was a view that these elections should not be held at all because, according to Lieutenant-Colonel Walter Guinness, 'no one in the South, except the Sinn Féiners, wished them to be held under present conditions'. He was referring to the increasing hostilities between the IRA and crown forces, and he rightly predicted that it would lead to 'an unchallenged mandate for the extreme Republican demand' and that the 'election would not show the gradations in Irish opinion'.[103] The gradations were evident in the municipal elections of 1920, but the lack of contest in 1921 for the southern parliament makes it impossible to discern voter opinion at any great level because of the lack of competitive political propaganda.

No constitutional nationalists contested the elections mainly because Dillon issued a statement that any contests would lead to 'the bitterest possible feeling, and might result in disorder and bloodshed' and he could 'not consent to be in any degree responsible'. His primary concern was that any opposition to Sinn Féin would lay open the charge of supporting the Black and Tans, and that the British government had made it impossible over the past three years for any nationalist to fight Sinn Féin at this election. He remained steadfast in his belief that Sinn Féin was on the path of 'war between the two nations' and the IPP sought 'compromise and peaceful means'. 'Time', he added, 'will tell which is right'.[104] Unfortunately for Dillon, in providing this time he paved the way for the death of the IPP. The lack of competition led to voter apathy, with the *Nationalist and Leinster Times* reporting that 'the masses of the people took no direct interest in the matter' aside from the opinion that 'none with any scintilla of nationality wanted the Partition Act'. As will be seen later, this election became known as the 'partition election' and this may have reinforced belief among constitutional nationalists to follow Dillon's advice and hold back on challenging Sinn Féin in an effort to

103 *IT*, 29 Apr. 1921.   104 *BNL*, 9 Apr. 1921.

Table 1.10 Candidates elected by party in 1921 for northern parliament, based on first-preference votes before transfers

Party	Seats	% of seats	Votes	% of valid votes
Unionists (partitionists)	40	76.9	343,347	74.6
Sinn Féin (anti-partitionist)	6	11.5	69,293	15.1
Nationalist Party (IPP) (anti-partitionists)	6	11.5	47,631	10.3
Total	52	100.0	460,271	100.0

avoid acrimony among nationalists that might fuel unionist demands. The success of Sinn Féin in 1918 and at local level in 1920 gave them a walk-over in 1921 in the three southern provinces.

Voting did take place for the northern parliament and it was polarized between unionists and nationalists – partition versus anti-partition. The Belfast Labour Party did not contest (although five members of the Independent Labour Party contested, with all combined polling less than 1 per cent of the total votes). The overall final result in the north was a unionist victory, with a win of 40 of the 52 seats, gaining 74.6 per cent of the total vote. Sinn Féin won six seats, with 15.1 per cent of the votes and nationalists won six seats but with only 10.3 per cent of the votes. Voters in the six counties and north-east Ulster particularly were largely with the unionist viewpoint (see table 1.10).[105]

The highest percentage of unionist votes was in east Ulster, corresponding closely with the population distribution of Protestants – although they were strong in all constituencies, allowing even the least supported candidate to gain enough votes to reach the quota. They fielded forty candidates and attained forty seats and reached the quota each time. They had very accurately gauged the number of seats they could win and this was largely because they had made calculations based on religious affiliation, i.e. Protestant voters voted unionist.[106]

Nationalists did not appoint enough candidates to challenge unionists, and this was also problematic when it came to transferring surplus votes under PR-STV. Because nationalists did not give later transfers to unionists, many votes were unused, and because there was a reluctance to cast outside of party interests some candidates failed to reach the quota – Devlin did not reach the quota in either of the two constituencies he contested. Sinn Féin fared better in the rural west, although in the east the nationalists managed to out-poll Sinn Féin only in Antrim and West

105 See appendix 4 for Northern Ireland results.   **106** D.G. Pringle, 'Electoral systems and political manipulation: a case study of Northern Ireland in the 1920s', *Economic and Social Review*, 11:3 (Apr. 1980), 187–205.

Belfast (Devlin's constituencies). The low percentage of votes transferred between all parties – despite an agreement that nationalists of both hues would encourage voters to give later preferences to other nationalists – also points to ardent party views being held by the electorate in these constituencies.

Taking the entire six counties, the anti-partitionist wins were roughly 116,924 and the partitionist poll was 343,347. So, the partitionist percentage of votes won was 74.6 against 25.4 per cent for anti-partitionists. Therefore, in 1921 in Ulster, opinion had not changed since the third home rule bill crisis in 1912.

FACTORS AFFECTING ELECTION RESULTS 1918–21

The total registered electorate in contested constituencies in 1918 was 1,462,895 and the total valid poll for contested constituencies was 1,039,143, therefore 423,752 did not turn out on election day. The Great War, erroneous registers (despite attempts to update them), distance from polling booths, deceased voters and emigration did cause a lot of the absenteeism in 1918, but it does not account for figures running into thousands more. In Galway Connemara, for instance, the Sinn Féin candidate attained 11,754 votes and the IPP 3,482, where the total electorate was 24,956. Therefore, 9,720 voters did not go to the poll. In Leitrim, where Dolan defeated the IPP candidate by massive 14,615 votes, 9,272 eligible electors abstained from voting. As mentioned, in Dillon's constituency the total electorate was 21,635, yet 8,146 stayed away from the ballot box. The intimate reasons for voter disaffection will remain forever unknown, but a palpable spurning of both nationalist parties or a dislike of the candidates was evident. A desired (but unavailable) alternative such as the Labour Party may have captured these votes, and the 1920 urban election results hint at this. It seems the choice between Sinn Féin separatism and IPP constitutionalism was too limited or entirely deficient to meet the hopes and wants of abstaining voters.

Over the course of the Great War 210,000 had enlisted, and of those it is estimated that between 30,000 and 35,000 Irish people died.[107] Men, and women, who might previously have campaigned on behalf of or voted for unionism or constitutional nationalism in the 1918 election were either still at the frontlines, making their way home or were killed or missing in action. Many would not return in time to cast their votes on 14 December 1918. The *Northern Whig* estimated that the number of absent voters was in the region of 'something like 22,000'.[108] The

---

107 See Fitzpatrick, 'Militarism in Ireland, 1900–1922' in Thomas Bartlett and Keith Jeffery (eds), *A military history of Ireland* (Cambridge, 1996), p. 388; War Office, *Statistics of the military effort of the British empire during the Great War*, p. 192; Fionnuala Walsh, 'The impact of the Great War on women in Ireland, 1914 to 1919' (TCD, PhD, 2017), pp 182–3; Philip Orr, '200,000 volunteer soldiers' in John Horne (ed.), *Our war: Ireland and the Great War* (Dublin, 2008), pp 63, 76. The number of Irish deaths in the British army recorded by the registrar general was 27,405. 108 *Northern Whig (NW)*, 14 Dec. 1918.

Table 1.11 Absent voters and votes returned in the 1918 general election

Constituency	Registered absent voters	Votes returned	Percentage returned
Rathmines (Dublin)	1,500	539	35.9
Wexford South	752	248	33.0
Cork	5,665	1,553	27.4
Queen's County	1,193	316	26.5
Kildare South	755	189	25.0
Pembroke (Dublin)	2,337	495	21.2
Wexford North	900	150	16.7
Total	13,102	3,490 (-9,612)	26.6

new Representation of the People Act allowed for servicemen over 19 to vote and to vote absently if in France or Belgium; all others could appoint proxies,[109] but there were problems with these votes. As the *Irish Times* reported, in Dublin's St James' Division, 84 papers from absent electors were disallowed because they were unstamped. In the Pembroke Division, only 495 absentee votes were polled out of a total of 2,337; in the Rathmines Division, only 539 absent electors out of 1,500 sent in papers; and, in Cork only 1,553 absent votes were recorded out of a potential 5,665. The selection of constituencies in table 1.11 gives some indication of the impact.[110]

While it is unlikely that, say, John Good in Pembroke would have attained all the registered absent votes, speculatively, if the 1,842 votes (figure minus those that were returned) had been added, he could have defeated Desmond FitzGerald; and Peter Ffrench would certainly have defeated James Ryan of Sinn Féin in Wexford South. Yet, in the other constituencies in table 1.11, Sinn Féin's results were too strong to affect change even if absent votes were added. The sample given here was all that was available, and perhaps in other constituencies absent voter numbers were higher. There is wide variation in the registered absent voters and the votes returned in table 1.11, particularly between, for example, Pembroke and Wexford North. Comprehending the reason for this is difficult because the whereabouts of these voters is unknown. They may have been too distant to have received their voting papers in a timely manner for the three-week election lead in, they may have been missing-in-action, or the registers may have been incorrect. Their absence no doubt affected overall results, as Sir Thomas Robinson, the unionist candidate for Dublin South County, lamented that it was 'most discreditable that the Act passed for the purpose of enabling absent voters to record their votes should have so failed

109 HC, PD, vol. 110, cc 1780–3, 4 Nov. 1918: president of the Local Government Board (Mr Hayes Fisher). **110** Figures calculated from *IT*, 30 Nov. 1918 and *CE*, 30 Dec. 1918.

its aim'. He further asserted that 'many thousands' were 'deprived of the opportunity of voting at this election'.[111] A Sinn Féin supporter writing to the *Irish Times* on 15 January 1920 upheld this claim, remarking that there was 'ample proof' that the voting papers reached 'but a small percentage of the men at sea and the men in the trenches' in 1918. However, contrary to the opinion that these men would vote unionist or IPP, he ardently maintained that in the municipal elections of 1920 'the men who were deprived of their votes in 1918 will vote, and in Rathmines the majority will vote Sinn Féin'.

Again in the 1920 municipal elections there was a significant number of uncontested seats and voter turnout was low, for instance in Galway's South ward out of a register of 941 only 542 polled (in the Dublin County contests it was estimated that only half the electorate went to the polls).[112] The vigorous and at times rancorous 1918 general election campaign may have generated electoral fatigue. The mundanity of battling over everyday issues resulted in bland and featureless propaganda campaigns. And, the overall uncertainty of Ireland's future governance may also have caused voters to believe it not worth their while casting votes until final decisions were made. This is mere speculation because whether urban or rural no reasons were provided for this voter apathy. The *Freeman's Journal* reported that by evening there was a little more life at the various centres.[113]

In the 1800s at the local level electoral politics had been intimate, bound up in ties of kinship, which as Hoppen points out 'ran like a leitmotif through Irish life and politics'.[114] 'Parish-pump' politics still existed in 1918, 1920 and 1921, but the relationship between town and country was changing and there were now more voters, and, as will be seen in the next chapter, very few candidates (or voters) were of the old landlord class. While many were still influenced by family and business connections and by religious beliefs, new and unknown candidates appealing for votes weakened the old kinship battles, and localism began to fragment (if only for a brief period). Politics from 1917 to 1921, and slightly beyond, was motivated by the immediate polarized concerns of nationalists and unionists to a large degree, with undercurrents of concern on local issues that really came to light only in the 1920 local elections.

The absence of long-term emigration opportunities due to the war also affected voter numbers. According to the registrar general's report, between 1851 and the outbreak of the Great War, annual emigration overseas never fell below 23,300 and was rarely less than 35,000. Between 1904 and 1913, the average number of migrants was 31,872. If we take the year 1911 as an example, the total number of native Irish emigrants was 30,573, which was equivalent to 7.0 per 1,000 of the population of Ireland. By 1914 the total number of emigrants leaving Ireland fell to 20,314 – 4.6 per 1,000 of the population – a decrease of 10,653 since 1913 (and 10,259 by 1911 figures). In the year 1916, only 7,302 Irish natives emigrated,

111 *IT*, 29 and 30 Nov. 1918. 112 *FJ*, 8 June 1920. 113 Ibid., 8 June 1920. 114 Hoppen, *Elections, politics and society*, p. 66.

which represented a rate of 1.7 per 1,000 of the estimated population.[115] By 1918 the figures had dropped hugely, with the total number of Irish native emigrants being only 980 (442 males and 538 females) representing 0.2 per 1,000 of the estimated population. The majority were now opting for England, Wales and Scotland as opposed to North America or elsewhere. Many who did not migrate may have enlisted for war service, but those who did neither may have been persuaded by or supported the anti-war rhetoric in Sinn Féin propaganda.

Voter turnout was also affected by the influenza pandemic in 1918–19, which killed at least 20,057 people and infected an estimated 800,000 people on the island. According to Ida Milne, the pandemic occurred in three waves in Ireland; a mild wave in the early summer of 1918, and two much more severe waves in the autumn of 1918 and spring of 1919. Milne's research into the medical reports of the Adelaide Hospital in 1918 reveals that 'the peak months for hospital admissions were June, and October, November and December. In many households, entire families were incapacitated by the disease'.[116]

Spoiled votes, either through ignorance or intention, were also uncounted across the elections. Some ballot sheets had 'God Save the King' written across them, indicating that they were unionist in a constituency with no representative candidate, and others wrote 'unionist' or 'nationalist' according to their bias. Some errors saw voters put crosses against two and even three candidates, and one individual placed a huge cross that covered all three names in the constituency showing his or her obvious contempt for the candidates, while another put a zero against the names of rejected candidates.[117]

Many may have stayed away from the polls in hostile constituencies, where volunteer aggression created a state of fear (see chapter 4). Nearly 3,000 failed to vote in Waterford city in 1918, which was ridden with violence. In Wexford, despite William Redmond's determined efforts to instruct IPP supporters to 'allow freedom of speech to our political opponents', disorder prevailed. During a speech by Fr O'Flanagan 'a fracas' quickly assumed the dimensions of a riot and a 'battle royal[e]' took place.[118] Of the 46,190 on the register of electors in Wexford, 12,199 did not vote.

Another oft-made and truthful claim was that Sinn Féin's success was the result of the youth vote. As Garvin phrased it, 'the young were released from any

115 HC, PD, CD 6131, 1912–13, CV, p. 595; HC 1913, CD 6727, LV, p. 933; HC 1914, CD 7313, LXIX, p. 1001; HC 1914–16, CD 7883, LXXX, p. 319; HC 1916, CD 8230, XXXII, p. 915; HC 1917–18, CD 8520, XXXXVII, p. 269; HC 1918, CD 9013, XXV, p. 17. See also Vaughan and Fitzpatrick, *Irish historical statistics*. These figures do not include men and women recruited through labour exchanges for work in Great Britain, as they do not count as emigrants because they were not *permanently* leaving. For migrant war workers, check: NAI CSO RP/1918/33366, Chief Secretary Office Papers.   116 Ida Milne, 'Influenza: the Irish Local Government Board's last great crisis' in Donnacha Seán Lucey and Virginia Crossman, *Healthcare in Ireland and Britain from 1850: voluntary, regional and comparative perspectives* (London, 2015), pp 217–36.   117 *IT*, 30 Dec. 1918.   118 Ibid., 29 Nov. 1918.

restraint [after the conscription crisis] and rushed into Sinn Féin'.[119] Newspapers claimed that 'Sinn Féin has a powerful hold on the youth of the country'.[120] Hart explains that Sinn Féin was a coalition of interests and 'this omnibus "Sinn Féin" flew a republican flag' that was also 'a voice for youth and women'.[121] Youths had been called on to join Sinn Féin clubs in order to receive military instruction, with Eoin MacNeill stating that 'every man should join a Sinn Féin Club and be a soldier and be prepared to act as a soldier'.[122] As will be seen in chapters 2 and 3, like the IPP's UIL and unionist associations, Sinn Féin established clubs at the constituency level in many counties and this enhanced electioneering, enriched fundraising efforts and generated votes.

Accusations of personation and falsifying the register of electors were widespread during the elections in this era and all parties engaged in these practices. In 1918 Patrick Cassidy of Mayo maintained that the IPP was beaten in Dillon's constituency of Ballaghaderreen because of the 'great volume of personation and by falsifying the register of voters and so forth. Dead and absent voters "recorded" their votes.' Eugene Kilkenny of Leitrim remarked that 'in an all-out effort to win the election and finally oust the Redmond Party ... personation was resorted to on a large basis. I myself voted at least fifty times.'[123] In 1920 Sinn Féin in Co. Tyrone accused unionists of personation, stating that 'the booths were not long open on the day of the poll when it became known that a large number of prominent unionists had voted twice, and also that numerous attempts at personation had been made, a good many of which were successful'.[124] However, Sinn Féin's overall support of 47 per cent (from the 69 per cent of the electorate who cast a vote in contested constituencies) in 1918 was a considerable victory margin that offset any advantage secured through internal personation, and it overshadowed competitive personation by the IPP or unionists. All parties were equally culpable of personation so they effectively cancelled each other out. The negative impact on nationalists by unionists impersonating voters in 1921 is more difficult to measure as there was widespread reporting that unionists regularly carried out this activity. For instance, 'In the Ballymacarett district those who were driven from their houses ... were personated in large numbers.' Devlin also accused unionists of personating nationalist voters, stating that they had lost 'hundreds of votes by intimidation' and because the 'unionists have personated our voters'. The *Anglo-Celt* reported that 'when a nationalist family of five voters from Mayo Street, West Belfast, arrived at the booth, they found they had all been personated'.[125]

119 Garvin, *The evolution*, p. 130.   **120** *IT*, 7 and 8 May 1917; *Westmeath Nationalist* and *Midland Reporter*, 26 Apr. 1917.   **121** Peter Hart, *The IRA at war, 1916–23* (Oxford, 2005), p. 17.   **122** Précis of Sinn Féin meetings, 1917, CO 904/23/3 (A 30, iii) in Fitzpatrick, *Politics and Irish life*, p. 174.   **123** BMH WS 1017: Garda Patrick Cassidy; WS 1146: Eugene Kilkenny. For examples see also: WS 1366: Patrick Lennon (Westmeath), WS 1436: Walter Brown (Fingal).   **124** *UH*, 12 June 1920.   **125** *FJ*, 26 May, *II*, 26 May and *Anglo-Celt (AC)*, 28 May 1921.

The claim is also regularly made that Ireland in 1918 had new characters in its political elite that were younger men in their late twenties or thirties – a generation younger than IPP leaders. While this is true when compared against Dillon and O'Connor, it is not true of all IPP candidates. Devlin was 47 years old at the time, only a year older than Griffith. Sinn Féin had also selected the 67-year-old Count Plunkett in 1918 for Roscommon North. An examination of the contested elections shows that most IPP and Sinn Féin candidates were of similar age, with the exception of thirteen. Within this thirteen the candidates of both nationalist parties were similarly older in Fermanagh South, Kildare North, Mayo West and Westmeath. Unionist candidates were inclined to be older, ranging in age from 35 to 67, with the majority being in their late forties to early fifties. Where Sinn Féin benefited in terms of youth was in their Volunteer members. Taking Hart's figures, the majority of Volunteers were 20 to 29 years old, making them useful canvassers and 'peace patrollers' and, if male, eligible voters.[126] Therefore, the youthfulness of the candidates was not as crucial as the youthfulness of those necessary to conduct the propaganda war and cast a vote. Even Dillon conceded that Sinn Féin's by-election victories in Roscommon, Longford and Clare were because of 'the frantic activity of the young Irish, who seem to be possessed by poisonous hatred of the party'.[127] The Irish Volunteer movement (and Cumann na mBan) attracted the young, and imagery in Sinn Féin propaganda regularly portrayed de Valera in military uniform, emphasizing manliness and youth, as shown in plates 1 and 9.[128] Using minimal text and strong imagery, a soldierly de Valera in plate 1 suggested that the coherent path to freedom and prosperity lies with Sinn Féin's plan to appeal to the peace conference. The IPP road promised only high taxation, conscription and famine. De Valera presaged a self-determined future Ireland with an internationalist flair.

'A large number of clergy voted during the day' and Roman Catholic clergymen voted in large numbers in Dublin city in 1918. The Most Reverend Dr John Bernard, Church of Ireland archbishop of Dublin, voted in the Kevin Street polling station at midday and the Most Reverend Dr William Walsh, Roman Catholic archbishop of Dublin, voted at Drumcondra and Finglas, and it was reported that he 'voted in each case for the Sinn Féin candidate'.[129] If the vociferous propagandistic support of separatism by the Catholic clerics is to be believed and if devout members of the electorate followed, the majority of the clergy voiced favour for Sinn Féin (see chapter 4). The *Irish Times* claimed that the Roman Catholic bishops had 'strengthened the hands of Sinn Féin and weakened the hands of the Nationalist party' and they were 'using Sinn Féin as a means of killing home rule'.[130] When enclosing a subscription of £25 to the Sinn Féin election fund Dr

126 Hart, *The IRA at war*, p. 121; and Townshend, *The republic*, p. 43. 127 TCD, JD, 6741/416: Dillon to O'Connor, n.d. 128 See also Aidan Beatty, *Masculinity and power in Irish nationalism, 1884–1938* (London, 2016), pp 21–57. 129 *IT*, 23 Dec. 1918. Mordechai Feingold, *History of universities*, vol. 23/1 (Oxford, 2008), p. 121. 130 *IT*, 5 Dec. 1918.

Michael Fogarty, the Roman Catholic bishop of Killaloe, condemned the IPP's policy of 'massaging' English ministers. He irately maintained that abstention was 'not only a logical and long-called for protest against the pillage of our national rights in the infamous Union', but that 'no other course is open to us if we have a particle of self-respect'.[131] He indignantly accused unionists of working 'its shameless will on Ireland' and saw little point in sending members to the Commons to be

> spat upon as paupers, to come back to us with empty hands, or with a few crumbs from the English kitchen garnished with rhetoric, but, as always, with the leprosy of Anglicization visibly developed on their person for the ruin of our national spirit.[132]

So powerful was the influence of clerical rhetoric that Dillon credited the success of Cavan East to the priests who 'went the length of working minds' through 'spiritive intimidation'.[133] Many in the Roman Catholic Church, from the local curate up to the bishop, had gradually switched to the separatist ideology of abstention and encouraged parishioners to follow suit.[134]

Candidates in all parties hailed from a mixed bag of middle-class occupations, including university lecturers, teachers, civil servants and journalists. In 1918 Sinn Féin had eight doctors, five solicitors, eight barristers and one king's counsel running as candidates. After the election unionists comprised three doctors, six king's counsel, seven barristers and seven military officers as members. Among Sinn Féin there were three doctors, two solicitors and a barrister. And, of the six IPP MPs elected, there were three barristers and two solicitors, with Devlin being the only layman.[135] Therefore, with such similarities of occupations across the political divides, it is safe to conclude that a candidate's means of earning a livelihood had little bearing on election success.

Women, on the other hand, did influence electoral outcomes and the evidence lies in the newspaper reports across the entire island on election day. Comprehensive studies on the history of the nationalist and unionist suffrage campaign in Ireland have already been carried out by many authors on the topic, so it is unnecessary to repeat research already available.[136] This work intends to investigate the turnout of women in 1918 and 1920, and to ask if the parties that petitioned for women's votes were more successful than those that did not. Chapter 5 will demonstrate that Sinn Féin and unionist propaganda resolutely pursued women voters or addressed

---

131 Ibid., 30 Nov. 1918.   **132** Ibid.   **133** TCD, JD, MSS 6742/499: Dillon to O'Connor, 22 June 1918.   **134** See Coleman, *County Longford*, pp 54–5.   **135** *II*, 30 Dec. 1918.   **136** For examples see Diane Urquhart, *The minutes of the Ulster Women's Unionist Council and executive committee, 1911–40* (Dublin, 2001); idem, *Women in Ulster politics, 1890–1940* (Newbridge, Co. Kildare, 2000); Janice Holmes and Diane Urquhart (eds), *Coming into the light: the work, politics and religion of women in Ulster, 1840–1940* (Belfast, 1994); Senia Pašeta, *Irish nationalist women, 1900–1918* (Cambridge, 2013); Rosemary Cullen Owens, *Smashing times: a history of the Irish women's suffrage movement, 1889–1922* (Cork, 1984); Margaret Ward, *In their own voice* (Dublin, 1995) and *Unmanageable revolutionaries*.

both sexes, although women were influenced by the main propaganda of all parties. Sinn Féin had the advantage of having as its founder Arthur Griffith, who
even though he was concerned that women's suffrage might distract from attaining
independence, had backed the cause. Sinn Féin (unlike the IPP) had no long-term
history on suffrage that could be pitched against them during election campaigns.
Contrary to the IPP they had encouraged women's organizations such as Cumann
na mBan, albeit as an auxiliary to the Volunteers.

Back in 1912 Redmond had told a delegation from the Irish Women's Franchise
League (IWFL) that he would not support the extension of the franchise to women
either before or after home rule. This proved an error of judgement and because
of past policies the IPP may have failed to draw women voters in 1918. They did
attract vocal support from 'separation women' – so called because they were paid
'separation money' while their husbands (or other male family members) served
in the war – during election campaigns. But, despite their bellicose campaign tactics on behalf of the IPP many of the separation women did not have the vote in
1918 because of the property qualifications imposed on women voters. According
to Borgonovo, their turnout in Cork was only 27 per cent.[137] Unlike unionists and
Sinn Féin the IPP had neglected to create targeted propaganda to appeal to the
female voter, aside from Devlin, who made specific mention of issues that affected
women in this era. Whether Devlin's policies appealed or whether women voters
were swayed because of his inclusivity is hard to tell, but he was one of six IPP
MPs in Ireland to hold his seat in 1918.

In a letter to the editor of the *Irish Independent* in November 1918 the 'chairman' and honorary secretary of the IWFL pointed out that 'the number of women
voters on the register is very large; in Belfast alone there are 85,000, in one of the
Tipperary divisions women are half the total electorate'.[138] The *Freeman's Journal*
highlighted that 'the women's vote is a new factor in the election campaign, and as
it roughly represents from forty to fifty per cent of the electorate, it will exercise
an enormous influence on the result of the elections'. According to this newspaper,
in the city of Dublin, out of a total electorate of 124,426, there were 49,351 women
parliamentary voters, representing roughly two-fifths (or 39.7 per cent) of the electors. In the county of Dublin, out of a total electorate of 75,524, there were 30,609
women voters, comprising 40.5 per cent of the electorate.[139] In table 1.12, figures
from the *Freeman's Journal* of 26 November 1918 show the total number of electors
and women electors in various city and county constituencies and this gives some
indication of the strength of their voting power.

In Tipperary South, the women voters were nearly 35 per cent, and in Cavan
about 33.25 per cent of the entire electorate.[140] While the sample provided here
is small (and includes the only examples provided in the newspapers), given that

---

137 John Borgonovo, *Dynamics of war and revolution* (Cork, 2013), p. 228; see also Keith Jeffery, *Ireland
and the Great War* (Cambridge, 2000), pp 44–6; and Walsh, 'The impact of the Great War on women
in Ireland', pp 90–109. 138 *II*, 18 Nov. 1918. 139 *FJ*, 26 Nov. 1918. 140 Ibid. 141 Ibid., 26
Nov. 1918.

Table 1.12 Percentage of women electors in 1918

Constituency	Total electors	Women electors	Percentage of votes
Cavan East	15,148	6,956	45.9
Rathmines	19,002	8,233	43.3
Cork City	43,017	17,701	41.1
Pembroke	17,951	7,358	41.0
Dublin South	18,144	7,371	40.6
Dublin (St Patrick's)	18,785	7,595	40.4
Belfast (Cromac)	21,975	8,834	40.2
Belfast (Falls)	15,859	6,359	40.1
Dublin (College Green)	21,345	8,433	39.5
Belfast (Ormeau)	16,408	6,471	39.4
Dublin (St James')	13,134	5,156	39.3
Down South	18,708	7,310	39.1
Dublin (St Michan's)	17,588	6,742	38.3
Mayo East	21,635	8,237	38.1
Dublin North	20,427	7,627	37.3
Tyrone North East	22,963	8,162	35.5
Tipperary South	14,716	5,119	34.8
Wexford South	23,168	8,011	34.6
Tipperary Mid	17,458	5,925	33.9
Mayo North	20,212	6,744	33.4
Wexford North	23,022	7,331	31.8

there were eighty contested constituencies, it is unlikely there were great variances for the rest of the country. In general women averaged at 38.5 per cent of the total electorate (based on the figures in table 1.12).[141] There is a wide variation between rural and urban constituencies in the number of female registered electors (although Cavan East is an anomaly). Many women had moved to the cities in search of employment mainly as domestic servants and factory workers.[142]

The novelty of being able to cast a vote and participate at the political level sparked enthusiasm among women. Some have argued that women did not

142 HC, PD, Cmd 721, 1919.   143 For an interesting analysis of this election based on the 1911 census, see Alan de Bromhead, Alan Fernihough, and Enda Hargaden, 'The Sinn Féin election in Ireland, 1918', working paper 2018-08, Queen's University Centre for Economic History, June 2018, http://www.quceh.org.uk/uploads/1/0/5/5/10558478/wp18-08.pdf, accessed June 2019.

participate in large numbers in the election and did not sway election outcomes, but the numbers above contradict this, and contemporary newspaper reports consistently comment on the high turnout of women at the 1918 election in particular.[143] The *Irish Times* stated that 'from all quarters ... women voted in large numbers, and early in the day', and in Belfast women also voted 'in larger numbers than was generally anticipated'. The *Cork Examiner* on 16 December 1918 reported that a feature of the election was 'the large number of women voters who came to exercise the franchise'. It was pointed out that women voted across the parties, with a 'considerable number of those favouring the Union', but 'the majority support either Sinn Féin or the nationalist candidates'. The *Irish Independent* remarked that the poll in Cork was a heavy one and 'women polled in large numbers', with their votes amounting 'to nearly one-third of the total'. They maintained that 'this was to a great extent a women's election, and out of 18,000 voters they [Sinn Féin] had nearly 8,000 women voters'. In Dublin the newspapers reported that 'women marched in procession through some of the leading thoroughfares in celebration of their right to exercise the parliamentary franchise', and that 'some women voters in their enthusiasm for Sinn Féin candidates wrote on the voting papers "Up de Valera"'. According to the Tipperary *Nationalist* on 28 December 1918, women 'alone added about 60 per cent to the total polling strength'.[144] The *Irish Citizen*, the newspaper of the women's suffrage movement, remarked that

> Babies were washed and husbands fed on Election Day just as they are Washing Day or at spring cleaning. The Police Court returns showed no increase in domestic strife, such as was predicted by the duties if a wife voted against her husband's favourite ... Babies were wheeled along to the booths and policemen looked after them while mothers voted – sometimes even fathers condescended to the task.[145]

Women were not successful in fielding candidates, and despite Cumann na mBan urging Sinn Féin to select women candidates only two ran in urban constituencies.[146] As previously mentioned, Constance Markievicz was elected in Dublin's St Patrick's Division, with 66 per cent of the vote. The other Sinn Féin woman candidate, Winifred Carney, contested in the highly unionist constituency of Belfast's Victoria and received only 539 votes (4 per cent). Hanna Sheehy Skeffington had declined the nomination to run for Sinn Féin. Labour had nominated Helena Molony, but she too refused to run, even before the decision was taken not to contest the election.[147] Greater numbers of women contested elections in 1920, but in Ulster only three women were elected outside Belfast. In Dublin city five

144 *FJ*, 26 Nov. 1918; *IT*, 21 Dec. 1918; *II*, 16 Dec. 1918; *Derry Journal*, 16 Dec. 1918; *NLT*, 21 Dec. 1918; and *Munster Express*, 14 Dec. 1918. 145 *Irish Citizen*, Jan. 1919. 146 SFSCM, 12 Sept. 1918. 147 Laffan, *The resurrection*, p. 154. 148 *II*, 19 Jan. 1920.

women were returned (one of them for two seats) and in the townships they fared better, with twelve were returned. Eight of the twelve women elected represented Sinn Féin, two were unionist, and was one nationalist and one was Ratepayer.[148] Kathleen Clarke maintained that while she had been considered for Dublin North City and Limerick City she was ultimately disregarded in favour of male candidates.[149] Anna Haslam believed that women were 'withheld by the heavy expense involved' in contesting elections.[150]

In 1921 Lady Craig pointed out that the women's vote would be the 'great determining factor in the coming election, and every possible vote must be recorded'.[151] Unionists and nationalists called on women to canvass and to vote. In the southern provinces Sinn Féin made increases in women representatives compared to 1918, but still, out of a total of 128 candidates only six were women, and no women contested for seats in the northern parliament. Unionists put forward two female candidates: Julia McMordie in Belfast South and Dehra Chichester in Londonderry, and both were elected under the PR voting system. Writing to the editor of the *Belfast News-Letter*, a female voter commented that women had 'not been quite ignored in the choice of Unionist candidates', with 'at least two representatives', and she pointed out that 'it is not an alarming advance two out of forty, but it is at least a step in the right direction'.[152]

While we will never know exactly how women (or men) voted in these elections, their high turnout did not bode well for the IPP in 1918, particularly when the IWFL at a meeting accused 'Mr Dillon's Party' of being 'from the beginning hostile to their League'. They recalled that Dillon had previously stated 'he hoped they [women] would never get the vote as it would mean the "disturbing of Western civilization"'.[153]

The final results of the 1918 general election saw 69 per cent of the electorate cast a vote in contested constituencies in 1918, and of this 47 per cent favoured Sinn Féin.[154] If the uncontested constituencies are taken into account Sinn Féin had voter support of between 52 per cent and 64 per cent. The results in the southern provinces differed considerably from those in many of the Ulster constituencies.[155] The IPP managed to win 21.8 per cent of the total vote and polled well in some areas, particularly Ulster. This leaves a majority of the electors in the southern provinces endorsing the Sinn Féin programme, with the IPP being reduced from sixty-eight MPs in 1910 to just six seats. As will be seen in later chapters Sinn Féin maintained that this provided them with a mandate to establish Dáil Éireann in 1919.

In the southern provinces all had dramatically changed in the eight years between general elections – from 1910 to 1918. The once successful IPP that had

---

149 Kathleen Clarke, *Revolutionary woman: Kathleen Clarke, 1978–1972*, ed. H. Litton (Dublin, 1991).   150 *IT*, 23 Dec. 1919.   151 *BNL*, 23 Apr. 1921.   152 Ibid., 17 May 1921.   153 Ibid.; *II*, 4 Dec. 1918 and 11 and 18 Nov. 1918.   154 See also O'Leary, p. 8. For examples, see: Garvin, *The evolution*, p. 130; Kissane, *Explaining Irish democracy*, p. 10.   155 J. Coakley, 'The election that made the first dáil' in Brian Farrell (ed.), *The creation of the dáil* (Dublin, 1994), pp 31–44.

dominated Irish politics and had held the balance of power in 1910 to facilitate the launch of the third home rule bill was now redundant. The new separatist nationalist challenge had altered the mindset of many to defeat the IPP and they had done so in under two years to usher in a new political order.

The results, however, only tell us how much Sinn Féin swayed the electorate in their favour, numerically. They do not reveal how this was achieved, how Sinn Féin reached maturity of political form and ideology, or how the IPP and southern unionists challenged this new separatist threat. They also do not provide any depth to the Ulster contests where unionists and nationalists waged electoral war to obtain mass support.

By investigating the electioneering and propaganda efforts of all parties during these elections it is possible to comprehend the motivations that inspired voters to turn from over forty years of battling for home rule versus union to a new alternative. It is necessary to return to the beginning of these electoral campaigns to examine how candidates were selected, how funds were raised to finance electoral campaigns, what methods of propaganda were used and what messages were propagated to the voting public to find out how the course of Irish history changed in this era.

2

Candidate selection

Candidates revealed and promoted party policies and they were the practical medium through which concepts and ideologies were disseminated to voters at the local constituency level. How parties selected candidates for elections shows the importance that was placed on this essential role. This chapter will examine the past practices of the established IPP and unionists leading into the by-elections and the 1918 general election to analyse if the methods of choosing party representatives remained constant or if they evolved. Sinn Féin and the Labour Party were new contestants in the political arena and an investigation into their methods of selecting party candidates will show whether novel techniques were applied or older techniques were emulated. Independent candidates also contested elections in this era and, in Ulster, Labour associations and Belfast Labour nominated candidates, but with only moderate success, and their numbers were low so they will not form part of the analysis. They mainly challenged the larger parties whose competition dominated the selection process and propaganda efforts.

There were similarities and variances between the parties in the degree of control over the candidate-selection process and an individual examination, beginning with the nationalist parties, will highlight how the processes were born, how they evolved and where complications arose.

NATIONALISTS

IPP candidate selection under Charles Stewart Parnell's leadership has been well documented in a number of excellent works, such as Conor Cruise O'Brien's *Parnell and his party, 1880–1890*; F.S.L. Lyons' *The Irish Parliamentary Party, 1890–1910* and more recently James McConnel's *The Irish Parliamentary Party and the third home rule crisis.*[1] Suffice to say here that in October 1882 Parnell replaced the semi-revolutionary Land League with the more disciplined and pledge-bound Irish National League, which became centralized under his control. Supplanting the weaker system with a more co-ordinated approach to candidate selection allowed for the creation of an efficient party election machine. Candidates were often chosen privately and prior to a convention with, as T.P. O'Connor stated, 'everything

---

1 Cruise O'Brien, *Parnell and his party*, ch. 4; Lyons, *The Irish Parliamentary Party;* and McConnel, ch. 2. **2** *FJ*, 6 Oct. 1885; Jackson, *Ireland, 1798–1998*, p. 123; T.M. Healy, *Letters and leaders of my day* (London, 1928), i, p. 250; and T.P. O'Connor, *Memoires of an old parliamentarian* (London, 1929), ii, p. 14.

[being] done subject to the approval or disapproval of Mr. P.'² A 'façade of popular selection' at conventions provided credence to the successful candidate.³ This centralized control facilitated the monopoly of national political sentiment that actively set out to pursue home rule; however, it silenced the local voice at constituency level.

After the fall of Parnell, William O'Brien launched the UIL in 1898 with its motto 'The Land for the People'. O'Brien drafted a new constitution, replacing Parnell's system of candidate selection in favour of 'absolute local control'.⁴ Conventions were summoned in each parliamentary division to nominate candidates, and the decision of the majority bound the minority.⁵ An IPP representative could still attend the local conventions, but now only in the role of observer who could proffer no advice on the selection of candidates except at the invitation of the convention. The party pledge devised by Parnell was retained and a candidate had to sign the pledge before being forwarded to the convention. This pledge stipulated that each MP was required to sit, act and vote with the party at Westminster. The advantage of this system was that it increased audience numbers at conventions because representatives of public bodies and nationalist organizations could now be present (prior to this, attendance was determined by the party). The drawback was that power lay entirely with the constituency.

This was the system that the new leader, John Redmond, inherited in 1900 and there were times when he aspired to a more 'potent role' in the selection process.⁶ The fact that candidates 'were often chosen purely for local and even personal considerations' caused concern, as he wanted to find 'the man best fitted to do Ireland's work at Westminster'.⁷ Redmond and his second in command, John Dillon, had also voiced concerns about 'the pernicious influence of localism', which they believed 'had to be checked'.⁸ Political localism, as Hoppen points out, was motivated by what could be delivered to the local community. In 1918 however, the majority of voters were no longer shopkeepers and publicans and new separatist politicians were not affected by the influence of family or business connections. But, for the IPP the constituency selection process was still often the medium for the settlement of local scores.⁹

By 1915 Redmond's confidence in the UIL's methods for candidate selection had strengthened, which was apparent in his statement 'that the candidates selected shall represent the full, free choice of the nationalist electors of every class and creed in the constituency; … promote harmony; and prevent division'. The system, he maintained, took into consideration the opinion of 'the greatest number possible of the electors' to 'avoid local and personal feuds and cabals …

3 Alan O'Day, *The English face of Irish nationalism: Parnellite involvement in British politics, 1880–86* (Dublin, 1979), p. 26.   4 *FJ*, 21 June 1900.   5 Ibid., 20 Sept. 1900. See also Lyons, *The Irish Parliamentary Party*, pp 150–1.   6 David W. Miller, *Church, state and nation in Ireland, 1898–1921* (Pittsburgh, PA, 1973), p. 141.   7 Gwynn, *John Redmond's last years*, p. 39. See also *II*, 30 June 1900, and McConnel, pp 50–2.   8 Miller, *Church, state and nation*, p. 141.   9 Hoppen, *Elections, politics and society*, pp 47, 71, 244–5 and 445.

to ensure that the best man shall be selected, men known to the people and worthy of their trust'. This made the IPP, in his view, the most democratic and popular in its selection process and in its personnel.[10] This speech was made at a UIL meeting in the second year of the Great War, so the impetus may merely have been to rally members.

UIL disorganization and incompetence was evident by 1917–18 in their lack of meetings and they displayed a growing detachment from the lives of ordinary people. Prior to 1910 there had been two or three annual meetings, but by 1916 only one had been organized to discuss important issues such as membership and affiliation fees. According to O'Brien and Garvin, the League's listing in Ireland in 1900 showed 462 branches, representing between 60,000 and 80,000 members in twenty-five counties, and within two years this had grown to 1,150 branches and 85,355 members.[11] Membership numbers, according to the inspector general reports, had not increased by the time the 1918 general election loomed, as there were 110,972 members with 1,025 branches by December. However, when compared against the emergent Sinn Féin – a novice party and growing adversary – rivalry within nationalism was now tense. Sinn Féin's 1,255 clubs boasted 105,132 members. Even though there was parity of membership Sinn Féin was clearly absorbing nationalists who were discontent with the constitutional approach.[12] These figures may also simply indicate that many were registered as members of both organizations.

The flaws in the UIL system came to light during the 1917 by-elections in Roscommon North, Longford South and Clare East, where delays and local competition caused difficulties. In Roscommon North, the party candidate, Thomas Devine, was nominated one month after the opposition candidates. In Longford South the IPP had three candidates in the field vying for voter attention and local selection. The party's favoured candidate was a local businessman, Patrick McKenna, who was a cattle dealer and according to some 'had all the cattle dealers and ranchers behind him'.[13] McKenna was not the choice of the Roman Catholic bishop of Ardagh and Clonmacnoise, Dr Joseph Hoare, who summoned a meeting of all priests in the diocese, during which he proposed the nomination of the barrister Joseph M. Flood, much to the fury of the IPP. His choice was sanctioned by a majority of the priests – fifteen to two, with four abstentions.[14] 'Outrageous', 'treacherous' and 'scandalous' was Dillon's angry observation on the bishop's actions, which he called the 'most deplorable of affairs'.[15] To complicate matters further, another candidate, Hugh Garrahan, a local farmer, entered the field.

10 NLI, MS 708, UIL National Directory, Thirty-third Meeting (Fifteenth Annual Meeting), 12 Jan. 1915; see also TCD, JD, MSS 6762: United Irish League: objects, constitution and rules. 11 O'Brien, *William O'Brien*, p. 112; Garvin, *The evolution*, p. 101, see table. 12 The National Archives, Kew, London (NA), Dublin Castle Records, 'The British in Ireland', *Irish government police reports, 1914–1921* (CO 904, Boxes 92–122 and 148–156A), Sept.–Dec. 1918 CO 904/107 – some reports are missing so the figures may be ambiguous. 13 BMH WS 707: Michael Noyk. 14 NLI, JR, MS 15,182/24: letter from D. Reynolds, Parochial House to J.P. Farrell, 1917. 15 Ibid., Dillon to Redmond, 12 Apr. 1917.

Redmond was lobbied to select one candidate by a number of interest groups aiming to influence his decision. He received telegrams from five UIL branches and two divisions of AOH as well as the Town Tenants' League, the board of guardians, and Irish National Forresters in Garrahan's home town of Ballymahon.[16]

The battle among IPP members for candidature meant there was no single-voice argument or clear party message. It was a situation Dillon described as a 'deplorable tangle'.[17] Redmond reluctantly took on the task of arbitrator and the crisis was finally resolved on 24 April when McKenna was selected. This ran contrary to the League's constitution for candidate selection. But, as McConnel points out, while Redmond did advocate for certain candidates he 'did so at the request of senior local nationalists'.[18] The *Longford Leader* reported that 'there was much satisfaction on all sides of the town' with McKenna's nomination; and it incorrectly predicted that he was 'the one most likely to defeat the dangerous enemy [Sinn Féin]'.[19]

In Clare East internal disputes again erupted when local selection contrasted with leadership aspirations. A native lawyer, Patrick Lynch, was nominated by John Moroney, vice chairman of the Ennis Urban District Council, and was seconded by George Frost, a member of Clare County Council.[20] Dillon was 'strongly against the party identifying itself with Lynch's candidature', because Dillon believed that the IPP was being 'dragged in' to an election 'without being consulted on the selection of the candidate'.[21] Sensitivity was high for this by-election. It had come about because of the death of John Redmond's brother William at the Battle of Messines in the Great War. Sinn Féin was fielding Éamon de Valera, their most celebrated candidate. Dillon was fully cognizant that a propaganda war of maximum strength would be waged against the IPP, and he no doubt wanted a voice in selecting a suitable adversary. Dillon withdrew his objection to Lynch in response to a request for party backing from supporters in Clare and Limerick.[22] The party weakly admitted that Lynch provided the better choice to represent them, but they distanced themselves from the by-election in the hope that public opinion might not identify them with his defeat.

Problems continued into the Kilkenny city by-election in 1918 as confusion once again delayed the nomination of a candidate. A conference due to take place did not occur because the party had vacillated as to whether they should take part in the by-election at all. Eventually a private conference was held and presided over by the mayor, John Slater, with twenty others present including eight members of the corporation and a UIL organizer. Attendees only acceded to running John

16 Ibid., MS 15,263/2: letters to Redmond re: Garrahan. See also Coleman, *County Longford*, p. 47.   17 Ibid., MS 15,182/24: Dillon to Redmond, 12 Apr. 1917.   18 McConnel, p. 54.   19 *LL*, 28 Apr. 1917; Coleman, *County Longford*, pp 46–7.   20 NLI, JR, MS 15,263/2: Letter to IPP, 17 June 1917 from Patrick McNamara and P. Howard, secretaries, East Clare Division parliamentary election.   21 Ibid., MS 15,182/24: Dillon to Redmond, 21 June 1917.   22 Ibid., Dillon to Redmond, 26 June 1917 and 3 Aug. 1917.

Table 2.1 Retiring Irish MPs in 1918

Party	Number
IPP	35
AFIL	7
Independent nationalists	1
Liberals	2
Unionists	6

Magennis as their candidate out of fear that an independent candidate might 'be put forward in the party interests'.[23]

Fielding candidates for the 1918 general election proved deeply problematic because of the number of retiring IPP MPs. Of the 105 Irish members of parliament at the dissolution, a total of 51 failed to face their old constituents and of these the IPP lost the most candidates (see table 2.1).[24]

Inefficiency and disorder in appointing replacement candidates, particularly because so many retirements came at late notice, left the party in disarray. Three candidates sought election in other constituencies – Richard Hazleton went to Louth, John T. Donovan went to Donegal South and Stephen Gwynn contested Dublin University. Sir Walter Nugent, a former member of the IPP, contested in Westmeath as an independent nationalist.[25] IPP MPs provided an assortment of excuses for retirement, from ill-health to old age. The party could not restore internal equilibrium to replace defecting MPs in time to contest twenty-five of the 105 seats for the general election. Sinn Féin fielded candidates in these constituencies who secured walk-overs, signifying a lack of IPP efficacy in a transformed electoral environment.

Sinn Féin had enticed new voters by operating a propaganda war to successfully secure wins in four by-elections throughout 1917, as discussed in chapter 1. They also established a tightly controlled and methodical system of candidate selection, whereas IPP disorganization was manifested in the candidate-selection process in many constituencies from the outset of the by-elections, and at the foremost levels of structure. Their decentralized approach failed because of limited guidance to UIL organizations in selecting candidates, which resulted in potential contenders publically jostling with each other for supremacy. The regular distancing of the IPP elite from candidates out of fear of possible electoral defeat resulted in confused, fragmented and localized propaganda efforts where the only constant was continued support for home rule. A disillusioned Dillon failed to gear up the party machine at the end of the war to provide a centre of operations to oversee a

23 *IT*, 28 July 1917. See also *Nenagh Guardian*, 28 July 1917 on Magennis' selection.   **24** *IT*, 30 Dec. 1918.   **25** *Weekly IT*, 30 Nov. 1918; *II*, 30 Nov. 1918.

coherent candidate-selection process and consistent propaganda themes, and this continued into 1921. Constituencies in Ulster fared better under the guidance of Devlin, but the conflicting unionist challenge and the threat of partition also aided IPP success there.

Throughout the entire island the UIL and IPP went into decline after their 1918 election losses. No annual meetings were held by the UIL from September 1919 through to May 1920, although at the local or constituency level there were still weekly meetings and activities.²⁶As the local-government elections loomed in 1920 approximately 696 branches and 72,525 members remained.²⁷ Wheatley and Fitzpatrick report on the degeneration of the UIL after 1903 in their county studies and using their figures and those of the inspector general for 1920 in Ireland there is evidence of branch and membership decline. Taking the three counties of Leitrim, Longford and Clare as examples, between 1913 and 1916 Leitrim had 37 UIL branches with 5,663 members and by 1920 this had fallen to 18 branches and 2,381 members. Longford had fallen from 22 to 18 branches and 2,982 members to 1,730. Clare had 50 branches with 3,000 members in 1913 whereas by 1920 they had only 7 branches and 433 members – a significant decline.²⁸

Devlin's sanguine approach for the 1920 local elections was to focus on 'those constituencies where we have a good hold, such as Donegal, Wexford and Louth'. He emphasized that in Donegal John Donovan had been doing well and that he had only been beaten in 1918 by 1,000 votes and that was because 'he had no vehicles to carry the voters'. He also pointed out that 'half the voters did not poll' and concluded that because of this a good campaign 'could be effectively carried out' going forward.²⁹ He acknowledged that in Britain 'nobody is in a mood to discuss the matter [Ireland] rationally, nor do I think there is any possibility of a settlement until things become better or worse'. And, he anticipated a 'fierce conflict' between the British government and Sinn Féin, with the country being 'in for a very bad time'.³⁰ There was mounting concern over Sinn Féin's support at local level, although Devlin was less concerned than Dillon, and he believed that Dillon was taking 'too serious a view of it'.³¹ Just how seriously the IPP leaders took the local elections is questionable because between the municipal and rural elections O'Connor and Devlin spent their time in Great Britain petitioning Irish voters to support Labour Party candidates in a series of by-elections.

In the past the IPP – since the introduction of the Local Government (Ireland) Act 1898 – had deliberately targeted the county and district councils, and appointed candidates at local UIL meetings. In 1899 these UIL candidates had swept the

26 NA, 1916–20 CO 904/21, nationalist organizations, Irish government, anti-government organizations, 1892–1921, CO 904, vols/boxes 7–23, 27–9 and 157, UIL reports of meetings.   27 Ibid., police reports: inspector general's and county inspectors' monthly confidential reports: CO 904, boxes 92–122 and 148–56A: Sept.–Dec. 1919 CO 904/110.   28 Fitzpatrick, *Politics and Irish life*, p. 80; Wheatley, *Nationalism and the Irish Party*, p. 45; TCD, Dublin Castle records, inspector general reports, June 1920.   29 TCD, JD, MSS 6730/225: Devlin to Dillon, 22 May 1919.   30 Ibid., 6730/224: Devlin to Dillon, 15 May 1919.   31 Ibid., 6730/254: Devlin to Dillon, 5 Mar. 1920.

field, displacing unionists in many areas, and new councillors began to administer county affairs previously overseen by the landlord-dominated grand juries. By 1920, nationalists had to rely on localism, because their centre had fallen apart after the 1918 electoral defeat. Indicative of the selection process was the *Anglo-Celt*'s report that in Clones, Co. Monaghan, a plebiscite was taken for the selection of seven candidates to represent all sections of Catholics and nationalists in the 1920 urban district elections.[32] Despite the lacklustre approach by the now disaffected IPP leaders, independent nationalists contested seats in many constituencies for the local elections and as discussed in chapter 1 managed to gain moderate success.

In 1921 constitutional nationalists contested seats for the Northern Ireland parliament, but their candidates (aside from Devlin) were weak. The IPP appointed no candidates for the southern election and the reason was made clear by Dillon in a letter to nationalists who were keen to contest – particularly J.P. McCabe of Dublin County – which was published in the newspapers. Dillon argued that it was the 'wisest and most patriotic course for members of the Nationalist Party to take no part in the coming elections for the Dublin Parliament'. His reasoning was that 'any attempt on the part of nationalists to secure a share of the representation in the South would be treated as a hostile act by the Republicans, and that all the resources of the Republican organization would be used to defeat it'. He pointed to 'the horrible condition of disorder and anarchy' that existed in the country because of the War of Independence and maintained that he could not take responsibility of advising anyone 'to adopt at this crisis a course calculated to lead to bitter contests between Irish Republicans and Irish Nationalists'.[33] He made this case emphatically on a number of occasions to T.P. O'Connor, while also saying he wanted to avoid the threatened postponement of the elections. He maintained that:

> I should on the whole prefer to see the elections go on, and I do not see how the government can adjourn them without making themselves utterly contemptible, and sowing the seed of even bloodier tragedies in Ireland than we have yet suffered.

But he admitted that 'it would never do for any of us to state publicly that view'.[34] In his letters to O'Connor, Dillon oscillated between utter contempt for Sinn Féin's tactics and grudging admiration. He constantly referred to the 'persistence of Sinn Féin ambushes' and 'beastly murders' and believed that the IPP needed to lie in wait for the 'subterranean' peace negotiations between Lloyd George and de Valera ('not a strong man, and … completely under the control of the Secret Executive') to take place and subsequently leave Sinn Féin with no mandate. O'Connor agreed and argued that 'the Dail Eirann [*sic*] on the other hand has a mandate now pretty old, which is more or less in the hands of a few men'. O'Connor phrased the

---

32 *AC*, 3 Jan. 1920; *CT*, 3 Jan. 1920.   33 *CE*, 11 May 1921.   34 TCD, JD, MSS 6744/832: John Dillon to T.P. O'Connor, 27 Apr. 1921.

underlying thinking of the IPP clearly in a letter to Dillon in October 1921 when he referred to a discussion with Devlin, taking the view that 'for the moment all of us of the constitutional party are entirely out of it, not merely now but for some time to come', and he laid the blame squarely with Lloyd George, who he argued 'helped to create and has also succeeded in making the S.F. party omnipotent'.[35] As early as March 1921 O'Connor pointed out that 'the real obstacle I think to a good peace now is the gunmen ... At the same time it is quite evident that the Government are quite ready to grasp at any excuse that would enable them to bring the present situation to an end'.[36] By May 1921 Dillon was despondent about the IPP and seemed ready to take a back seat, leaving constitutional nationalists in southern Ireland without strong leadership.

After the Roscommon North by-election Sinn Féin established a novel approach to the selection of candidates, which evolved from Griffith's original monarchical movement with similar ideology to the IPP, to one with a defined separatist agenda.[37] Griffith's conciliatory methods had been based on an emulation of the Austro-Hungarian Compromise of 1867, which he wrote about in his *The resurrection of Hungary*.[38] Laffan's seminal work *The resurrection of Ireland* provides much insight into the formation of Sinn Féin and he maintains that they were 'the most important of several new political movements which emerged in the first decade of the twentieth century'.[39] Fitzpatrick described the separatist movement in this period as more of a mood than a party; it reflected the growing public sentiment against home rule which, as yet, had no political party to which it could rally.[40] The tenets of the Gaelic Revival movement and the GAA and the ethos of Irish identity were to become embedded in the philosophy of Sinn Féin as it absorbed new followers. Membership increased gradually in the early years to combine this assortment of diverse beliefs and among them were those who aspired to more radical methods for attaining self-government.

The movement needed a distinctive and significant propaganda concept to distinguish its members from their IPP rivals and provide impetus for selecting candidates. Militant and restless voices within separatism gained momentum and emergent radical ideals manifested in the Easter Rising of 1916. For six days the leaders of the Rising theatrically played out their eschatology of 'blood sacrifice' in Dublin city and proclaimed the Irish republic a sovereign independent state.[41] No political party could claim the legacy of the Easter Rising. The Irish Volunteers, the IRB and the Irish Citizen Army were all mentioned in the 1916 proclamation, but they were not political parties. The British government and Irish newspapers

35 Ibid., 860: O'Connor to Dillon, 17 Oct. 1921.   36 Ibid., 820: O'Connor to Dillon, 8 Mar. 1921; 823, Good Friday 1921 and 831, 26 Apr. 1921.   37 John Coakley, 'The significance of names: the evolution of Irish party labels', *Études Irlandaises*, 5 (1980), 171–81; see also Laffan, *The resurrection*, pp 23–5.   38 Arthur Griffith, *The resurrection of Hungary: a parallel for Ireland* (Dublin, 2003); Eoin Ó Broin, *Sinn Féin and the politics of left republicanism* (London, 2009), p. 178.   39 Laffan, *The resurrection*, pp 16–25.   40 Fitzpatrick, *Politics and Irish life*, p. 174.   41 Charles Townshend, *Easter 1916: the Irish rebellion* (London, 2005).

incorrectly blamed Sinn Féin – a charge they happily appropriated – delivering them a propaganda victory. Irish Volunteer Sean Prendergast stated 'what matter if the Volunteers were styled "the Sinn Féin Volunteers"; the intention was good and laudable enough'.[42]

The popular mood began to change in the months after the Rising when sixteen leaders were executed and widespread arrests brought internment for approximately 3,500 suspected revolutionaries (many were swiftly released). This caused extensive acrimony towards the British government. Commemorative photographs of the executed leaders were published and disseminated, and ballads were written to celebrate their deeds to create cult-hero status. The effect was to immortalize the leaders of the Rising and provide a permanence to Easter week 1916. As a propaganda exercise the Rising was a consummate success.

The 1916 by-election in Cork West instigated by the death of the incumbent AFIL MP James Gilhooly did not see Sinn Féin field a candidate, but the spread of separatist views by republican prisoners in Reading Jail led to AFIL candidates promising amnesty for prisoners to gain their support and win votes.[43] The death of James O'Kelly, the IPP MP for Roscommon North, opened the way for a by-election in February 1917 and lessons from this campaign were quickly learned. A number of political interests sought candidates to fill the vacancy, and among them was Sinn Féin. Candidate selection was spearheaded by Fr Michael O'Flanagan, a Roman Catholic curate from Crossna, Roscommon, who favoured Count George Noble Plunkett mainly because three of his sons – Joseph, George and Jack – had been actively involved in the Easter Rising. All three had been sentenced to death, but only Joseph had been executed. Plunkett's past political associations and aspirations made him a curious choice to represent more radical nationalism. He was a 67-year-old papal count who had received his title from Pope Leo XIII for donating money and property to the Sisters of the Little Company of Mary, a Roman Catholic nursing order. He had also served as director of the National Museum of Science and Art in Dublin, and had applied for the post of undersecretary in Dublin Castle.[44] Critics called him a 'place-hunter' and a 'place-holder', and the local Roscommon newspaper criticized his age, calling him 'a very feeble old man and a delicate man'.[45] However, Plunkett's familial association with the Rising and his subsequent electoral success initiated a process whereby Sinn Féin aimed to select candidates directly involved in or associated with Easter week 1916.

Plunkett had also been discussed as a potential candidate by William O'Brien and Arthur Griffith, and subsequently by O'Brien and P.T. Keohane, because of his association to the Rising.[46] Moreover, he was nominated by the recently formed

---

42 BMH WS 755 (ii), Sean Prendergast.   **43** William Murphy, *Political imprisonment and the Irish, 1912–1921* (Oxford, 2014), p. 77; Laffan, *The resurrection*, pp 73–5.   **44** D.R. O'Connor Lysaght, 'Plunkett, George Noble, Count Plunkett in the papal nobility (1851–1948)', *Oxford dictionary of national biography* (Oxford, 2004); and Michael Laffan, 'The unification of Sinn Féin in 1917', *Irish Historical Studies*, 17:67 (Mar. 1971), 353–79.   **45** *FJ*, 6 Feb. 1917 and *RH*, 27 Jan. and 3 Feb. 1917.   **46** BMH WS 1,766: William O'Brien.

Irish Nation League (also called the League of Seven Attorneys), created in Ulster to support the anti-partitionist stance.[47] Therefore, Plunkett was not just a Sinn Féin candidate, but an independent candidate with a number of sponsors.

In the aftermath of the by-election Plunkett's relationship with Sinn Féin became strained. The Roscommon North success and the subsequent Longford South triumph later that year prompted Plunkett, Rory O'Connor and some other younger men to seek to gain control of the movement.[48] They attempted to establish Liberty clubs to replace Sinn Féin clubs, but found little success. Sinn Féin as a political entity had gained national (and international) recognition in the wake of the Rising. Now they had to organize themselves as a political party, and it took until the October convention of 1917 to agree on their aims and form a constitution.

Prior to the convention the party had contested and won three further by-elections in 1917. In Longford South in May Joseph McGuinness, who was serving a prison sentence in Lewes Jail because of his role in the Rising, was selected to represent Sinn Féin. He was also a native of south Longford and considered popular.[49] A group comprising Griffith, Plunkett, Kelly, Collins, Rory O'Connor and William O'Brien, among others, met and decided Sinn Féin should contest the seat.[50] However, not all within Sinn Féin were amenable to contesting elections, and even McGuinness, according to Dan McCarthy, had written to Griffith and Collins demanding that his name be withdrawn as a candidate.[51] De Valera, also imprisoned at the time, was concerned about defeat, and maintained that if their candidate lost 'it would mean the ruin of the hopes – not to say the ideals – which prompted our comrades to give the word last Easter'. De Valera insisted that 'his [McGuinness'] defeat would mean our defeat' and he believed a guarantee of success was essential before an electoral gamble should be taken.[52] Collins and Griffith decided to proceed with McGuinness as a candidate, arguing that 'a man in gaol could not know what the position was like outside'.[53] The intervention of Thomas Ashe in support of the decision to field McGuinness bolstered Collins' confidence in going forward, and mollified the prisoners' concerns. Ashe argued that those at liberty in Ireland should be allowed discretion.[54] The decision of the new movement to select rebel candidates to foster its association with the Rising was cemented in this by-election. Joseph McGuinness' brother Frank conducted much of the propaganda campaign and continuously promoted the link with the Rising, pointing out that Joseph McGuinness represented 'unity in the cause of Ireland for which he had fought in Dublin in Easter Week'.[55]

---

47 Brian Farrell, 'Labour and the Irish political party system, a suggested approach to analysis', *Economic and Social Review*, Tara, TCD; Patrick Maume, *The long gestation: Irish nationalist life, 1891–1918* (Dublin, 1999), p. 188. **48** BMH WS 707: Michael Noyk. **49** Ibid., 907: Laurence Nugent. **50** NLI, MS 15,705: William O'Brien Diary, 4 Apr. 1917. **51** Ibid.; BMH WS 722: Dan McCarthy. **52** UCDA, de Valera Papers P150: memo Easter Sunday 1917. **53** BMH WS 722: Dan McCarthy. **54** Laffan, *The resurrection*, p. 98, quote of draft reply suggested by Ashe [n.d.] in Éamon de Valera Papers. **55** *Roscommon Herald (RH)*, 14 Apr. 1917; *LL*, 14 Apr. 1917.

New energy was infused into Sinn Féin with the release of rebel Irish prisoners by Lloyd George in June 1917. Lloyd George hoped for resolution and compromise between disparate Irish ideologies where a political settlement on the Irish question could be found, and cleverly he placed the burden of finding a resolution onto Irish politicians by establishing the Irish Convention. Meanwhile, the released prisoners arrived into Dublin to a jubilant welcome from the public, signifying the growth of separatist nationalist sentiment. They found a robust and dynamic party that readily accepted them into the fold, and this favoured unification, cohesion and stability. Rejection could easily have split separatist nationalism into two parallel and competitive movements. It also allowed Éamon de Valera to take his place in politics, and the timing was perfect as the death of Major William Redmond paved the way for a by-election in Clare East.

Clare East had been a home rule constituency that had not been contested since 1885, and, as mentioned, William Redmond had been its representative for twenty-five years at Westminster. But, there was no certainty of victory for the IPP as the county had become unstable in the post-Rising months. As Fitzpatrick points out, 'during February 1917 twenty Republican flags were hoisted on trees, schoolhouses and telegraph wires in the county. And three months later all three symbols of disaffection – badges, flags and seditious remarks – were again in fashion.'[56] According to Laffan, 'as far back as 1909 Clare had the third highest number of paid-up members of Griffith's Sinn Féin party of any county in Ireland'.[57]

Sinn Féin members met at the Clare Hotel to get the election machinery going and to select a suitable candidate. The names of three potential candidates were put forward: de Valera, Peadar Clancy and Eoin MacNeill. Initially Clancy, who was a Clare man and had also taken part in the Easter Rising, was favoured. A second meeting in the same hotel a week later with twenty present, including five or six priests, made the decision to hold a convention to select a candidate. Prior to the convention a 'steady quiet canvass went on for MacNeill by the clergy and their supporters', and a 'more forceful and organized canvass for Dev' was made by others.[58] At the convention, held in the Old Ground Hotel in Ennis, with over two hundred delegates attending, Clancy and the other candidates withdrew, leaving the way clear for de Valera. There was no explanation for their withdrawal, but de Valera's Easter Rising status was obviously significant and his supporters persuasive and MacNeill's countermanding order in 1916 had not been forgotten.

Just over a month after the Clare East by-election a fourth by-election was held in August 1917 in Kilkenny city due to the death of the incumbent IPP MP, Pat O'Brien. William T. Cosgrave was appointed by Sinn Féin because of his participation in the Rising, and because of his strong service in Dublin Corporation. He had been among those released from prison about two months before the election.[59]

56 Fitzpatrick, *Politics and Irish life*, p. 111. **57** *Sinn Féin*, 28 Aug. 1909, quoted in Laffan, *The resurrection*, p. 108. **58** UCDA, de Valera Papers, P150/548: letter from Joe Barrett, Barrett Brothers, Kilrush, Clare on 17 Apr. 1917. **59** *CE*, 17 July 1917; BMH WS 1,006: Martin Kealy.

On his nomination paper he was described as a 'grocer of Dublin' and, alongside eleven nomination papers, his supporters included 'prominent city merchants and farmers'. In a method very similar to Parnell, Cosgrave had been appointed by de Valera as the Sinn Féin candidate at a private meeting held in one of the anterooms in City Hall before the convention. After the meeting Cosgrave was presented to the convention delegates in the council chamber, where E.T. Keane, editor of the *Kilkenny People*, announced that Cosgrave had been selected. He was seconded by businessman W.F. O'Meara, director, St Francis Abbey Smithwicks Brewery. Clearly the insidious power of localism was creeping into Sinn Féin with the use of local businessmen to authenticate their candidate. To ensure that Cosgrave's candidature became the 'unanimous' decision of the convention and to ensure there was 'no opposition' to the 'official candidate' Seán Milroy gave an address to the delegates. He praised Cosgrave for his part in the Rising and spoke of his activities in public life as a member of Dublin Corporation, promoting his 'general suitability as public representative'.[60] Cosgrave won the election with 722 votes, defeating the IPP candidate John Magennis.

Four by-election victories inspired encouragement for the party to officially organize and develop a competent structure. De Valera was unanimously elected president (Griffith decided not to contest) at the October convention, where 1,700 delegates attended. Griffith and O'Flanagan were elected vice presidents. The by-elections stimulated the administrative upscaling and desire for efficiency within Sinn Féin that led to the formation of a constitution.[61]

Success bred complacency, and perhaps arrogance, as Sinn Féin suffered a reversal of fortune in the next three by-elections. The first, in Armagh South in February 1918, saw Sinn Féin select Dr Patrick McCartan because he was a native of Ulster, being from Eskerbuoy in Co. Tyrone. He had emigrated to the USA as a young man and became a member of Clan na Gael in Philadelphia. In 1916 he had been due to take part in the Easter Rising with the Tyrone Volunteers but fell victim to MacNeill's countermanding order. He was arrested in the aftermath and interned in an open prison in England. After his release he travelled to the USA to secure publicity and funds for Sinn Féin, but was again arrested and interned in New York as the by-election was taking place. His selection was based on the fact that he strongly represented separatist ideology. Armagh South was a nationalist constituency where the incumbent IPP MP, Charles O'Neill, had held his seat since 1909, and the Hibernians were well organized.[62] McCartan was selected at a conference held in Whitecross, Co. Armagh, where only two names were submitted – Dr McCartan and Dr McKee of Banbridge – but the latter withdrew (in favour of McCartan). MacCartan was defeated by the IPP candidate Patrick Donnelly.

60 BMH, WS 1,032: James Lalor; WS 1,765: Sean T. O'Kelly; and see *II*, 8 Aug. 1917 for nominations in Kilkenny.   61 See Laffan, *The resurrection*, pp 116–21 for details on October Convention.   62 *II*, 15 Jan. 1918; BMH WS 492: John McCoy; BMH WS 687 (section 1): Revd Monsignor M. Curran.

Waterford city in March 1918 presented a bitter and violent by-election contest between Sinn Féin and the IPP. Dr Vincent White was selected at a late-night private meeting of the Sinn Féin Waterford executive. White expressed concern at his own selection, stating that 'it was not his ambition to go forward, but it was the wish of the central and local Executives'.[63] He was an interesting selection because he was not a 1916 veteran, and did not have any familial connection to it.[64] Sinn Féin needed a convincing, well-known local candidate because Waterford was an IPP stronghold, and William Archer Redmond – John Redmond's son – was contesting on behalf of the IPP. The *Freeman's Journal* emphasized that 'Dr White is a local man, and this fact has undoubtedly had considerable influence on his selection', although they also highlighted that 'he is only a politician of very recent date, with little experience in public affairs' – which was common among Sinn Féin candidates in the by-elections and the 1918 general election. The *Evening Star* maintained that White's selection was 'intended to make a direct appeal to local sentiment, local associations', indicating that national aspirations were central in by-elections, but local interests were important too.[65] Reference to or close links with Easter week would not work in Sinn Féin's favour in Waterford city and they were aware of this. Sinn Féin faced not only a city that was an IPP bastion, but one that was still mourning John Redmond who had died exhausted and in his own words 'a broken hearted man' on 6 March 1918. William Archer Redmond won with a clear majority.

William Archer Redmond had resigned his Tyrone East seat to contest Waterford, activating a by-election. Tyrone East proved a disaster for Sinn Féin. The party headquarters believed that contesting this election would be 'a hopeless proposition and that a defeat during the acute conscription crisis would not be good politics'.[66] Belfast, however, did not agree with the Dublin decision and Seán Milroy requested permission to challenge, promising that the costs to headquarters would be minimal. In a moment of weakness Sinn Féin agreed, but ultimately it was an imprudent decision, as they were defeated by the IPP, which attained 60 per cent of the vote.

Misfortune turned to triumph in the final by-election of 1918, in Cavan East, again due to the death of an IPP MP. Sinn Féin's candidate was the founder of their movement, Arthur Griffith. He had also been imprisoned after the Rising even though he did not actively participate. Sinn Féin was determined not to repeat the outcome of the previous three by-elections in Cavan East, but they faced a major threat in the Irish Convention, which they had boycotted, because it was about to present its proposals for implementing home rule, so there was the possibility that support for Sinn Féin could diminish.

Two incidents provided rescue. First, the coalition government, under Lloyd George, decided to extend the military service bill, introduced in Britain in 1916,

63 *FJ*, 11 Mar. 1918.   64 BMH, WS 1,764: Vincent White.   65 *FJ*, 12 Mar. 1918; *Evening Star*, 12 Mar. 1918.   66 BMH WS 353: James McGuill.

to Ireland. This conscription legislation was connected to a new home rule set-tlement that had the effect of alienating most nationalists.[67] With the passing of the bill by 296 votes to 123, IPP MPs walked out of the house of commons and returned to Ireland to wage an anti-conscription battle. Labour and Sinn Féin became active and vocal in the cause, with the former introducing a one-day gen-eral strike and the latter rallying the anti-conscription campaign.

At the height of the anti-conscription crisis, a by-election was due to take place in Tullamore, King's County (Offaly) on 19 April 1918, due to the death of the incumbent IPP MP, Edward John Graham. To offer a display of national-ist unity against conscription the IPP candidate withdrew, allowing Sinn Féin's McCartan take the seat. When the by-election in Cavan East opened in June 1918, Dillon, who was now the leader of the IPP, expected Sinn Féin to recipro-cate in kind so he called for Griffith to stand down in favour of the neutral mayor of Dublin, Laurence O'Neill. Griffith's refusal to do so was seen by Dillon as 'wanton provocation' and he stated that 'no other choice could have been calcu-lated to add bitterness to the contest'. The Roman Catholic church stepped in to support Dillon, but without success, and the IPP selected John O'Hanlon.[68] Public sympathy began to favour Griffith by May 1918 because of his arrest due to 'the German Plot'. Dillon was now asked to withdraw the IPP candi-date, but he refused, stating it 'would be taken as a sign of weakness of the Irish Parliamentary Party were they to withdraw their candidate'. They lost the seat to Griffith.[69]

The by-elections and October convention advanced an ordered system of can-didate selection for Sinn Féin, and this became firmly established for the 1918 general election. By now Sinn Féin candidates were largely nominated by the *comhairlí ceantair* (area council) and the result was submitted to the standing com-mittee for authorization and approval. The standing committee at times requested further information, but only rarely rejected a candidate, mainly to avoid doubling up.[70] Obedience, compliance and, in some instances, capitulation to this central authority ensured that little was left to electoral chance.[71]

A new party structure was also outlined by the leaders and it consisted of an intricate system of assemblies and committees. At the top was the officer board elected at the *ard fheis* (high assembly) and the *coiste seasta* (standing committee) of ten to fifteen members elected by the *ard chomhairle* (national executive). A new *ard chomhairle* met on 17 December 1917 and elected the standing committee, which joined the officer board that had already been chosen at the *ard fheis*. At the lowest level were the Sinn Féin clubs, which reported to the constituency execu-tive, who in turn reported to the standing committee. The executive, elected at the October convention, had established eighty-six constituency executives before

---

67 Alan J. Ward, 'Lloyd George and the 1918 Irish conscription crisis', *Historical Journal*, 17:1 (1974), 111. **68** Laffan, *The resurrection*, pp 147–9. **69** *Times*, 27 May 1918. **70** SFSCM, 26 Sept. 1918. **71** Ibid., 29 Aug. and 6 Sept. 1918.

disbanding.[72] Laffan states that de Valera's structure was an 'interlocking system which involved endless meetings, elections and delegations … It was democratic almost to excess.'[73] The structural benefit was that regular standing committee meetings provided a forum for collecting opinion on constituency happenings in a timely manner. Sinn Féin, however, was on the road to a top-down communication set-up, with de Valera emulating the managerial leadership style of Parnell.

While there were aberrations in that not all candidates had been involved in the Rising, the prerequisite for any candidate was proof of non-compliance with the status quo. By September 1918 candidate selections had been made for twelve constituencies facing contests. Concerns remained on Carlow (subsequently uncontested), Clare West (uncontested), Donegal East, Mayo East, Monaghan North and South, Kerry West (uncontested), Galway East (uncontested), Tyrone North-West, Cavan West (uncontested), Louth County and Tipperary Mid (uncontested) either because of duplication of candidates or because further information was required on a proposed candidate (as was the case for James Lennon of Borris, Carlow who was serving a jail sentence in Belfast at the time).[74]

Cumann na mBan petitioned for female candidates, reminding the standing committee that the 1916 proclamation had addressed both Irishmen and Irishwomen.[75] The standing committee argued that selection resided with the *comhairlí ceantair* and not with themselves, but these appeals indicate that there was no general consensus and opinions differed.[76] By 1920 there was more resolve to forward female candidates for selection. Early and efficient organization paid off as a high number of women became Sinn Féin councillors and poor law guardians.[77] However, on a national level, women remained underrepresented by 1921, as only six female candidates were appointed by Sinn Féin out of 128 (including university seats).

Selecting Irish-speaking candidates for the Gaeltacht areas of Ireland and creating literature *as Gaelige* (in Irish) proved problematic. There was a dearth of proficient linguists within the party, so a decision was taken to acquire the assistance of the Gaelic League to support the canvass. A newly formed deputation was created which introduced a 'detailed scheme' to assist with the Irish language in the election and generally throughout the country.[78] Cork West and Galway North became particular concerns. Candidate selection was deferred to inquire into whether proposed candidates for these constituencies spoke Irish.[79] Ultimately, disquiet about the influence of the Gaelic League in Sinn Féin politics led the party to distance themselves for the 1920 local elections. Sinn Féin was adamant

72 NLI, MS 11,405/2: Count Plunkett Papers, Report on the national organization of Sinn Féin by Austin Stack and Darrel Figgis, 19 Dec. 1917. See also MS 11,405/3: Report on organization of Sinn Féin; and, Laffan, *The resurrection*, pp 170–1.   **73** Laffan, *The resurrection*, p. 173.   **74** John O'Donovan, *Members and messengers: Carlow's 20th century parliamentarians* (Carlow, 2003), p. 33.   **75** Ward, *In their own voice*, p. 83.   **76** SFSCM, 18 Sept. 1918.   **77** Ward, *Unmanageable revolutionaries*.   **78** SFSCM, 16 Oct. 1918.   **79** Ibid., 19 Aug. 1918.

that only their representatives could select candidates, but they assured the Gaelic League that they were 'always ready to help' the League to 'carry through its pro- gramme of Irish'.[80]

Sinn Féin was determined to emulate past IPP local-election success, so they began preparations in earnest in early 1919. For the January municipal contests, Liam O'Broin, secretary of the party's Dublin elections committee, suggested creating a permanent registration office and advisory board for the municipal elec- tions.[81] By 16 January 1919 a committee was appointed to draft instructions with regard to local elections. It comprised Alderman Tom Kelly, Jennie Wyse Power, James J. Walsh, Con Collins, Robert Barton and Dr Kathleen Lynn.[82] Strict direc- tions were distributed to all *cumainn* (branches), which had been passed by a resolution of the *ard comhairle* on 20 February 1919, regarding the selection of candidates for local elections and boards of guardians. They said 'the selection of candidates ... [should] be left in the first instance to the Sinn Féin Club, or Clubs, in consultation with other organizations pledged to Republican principles in their respective areas'; and for county councillors:

> that the selection of candidates ... [will] be left to a Convention of those
> representatives from each Sinn Féin Club in the County Electoral area ...
> In the event of the County Council failing to approve of the candidate so
> selected that the reason for so doing be put in writing, and be forwarded to
> the standing committee for final jurisdiction.[83]

The sheer number of candidates required to successfully capture seats in the January municipal contests and June rural district council elections compelled Sinn Féin to release selection to local clubs. The standing committee could not deliberate over each potential candidate in a manner similar to 1918, but they could intervene if difficulties emerged. They also restricted the franchise to those who had joined clubs before 22 January 1919 to avoid the entry of new and unknown candidates.[84] Local Sinn Féin Volunteers took up the mantle and ran for council positions because of the dearth of candidates. To ensure adherence to Sinn Féin manifestos and policies a pledge was drafted which had to be signed by those contesting for county boards and offices.[85] In a style that emulated Parnell's requirement for IPP candidates to adhere to home rule policy, Sinn Féin candidates had to pledge their allegiance to the Irish republic. To make sure that only the party faithful became candidates those who did not subscribe to the pledge received no support.[86]

Candidates in Tyrone, Fermanagh and other northern counties did not have to adhere to this rule; instead, all arrangements were left to be decided locally. Sinn Féin was anxious about repelling or deterring potential voters in these areas,

---

80 Ibid., 20 Apr. 1920.   81 Ibid., 9 Jan. 1919.   82 Ibid., 16 Jan. 1919.   83 Ibid., 20 Nov. 1919.   84 Fitzpatrick, *Politics and Irish life*, p. 155.   85 SFSCM, 23 Oct. 1919; BMH WS 353: James McGuill; WS 702: Frank Drohan.   86 SFSCM, 29 Oct. 1919 and 20 Nov. 1919.

particularly those who had previously voted for the IPP. They were also apprehensive of robust unionist reaction if the word 'republic' was uttered in the northern counties. An acceptance of the potential reality of partition was acknowledged, although not an acquiescence to its premise. According to the Sinn Féin honorary secretary's report from the *ard fheis* of 27 November 1921, '[I]t became clear to us in September, 1920, that the British Government was determined to put the Partition Act into operation in order to create a division of the people.'

Foreboding about partition elicited immediate organization in the party for 'the weaker parts of the country thoroughly' to ensure that the results of the 1920 elections proved that the 'the people renewed their Republican Mandate of 1918, and increased its representation'.[87] There was a suggestion at a Sinn Féin election subcommittee meeting in November 1919 for the *ceann comhairle* (chairperson/speaker) of the constituencies that were defeated at the general election (such as Rathmines, Fermanagh North) be empowered to nominate a candidate and forward the name for ratification by the standing committee. This decision was postponed, but it demonstrates that the party was determined to succeed in 1920 wherever they had lost out in 1918.[88] Agreements were also made with the Labour Party, particularly in Cork, in an attempt to capture the working-class vote, and this will be discussed later in this chapter.

The 1921 elections came about because of a modified Home Rule Act being introduced by the British government, and to battle against partition Sinn Féin felt compelled to contest the elections for the northern parliament. Because of IPP capitulation they could appoint candidates uncontested for the second dáil. For the northern elections de Valera, in a letter to all members of the dáil ministry, weighed up the advantages and disadvantages of a contest. The fundamental question was: how many Ulster representatives can be elected on the 'abstention' policy? He calculated that, 'if we get over one-fourth or so of the representation I think that the arguments are altogether in favour of vigorously contesting the seats, it being understood that the representatives elected will become members of Dáil Éireann'. He maintained that engaging in an electoral contest was the action least liable to misrepresentation in foreign countries and it would prove republican sentiment throughout Ireland. He was concerned that if Sinn Féin let the elections go by default it could be taken that the party had given way to 'partition', and that 'the North will be thrown of necessity into the Nationalist, or old Party camp'. He feared a later, dangerous reactionary effect, by contagion, on the south. Sinn Féin hoped to strengthen their movement in the north and aimed to defeat independents and unionists and eliminate the IPP entirely. A win could also provide a great moral effect if, having contested the election and won, a substantial proportion of the representation then boycotted the northern parliament and attached their representation to Dáil Éireann.

---

87 NLI, Piaras Béaslaí Papers (PB), MS 33,921(9): Sinn Féin Ard Fheis, honorary secretary's report, 27 Nov. 1921. **88** SFSCM, 13 Nov. 1919.

The decision was taken in February 1921 to 'contest all the seats for the northern parliament'. Candidates were appointed, but this time under the stringent eye of an eight-member subcommittee and the standing committee. Darrell Figgis and Jennie Wyse Power were co-opted onto the subcommittee – the former as director of propaganda and the latter as financial director. It was agreed that candidates were to run on an anti-partition ticket pledged to self-determination and abstention from 'the so-called Parliament of Northern Ireland'.[89] A decision was taken to run nineteen candidates (this subsequently increased to twenty): two in Antrim, two in Armagh, two in Derry, three in Down, four in Fermanagh-Tyrone, two in Belfast (West), one in Belfast (East), one in Belfast (North), one in Belfast (South), one in Belfast (University). Candidates were ratified by the standing committee in April and May 1921. In both southern and northern Ireland, candidates were selected by local clubs and ratified by the standing committee. The party had high expectations for Ulster wins, but as evidenced in chapter 1, the end result was a disappointing six seats. Unionists, however, polled very well in 1921 exceeding their expectations by two seats to gain forty in total.[90]

UNIONISTS

Unionists had been determined to hold onto their Ulster seats ever since the threat of home rule became a reality during the reign of Parnell.[91] The defeat of the first home rule bill brought this crisis to an end but it triggered a general election that galvanized unionists into action. Canvassing and registering voters in rural areas back in the 1886 election produced a system of local unionist associations. These associations began to organize the electorate and continued to select and appoint candidates for all future elections. The election outcome was a Conservative victory, and in Ulster it demonstrated that unionism was highly organized and efficient and was ready to repel any attack.[92]

In early 1891 Belfast unionists convened a conference to reinforce and stimulate support for the future protection of the union.[93] The principle resolution, moved by Sir William Ewart, set the path for the unionist stance against home rule, and they announced their 'resolve to take no part in the election or proceedings of such a [home rule] parliament'.[94] Out of this convention emerged the Ulster Convention League, which became established in every polling district. It provided the permanent electoral machine that became the framework of the Ulster Unionist Council (UUC), although it did not attain this name until 1905.

89 SFSCM, 10 Feb., 19 Mar., 13 Apr., 9 May, 10 May, 12 May 1921.   **90** *NW*, 28 May 1921.   **91** J.L. Hamond, *Gladstone and the Irish nation* (London, 1928); Paul Adelman, *Gladstone, Disraeli and later Victorian policies* (NY, 2014), pp 39–42.   **92** Harbinson, p. 13.   **93** See special convention issue of the *Belfast Weekly Telegraph*, 25 June 1892. Also, R. McNeill, *Ulster's stand for union* (London, 1922), pp 32–4; and Harbinson, p. 17.   **94** Harbinson, p. 18.

The Irish Unionist Alliance (IUA), or Irish Unionist Party, was founded in 1891 from the Irish Loyal and Patriotic Union (ILPU) to oppose any plans for home rule within the United Kingdom.[95] The ILPU had been established to prevent electoral competition between Liberals and Conservatives in the three southern provinces, on a common platform of maintenance of the union. The IUA united unionists, particularly in Ulster where unionist sentiment and support was strongest.[96] Its primary function was to represent unionism on an all-Ireland basis, and co-ordinate electoral and lobbying activities. With the introduction of Gladstone's second home rule bill in 1893 unionists immediately launched logistical and bellicose activities to protest against any measure that would 'separate them from their inheritance in the imperial legislature'.[97] By May of that year over two hundred clubs were established throughout the province of Ulster.[98] Laws and a constitution were drafted that determined to defend the legislative union between Great Britain and Ireland, and render assistance to their members and others in carrying out that policy.[99] The duty of clubs was to enrol members over the age of 16 and unite all in common cause.

With the defeat of the second home rule bill and the Liberal Party loss in the general election, unionists clubs went into decline. The 'devolution crisis' of 1904–5 sparked another conference, which was held in Belfast on 2 December 1904 to 'form an Ulster union for bringing into line all local unionist associations in the province ... to advance and defend the interests of Ulster unionists in the Unionist Party'.[100] This led to the formation of the UUC, which was largely controlled by a few landowners and professional men, even though they had aspired to encouraging a wide range of opinion and representation. The UUC was highly influenced by Ulster's Loyal Orange Institution, with the first standing committee comprising six prominent Orangemen led by the earl of Erne, grand master of Ireland, and four deputy grand masters.[101]

With a steady increase in prominence over the next few years, the UUC became the leading influence of Ulster unionism. Day-to-day activities were managed by a standing committee comprised of ten members nominated by the chairman of the Parliamentary Unionist Party and twenty elected by regional delegates. As Lyons states, the formation of the UUC 'provided Ulster unionism with an instrument whose political importance in succeeding years is difficult to exaggerate'.[102] According to Jackson, the constituency association within the UUC structure had three functions: supervising and financing the registration of voters, selecting

95 Walker, *A history of the Ulster Unionist Party*, p. 11. 96 Grenfell Morton, *Home rule and the Irish question*, ed. Patrick Richardson (London, 2014), p. 32. 97 Buckland, *Ulster unionism*, ii, p. 1. 98 Ibid., p. 16. 99 Laws and constitution of the unionist clubs, 2 May 1893, clause 1 in Harbinson, p. 21. 100 *IT*, 3 Dec. 1904. 101 Thomas C. Kennedy, 'War, patriotism and the Ulster Unionist Council, 1914–1918', *Éire-Ireland*, 40:3 (Fall/Winter, 2005), 189–211; Fitzpatrick, *The two Irelands*, pp 10–11 and *Descendancy, Irish Protestant histories since 1795* (Cambridge, 2014), particularly part 1, pp 19–78. 102 F.S.L. Lyons, 'The Irish Unionist Party and the devolution crisis', *Irish Historical Studies*, 6:21 (1948), 1–22.

parliamentary candidates, and working for their election.[103] The formation of the UUC fostered new energy to constituency organization and the council came into its own in the battle against the third home rule bill in 1912.[104]

Unionist clubs and the UUC grew steadily and by February 1914, 371 clubs had been formed, with 372 in existence between 1915 and 1919.[105] The unionist organizational structure and propaganda skills behind the drive to defeat home rule were easily transferable to election campaigns in 1918, although, because of voluntary enlistment during the Great War unionists found they could no longer attack home rule in traditional terms. For instance, Bryan Cooper, a former unionist MP for Dublin South County, and a prominent member of the IUA, joined Redmond's National Volunteers and openly encouraged other unionists to do so. On the other hand, George Richardson, general of the Ulster Volunteers, stated in the *Daily Chronicle* that 'when the war was over and their [army and navy] ranks were reinforced by some 12,000 men thoroughly well-trained and with vast field experience, they would return to the attack and relegate home rule to the devil'.[106]

Unionists did not field candidates in any of the by-elections, even though two were held in Ulster, in Armagh South and Tyrone East, because, as stated in chapter 1, they were in predominantly nationalist areas. In Armagh South an unofficial independent unionist and temperance reformer, Thomas Wakefield Richardson, put himself forward, much to the anger and disgust of unionists in the region. A unionist association meeting in Poyntzpass on 28 January 1918 refused to support him, with the majority expressing disapproval of his candidature.[107] Richardson was forced to withdraw due to pressure and opposition (although he received forty votes because there was insufficient time to remove his name from the ballot papers). This demonstrates the strength and cohesion of the unionist approach to candidate selection.

For the 1918 general election candidates were nominated by unionist associations in almost every Ulster constituency, except for Armagh South, Belfast (Falls, St Anne's, Shankill, Victoria – although a Unionist Labour candidate often contested), Cavan, Donegal and Monaghan South. In the other three provinces there were many areas with no unionist representatives, and contests only took place in Cork, Dublin and Wicklow East across Leinster, Munster and Connacht candidate selection and electoral support was mainly drawn from the Protestant population.

---

103 Jackson, *The Ulster Party: Irish unionists in the house of commons, 1884–1911* (Oxford, 1989), p. 200. **104** See Harbinson, pp 14–19. **105** PRONI, UUC Papers, D1327/1/2: minutes of the meetings of the executive committee of Unionist Clubs Council, 25 Feb. 1914, 26 Mar. 1916 and 30 Apr. 1919; see also NA, Irish government police reports, 1914–21, CO 904, boxes 92–122 and 148–56A, Sept.–Dec. 1918, CO 904/107 (there was some overlap in these records of membership of Unionist Clubs and the Orange Order). **106** *IT*, 8 Aug. 1914; NLI, JR, MS 15,215/2/1, *Daily Chronicle*, 26 Oct. 1914. According to unionist propaganda, 75,000–80,000 Ulstermen voluntarily enlisted to serve in the Great War: see D1327/20/4/142, U.C. 132, *The two Irelands. Facts. Not fiction!* And *Ulster's claim on Britain, a proud record*. The 12,000 returning ex-servicemen mentioned by Richardson is, therefore, a rather low number. **107** *Armagh Standard*, 2 Feb. 1918.

Here many unionists were farmers, small business owners or Church of Ireland clergymen. Unionist associations in these provinces followed a geographic pattern of Protestant population density. But their numbers and electoral powers had fallen. Maurice Dockrell (unionist MP for Rathmines in Co. Dublin) informed the commons in 1919 that contrary to popular belief there were unionists outside Ulster, and in making this point he provided a population figure for the southern provinces when he accused members of believing that

> outside Ulster there did not exist such a thing as a Unionist – in fact, that Unionists were almost as extinct as the Dodo … they are so few in number. Perhaps some honorable Members will be surprised to hear that I am the sole representative in this House of about 350,000 Unionists.[108]

The Dublin Unionist Association met in their offices at 10 Leinster Street in late November 1918 to select candidates for a number of constituencies. John Good, a building contractor, was unanimously selected for the Pembroke Division; Simon Maddock, member of the executive committee of the Unionist Alliance and honorary secretary to the South County Dublin Unionist Association and a justice of the peace, was selected for the St Patrick's Division (although he withdrew before the election), and Henry Hanna, a commercial and labour lawyer, was unanimously chosen for the St Stephen's Green Division.[109] A meeting of the South Dublin Unionist Association, held in the Shelbourne Hotel on 22 November, approved Dockrell and Sir Thomas Robinson as candidates after their selection by the executive council for the Rathmines and Dublin South divisions, respectively. In Dublin all candidates received undisputed support at unionist association meetings. Unionists in Cork city selected two candidates, Daniel Williams and Thomas Farrington, who were subsequently heavily defeated. Alexander Keane came forward as a unionist candidate in Wicklow East.

In Ulster, unionist associations played a pivotal role in candidate selection and in many instances a poll was taken to select one of a number of potential candidates. For instance, the East Antrim Unionist Association at Ballyclare selected Lieutenant-Colonel McClamont, who had succeeded his father in the representation of Antrim East in 1913, and the South Antrim Unionist Association selected Captain Charles C. Craig (brother of James). In Down West two names were put forward to the unionist association – William MacGeagh MacCaw, who was the sitting member, and Daniel Wilson. Wilson was selected by eighty-eight votes to sixty-three over MacGeagh MacCaw (who had been returned unopposed in the 1910 elections) and he went on to defeat the Sinn Féin opposition by a huge majority.[110]

Carson and the businessman John Miller Andrews also founded the Ulster Unionist Labour Association (UULA) in order to create a party of loyal workers

---

108 HC, PD, vol. 114, cc 126–7, 24 Mar. 1919: Sir Maurice Dockrell. 109 *IT*, 23 and 25 Nov. 1918. 110 Ibid., 27 and 29 Nov. 1918; Walker, *Parliamentary election results*, p. 6.

and dilute class conflicts, and to reduce the threat posed by British Labour, and Sinn Féin.[111] These intentions were set out by the secretary of the UUC, Richard Dawson Bates, in a letter to Carson where he stated that the UULA would be used as a means of distracting younger members of the working class from the socialist views of the Independent Labour Party (of Britain).[112] The UULA put forward three candidates who were elected in 1918 for Belfast seats, and on the basis of a commitment to vote with the Unionist Party on 'questions affecting the union'.[113] Belfast Labour – founded in 1892 by a conference of Belfast Independent Labour activists and trade unions – also put forward four candidates but they lost out to two UULA and two unionist candidates.[114]

Sinn Féin was perceived as a threat to unionism, particularly at the local level on urban and rural councils. Carson was aware of their potential to secure a footing as early as May 1917 and discussed the matter with Dawson Bates. In a further letter to the British prime minister he admitted that if local elections were to take place in 1917 the 'Sinn Féiners would have a very much increased representation in the County Councils'.[115] His predictions proved correct in many areas of Ulster during the 1920 rural elections.

Precision in organization and candidate selection did not avert problems. Unionists had struggled to find a candidate for Londonderry in 1918 despite the best efforts of the Londonderry Unionist Association. The president of the City of Londonderry Unionist Association wrote to Carson requesting assistance in finding a suitable candidate as they were 'unable to find one in our own locality'.[116] Lord Armadale, Chairman of the Irish unionist MPs, took it upon himself to find a candidate and the president of the unionist association assured Carson that they were devoting all their resources 'to the duty of having all available unionists duly qualified' to see if a 'candidate can be found'. They found one in Sir Robert Newton Anderson, a hosiery merchant and manufacturer, but he narrowly lost to Sinn Féin's Eoin MacNeill. When faced again with serious opposition from nationalists in the 1920 municipal elections, seven candidates were nominated.[117] Anderson was again selected in 1921 and this time he beat MacNeill by 1,600 votes.[118]

Another appeal was made to Carson in 1919 to solve friction in Antrim East for a by-election, because two contestants were forwarded as potential candidates but one refused to abide by the unionist rules and opted to run as an independent. The division became amplified because the candidate, George Hanna, was

111 Brian Lalor (ed.), *The encyclopaedia of Ireland* (Dublin, 2003), pp 23–4.   112 PRONI, Carson Papers, D1507/1/3/41: Dawson Bates to Carson, [n.d.], 1918.   113 Ibid., UUC Papers, D1327/11/4/1: 8 Nov. 1917.   114 Peter Barberis, John McHugh, Mike Tyldesley, *Encyclopaedia of British and Irish political organizations: parties, groups and movements of the 20th century* (London, 2000), p. 694.   115 PRONI, Carson Papers, D1507/A/23/37: confidential letter from Carson to prime minister, 22 May 1917.   116 Ibid., D1507/A/26/7: letter to Carson, 20 Mar. 1918.   117 Ibid., D1507/A/26/61: letter from City of Londonderry Unionist Association to Edward Carson, 20 Mar. 1918.   118 Walker, *Parliamentary election results*, p. 46.

an Orangeman and the independent, William Moore, was not. Carson could not solve the dilemma and the unionist vote was split, with Hanna getting the majority. Lessons were quickly learned. A reformation of the constituency was subsequently requested to allow for new delegates to be elected and for the enforcement of the rule for unsuccessful candidates to support successful candidates.[119]

Unionists operated a similar system to the IPP by selecting candidates through their associations, and generally these were given freedom to appoint representatives without intervention unless problems arose. However, there was keen supervision to steer attitudes in constituencies, to ensure that non-unionist adherents and the hazard of individualism were swiftly eliminated. The removal of Thomas Wakefield Richardson from the Armagh South contest demonstrated the refusal of the Poyntzpass Unionist Association to support his candidature. Unlike the IPP, which had to petition Redmond to cast the final verdict in Longford South, unionists generally relied on the direct pressure of peers. The central component for selection to represent unionism was strict adherence to upholding the Act of Union.

In the municipal and rural elections in the three southern provinces unionists faced difficulties nominating candidates because many had transferred allegiance to the Ratepayers' Association or Municipal Reform. According to a letter to the editor of the *Irish Times* from Robert Benson, the chairman of Rathmines and Rathgar Urban District Council, some candidates were 'soliciting the support of the ratepayers' and were not running in 'the interests of any political party, but merely as business men and women desirous of conducting the affairs of the township on business lines'.[120] The *Freeman's Journal* reported that unionists found difficulties fielding candidates in southern constituencies because they failed to understand the new PR-STV method of voting for the 1920 elections. They also accused the chamber of commerce of being unacquainted with the voting system because the 'reformers' showed 'a lack of courage in taking advantage of the new situation'.[121] It is highly unlikely that unfamiliarity with proportional representation was the cause, as unionists had instructed voters to cast their ballots in alphabetical order.[122] Many had attended the Proportional Representation Society of Ireland 'model elections', which had been set up to coach voters on the new system. Furthermore, Dawson Bates, in a letter to Carson in January 1920, had reported that unionists were 'at the present time engaged in the Municipal Elections'.[123]

With the introduction of women voters and candidates, selecting women candidates proved problematic. There was even confusion among women themselves. Women's unionist associations existed in many constituencies in Ulster, and the president of the Ulster Women's Unionist Council (UWUC) offered two paths forward. The first called for a fusion of men and women in one association and the

119 PRONI, Carson Papers, D1507/A/29/27: letter to Carson, 15 Apr. 1919. 120 *IT*, 7 Jan. 1920. 121 *FJ*, 6 and 7 Jan. 1920. 122 *IT*, 20 and 21 Jan. 1920; *Strabane Chronicle*, 24 Jan. 1920. 123 PRONI, Carson Papers, D1507/33/1: letter from Bates to Carson, 3 Jan. 1920.

other for separate associations united at the top in one joint executive.[124] However, the UWUC failed to initiate a definite programme for selecting and appointing women candidates.[125] Instruction was given to every woman above the age of 30 to ensure she was placed on the register. They were also called on to carry out 'vigorous and persistent propaganda work' prior to the election, and advised that the 'greatest care should be taken to select as office-bearers and members of the committee only those who are prepared whole-heartedly and enthusiastically to throw themselves into the work of the Association'. There was no specific call to nominate women candidates or to solicit support for potential women candidates, but the move towards inclusivity was evident.

In September 1918 a resolution was passed by the UWUC 'to provide for the inclusion of representatives elected by the Ulster Women's Unionist Council, in the same way as the Orange Order and Unionist Clubs', but this did not require that any of these candidates specifically be women.[126] Lady Dufferin wrote to Carson insisting on the direct representation of women on the UUC, but the UUC's reply was that the 'proper way women should get on to the Council is in the ordinary course, similar to the men, and not by nomination from the Ulster Women's Unionist Council', which they chauvinistically termed a 'more or less effete organization'. The UUC expressed hope that women would get 'their due representation on each of the Parliamentary Associations' because 'when they do that any necessity for direct representation will pass away'. Six members of the UWUC met with Carson in June 1918 to voice their grievances and as a result they were granted twelve UWUC representatives in the UUC.[127] No female unionists were selected as candidates for the 1918 general election, but as will be seen in later chapters, the move to entice the female vote was essential for success.

By 1920 advances had been made and women candidates were nominated. For example, Margaret Kerr Dixon was nominated as the unionist candidate for the No. 2 West Urban Rathmines Division of Dublin and Mary Weldrick ran as a Municipal Reform candidate in the Mountjoy Ward of Dublin. By 1921 the Unionist Central Office parliamentary election manual still made no mention of selecting women candidates, suggesting only that 'special meetings for women' should be arranged and 'addressed by the candidate and women speakers whenever possible'.[128] As mentioned in chapter 1, unionists selected only two female candidates out of forty (including Queen's University): Julia McMordie for Belfast's Cromac-Ormeau Division and Dehra Chichester in Londonderry.

Unionists in the three southern provinces – whether male or female – were never able to attain enough votes to gain majority representation, because their

124 Rachel Ward, *Women, unionism and loyalism in Northern Ireland* (Dublin, 2006), p. 115. 125 PRONI, Carson Papers, D1507/A/27/3: address by the president of the UWUC to council members. 126 Ibid., D1507/A/28/34: resolution passed by the UWUC, 11 Sept. 1918. 127 Ferriter, *The transformation of Ireland*, p. 119; Diane Urquhart, *The ladies of Londonderry: women and political patronage* (London, 2007), pp 136–210. 128 PRONI, UUC Papers, D1327/20/4/148: *Unionist Central Office parliamentary election manual*.

local branches varied in strength. This was part of the reason why the PR-STV method of voting was introduced in 1920. Unionist support was limited to certain sections of the population, described as being usually 'Protestant, anglicized, propertied and aristocratic'.[129] It was from this small pool that candidates had to be selected and supported. Lord Midleton stated that a key reason for lack of electoral success among southern unionists was that they were 'lacking political insight and cohesion' and 'restricting themselves to the easy task of attending meetings in Dublin'.[130]

In 1918 unionist associations successfully selected strong candidates in many areas of Ulster, ensuring electoral success. In 1921 they were vehement in their determination to secure success for the Northern Ireland parliament. The unionist electors of Waringtown District in Co. Down provide a good example. A meeting was held in May 1921 to select the six official candidates for the county and the hall was 'packed to overflowing with a representative attendance of the Loyalist electors of the populous district'. Robert McBride of Gilford, one of the selected unionist candidates, voiced the principles of unionism for this contest in his speech, stating:

> if they didn't come out on Empire Day and record their votes for the stalwart six, and let their Ulster Parliament go down, and be brought under the domination of a Dublin Parliament and under the heel of the Church of Rome, could they ever lift their heads again having failed to do their duty?

Miller Andrews, in the same constituency, maintained that it 'was a fight for their lives, and were they going to establish their Parliament in Ulster on sound, firm democratic lines, or were they going to be put into a Sinn Féin Parliament in Dublin?'[131] The 1921 elections were a call for loyalists to 'hark to the beat of the drums' because 'the battle has begun', and candidates were selected because 'these are the men who stand for the throne'.[132] For unionists the threat was now Sinn Féin and their anti-partition stance, as espoused by Michael Collins in his address for the constituency of Armagh on 10 May 1921, when he stated that 'we go forward not accepting the Partition of Ireland Act, but rejecting it … We ask our friends to vote for us on the ground that Ireland is one and indivisible …'[133]

THE LABOUR PARTY

Nationalists and unionists dominated politics across the island and this proved difficult for the Labour Party. In the southern provinces the main difficulty was that political labour remained an appendage of the trade unions and as Laffan points out, this was illustrated by the sequence of words in the movement's official title. It was not until 1919 that the words 'Labour Party' featured before rather than

129 Alan O'Day, *Reactions to Irish nationalism, 1865–1914* (London, 1987), pp 369–71. 130 Ibid. 131 *BNL*, 20 May 1921. 132 Ibid., 21 May 1921. 133 *FJ*, 21 May 1921.

after 'Trade(s) Union Congress'.[134] There were also concerns that the formation of an Irish Labour Party would antagonize members of the Ulster trade unions. In 1912, as O'Brien states, the Irish Labour party reflected the full gamut of Irish political opinion even though cleavages continued to exist between nationalist and unionists, constitutionalists and separatists, artisan and general trade unions and old and new trade unions.[135] From 1911 to 1915 Labour Party representation in local government was established on a solid basis in Dublin, but in the rest of Ireland the party was active only in the larger towns. According to James Larkin Jnr political activity at the time was seen by the supporters of 'new unionism' as primarily another weapon in the industrial struggle.[136] The formation of a united trade-union movement was the party's primary objective.

The powerful ideological legacy left by Connolly after the Rising may have inspired the substantial increase in trade-union membership, which rose from 5,000 to 120,000 between 1916 and 1920. In 1918 the ITGWU's membership was 43,788 and the *Manchester Guardian* reported on the 'spread of the Labour organization throughout the length and breadth of Ireland', which it maintained would be 'a fact that must be reckoned with in the future'.[137] Connolly was succeeded as leader by Thomas Johnson in 1917, who led a successful anti-conscription protest strike in 1918. Labour should have been able to emulate Sinn Féin's anti-conscription success to capitalize on their strike actions during the conscription crisis, and while it gave impetus to the movement the general variation in political interests destabilized the party.[138] There was also the difficulty of inconsistency of trade-union movements in the smaller towns of Ireland, 'who are at present unorganized either for industrial purposes or political'. Many towns of 1,000 to 10,000 inhabitants had no trade-union branches, while others had two or three societies (such as the Drapers' Assistants). The national executive planned to organize unions in these towns and rural districts to create local trades and labour councils, but by 1918 this was yet to be activated.[139]

In preparation for the 1918 general election P.T. Daly, under the auspices of the national executive of the ITUC&LP, issued a circular with a list of questions. Trade union councils were asked whether constituencies in their districts should be contested, what the financial responsibility would be and what organizational work needed to be undertaken. The circular then honed in on the prospects for a

---

134 Laffan, 'In the shadow of the national question' in Paul Daly, Paul Rouse and Rónán O'Brien (eds), *Making the difference? The Irish Labour Party, 1912–2012* (Cork, 2012), p. 36.   **135** Rónán O'Brien, 'A divided house: the Irish Trades Union Congress and the origins of the Irish Labour Party' in Rouse et al., *Making the difference?*, p. 18.   **136** Interview with James Larkin Jnr, 3 Feb. 1966 in Arthur Mitchell, *Labour in Irish politics* (Dublin, 1973), p. 27.   **137** C.D. Greaves, *The Irish Transport and General Workers' Union: the formative years, 1909–1923* (Dublin, 1982), pp 207–8; *Manchester Guardian*, 3 Sept. 1918.   **138** Emmet O'Connor, 'Labour and politics 1830–1945: colonisation and mental colonisation' in Fintan Lane and Donal Ó Drisceoil (eds), *Politics and the Irish working class, 1830–1945* (Basingstoke, 2005), p. 34.   **139** NLI, ITUC&LP, Report of the Annual Congress, Waterford, 5, 6 and 7 Aug. 1918, p. 19.

local Labour Party representative, asking about the number of candidates required to run in the district and how women voters could be organized and associated with the party.[140] William O'Brien maintained that the Labour Party was 'a political party, independent, erect, free … [W]e must bend at all events some of the energies to building up from within our political machinery …'[141] He also called for securing 'independent, able, strong, efficient and constructive' Labour Party representation on 'all our public elective bodies, both national and local'.[142] There was, at this point, resolute determination to field candidates, but a lack of order was evident in the acknowledgment that with 'many places in the country calling out for organization there was absolutely none'.[143]

The disparity between the political organization and the trade unions continued, with the result that labour was more of a movement in Ireland than an articulate political party. Johnson was still confident that the election could be contested and he released a circular on 20 September 1918 stating that the party had 'decided unanimously in favour of entering the field at the coming General Election … to provide an opportunity for the workers to declare their adhesion to the principles and policy of the Labour Party'.[144] A directive from the National Executive instructed that trades councils should call a conference of trade unions in each constituency to decide whether Labour Party candidates should be nominated for the election. Nominated candidates had to be approved by the congress executive and they had to pledge their support for the constitution and pronouncements of the congress. Mitchell states that the Labour Party voted for strict controls over the candidates; they were allowed to remain members of their unions if elected, but could not support other parties.[145]

The decision was ultimately taken to contest four seats in Dublin – Harbour, College Green, St Patrick's and St Michan's – and five names were proposed, including James Larkin (he was in the USA at the time, but his name carried weight), Thomas MacPartlin, Thomas Farren, Louie Bennett (a female candidate) and William O'Brien.[146] With ideological divisions mounting between constitutional and separatist nationalism, adhering to the directive to withhold support from other parties proved problematic. Similarities in policy between Labour and Sinn Féin caused difficulties in constituencies, causing many, particularly outside Dublin, not to field candidates. The Kilkenny Trades Council, for instance, disapproved of running a candidate or running Labour as a separate political party, 'being convinced that by doing so they would be doing the movement an immense disservice to itself and the country'.[147] Dublin candidates also had concerns and declared that they stood for a free and democratic workers' republic, and maintained 'the right of the Irish people to full, absolute and untrammelled self-determination'.[148]

140 Ibid., p. 20. **141** In Hart, *The IRA at war*, p. 21. **142** NLI, ITUC&LP, Twenty-fourth Report of the Irish Trade Union Congress and Labour Party, p. 17. **143** Ibid., p. 19. **144** NLI, Thomas Johnson Papers, MS 17,203. **145** Mitchell, *Labour in Irish politics*, p. 38. **146** NLI, MS 15,705–10, William O'Brien Papers: diary. **147** Ibid. **148** Irish Labour History Society: *Voice of Labour*, 26 Oct. 1918.

To address the growing disquiet of labour members a pamphlet was issued, titled *Sinn Féin and the Labour Movement*. This elaborated on Labour's national position, stating that 'Sinn Féin may claim to be the national movement of Ireland … [but] the movement for National Independence cannot possibly hurt the Labour Movement, and the Labour Movement ought not to hurt the National Movement'.[149] In the background Labour and Sinn Féin began negotiations on the electoral contest and the possibility of an electoral pact was proposed for some constituencies. At a Sinn Féin standing committee meeting in July 1918 the suggestion was made that 'if Labour put up a good man [for Wood Quay] Sinn Féin would support them'.[150] Harry Boland was assigned as the Sinn Féin intermediary and instructed to arrange a conference with 'representative Labour men' in August 1918. Despite many attempts he eventually reported that 'his efforts to bring about a conference with Labour were fruitless … that Labour intended to contest some fifteen seats and to declare for abstention from the English parliament but not as a principle but as an expedient'.[151] The Labour Party's election intentions were 'discussed at length' by Sinn Féin.[152]

In the end Sinn Féin proceeded with their own ratification of candidates for Dublin's Clontarf, College Green, Harbour, St Michan's, St James', St Patrick's and St Stephen's Green.[153] Conflicting motions were put forward by Sinn Féin throughout the month of November on the Labour Party's position. George Gavan Duffy proposed that 'at least 10 seats be given to labour at the present election' but Seán T. O'Kelly vehemently ruled out any form of co-operation, maintaining that all seats were to be contested by Sinn Féin.[154] Despite warnings from Boland that Sinn Féin could not afford to antagonize the Labour Party and lose votes to them, an audacious pledge was drafted that all Labour candidates had to adhere to if Sinn Féin agreed not to contest against them in certain constituencies:

> I hereby pledge myself to work for the establishment of an Independent Irish Republic and that I will accept nothing less than complete separation from England in settlement of Ireland's claim: that I will abstain from attending the English parliament: and that if I am ordered by the Labour Congress to attend the English parliament I will place my resignation in the hands of my constituents.

This sparked confusion among Labour Party members and caused consternation among some within Sinn Féin. The secretary of the Sinn Féin College Green *ceantar* disagreed with the pledge and refused to offer it to the local Labour Party candidate.[155]

---

149 NLI, P1084: *Spálpín*, Sinn Féin and the labour movement (Dublin, *c.*1917), p. 15.   **150** SFSCM, 23 July 1918.   **151** David Fitzpatrick, *Harry Boland's Irish Revolution* (Cork, 2003), pp 106–8.   **152** SFSCM, 19 Aug., 12 and 30 Sept. 1918.   **153** Ibid., 30 Sept. 1918.   **154** Ibid., 7 Nov. 1918.   **155** Ibid., 24 Oct. 1918.

Signing such a pledge and being subject to Sinn Féin authority was a step too far for the Labour Party. They were keen to have their own policies and principles, espoused by Connolly in 1916, included in the formation of any new state. Editorial comments in newspapers also agreed that the economic and social concerns of the Labour Party were a luxury that needed to be postponed until the political struggles were overcome.[156] Furthermore, alarm was raised that trade-union members would vote for Sinn Féin over a Labour Party candidate. A delegate at a special conference stated that 'he had heard organized bodies of labour down south stating that they would vote Sinn Féin against any man'.[157] The fact that the Labour Party could not field a sufficient number of candidates to effect their political programme was evident in Johnson's admission that the election of five or six or ten or twenty MPs was not their end purpose.[158]

Sinn Féin's doctrinaire approach and the internal conflicting attitudes towards divergent nationalist approaches to self-government were not the only complications facing the Labour Party. Widespread disorganization also prompted an escape from the stresses of the general election. The Labour Party ultimately capitulated to all the internal and external pressures, but they needed to publicize a viable explanation (or excuse). Johnson called a special conference of the ITUC&LP on 1 November and made a grand and elaborate announcement on the reason for their withdrawal from the electoral contest. He explained that the Labour Party perceived a difference between the election that was originally anticipated and the reality of the one they were facing into. They had intended to nominate candidates for a 'war election', but the current 'peace election' (because the Great War had ended) called for a 'demonstration of unity' on the question of self-determination to allow to voters cast in favour of home rule or republic. The workers of Ireland, Johnson stated, 'would willingly sacrifice, for a brief period, their aspirations towards political power'. McPartlin, seconder to the motion, maintained that Labour Party workers would continue to unite 'for the fight that would come in the future'.[159]

The Labour Party overestimated the electoral ability of Sinn Féin and could have secured many of the votes from those who failed to turn out in 1918.[160] As Farrell states, 'they did not recognize in it a political weapon that might be captured by a vigorous labour leadership and shaped into a socialist sword'.[161] On the positive side, the Labour Party's abstention in 1918 allowed for the inclusion of some of their socialist principles in the first dáil's democratic programme.[162]

The Labour Party's 'brief period' of national political absence lasted until the general election of 1922. Prior to that, a political voice awakened at the local level for the municipal and rural elections. As early as October 1918 Daly had asserted

---

156 *FJ*, 18 Sept. 1918; *SC*, 12 Oct. 1918; and Laffan, 'In the shadow', pp 36–7.   157 Ibid., pp 103, 108 and 114.   158 Ibid., pp 102–3.   159 ITUC&LP, Report of Special Conference, 1 and 2 Nov. 1918, pp 103–5.   160 See ch. 1.   161 Farrell, 'Labour and the Irish political party system, p. 488.   162 Dáil Éireann Debates (DÉD), 21 Jan. 1919.

that the Labour Party needed to focus on contesting the municipal seats in the next local elections. By mid-1919 the ITGWU had matured into a sizeable body that included 959 small farmers and by now the Labour Party was powerless to resist their encroachment. Joining a union had also become a condition for securing employment in many places. Pat Purcell from Queen's County recalled that a firm of builders, Connolly and Cullen from Kilkenny, were contracted to carry out work on the Munster & Leinster Bank. When he and a colleague 'went to them looking for work' they were refused 'because we weren't in a union'. This motivated the establishment of an ITGWU branch in their locality.[163]

Election candidates were nominated through the trades councils, as in Galway, where the various trades and labour bodies held a meeting to select representatives for the urban council elections. To lure support an article was issued that carried an appeal to voters for 'a clean administration'. In true socialist style the author stated that the

> greedy profiteers and landlords have had full control of the steering gear, and have run the Urban Council, of course, to the benefit of their own pockets. As for the working class, they forget all about them until the election comes around.[164]

A conference was called in Dublin in October 1919 to ensure strong central control of candidates and election propaganda. Farren stated that this conference would define Labour Party candidates, pledge them to act as a distinct Labour Party, 'and remain independent of all other parties when elected'. To be eligible to stand, a Labour Party candidate had to be nominated and financed by a legitimate labour body and/or be bona fide members of trade unions selected by a recognized Labour Party conference. The candidate also had to consent to adhere to the decisions of the Trade and Labour Council and to 'sit, act and vote with other Labour representatives on the Council as a Labour Party in the carrying out of these decisions'. The Labour Party, too, were emulating and implementing past effective IPP methods. Their entry into political contests sparked political concern and voter interest. The *Anglo-Celt* reported that the participation of 'fourteen workers' had 'caused much fluttering in the dove cotes of the reactionaries'. Workers were called on to 'down tools' at 1 p.m. on election day to cast their votes.[165]

The Labour Party and Sinn Féin co-operated effectively in 1920 in a number of constituencies. As mentioned in chapter 1, in Cork city, for instance, the parties combined to secure control of the corporation as the ITGWU had received fourteen nominations and Sinn Féin forty-two. However, not all trade unions were happy with the amalgamation, as the Cork District Trades and Labour Council ran thirteen candidates in an attempt to defeat the coalition. In Londonderry

---

163 *NLT*, supplement June 1993: *SIPTU celebrates 75th anniversary.*   164 *CT*, 10 Jan. 1920: article by Stephen Cremin.   165 *AC*, 10 Jan. 1920.

constitutional nationalists, Sinn Féin and the Labour Party joined forces to defeat unionists and they successfully took control of the council. The Labour Party's 18 per cent of the first-preference votes in January 1920 (Sinn Féin secured 27 per cent) proved that withdrawal in 1918 had not necessarily resulted in long-term difficulties. The Labour Party had fielded and successfully secured enough candidates to become the largest opposition party in Dublin Corporation. In 120 urban districts, Labour Party candidates were nominated and the results across the country as a whole returned 341 Labour Party candidates with 116 trade unionists also returned (although nominated by other political organizations).

The pattern in the rural elections of June 1920 was very different as Sinn Féin came in strongly to defeat almost all other contestants, taking 338 of the 393 boards of guardians, rural district councils and county councils. In many instances, outside Ulster, there had been no contest. The Labour Party's weaker performance was either due to a lack of industrial interests outside the major cities, which worked against them, or the fact that Sinn Féin was strong in rural areas, or both. The chairman of Sligo Rural District Council maintained that Sinn Féin's return 'was a sufficient answer to the British Government to clear out'.[166] Even though the Labour Party had aspired to centrally control the mechanisms for candidate selection, their inefficiency in mobilizing support at the local constituency level sometimes resulted in a scarcity of candidates, particularly in 1918 and June 1920.

The Labour Party had maintained that by refusing to interfere in the 1918 general election they had recorded their patriotic actions, but they again abstained from the electoral contest in 1921. Their reason this time was to record their protest 'against the partition of our country'. It was argued by James Nolan of the Bookbinders and Machine Rulers that 'they should not go to the truncated Parliament'. However, the chairman, J.J. Farrell, argued that 'the working class could always be called upon to make the sacrifices, but they seemed to be forgotten when the time came for the distribution of the honours'. While he approved of the principle of not recognizing the 'Partition Parliament' he was more in favour of the working class having representation. The motion was put and abstention from the election was carried unanimously.[167]

CONCLUSION

Sinn Féin and the Labour Party steered the candidate-selection process from a centre of operations. However, after their 1918 victory Sinn Féin party leadership confidence prompted them to imitate the old ways of Parnell and the IPP. The IPP and unionists retreated from central control to a devolved localized system, while unionists kept some power over candidate selection.

---

166 *IT*, 19 June 1920.   **167** *FJ*, 9 May 1921.   **168** Giovanni Sartori, *Parties and party systems: a framework for analysis* (Cambridge, 1976), i, p. 64.

The significance of candidate selection as a propaganda and electioneering function is stressed by the more modern political scientist Giovanni Sartori, who points out that 'the way in which political parties select their candidates may be used as an acid test of how democratically they conduct their internal affairs'.[168] The IPP candidate-selection process was democratic to the extreme under the UIL system, but torpor had set in and dispiritedness reduced the power of leaders to raise objections to unsuitable candidates and unnecessary rivalries at local level. Ergo, while they appeared internally democratic, in theory, it was not the case in practice, and even Redmond continued to have concerns over localism. Unionists operated in similar style to the IPP, however their rigid emphasis on maintaining the union ensured adequate peer pressure was mounted against those who deviated. The devolution of control to local organizations worked for unionists, but with a focus on Ulster decision-making was more straightforward and monitoring candidate selection was easier. The Labour Party suffered from working-class apathy, particularly in 1920, and middle-class and clerical condemnation of their socialist principles as the electorate still favoured candidates who were small employers, publicans and shopkeepers. The results of the 1918 general election that had brought Sinn Féin victory altered the trajectory of the candidate-selection process for both the IPP and the Labour Party by 1921. The IPP could no longer field candidates in the volatile military and political climate because of their 1918 losses and resultant despondency. The Labour Party remained caught between fielding political opponents and supporting Sinn Féin's separatist ideals and the latter won out.

Candidate selection was vitally important for all parties in their campaigns to secure votes, but it was only one aspect of electioneering. Raising funds, incorporating a variety of propaganda methods and steadfast themes, as will be seen in the coming chapters, also proved necessary for a party's potential electoral success. Investigating the methods of raising finances to conduct election campaigns is central to determining the importance each party placed on electioneering and propaganda, and this will be investigated in the next chapter.

3

Funding

Raising a propaganda budget to conduct an effective electoral campaign and conceiving clever strategies to raise these funds became paramount. Generating handbills, posters and political ephemera, and placing advertisements in newspapers all cost money. Devising successful propaganda also required initiative, as not all propaganda was paid for. Sinn Féin, the Labour Party and unionists operated skilled and coherent fundraising campaigns although they differed on method, sources and distribution. Affiliation fees and voluntary donations were collected through the formation of clubs and associations, which were tactically controlled by central organizations. The IPP, on the other hand, scrambled at home and abroad to plug holes in an ailing balance sheet.[1]

Candidates and parties incurred personal administration expenses (office rental, postage, travel, accommodation costs and so on) and electoral administrative expenses. For the latter, the total administrative charges in each constituency were divided equally among all the candidates, but for all other expenses they were self or party reliant. Under the Representation of the People Act 1918, the maximum permitted administrative expenditure became 5*d*. per elector in a borough constituency and 7*d*. in a county. Therefore, if the electorate was 60,000 and there were joint candidates, the maximum total or combined administrative expenses of the two joint candidates for a borough constituency was £937 10s. (£468 15s. each).[2] The act removed from the candidates' responsibility expenses connected to returning officers, the £150 deposit, candidates' personal expenses, agents' fees, postal delivery and one copy of the electoral register. If a candidate did not win at least 12.5 per cent of the vote (exclusive of spoilt votes) this deposit was forfeit. Furthermore, the deposit was not returned to a successful candidate unless he or she took the oath as an MP, so all Sinn Féin candidates in 1918 lost their deposits.

In Britain in 1909 a successful challenge in the courts (the Osborne judgement) against financial support from trade unions to Labour MPs led directly to the introduction of an annual payment of £400 for MPs (except ministers) in 1911.[3] Lloyd George, then chancellor of the exchequer, stated that this was 'not a

---

1 Note: all monies have been rounded to the nearest pound value. There were 20 shillings in a pound, and a pound was 240 pence before decimalization. 2 F.W.S. Craig, *British electoral facts, 1885–1975*, 3rd ed. (London, 1976), pp 73–4; PRONI, UUC Papers, D1327/20/4/148: *Unionist Central Office parliamentary election manual*; Keith Ewing and Samuel Issarcharoff (eds), *Party funding and campaign financing in international perspective* (Oxford, 2006), pp 36–7; D. Butler, *British political facts* (Basingstoke, 2011). 3 House of commons committee on members' expenses, operation of the Parliamentary Standards Act 2009, first report of session 2010–12, vol. 1.

remuneration, it is not a recompense, it is not even a salary. It is just an allowance
... to enable men to come here ... but who cannot be here because their means do
not allow it.'[4] IPP and unionist MPs benefited, but for the former the introduction
of the payment was controversial and roused condemnation in Sinn Féin propaganda. Laurence Ginnell, for instance, remarked that 'it was an evil day for Ireland
that the £400 was granted to Irish members.' In turn, IPP supporters defended
their MPs, arguing that Sinn Féin

> were making a lot of bother too about £400 a year, but did any of them
> think that £400 a year was the reason why John Redmond was their leader
> in Parliament? Could he not make £1,000 or £2,000 a year if he devoted
> himself to his profession and not bother at all about Parliament?[5]

The £400 was intended to cover both personal income and expenses. Prior to the
allowance, MPs received small stipends from party funds, now this money could
be redirected to cover electoral expenses and augment financial support for prospective candidates. But the IPP and unionists still had to raise substantial funds
in this era to promote candidates yet to be elected and promote party manifestos
and policies.

By 1920 new parties such as the Municipal Reform Party and Ratepayers'
Association also contested the local-government elections, but due to their
small numbers or divergent views they will only be interwoven into the analysis.
Computing a full account of receipts and expenditure for parties is not feasible
due to inconsistent methods of documenting income and expenditure, an arbitrary
application of finances to fund propaganda, clustering of expenditures of which
propaganda formed only part, and belated applications for expenses accrued. It
is highly likely that there were many clandestine donations for all parties as some
benefactors may not have wanted to be publicly associated with a particular party
for commercial or personal reasons and others may simply not have wanted it
known that they had switched allegiance. Therefore, investigating the collection
and dispersal of funds confronts the historian with difficulties because of the lack
of transparency.

NATIONALISTS

The organizational changes within the IPP, new leaders and the entry into an era of
competitive elections altered the party's approach to fundraising. In the early 1800s,
as Conor Cruise O'Brien highlights, 'candidates were substantial people capable of
defraying their own expenses'.[6] By the late 1800s candidates had come on board
from outside this elite class so the formation of a system to provide election funds

---

4 HC, PD, ser. 5, vol. 29, c. 1383: 10 Aug. 1911.   5 *LL*, 21 Apr. 1917.   6 Cruise O'Brien, *Parnell
and his party*, p. 137.

became essential.[7] Initially candidates began to obtain funds through small individual payments from the Land League; for example, T.M. Healy received £290 [£19,194] in 1880.[8] The National League subsequently became a source of revenue, and a total of £1,267 was provided for by-election expenses in 1883. The result was victory for the IPP in the six by-elections held in Monaghan, Tipperary, Mallow, Wexford, Waterford and Sligo. The total IPP funds from the National League for elections before the 1885 general election amounted to £2,325.[9] However, as this general election approached it became necessary to establish a special parliamentary fund where money was successfully raised through the League and in the USA. By the end of 1885, £17,950 [£1,188,015] was accumulated, and of that £14,610 was distributed, or as Timothy Harrington stated, the campaign cost 'about £15,000'.[10]

Under the leadership of Redmond and prior to the Great War the IPP created the Home Rule Fund and the amount collected in 1913 provided the party with £20,718 [£1,222,200]. At the thirty-first meeting of the UIL it was claimed that this collection 'beats all records and is nearly three times the amount subscribed in the very height of the Land League agitation'. In the euphoria of such riches and being blissfully ignorant of Ireland's impending entry into the Great War, the party announced that there was to be no appeal for funds in 1914 because of 'the generosity of the Irish people'.[11] Since the formation of the UIL, the IPP had depended on their revenue, and they in turn relied on the general support of members at constituency level through the provision of affiliation fees. In 1912 £2,764 was raised, it was £2,519 in 1913 and in 1914 branch affiliation fees increased by £50 to £2,570. Between the introduction of the third home rule bill and the UIL meeting of 1914 there had been an overall slight drop in affiliation fees amounting to approximately £194. Nonetheless, the IPP could claim at their thirty-second meeting in January 1914 that the UIL 'was never more widespread, more efficient, or more powerful than it is today'.[12]

By 1916 matters had substantially changed and at the thirty-forth meeting of the UIL (held in February 1916 – during the war, but before the Easter Rising) the party announced an expansion of affiliated branches since 1915. This increase of 276 branches – Cork (33), Donegal (28), Limerick (25), Louth (17), Kerry and Sligo (15 each), Armagh and Mayo (14 each), Cavan and Tyrone (12 each), Dublin and Derry (11 each), Down (10), Waterford (9), Meath and King's County (8 each), Queen's County (7), Carlow, Fermanagh, Galway and Leitrim (6 each) and

7 See Tadhg Moloney, *Limerick constitutional nationalism, 1898–1918: change and continuity* (Cambridge, 2010), pp 96–108 for information on the IPP fund to support MPs at Westminster in the early 1900s. 8 Healy, *Letters and leaders*, pp 95, 100. Note: the National Archives online currency converter was used for modern values (in the year 2017) and will be presented in square brackets: http://www.nationalarchives.gov.uk/currency-converter. 9 NLI, Harrington Papers, MS 16,292: Harrington affidavit. 10 Ibid., J.F.X. O'Brien Papers, MS 13,418–77: letters, memoranda, account books, etc., c.1879–1917. See also Cruise O'Brien, *Parnell and his party*, pp 133–9; *FJ*, 17 Dec. 1885. 11 NLI, UIL, MS 708: minutes of the National Directory, 7 Feb. 1913: Home Rule Fund. 12 Ibid., minutes of Thirty-Second Meeting (Fourteenth Annual Meeting), 29 Jan. 1914.

Wicklow (3) – accrued an extra £1,000 a year in affiliation fees. Yet, as Paul Bew argues, there was 'a degree of rustiness' in the League machinery: 'throughout 1915 Irish MPs were increasingly frank about the weakness of the UIL structure'.[13]

To remedy this weakness a national organizer was sent to Longford South to revitalize the League in advance of the expected 1917 by-election. However, an assertive propaganda campaign and the resultant success of Joseph McGuinness saw financial contributions moving to Sinn Féin. In 1918 IPP election committees were established or reawakened to garner funds to finance the necessary canvassing and campaigning for the general election. In Westmeath, for example, where businessman Patrick J. Weymes was unanimously selected at a UIL convention, an election committee was appointed and approximately £155 was contributed to election funds (including £50 from Weymes himself). The list of donations demonstrated that the breakdown of funds was one payment of £10, ten of £5, three of £3, eleven of £2, fourteen of £1, three contributed 10s., two 2s. 6d., one 5s. and one 4s.[14] Aside from monies raised by T.P. O'Connor in the USA, which will be discussed later, this piecemeal style of contribution was the manner in which most of the election monies for the IPP was raised.

In November 1918 Dillon opened the election campaign appealing for funds by announcing that 'under the new law electoral contests will be less expensive than they have been'. But, an immediate qualification added that since all the seats in Ireland were to be contested, 'the present general election will require a larger sum than has been required [heretofore]'. Impetus was needed to galvanize support in a short time frame. Under the auspices of the 'Irish National Trustees' a fund was established and Dillon appealed for subscriptions, and acknowledged receipt of £2,951 by November 1918. This amount was followed by a list of 173 further subscribers who contributed from £50 (only two) to £10 (only six) to smaller sums of 5s. Twenty-nine had contributed a sum of between £3 and £5, the majority contributed between £1 and £2 5s. (96), with the rest coming in smaller values.[15] Contributors in this instance came mainly from Dublin and areas of Ulster, and a few interestingly referred to themselves as 'A Friend' or 'A Hibernian' – proving that not all wanted their party affiliation known publicly, perhaps fearing intimidation or loss of business from opposing electors.[16]

In the same month, Dillon praised the small farmers in Loughglynn, North Roscommon who had donated to the IPP cause 'without any outside appeal or organization'. He hoped to create optimism and encouraged subscribers in other parts of the country 'to take action spontaneously in support of the Fund'. The nationalists of the townland of Kiltobranks subscribed £15 even though they had 'no representatives for North Roscommon to look after the interests of the people of this district' in the hope that their contribution would 'secure one at the general election'. Again, contributions came mainly in smaller denominations of 15s., 10s. and 3s.[17]

13 Bew, *Ideology and the Irish question*, pp 146–50. 14 *AC*, 30 Nov. 1918; *Westmeath Examiner*, 14. Dec. 1918. 15 *FJ*, 16 Nov. 1918. 16 Ibid. 17 Ibid., 19 Nov. 1918.

By early December an urgent appeal in the same newspaper requested that all outstanding funds be forwarded, indicating that collecting and releasing funds from constituencies was slow.[18] For instance, the St Patrick's Division in Dublin had gathered £243 by December plus £190 from their first instalment and £55 in the second instalment with further subscriptions still to be taken up just two days prior to polling. Seven days preceding the election Westmeath had raised £131, and constitutional nationalists in the village of Augher, Tyrone South had raised £7 and maintained that 'there is no waning here in the spirit of loyalty and devotion to the great national principles for which we stand'.[19] These examples demonstrate that the IPP was able to secure funds prior to the general election, but they came in dribs and drabs, and often too late in the day to mount a constituency-funded and focused poster or pamphlet campaign.

The IPP also hoped to raise funds from previously lucrative sources in the USA. By 1900 it had been estimated that 4,862,904 Americans were Irish-born or born to Irish-born parents, but by 1920 there were scarcely a million natives of Ireland in the USA, and many of the other millions with Irish parentage were no longer self-consciously Irish.[20] Most emigrants from Ireland in the mid-1800s had been young, single, uneducated Catholic unskilled male labourers, but by the early 1900s second- and third-generation Irish had become more upwardly mobile.[21] By 1918 the UIL's organization in America had collapsed, eliminating a major source of funding.[22] Redmond's defence of the British war effort had negatively affected his popularity among Irish-Americans, particularly within the AOH. Michael Ryan, the leader of the UIL in the USA, and publications like the *Irish World*, had withdrawn their support. The latter stated in 1915 that for Redmond to 'fritter away any part of her [Ireland's] military resources by going to England's defence would be treason of the blackest kind'.[23] The UIL's decline was so rapid that by 1915, in a complete reversal of fortune, the IPP had to finance the American organization.[24]

Fearing Sinn Féin's potential electoral success, and realizing that funds needed to be bolstered, the 69-year-old T.P. O'Connor travelled to the USA in 1917. He hoped to expeditiously revitalize past connections to source money from former advocates, such as those on Redmond's 1904 tour.[25] Doubt quickly dawned that they would rally to the party cause. O'Connor aimed to 'get the necessary funds at

18 Ibid., 9 Dec. 1918. **19** Ibid., 7 Dec. 1918, and 20 Dec. 1918: letter from John Skeffington, Dungannon, Co. Tyrone to Joseph Devlin. **20** F.M. Carroll, *American opinion and the Irish question, 1910–1923: a study in opinion and policy* (Dublin, 1978), p. 3; Fitzpatrick, *Harry Boland*, p. 137; US Department of Commerce, Bureau of the Census, Fourteenth Census of the United States, Taken in the Year 1920, 9 vols (Washington DC, 1922), ii, pp 693, 897 in ibid. **21** Kevin Kenny, *The American Irish: a history* (Abingdon, 2000), pp 131–209; Kerby A. Miller, 'Emigrants and exiles: Irish cultures and Irish emigration to North America, 1790–1922', *Irish Historical Studies*, 22:86 (Sept. 1980), 97–125. **22** NLI, JR, MS PC 262(1); O'Brien, *William O'Brien*, pp 215–16. **23** *Irish World*, 15 Aug. 1914. **24** Alan J. Ward, *Ireland and Anglo-American relations, 1899–1921* (London, 1969), p. 80. **25** Michael Wheatley, 'John Redmond and federalism in 1910', *Irish Historical Studies*, 32:127 (May 2001), 343–64.

private meetings and not to take the risk of any public gatherings', no doubt in an attempt to avoid public confrontations with or heckling from Sinn Féin supporters. He found that the party still had some friends 'stalwart and loyal as ever' in the county associations and from branches of the Hibernians. Samuel Insull, a leading Chicago industrialist, was one and he enthusiastically provided money and propaganda, promising $25,000 to O'Connor. The Irish Fellowship Club, at a meeting in December with 150–200 in attendance, also promised $25,000, although there was a lack of confidence that this would be forthcoming.[26]

O'Connor consistently complained that past friends were now hostile or were largely quiet and inactive, while those of Sinn Féin were 'vocal and had several [news]papers'.[27] In a letter from Washington he expressed his concerns to Dillon, stating that 'they [the Irish] seem to be just back in 1846 ... From the very first hour of my landing I was given proof of the hatred for us as well as for England'. He remarked that the hotel manageress where they were staying had slighted his travelling companion Richard Hazleton (MP for Louth North) by saying that 'we were not real Irishmen'. Another affront came from the *Irish World*, when they compared O'Connor to Benedict Arnold, casting him in the role of traitor to Ireland.

To add to his difficulties personal funds were also running low by December 1917 and he requested that Redmond 'put immediately £800 to my credit at the Bank of Scotland'.[28] While lobbying for party funds O'Connor had to earn his own living and to do this he wrote articles for various newspapers. By early 1918 he could no longer raise personal funds from this source because Sinn Féin activists had been thwarting his efforts in many cities by holding their own fundraising campaigns – although how much they gained is unknown. The impact of the conscription crisis in 1918 also affected his ability to raise funds, as did news of the 'toll of wounded and dead every day' in the Great War.[29]

O'Connor was successful in some areas of the USA because of the growing seriousness of the war, which made it more difficult for Clan na Gael, the Irish republican organization in America, to openly avow hostile sentiments against England or appeal for support for an Irish rebellion. The Clan had worked closely with German-Americans to defeat the Arbitration Treaty of 1911,[30] but American opinion generally did not support Germany after 1914.[31] At the outbreak of the

---

26 TCD, JD, MSS 6741/430: T.P. O'Connor to John Dillon, 28 Dec. 1917 and MSS 6741/437: T.P. O'Connor to John Dillon (undated but written from Chicago); Erica Doherty, '"The party hack, and tool of the British government": T.P. O'Connor, America and Irish Party resilience at the February 1918 South Armagh by-election', *Parliamentary History*, 34:3 (2015), 339–64.   27 TCD, JD, MSS 6741/411: T.P. O'Connor to John Dillon, 10 July 1917.   28 Ibid., MSS 6741/430: O'Connor to Dillon, 28 Dec. 1917.   29 Ibid., MSS 6741/501: O'Connor to Dillon, 20 June 1918.   30 A treaty involving the USA, UK and France for diputes to be submitted to the Hague Court for arbitration.   31 Michael Doorley, *Irish-American diaspora nationalism: the Friends of Irish Freedom, 1916–1935* (Dublin, 2005), p. 35; John E. Noyes, 'William Howard Taft and the Taft Arbitration Treaties', *Villanova Law Review*, 56 (2011), 535; Alan J. Ward, 'America and the Irish problem 1899–1921', *Irish Historical Studies*, 16:61 (Mar. 1968), 64–90, 70–3.

war, most of the USA's news originated from English sources, which recounted sensational details of German atrocities. IPP support of the war should have assisted O'Connor, but he lamented that the 'money is coming in with dreadful slowness'. O'Connor made assurances that there were promises of a further $5,000, plus subscriptions of $1,000 from several party supporters. He also believed that a considerable number of smaller subscriptions ranging from $100 to $500 were imminent, and was confident that the total raised from Chicago would be $100,000.

By December 1917 he claimed he had accumulated $50,000 for the IPP and assured those at home that if he reached his expectations the IPP would attain £30,000.[32] If £30,000 was obtained this should have gone a long way to augmenting the election fund. O'Connor continued his USA tour with some level of success (although perhaps not the £30,000), and he vowed to remain – celebrating his seventieth birthday there – until he had exceeded £40,000–£50,000. In January 1918 he dispatched £3,000 and maintained that the total sum sent to date was £13,000 [£767,000]. He aspired to raise a further £3,000–£4,000, promising its arrival within the week, and was confident that £10,000 would be accrued by the end of the month, with a total of $20,000 by June/July 1918. O'Connor commented that his sole source for funds was 'rich and patriotic Americans'.[33]

Meanwhile, back in Ireland, Dillon was despondent about the IPP's chances in the general election. He pleaded with O'Connor for 'financial support to fight the seventy or eighty contests Sinn Féiners are forcing upon us'. Yet, in November 1918 he stated that 'money is coming in very well indeed in Ireland' although he highlighted that this was 'ear-marked for the actual expenses of candidates in the different constituencies'.[34] His expectation seemed to have been that O'Connor's fundraising efforts would underwrite the other election expenses, such as propaganda, in order to mount 'an effective fight'.[35] He still held out for a substantial sum from benefactors in the USA, because 'with £50,000, or better £100,000, of American money and the moral support of the American-Irish I think this country could be brought back to sanity and the constitutional movement saved'.[36]

By 12 December, the Irish National Trustees again earnestly appealed for funds 'to enable the IPP to meet the expenses of the approaching contests'. The total amount received had been £7,715, and this was added to by further donations. Bequests by various county nationalist organizations came in larger denominations, such as the first instalment from Queen's County, which amounted to £165. Nationalists in Lurgan and district contributed £126, the London city committee gave £123, Co. Louth nationalists' second instalment was £100, Portadown (Armagh), per the *Irish News*, provided £87, and the rest arrived in smaller sums from UIL organizations or individuals.[37]

32 TCD, JD, MSS 6741/430: O'Connor to Dillon, 28 Dec. 1917. 33 Ibid., MSS 6741/444: O'Connor to Dillon, 29 Jan. 1918. 34 Ibid., MSS 6741/552: Dillon to O'Connor, 22 Nov. 1918. 35 Ibid. 36 Ibid., MSS 6741, Dillon to T.P. O'Connor, 3 June 1917. 37 *FJ*, 12 Dec. 1918.

Motivating supporters across all UIL branches to contribute generously to the election fund was a key propaganda exercise of the IPP. The Armagh Mid executive of the UIL took up the baton and passed a motion in early December calling on all nationalists of the division 'at once and generously to subscribe to the fund being raised for the expenses of the General Election'.[38] Church-gate collections were held in many parishes to garner financial support for the local candidate. In Meath South, for example, it was hoped that nationalists would 'rise to the occasion and provide the sinews of war for the coming struggle'.[39] Where held, these collections proved rewarding, as Thomas Nagle, honorary secretary of the Kilrush UIL branch in Clare West, said he could not remember 'a more generous and spontaneous response as we had on Sunday', when 'the collection was a record one'.[40] Church-gate collections were also useful as a propaganda exercise in alerting voters to candidates and party aims, and in 1918 there was a guaranteed audience for speeches. Funds were also sourced from UIL branches in Great Britain, where, for instance, the Irishwomen's Committee in London provided £29, to raise a total subscription of £51 by early December.

By 11 December 1918 the total received was £8,968 [£530,000].[41] Not all benefactors had desired publication of their names in the national press so some contributions were unpublished, making it difficult to assess the overall IPP gain. For instance, Alderman Alfred (Alfie) Byrne, the IPP candidate in Dublin's Harbour Division, advertised in the *Freeman's Journal* appealing for donations from 'friends and supporters' to cover election expenses, and assured prospective contributors that 'subscriptions will be acknowledged privately and not to the press (unless desired)'.[42] If we accept that O'Connor raised £13,000, and perhaps another £1,000–£2,000 in his final months in the USA, and add this to the £9,000–£10,000 collected by Dillon, the IPP entered the general election with approximately £23,000 [£1,357,000]. This was not an insubstantial sum. However, with eighty seats to be challenged in the 1918 election, this gave them only £287 per contested seat to mount a defence. While these numbers are conservative estimates, they also do not take into account any of the monies spent on the by-elections during this time.

Another difficulty that the IPP faced was their failing party organ, the *Freeman's Journal*, and this consumed party finances. The newspaper had gone into rapid decline since 1912, largely because of competition from the *Irish Independent*, and because of the destruction of its premises in Easter week 1916.[43] However in June 1917 Dillon confessed to O'Connor that he needed a further £10,000 to carry the *Freeman's Journal* on through another year.[44] By the end of 1918 the newspaper was making a loss of over £100 a week, and even Dillon had to admit that 75 per cent was due to bad management and 25 per cent to the changed situation after the

38 Ibid., 4 Dec. 1918. 39 Ibid., 28 Nov. 1918. 40 Ibid., 11 Dec. 1918. 41 Ibid., 12 Dec. 1918. 42 Ibid. 43 Brian Farrell, *Communications and community in Ireland* (Dublin, 1984), pp 24–6. 44 Lyons, *John Dillon*, pp 419–20.

Table 3.1 Elected candidates for 1920 municipal elections

Province	Total members elected	Unionist	Sinn Féin	Labour	Nationalist	Reform	Independents
Ulster	646	302	103	109	94	5	33
Leinster	590	57	206	151	69	62	45
Munster	481	7	201	111	58	36	68
Connacht	130	2	51	29	15	12	21
All Ireland	1,847	368	561	400	236	115	167

election.[45] The IPP simply did not have enough finances to rescue a newspaper and fund an election campaign. Election expenses (detailed later in this and following chapters) highlight that substantial funds were needed by all parties to generate and disseminate challenging and adversarial propaganda.

Disorder in leadership and fiscal liabilities rendered the propaganda efforts of the IPP impotent, leaving candidates to fend for themselves. As will be seen later, this resulted in haphazard campaigns and asymmetry of themes, and despondency quickly took root. By 1920 the party had virtually disappeared as a coherent force (but constitutional nationalists still contested for seats), Sinn Féin had fully awakened, and the Labour Party had taken up its mantle to represent the working classes. The number of elected candidates for the municipal elections in January 1920 can be seen in table 3.1.[46]

The number of constitutional-nationalist candidates elected had fallen drastically, to half the number Sinn Féin had, and 117 fewer than unionists, but they had not been completed annihilated. Unfortunately, there is little information regarding fundraising by these candidates, as their campaigns seem to have been largely self-financed, or financed by the local UIL (if it had selected the candidate).

The Cork Ratepayers' Association, at a meeting of their committee in December 1919, maintained that £100 was required to defray elections expenses. They opened a local election fund and invited subscriptions from ratepayers towards it.[47] This provides some indication of the minimum funding required by candidates intent on securing seats in 1920. The expenses incurred for the local elections were substantially less than that of a general election. Far less literature was needed to sway local votes, as evidenced by a remark in the *Irish Times* of 3 January 1920, which stated that 'up to the present the election has not been marked by any exceptional display of election literature'. Unlike Sinn Féin and the Unionist Party,

45 TCD, JD, MSS 6730: Dillon to T.P. O'Connor, 20 Feb. and 10 May 1919.   **46** Results published in *IT*, *II* and *CE*, 20 Jan. 1920.   **47** *CE*, 24 Dec. 1919.

constitutional nationalists were now leaderless and no longer functioned as a party force, so no central authority managed a fundraising initiative, and by 1921 funds were needed only for the Northern Ireland elections, and these seemed to come from local sources under Devlin's management.

During the Roscommon North by-election Sinn Féin became aware of the importance of accumulating finances to successfully contest elections, and by May 1917 a fund was created to organize clubs and meet expenses. To challenge a seat in the Longford South by-election – a constituency that had always favoured an IPP candidate – Sinn Féin mounted an aggressive fundraising campaign through the pages of *Nationality*. Contributions came in that ranged from small amounts up to £50, from all parts of the country (£50 was donated by the working committee of Limerick nationalists and the executive of Sinn Féin in Cork) and £1,288 was speedily raised.[48] The expenses accrued during this electoral contest amounted to £491, leaving a surplus of £797, which was then directed towards the Clare East campaign.[49] At the October convention Sinn Féin affiliation fees had reached £1,010, subscriptions had reached £1,988, £239 had been gained from the resourceful sale of membership cards and literature, and the Longford fund contributed £1,288. The expenses accrued were £1,034 for organizing, and £378 for printing, and election expenses at Longford were £491, at Clare were £766 and at Kilkenny were £210, leaving a balance of £1,946.[50] An adroit fundraising campaign in these early days of the by-elections positioned Sinn Féin as a serious electoral contender.

Sinn Féin was also the first and only party to establish a dedicated department of propaganda, at 6 Harcourt Street, Dublin, in April 1918, which was staffed with paid workers. Robert Brennan became the first director of publicity, earning £5 a week, with £1 5s. for a boy assistant, £4 for a chief assistant and £1 10s. for a typist. The advantage was the centralization of propaganda efforts and some degree of control over finances, until the standing committee was established – responsibility for managing finances came under their remit in January 1918.[51]

The aggregate funds were sufficient for the by-elections, but Sinn Féin's determination for victory in the 1918 general election necessitated collecting larger amounts. The derisory sums available in Ireland inspired the party to seek alternative sources, so in similar fashion to the IPP before them, Sinn Féin looked outwards – to Britain, Australia and the USA. The Irish in Britain were largely unskilled or semi-skilled workers and it was only with the rise of labour that Irish workers became more organized.[52] However, Sinn Féin had some experience in Britain as Art Ó Briain had created the Irish National Relief Fund in London after the 1916 Rising and later he established the Irish Self-Determination League of Great Britain. The former organization mainly collected funds for the relief of

48 *II*, 4 May 1917, *Nationality*, 5 May 1917, and *Factionist*, 17 May 1917. 49 Laffan, *The resurrection*, p. 100. 50 *II*, 26 Oct. 1917. 51 SFSCM, 20 May 1919; Laffan, *The resurrection*, p. 177. 52 Fitzpatrick, 'The Irish in Britain 1871–21' in Vaughan, *A new history*, pp 653–702.

distress in Ireland and the latter was more propagandistic, organizing large nationalist demonstrations.[53]

By 1920 targeting Britain became important because the circulation of news from Ireland to a British and international audience was dependent on newspaper correspondents who were resident in London. Travel to interview these foreign pressmen in London and issuing pamphlets to be circulated onwards to 'practically every European country as well as the USA, Canada, South America, South Africa, Australia and Japan' proved costly.[54] In November 1919 Sinn Féin's propaganda department had received £300, and of this, travel to London cost £89, printing of pamphlets for the domestic and international markets cost £28, postage was £94, newspapers and photographs cost £19 and there were additional costs including rent and office fittings at £46, bringing the total to £276. By June 1920 Desmond FitzGerald was seeking £500 to continue to cover these expenses.[55] Disseminating weekly 'Acts of Aggression' committed by the British in Ireland became the barbed message that Sinn Féin wanted foreign journalists to repeat.[56] Voluntary distribution of pamphlets and the *Irish Bulletin* newspaper through the Self-Determination League of Great Britain and through the Sinn Féin organization in Ireland kept costs much reduced.

In terms of fundraising Britain did not prove as profitable as Australia, and particularly the USA. In February 1918 Australia was added to Sinn Féin's list as a possible external source for funds when Seán Milroy proposed that the Irish there be petitioned.[57] The difficulty with Australia was that the Irish were widely dispersed geographically and thinly spread on a vast continent.[58] Many Irish had prospered in business and thrived financially, however they had not retained their Irish cultural traditions and had assimilated quickly into their new country. Archbishop Daniel Mannix led the republican cause after the 1916 Rising, bringing the Irish demand for a republic to the fore in the Australian media. However, the overall response to republican causes was weaker than that afforded to home rule in the past. Tours by Redmond and Dillon in 1883 and 1889 had successfully collected substantial funds.[59]

In 1917–18 the Irish in the USA proved more generous, and they were easier to access in terms of travel distance than Australia. As mentioned earlier, O'Connor's account of his experiences in the USA demonstrated that Sinn Féin gained more support than the IPP. However, they too fought an uphill battle because of the USA's entry into the Great War in April 1917. As a result, Sinn Féin could no

---

53 NLI, Art Ó Briain Papers, MS 8436/27, 8422/11 and 8435/20: O'Brien, for example, had organized a demonstration in London's Trafalgar Square for the release of political prisoners. 54 UCDA, Desmond FitzGerald Papers, P80/14(6): report of propaganda department, 15 June 1920. 55 Ibid., P80/14(5): propaganda department invoice, 10 June 1920. 56 Ibid., P80/14(6): report of propaganda department, 15 June 1920. 57 SFSCM, P3269, 21 Feb. 1918. 58 Patrick O'Farrell, 'The Irish in Australia and New Zealand, 1870–1990' in Vaughan, *A new history*, p. 704. 59 Ibid., p. 719.

longer preach anti-war or pro-German opinions, but O'Connor reported in November 1917 that Sinn Féin was not 'out of business'.[60]

The Irish population residing in the USA had very diverse views of nationalism, and therefore financially backed both radical and constitutional approaches to Irish self-government. There were also many Irish-Americans who hailed from Scotch-Irish backgrounds and they continued to support the union between Britain and Ireland.[61] Walker states that a significant number of Protestants (mainly Presbyterians and Episcopalians) continued to emigrate to America from Ireland throughout the nineteenth and early twentieth centuries.[62] Similarly, in Australia, according to Fitzpatrick, there was recognition that what used to be viewed as an almost exclusively Irish Catholic community contained a significant Protestant component.[63]

The consequence of the diversity of the Irish-American diaspora was that finances could only be amassed by Irish political parties from those who supported their point of view. And, even at that, there were conditions imposed for support such as that by *The Liberty Digest* in February 1918, which claimed that Sinn Féin would continue to receive support from Irish-America if they made their 'fight for freedom a bloodless one'. However, they added the proviso that if England did not listen to reason then 'a revolt can be considered, and must be considered, after the present world war … Meanwhile, let them use the ballot wisely'.[64]

Mixed opinion in America on Sinn Féin was evident from a number of newspaper reports. The New York-based *Gaelic American* – the newspaper owned and edited by the radical and contentious John Devoy – complained that Sinn Féin was much maligned; J.P. Mahony, editor of the *Indiana Catholic* in Indianapolis, maintained that Sinn Féin was 'much misunderstood', and argued that 'if the same treatment was accorded Americans by a foreign military oppressor [as Britain was to Ireland] they would revolt in the same way'.[65] Sinn Féin, therefore, was reliant on a small number of organizations that advocated a more Fenian militant-style approach to gaining Irish self-governance, such as Clan na Gael. However, by 1915 Clan na Gael was in financial trouble and Devoy maintained in July that 'the organization is going down instead of up' and that raising money was now 'very serious'.[66] A convention was held on 4 March 1916 in the Hotel Astor in New

60 TCD, JD, MSS 6741(430): T.P. O'Connor to John Dillon, 5 Nov. 1917; see also 28 Dec. 1917 for comments on John Devoy and Clan na Gael. **61** Michael P. Carroll, *American Catholics in the Protestant imagination: rethinking the academic study of religion* (Baltimore, MD, 2007), pp 1–26; J.J. Lee, 'Interpreting Irish America' in J.J. Lee and Marion R. Casey (eds), *Making the Irish American: history and heritage of the Irish in the United States* (NY, 2006), pp 1–62; and Kerby A. Miller, *Emigrants and exiles: Ireland and the Irish exodus to North America* (Oxford, 1988). **62** Brian Walker, '"The lost tribes of Ireland": diversity, identity and loss among the Irish diaspora', *Irish Studies Review*, 15:3 (2007), 267–82. **63** David Fitzpatrick, *Oceans of consolation: personal accounts of Irish migration to Australia* (NY, 1994). **64** *Liberty Digest*, 2 Feb. 1918. **65** TCD, JD, MSS 6741(445): newspaper cuttings, the *Indiana Catholic*. **66** NLI, McGarrity Papers: MS 94109: Devoy to McGarrity, July 1915.

York City, and 2,300 delegates attended. A new Irish-American organization was founded and named the Friends of Irish Freedom (FOIF).

The FOIF had a seventeen-man executive committee, of which fifteen were Clan members, and they played a strong role in fundraising in 1916, establishing the Irish Relief Fund Committee.[67] The FOIF had strongly opposed O'Connor's visit to the USA, but in 1917 this had not been of grave concern because they were not numerically strong – support in the USA for the war had led to reduced membership, although they remained active in cities with large Irish populations, such as New York and Boston. Many branches of the FOIF ceased to function during the latter wartime years and in 1917 there were 2,891 paid up members and of these 1,495 were based in New York.[68]

Disillusionment with the FOIF led to the creation of the Irish Progressive League, and again Devoy was behind this operation. In the face of this new competition, the FOIF attempted to rejuvenate itself and an Irish Race Convention was organized for 18–19 May 1918 in the Central Opera House in New York. New officers were elected and Diarmuid Lynch was appointed national secretary on a salary of $3,000 per annum. Tighter discipline was imposed on the organization and the agreed objective was to petition US President Woodrow Wilson to allow for Irish representation at the Paris peace conference – a key message in Sinn Féin electoral propaganda. The proceeds of a collection taken up at the convention were $819, allowing the organization to meet its expenses, but leaving it little to spare.[69] As the collection demonstrates, attendance at the convention was much smaller than at previous conventions, but it did include members of Clan na Gael, the AOH, the Irish Progressive League and Irish-American literary societies.[70] In 1918 membership of the FOIF was still low at approximately 2,000, and this was distributed among forty branches. A further aim arising from the convention was the advancement of a firm recruitment drive to boost numbers, and membership and funds increased substantially by 1919 (in that year regular membership was recorded at 6,068 with associate membership estimated at 30,000).[71] But, in September 1918 the FOIF secretary, Diarmuid Lynch, reported that there was only a paltry $410 available.[72] Therefore, Sinn Féin had to rely on staging their own meetings and demonstrations to collect for the 1918 election. How much Sinn Féin actually harvested in 1918 is unknown, but the lessons learned and the funds gained were enough to send de Valera to the USA in 1919.

Back in Ireland it became critical for Sinn Féin to manage and centrally coordinate fundraising and fund distribution to local *cumainn* for the by-elections. Laurence Ginnell was appointed treasurer by the standing committee in January

67 John Devoy, *Recollections of an Irish rebel* (NY, 1929), p. 450; NLI, MS 32597: Diarmuid Lynch, 'History of the FOIF', p. 28.   68 Doorley, p. 48; Lynch, 'History of the FOIF'; and American Irish Historical Society (AIHS), Friends of Irish Freedom (FOIF) Papers, John D. Moore: 'Membership fees ledger, 1916–17'.   69 AIHS, FOIF Papers, Box 6, Folder 2: National Executive minutes, 1918–19; Charles Callan Tansill, *America and the fight for Irish freedom, 1866–1922* (NY, 1957), p. 270.   70 Doorley, pp 36 and 78; Lynch, 'History of the FOIF'.   71 Lynch, 'History of FOIF'.

1918 for the South Armagh by-election, and was empowered to spend £200 at his own discretion and appoint someone locally to manage funds. Local *cumainn* were allowed to retain a small amount for election expenses, but even this tight control failed to prevent over-expenditure. The Armagh South collection provided surplus income for the party but concerns were later raised that 'the expenditure in some of the departments … was most extravagant'.[73] Cosgrave proposed that all departments furnish detailed accounts of proposed expenditure to the executive committee at stated short intervals, and 'no orders [were] to be issued against the funds of the organization which shall not have the approval of the President'.[74] De Valera was president, and the man in charge, and now authorization for spending was his sole preserve. In a similar style to their candidate-selection process, Sinn Féin's financial-management structure was beginning to emulate that of the IPP when under the reign of Parnell.

Centralized control grew tighter as the distribution of funds for election campaigns became strictly managed. Payment of salaries to those in charge of registration work was agreed on in certain areas, but not in others. Registration work in Dublin was deemed important enough to warrant a salaried employee to be paid £2 per week and £3 if this proved insufficient.[75] Seán Milroy, director of elections in Cavan East, received £200 to secure victory there in April 1918,[76] but finances must have come from other sources because the projected expenses for this by-election were estimated at £1,600. By July only £480 had been received in subscriptions and it was agreed that supporters should be further petitioned to improve the situation. Tyrone East received £250 for their battle because a guarantee had been provided for a full treasury refund – but, by July only £11 had been paid back.[77]

Sinn Féin appointed five organizers for the 1918 general election, but the instruction was that their salaries would now be paid by local counties/constituencies while they were engaged there.[78] George Nesbitt became financial director in December 1918 replacing James O'Mara who was now director of elections. Jennie Wyse Power became financial director for North East Ulster and was provided with a sum of £2,250 and instructed to make haste to Belfast. Sinn Féin yearned for victory in Ulster, being determined to defeat partition, and this became more crucial during the 1921 partition election. In 1921 Sinn Féin and Dáil Éireann spent approximately £2,000 to fund a plan introduced by de Valera at a standing committee meeting of Sinn Féin. During the local elections a 'special effort' was made to secure a majorities in Armagh, Derry, Down, Fermanagh, Monaghan and Tyrone.[79] Seán Milroy applied for local organizers to manage the local elections and after some wrangling eight sub-organizers were retained for Ulster – two for Tyrone, one for Fermanagh North, two for Co. Down, one for Donegal East, one for Derry South and one for Armagh.[80]

72 Eileen McGough, *Diarmuid Lynch: a forgotten Irish patriot* (Cork, 2013), ch. 6. 73 SFSCM, 21 Feb. 1918. 74 Ibid. 75 Ibid., 10 Apr. 1918. 76 Ibid., 18 Apr. 1918. 77 Ibid., 8 July 1918. 78 Ibid., 6 Sept. 1918. 79 Ibid., 13 Apr. 1921 and 22 Jan.1919. 80 Ibid., 14 Oct. 1920.

At the outset of the 1918 general election campaign Sinn Féin's income was declared to be £17,360 [£1,024,000] and expenditure £9,718.[81] Expenditure on propaganda literature, posters, handbills and so on used up much of this income, as did salaries and travel expenses (cars were still a luxury, and petrol hard to come by in the war years). As the election loomed concerns were raised that debts accrued during the by-elections had not yet been fully paid – and many of them were in connection with the use of cars and car repairs (this was also the case after the 1918 election). In October 1919 the election subcommittee submitted and paid an account for £36 for repair to a motorcar used in the general election – over a year late. Non-payment for cars used in Waterford during the general election resulted in the Limerick city executive threatening to withhold affiliation fees until debts were paid in full.[82] Cosgrave moved that all expenses be paid at once, no doubt fearing that creditors had better memories than debtors, and that these same cars might be required in the general election.[83]

Funds for the general election were collected by door-to-door canvassers. Hurling and football matches were organized, as were dances, pilgrimages to local shrines, lectures and concerts.[84] Church-gate collections for Sinn Féin had commenced in 1914 and the process continued through the by-elections and into the general election. Polling day for the 1918 election was just a few months after the anti-conscription campaign, and it is interesting to query if the anti-conscription fund that was created and collected was used to support Sinn Féin's election campaign. Sinn Féin cleverly organized a party collection on the same day as the dispersal of these funds. There had been £17,000 accrued, but the return was not furnished until 1919.[85] However, some clubs donated their collections to the party (90 per cent of these funds had remained within parishes) such as £400 by Kilfinane in Co. Limerick, where only three demanded their £5 back as they 'all had sons fit for the front'.[86] Sinn Féin created a handbill to stimulate public donations, simply titled: *Sinn Féin general election fund*. This claimed that over a quarter of a million pounds had been collected to fight conscription, but that a 'much smaller sum' was needed to enable Sinn Féin make 'a bid for complete liberty'.[87]

According to RIC inspector general reports, Sinn Féin had collected approximately £42,613 from the provinces up to June 1918, of which £20,540 was sent to headquarters in Dublin; £11,449 was spent locally and £10,623 was in the hands of Sinn Féin clubs across the country. In the month of June alone £2,310 was collected, and 1,117 clubs paid the usual affiliation fee of £2, with 885 clubs having paid a special levy of £1 each. The general election fund had raised about £6,400 by June – £5,000 was collected by May, £5,595 by April, £4,500 by March

81 Ibid., 19 Nov. 1918. 82 Ibid., 30 Oct. 1919 and 20 July 1920. 83 Ibid., 19 Aug. 1918. 84 BMH WS 568: Eilis (Bean) Uí Chonaill (Ní Riáin); RIC inspector general's report, Jan. 1918, CO 904/105. 85 NA, CO 904/109: RIC inspector general's report, May 1919. Relying on information supplied by the inspector general is problematic due to inaccuracies, but it does provide a general indication of Sinn Féin finances. 86 BMH WS 1435: Daniel F. O'Shaughnessy. 87 NLI, Irish large books (ILB), p. 5: *Sinn Féin general election fund*.

and £2,000 by end of February, demonstrating that a sum £500 was being raised monthly (aside from the large leap from February to March).[88]

Despite monies raised, an outstanding debt for the 1918 general election for Sinn Féin amounted to £1,360, and regardless of motions by Cosgrave to finalize bills some were still outstanding six years later.[89] Election expenses incurred by candidates sanctioned in 1918 were still unpaid in 1919 and were then forwarded to the minister of finance (Eoin MacNeill January 1919 to April 1919, then Michael Collins until August 1922). These expenses amounted to a total of £712 and included: Donegal South (£92), Roscommon South (£14), Mayo West (£60), Down South (£52), Clontarf (£69), Dublin South (£68), Pembroke (£64), College Green (£40), St Patrick's (£79), Harbour (£85) and Dublin (£89).[90] Nesbitt reported in November 1918 that there had been a 'heavy drain on funds', stating that £5,000 had been spent on the contests in Ulster (although the party was still very much in credit, to the sum of £3,900). This led to a proposal by the standing committee that every elector who had voted Sinn Féin ought to be asked to contribute one penny to settle the debt (perhaps imitating Daniel O'Connell's 1824 'Catholic rent'). A motion was passed to the effect that £1 to a penny was to be levied on each individual, that Nesbitt was to take steps to organize the levy and that election staff be utilized to collect it.[91] This indicates that Sinn Féin had confidence in securing extra Irish fiscal backing and, with their sources in the USA, the party was sufficiently able to challenge in 1920. Most of the funding for the 1918 general election had been harvested from homegrown supporters, but the USA also proved lucrative because the party or its leaders returned again and again for financial aid.

After their 1918 general election win of 73 seats out of 105, in 1919 and 1920 Sinn Féin required substantial finance. Securing the majority vote had accorded the mandate, as far as they were concerned, to carry out their abstentionist policy, and this was made manifest in the creation of the unicameral Dáil Éireann in January 1919.[92] Ministers were appointed over various departments, but running these departments and a nation required not only internal support and recognition, but a serious amount of money. By gaining the USA's recognition for the 1918 electoral victory Sinn Féin also aspired to secure further funds to promote Dáil Éireann and finance electoral contests at local level in 1920. In 1919 the net sum of the 'Self Determination Fund', according to the minister for finance, was £12,237.[93]

In June 1919 Dr Patrick McCartan arrived in the USA as 'envoy of the Irish republic'. He met with infighting as well as external anger towards the FOIF's separatist position from those who considered their sentiments and behaviour

88 NA, CO 904/7–23, 27–9 and 157 and Nos. 19477/S, 18994/S, 18547/S: anti-government organizations, 1882–1921, Chief Secretary's Office No. 20379/S: Sinn Féin funds.   89 SFSCM, 25 Sept. 1919 and 22 Dec. 1924.   90 Ibid., 6 Nov. 1919.   91 Ibid., 19 Nov. 1918.   92 UCDA, Richard Mulcahy Papers, MS P7/A/37: proclamation by President de Valera, 2 May 1921.   93 DÉD, 27 Oct. 1919.

unpatriotic. This resulted in media hostility to his and Hanna Sheehy Skeffington's west-coast tours.[94] Sheehy Skeffington (like O'Connor in 1917) complained that the Irish in America were mainly timid 'comfortable, elderly gentlemen', who talked 'about old times … but the moment I talk of 1918 and what could be done now they close up!'[95] The decision was also taken to send de Valera to the USA and Harry Boland as 'envoy' to Clan na Gael. The predominant ambitions were three-fold: to attain support for admitting envoys to the peace conference, to acquire political and public support for Sinn Féin and Dáil Éireann through propaganda and political lobbying, and equally, to garner as much money as possible.

Fitzpatrick's work *Harry Boland's Irish Revolution* provides vivid background and a comprehensive account of Boland's activities in the USA; and a multiplicity of other works cover de Valera's.[96] Because this work is focused on domestic election propaganda, an impressionistic analysis of the USA's influence on Sinn Féin domestic propaganda campaigns will be conducted in chapter 5, and below briefly during the bond drive. De Valera's tour of the USA brought in substantial funds but was also costly. The income accumulated was enough to fund and maintain the programme of meetings and rallies, but only limited amounts were returned to Ireland to fund election campaigns or Dáil Éireann.

On 4 April 1919 the dáil voted to issue 'Republican Bonds to the value of £250,000'. Bonds were issued in denominations of £1, £5, £10, £20, £50 and £100, and accrued 5 per cent interest per annum. All bonds were redeemable within twenty years of the international recognition of the Irish republic. By 20 August 1919 the secretary for finance moved that an additional sum of $23,750,000 worth of bonds be issued for subscription as the 'Loan of the Government of the Irish Republic in the United States'. This increased the total amount for the issue to a ridiculously large $25,000,000 by late August and the loan campaign was launched in early September.[97] These bonds were to be redeemable only after the creation of a functioning independent state. Even though elections received only small amounts of the monies raised, the publicity proved enormously valuable in raising international awareness about Sinn Féin's policies, and lessons were learned on how to conduct a large-scale propaganda campaign (see chapter 4).

In Ireland, Collins managed the campaign, but the collection and promotion of the bonds was largely conducted at local level by the Sinn Féin clubs. By the end of October reports from certain parts of the country placed the amount of subscriptions promised at £30,700.[98] Promises were by no means guarantees so

94 Patrick McCartan, *With de Valera in America* (Dublin, 1932); Margaret Ward, *Hanna Sheehy Skeffington: a life* (Cork, 1997), pp 184–210. See also UCDA, P150/96, de Valera Papers: de Valera to Arthur Griffith, 13 Aug. 1919.   95 NLI, Peter Golden Papers, MS 1341: Sheehy Skeffington to Golden, n.d.   96 For further information on de Valera in the US see: Callan Tansill, *America and the fight for Irish freedom*, McCartan, *With de Valera in America*, Denis R. Gwynn, *De Valera* (London, 1933) and F.M. Carroll, *American opinion* and idem, 'De Valera and the Americans: the early years, 1916–1923', *Canadian Journal of Irish Studies*, 8:1 (June 1982), 36–54.   97 DÉD, 20 Aug., ministerial motions: finance.   98 DÉD, F:14, 27 Oct. 1919: statement of acting president – bond issue.

Collins decided to run advertisements in the newspapers to promote the bonds appeal further. The *Cork Examiner* printed the advertisements, but other national newspapers were reluctant to do so because Dublin Castle had warned that the act was illegal. Twenty-two other separatist and provincial weekly papers also printed the advertisement.[99] The result was the proscribing of Dáil Éireann and a raid on Sinn Féin offices in Harcourt Street. However, print advertisements to promote the purchase of bonds indirectly bolstered election campaigns. Creating recognition of the Sinn Féin agenda at local level cannot be underestimated and it no doubt influenced local councils to later pledge allegiance to Dáil Éireann because of instant recognition of the intent and programme.

A total of $5,500,000 was subscribed in the USA for Irish bonds, a huge amount by comparison to any previous campaign by Parnell or any IPP representative, and a figure that exceeded even de Valera's expectations (American subscriptions to the Land League in 1880 amounted to £66,000, and £250,000 between November 1879 and October 1882). Lynch had promised Boland $110,000 for the dáil by 1920, although not all of this had been delivered by the start of 1920. By the end of the year approximately $1 million had been slipped into Ireland, and a sum of only $400,000 ended up in the treasury of the Irish Free State. Later litigation battles between the Irish Free State and republicans in Irish and American courts saw over $2.5 million finally distributed to certificate holders by 1930.[100] The secrecy involved in preventing Crown Forces detecting the arrival into Ireland of funds amassed in the USA makes it problematic to account for their dispersal and to ascertain how much, if any, was allocated to the 1920 and 1921 election campaigns. American funds were needed and used to prop up the fledgling state and small amounts of revenue were directed into election campaigns to facilitate organization in constituencies that required special attention. Sinn Féin's determination to secure broad representation on councils hints that they were prepared to invest in propaganda to obtain votes. The fact that one of the first departments established by Dáil Éireann was the Local Government Department under Cosgrave indicates that the foundation of support at the local level was paramount. Grants were made to local constituencies to bolster electoral organization and propaganda. For instance, Seán Milroy proposed in July 1919, and Jennie Wyse Power seconded, that the dáil should grant loans to the constituencies to pay for organizers.[101] Loans amounting to £400 were agreed for certain constituencies who applied for funds, but in others (Cavan East, for example) loans were held over pending reports on performance.

The burden of debt repayment, however, was relegated to local constituencies because many still had outstanding financial liabilities after the general election.

99 F.M. Carroll, *Money for Ireland: finance, diplomacy, politics, and the first Dáil Éireann loans, 1919–1936* (Westport, CT, 2002), p. 7, and pp 15–30; Arthur Mitchell, *Revolutionary government in Ireland, Dáil Éireann, 1919–22* (Dublin, 1995), p. 60. **100** Dorothy Macardle, *The Irish republic* (London, 1937; NY, 1968), pp 1024–5; Katherine O'Doherty, *Assignment America: de Valera's mission to the United States* (NY, 1957), pp 66–9. **101** SFSCM, 10 July 1919.

The director of propaganda, Robert Brennan, highlighted that it was the responsibility for each *teachta dála* (TD) to clear these debts (although, as stated earlier some of these debts remained outstanding six years later).[102] Joseph McGuinness also called for all outstanding election debts to be paid, and a decision was taken to pay off £77 of the Mayo East debt as it was 'a special case'.[103] The 'special case' no doubt refers to the fact that the contest was against the IPP leader. Donegal West and Rathmines received £32 and £29, respectively, to clear their accounts, and Kildare South received £95. Belfast requested £137, but this 'claim could not be entertained' as Wyse Power maintained that 'ample financial assistance was given at the time'.[104] In September 1919, as previously stated, constituencies still owed the standing committee £1,360 in election loans, so the dáil agreed to liquidate these debts.[105]

In late December 1919 the election subcommittee applied for a grant of £300 to cover the cost of printing 750,000 copies of the Sinn Féin programme for the municipal elections. Cosgrave agreed to supply the grant and pay it into the account of the Sinn Féin executive. Where these funds were derived from is unknown, but managing the distribution of finance was kept under strict control, particularly in regard to election-literature expenses. The advantage was a central command to ensure that only agreed literature received the funds necessary for printing, and in turn only approved literature was circulated. Sinn Féin had raised a substantial amount of money by 1920, but for the rural elections, although 1,000 copies of the Sinn Féin manifesto were printed and sent to all election directors, every constituency or county council was asked to print sufficient copies locally to cover its own district. It was also considered 'very inadvisable' to pay the expenses of candidates during the local elections.[106] The numerous contenders required to contest seats meant that local *cumainn* and clubs had to bear most of the burden. General headquarters, the election committee, the standing committee and subsequently Dáil Éireann carried the weight of printing and circulating mainstream propaganda, but candidates and their nominators financed local election expenses and propaganda such as provincial newspaper advertisements and poster campaigns throughout all the elections.

According to Desmond FitzGerald's report in June 1920 the cost of running the propaganda department from November 1919 to May 1920 was £890 and of this £393 was paid in salaries, £235 on the printing of pamphlets and stationery, and £262 'has been paid out by me' which included the printing of pamphlets and handbills for £26.[107] George Gavan Duffy's campaign in France during the peace conference was not quite as economical, although the circulation of the *Irish Bulletin* newspaper created positive news coverage there also. He estimated that funding representation at the peace conference required 10,000 francs to set up

---

102 Ibid., 22 Dec. 1924. **103** Ibid., 17 July and 4 Oct. 1919. **104** Ibid., 29 Jan. 1920. **105** Ibid., 25 Sept. and 30 Oct. 1919. **106** Ibid., 17 Dec. 1919 and 26 Feb. 1920. **107** UCDA, Desmond FitzGerald Papers, P80/14(7): report of propaganda department, June 1920.

an office and pay a clerk, and that a further 30,000 francs would be needed to pay a high calibre representative. He maintained that when these and other costs were taken into account the total sum to present Ireland's case would be at least £50,000 [£1,452,885].[108]

Back in Ireland in 1920 a central office was required by the election committee to manage both the municipal and rural elections, and another outlay was required by the minister for local government to rent the backroom of the premises occupied by the election committee at a sum equal to half the rent and taxes. Agreement was reached between the Sinn Féin election committee and the Department of Local Government also to pay half the cost of maintenance (coal, light, and so on) and to avail of the services of Dan McCarthy, the election agent, at a payment of £2 per week. To cover expected expenses in the revision courts, Dan McCarthy applied for £1,000 from the standing committee, but the agreement reached was that each constituency was to be considered separately and on its own merits. McCarthy had requested this amount for election work in Dublin South, Rathmines, Pembroke, Wexford North and South, Waterford and certain northern constituencies – all the constituencies that had been problematic for Sinn Féin during the 1918 election. By July 1920 a sum of £340 had been granted for Pembroke, Rathmines, Dublin South, Louth, St Stephen's Green and College Green.[109] Salaries also had to be paid and included: Robert Brennan's salary, now at £6 per week, Dan McCarthy at £6 per week, and Michael Nunan at £2 per week. Salaries for the eight sub-organizers in Ulster at £5 per week was passed for payment, as was travel from Dublin to the north. The total for salaries by June 1919 was £65 per week for thirteen employees in party headquarters and three provincial organizers.[110]

As mentioned earlier, funding the administration of Dáil Éireann was also an expense that had to be absorbed, and forming Dáil Éireann was a propaganda exercise in and of itself. Running costs included ministerial salaries at about £4,100 per annum; the salary of the president was £500 and the seven ministers received £350 each, with the three directors of departments getting the same amount. TDs received no salaries but obtained travel and accommodation expenses and by September 1920 were given up to £250 annually for these expenses. Eight officials (ranging from the secretary to the minister) received £500–£600 per annum, with total salaries amounting to about £10,000 annually. The dáil also voted to allocate £10,000 yearly for new consular services and another £10,000 for a fisheries programme. Therefore, the new government needed a minimum of at least £25,000 every twelve months. And, this was only for the running of government; when financing the state is included costs add up fast.[111]

---

108 Ibid., Gavan Duffy, P152/115, 13 Apr. 1920; SFSCM, 19 Dec. 1918.   109 SFSCM, 4 May 1920 and 1 June 1920 and 20 July 1920.   110 NLI, Robert Barton Papers, MS 8786/1; and SFSCM, 5 June 1919, 22 June 1920 and 14 Oct. 1920.   111 DÉD, 18 June 1919; see also Mitchell, *Revolutionary government*, pp 57–8.

In October 1920 the director of organization, Seán Milroy, appointed eight sub-organizers for Ulster for the 1921 election – two for Tyrone (North-East and North-West), one for Fermanagh North, two for County Down (East and South), one for Donegal East, one for Derry South and one for Armagh South. It was decided that Dan McCarthy would remain on with a salary of £6 per week with £5 being granted for any extra expenditure (after the election McCarthy's services were dispensed with because there was no work for him and he was granted three months' salary (£80)).[112] To battle against unionists in 1921 £2,000 was allocated to propaganda, with the Dáil contributing £1,000 and Sinn Féin the other £1,000, demonstrating that Sinn Féin were resolute about securing Ulster seats. Costs were estimated as follows: 20,000 copies of propaganda per week for three weeks, £700; editorial, £250; newspaper advertisements, £500; and contingencies, £350. Archibald Savage, the Sinn Féin candidate for Belfast's Pottinger-Victoria District in 1921, explained that they had collected £400 in Belfast and were able to collect a further £400. The standing committee agreed to pay the sheriff's fees (or deposits), but believed the other expenses could be collected locally. There were heated requests from other constituencies, such as from the Fermanagh *comhairle ceantair*, who wrote stating that they had not yet collected the £300 sheriff's fee and would not or could not nominate a candidate if this fee was not forthcoming from the standing committee. There had also been an agreement between nationalists to give second-preference votes to other nationalists regardless of party affiliation as the 1921 election was conducted using the proportional representation method of voting. A further agreement was reached between Devlin and Sinn Féin that the balance of the anti-conscription fund was to be divided between the UIL and republican candidates in the six-county area to defray election expenses, but only on the proviso that the UIL kept their promise in regard to exchange of second preferences.[113]

It is difficult to calculate the full income and expenditure of Sinn Féin for elections because much funding was collected and used locally, and record- and book-keeping was inconsistent. In Clare East, for example, clubs had donated £703 and £523 had been spent locally.[114] Funds amassed from affiliation fees, local fundraising activities and profits from the sale of propaganda pamphlets and newsletters resulted in a profitable Sinn Féin, certainly after the 1918 general election. The dexterous and resourceful propaganda campaigns initiated by Sinn Féin, which included electioneering, the formation of Dáil Éireann and the drive for representation at the Paris peace conference, were financed chiefly from collections in Ireland and the USA. The distribution of funds to constituencies was managed closely and at times conservatively, yet the importance of propaganda was never underrated by Sinn Féin. Sinn Féin's ambition to contest practically every seat in 1918 and 1920 and Ulster in 1921 necessitated a full treasury, whereas the more regional geography of unionist interests allowed them to wage more targeted and economical campaigns.

112 Ibid., 7 June 1921.   113 Ibid., 4 May 1921.   114 *CC*, 26 July 1919.

UNIONISTS

Creating propaganda to protect the union during the third home rule crisis had provided unionists with good knowledge about raising substantial funds for political campaigns. Unionist patrons were usually landowners or businessmen and during the third home rule crisis they had risen to the challenge to mount an aggressive propaganda campaign by escalating their appeals for funds. Unionists were well-represented among UVF commanders, who had placed 'their wealth, their time and their property at the service of the force'. Unionism also had assumed the management of Edward Carson's Unionist Defence Fund – towards which he had contributed £10,000 of his own personal finances.[115] By January 1912 the chairman of the fund committee was able to disclose to Carson that 'the people connected with the Ulster industries will supply any money you may require in the course of the next two years'.[116] The UUC itself was supported by a Belfast bank which allowed them to write a cheque for £16,000 even though they knew 'full well that there was nothing in the bank account to cover it'.[117] Finances obtained from wealthy individuals, business donations and unionist associations funded the generation and public recognition of Orange lodges, the UVF and the Ulster Covenant (to mention a few), and generated anti-home rule propaganda with its captivating slogans such as 'Home rule means Rome rule' and 'Ulster will fight and Ulster will be right'. For example, Samuel McCaughey, a wealthy Ulster exile and sheep-station millionaire in New South Wales, sent £25,000 to Carson's fund.[118]

The anti-home rule income had been expended in the two-year battle from 1912 to 1914 by generating propaganda in newspapers and books, and creating postcards, posters, pamphlets, banners, films, badges and a host of other ephemeral items, but these fundraising skills and marketing abilities were rekindled for elections and managed by the UUC standing committee.[119] This was the organization that directed the path and policy of unionism until the 1920s.[120] Professional university-educated candidates within unionism rallied the political and business elite of Ulster, who donated large sums to ensure votes favoured unionist candidates. Unlike nationalists – militant and moderate – who petitioned for funds piecemeal, unionists were financed by a small number of wealthy individuals and commercial interests that rallied fellow elites to donate to the cause. Just how much was donated and by whom is unknown. However, by investigating UUC minutes, unionist associations' correspondence and the personal correspondence between higher-ranking politicians, some indication of unionist funding is possible.

115 Stewart, *The Ulster crisis*, p. 72. 116 PRONI, Carson Papers, D1507/1/1912/3: 2nd Baron Dunleath to Edward Carson, 19 Jan. 1912. 117 Ibid., PRB 987: report of interview between Sir Wilson Hungerford and staff of PRONI, Nov. 1965 in Buckland, *Ulster unionism*, p. 49. 118 Parkinson, *Friends in high places*, pp 90–1. 119 Stewart, *The Ulster crisis*; John Killen, *John Bull's famous circus: Ulster history through the postcard, 1905–1985* (Dublin, 1985); Ewan Morris, *Our own devices: national symbols and political conflict in twentieth-century Ireland* (Dublin, 2005). 120 Harbinson, pp 40–1.

To supplement larger donations unionists, like other parties, relied on local clubs to provide revenue and disseminate propaganda. By 1915 there were 369 clubs on the register and 133 clubs had sent in returns of officers for 1915. A further three clubs later joined, bringing the total to 372.[121] A UUC meeting of 30 April 1919 stated there were 372 clubs still in existence (although between 1917 and 1919 four were stated to have been wound up and two were described as virtually non-existent).[122] The laws and constitution of the UUC – adopted at a meeting of the council of clubs in Belfast on 2 May 1893 – stipulated that each club was free to make its own rules regarding subscriptions. However, a club had to subscribe no less than £1 annually to the funds of the Council if its membership was 100 or less, plus 10s. for each 100 (or part of 100) additional members. These funds were usually used to defray the expenses of the central offices.[123]

The revenue and expenditure for year ended 31 December 1918 for the UUC, calculated by accountants Stewart Blacker Quin and Company in Belfast, stated that the total cash in bank amounted to £182, and subscriptions from clubs were to the value of £318 (plus advances for 1919 of £5), giving a net income of £505. There was no specific figure provided for propaganda, but it was no doubt built into the expenses for printing and stationery, which amounted to £65, and post (literature was posted to constituency clubs), at £37.[124] This indicates that the central council absorbed the cost of creating and disseminating universal unionist propaganda, such as rules or decrees, to local constituencies and candidates during elections. This was conducted by appealing to local business interests and club members. There were funds received from the Unionist Central Office in London, who claimed that they had made provision for certain contests in Ireland to the value of £2,143, which was the remainder of a full donation of £4,000. This assistance was provided for the expenses of contests in Dublin and was issued through Arthur Samuels, MP for Dublin University. The Central Office disputed having to reimburse the election expenses of Alexander Parker Keane in Wicklow East, who had been defeated by Sinn Féin's Seán Etchingham by 3,316 votes.[125] Like the other parties, local unionist clubs and associations therefore needed to fundraise to support candidates and distribute specific local propaganda.

Unionists may have garnered sizeable funds, but they instructed candidates and constituencies to be frugal in their expenses. During the 1910 January election campaign 3,783,000 copies of eleven new or revised leaflets and large colour posters were put into circulation in Britain; but by December 1910 posters were dropped as being too expensive, and this no doubt influenced propaganda decisions by 1918 and 1921.[126] To defray election costs unionists were advised to order placards in moderate quantities, and keep leaflets and pamphlets brief to ensure

121 PRONI, UUC minutes, D1327/1/2: 23 Feb. 1914. 122 Ibid., D1327/1/2: minutes of the executive committee of the Unionist Clubs Council, 25 Feb. 1914, 26 Mar. 1915, and 30 Apr. 1919. 123 Ibid., D1327/1/1: UUC minutes (n.d.). 124 Ibid., D1327/14/5/7: UUC receipts and payments for year ended 31 Dec. 1918. 125 Ibid., Carson Papers, D1507/A/29/26: letter from Unionist Central Office, London to Carson, 9 Apr. 1919. 126 Buckland, *Irish unionism*, p. 73.

key messages were conveyed to voters at reduced printing costs. Candidates had to exercise 'great moderation' in advertising, which was to be limited to notices of meetings and the location of committee rooms. They were counselled to canvass directly and personally with the 'various classes of electors' because 'too much importance is attached to the display of bills and placards'. Admitting that placards were useful to attract attention, the effect upon the actual electors, it was maintained, was 'often out of proportion to the cost'. Targeted campaigning was advised whereby candidates had to 'carefully' select leaflets of special interest and send or hand them personally to voters. Furthermore, to attract attendance at open-air meetings, it was recommended that candidates 'use a motor-cyclist the day before' to put up explanatory notices in advance.[127] This advice attempted to limit overspending and assured private financers that their cash donations were being carefully disbursed.

As previously stated, the number of targeted constituencies was lower for the Unionist Party than for the IPP and the Labour Party, and much less than those for Sinn Féin, who contested nearly every seat. Unionists were determined to secure election victory mainly in Ulster constituencies, particularly where Protestants were in the majority. In the southern three provinces, unionists entered contests only in Cork (two candidates), Wicklow East (one candidate) and the Pembroke, Rathmines, St Patrick's and St Stephen's Green constituencies of Dublin, Dublin South and Dublin University (two candidates).[128] Therefore, finances collected only needed to be expended in twenty-six Ulster constituencies and eight southern constituencies (this figure includes Queen's University in Belfast, but does not include independent or labour unionists).

In the 1920 local-government elections new contestants had entered the field as Municipal Reform candidates and Ratepayers' Association candidates, and there were a large number of independents. All of these included previous Unionist Party candidates (and some IPP candidates, in the case of independents) who had been active at local level or were now eager for the reform of local rates. A letter to the editor of the *Irish Times*, 17 January 1920, pointed out that a number of candidates listed for the municipal elections in Rathmines and Ranelagh, Dublin, had been designated incorrectly as unionist when they were, in fact, Municipal Reform. In Pembroke, the Ratepayers' Association nominated four candidates, all of whom were already unionist members of the council.[129] Ratepayer candidates were usually owners of the local small businesses and shops visible on the high streets of towns and villages, and appeals were made to the 'middle classes' not to 'allow themselves be swamped' by Sinn Féin and Labour.[130] New Municipal Reform and independent candidates undermined unionist fundraising efforts (in constituencies where unionist candidates contested in January 1920) because the key concern among unionist contestants was also rates. Taking Kingstown (Dún Laoghaire) in

127 PRONI, UUC Papers, D1327/20/4/148: *Unionist Central Office parliamentary election manual.* 128 *Weekly IT*, 30 Nov. 1918. 129 *IT*, 3 Jan. 1920. 130 Ibid.

south Dublin as an example, an appeal was made to the electors to vote for unionist candidates because they had actively reduced rates while also improving local
services.[131] To solicit funds and votes unionists argued that ratepayers fared better
under their control of the urban council. Approximately forty candidates contested
for twenty-one seats in the Kingstown constituency, and unionist propaganda and
funding paid off as wins were gained in the four wards. However, this example only
gives an indication of unionist success where funds and propaganda gained votes.
To obtain a breakdown of more specific unionist fundraising at local level and to
investigate unionists in the highly contested region of Ulster, Co. Tyrone will be
the example, as these records were preserved and available.

Unionists contested the four urban Tyrone constituencies in January 1920
and six rural districts, and a concentrated effort was made to raise funds. The
county election and indemnity fund garnered subscriptions from a number of
local businessmen and politicians, who contributed in sums of £100 (10), £50 (4)
and £25 (7), giving a grand total of £1,375. Unionist associations and clubs in
the county towns held preliminary meetings and also raised funds to the sum of
£2,711 – from Omagh (£480), Dunamana (£483), Strabane (£100), Castlederg
(£200), Dungannon (£583), Mountjoy (£200), Dunmullan (£120), Seskinore
(£107), Dromore (£90), Edenderry (£60), Clanabogan (£80), Loughmuck (£123),
Mullagharn (£50) and Killyclogher (£35).[132]

As the rural district elections were playing out, widespread communal violence
erupted in July 1920 where Catholics, Protestants and members of the police and
British army were killed at the start of the 'Belfast pogroms'. Thousands of Catholics
were driven out of their jobs, homes, and businesses, so political parties in these
six counties began to prepare in earnest for future elections.[133] Unionist concern
in 1920 was focused on the formation of the new Northern Ireland parliament, so
motivating industrious fundraising campaigns for an election that eventually took
place in May 1921 became paramount. James Craig viewed the 1921 election as a
plebiscite on the single great issue before the voters: 'who is for Empire and who
is for a Republic?'[134] However, differentiating between fundraising carried out in
June 1920 for 1921 and for the rural elections proved difficult. For instance, by the
end of June 1920, after the rural elections, a handbill was drafted for the purpose
of raising £5,000 to meet election expenses in Co. Tyrone. The local secretary,
R.A. Parke, maintained that 'it is now a case of fighting our corner or disappear-
ing and knuckling down to Sinn Féin forever'. Obviously submitting to a Sinn
Féin regime was inconceivable so he called for unionists to increase the ordinary

---

131 Ibid., 13 Jan. 1920. **132** PRONI, D3110/1: County Tyrone Election Fund. **133** For further
information on violence in Northern Ireland see: Jonathan Bardon, *A history of Ulster* (Belfast, 1992),
p. 494; Brian Follis, *A state under siege: the establishment of Northern Ireland, 1920–1925* (Oxford, 1995),
pp 93–4; Dennis Kennedy, *The widening gulf: northern attitudes to the independent Irish state, 1919–1949*
(Belfast, 1988), p. 121; Eamon Phoenix, *Northern nationalism: nationalist politics: partition and the
Catholic minority in Northern Ireland, 1890–1940* (Belfast, 1994), pp 107–9; and Thomas Hennessy, *A
history of Northern Ireland, 1920–1996* (Dublin, 1997), pp 11–13. **134** *NW*, 14 May 1921.

subscription of £1, 'which the strong farmer and businessman usually gives'.[135] Results of collections across two of the Tyrone towns in 1920 show Omagh providing £438 and Dunamana £250, where the larger farmers and merchants gave £20 and the smaller ones, £10. This provided enough to start proceedings for 1921 as the sum total received was £1,200. This amount had been accumulated only seven days after the rural elections.[136] The receipts and payments accounts for the year ended 31 December 1920 show a cumulative income of £2,643, where the balance from two accounts was £1,471, and subscriptions collected were £1,172. There was also the sum of £1,700 explained as a 'grant from special funds', giving a total of £4,343.[137] Payments of salaries, wages, travelling expenses, stationery, literature, printing and advertising (excluding postage) amounted to £225. By the end of 1920 propaganda for 1921 had not yet started, so we can safely assume that the literature, printing and advertising costs were incurred for the local elections.

Despite higher levels of private funding unionists did not fare as well in the 1920 municipal elections as previously, although they had an overall majority in Ulster. Unionists, who formerly numbered fifty-two, were now thirty-seven – largely due to the number of seats captured by Labour, and because of proportional representation. In 1921, in similar manner to 1918, a drive to secure funds and votes began in earnest to ensure that unionists had substantial representation in the new northern parliament.

THE LABOUR PARTY

The Labour Party's uncertainty about raising funds and contesting the 1918 general election dated back to their formation in 1912 and provides some explanation as to why the ITUC&LP were divided on the issue of political representation. The organization was comprised of trade-union members. Some supported the IPP, others supported Sinn Féin and many trade unions were strongly linked with British trade unions. In Londonderry, for example, unions were loyal to the 'amalgamateds' (as cross-channel unions were called).[138] This led to difficulties in forming an Irish Labour Party, distinct from British trade unions, which would remain out of the Irish national struggle. Connolly's participation in the Easter Rising altered perspectives, and by 1918 he was hailed as a 'flaming torch pointing the way to freedom and happiness' to create a new social order. As William O'Brien stated, 'This, I say, was Connolly's ideal; and it is our ideal. For it we shall fight on, for it we shall toil on'.[139] As discussed in the previous chapter, the

---

135 PRONI, D3727/E/52/1–10, Armstrong of Deans Hill Papers: A5 handbill to unionists from R.A. Parke on 29 June 1920.   136 Ibid., D3110/1: letter to Parke from E.L. Hendman on 19 June 1920.   137 Ibid., D1327/14/5/9, receipts and payments account, year ended 31 Dec. 1920. Note the subscriptions include £3 from 1918 arrears, £38 from 1919 arrears, 1920 at £541 and a 1921 advance of £589 (figures rounded to nearest pound).   138 Emmet O'Connor, *Derry labour in the age of agitation, 1889–1923: Larkinism and syndicalism, 1907–23* (Dublin, 2016), p. 8.   139 Twenty-Fourth Annual Meeting, pp 18–19.

subsequent increase in trade-union membership and the success of the anti-conscription campaign energized the Labour Party and they developed confidence to contest elections.

The enormous growth of the ITGWU in rural Ireland, and a host of strikes for better pay, particularly among agricultural labourers during the years 1917 to 1919, should have made the Labour Party in southern Ireland a force to be reckoned with (by 1919 there were 66,000 members of the ITGWU).[140] According to ILP&TUC calculations in 1919, 250,000–300,000 workers were trade-union organized, and about 220,000 were associated through their unions with the ILP&TUC, out of 700,000 adult wage earners in Ireland.[141] The list of societies affiliated in 1919 to 1920 provides a total membership figure of 256,090. Londonderry, for example, saw a surge in trade union membership. Membership of the ITUC&LP jumped from under 100,000 in 1916 to 229,000 in 1920.[142] Therefore, the national executive unanimously decided to enter the 1918 electoral contest, so the Labour Party had to raise funds. Labour had £1,958 at this point, including £347 from the last congress, £708 from affiliation and delegates' fees, £15 from the sale of Congress reports, £833 from a special appeal fund collected to pay for strike actions and £55 from the Labour Representation Fund. Up to this point the party had spent a total of £3 on advertising in the city of Londonderry, £80 on printing, £9 on an anti-conscription meeting in Belfast and £66 on attendance at the Mansion House conference, so the total 'propaganda' expenditure was £158.[143] There were other expenses not associated with propaganda such as grants to unions, auditors' fees and so on, and total expenses amounted to £512. The net balance of £1,446 (excluding uncashed cheques, which amounted to £154) could have funded a reasonably substantial electoral propaganda campaign given that Labour intended to run a maximum of two dozen candidates.[144] Yet the funds raised were far less than those raised by the IPP, and substantially less than what Sinn Féin and unionists had raised. No specific election fund was established by the Labour Party, and their general guideline was that 'the expenses of candidates for election to Parliament shall be borne by the organization or organizations nominating the candidates, with such financial assistance as the Central Fund can afford'.[145]

In a complete volte-face, the Labour Party pulled out of the general election in November 1918. Their earlier lacklustre pronouncement that organizations were to bear the burden of financing candidates was practical, but it was not a rallying call – nor was there an impassioned appeal to engage in an aggressive unified battle of the workers, who would contribute into an election victory fund. Vague reference

---

140 Twenty-Fifth Annual Meeting, pp 152–63; David Fitzpatrick, 'The disappearance of the Irish agricultural labourer, 1883-1916', *Irish Economic and Social History*, 7 (1980), p. 81; *II*, 17 Jan. 1912.   141 Twenty-Fifth Annual Meeting, Appendix 1: memorandum respecting amalgamation, p. 61.   142 Ibid., pp 152–63: Names of Societies Affiliated, 1919–20 with Number of Members on 1 Jan. 1919; Donal Nevin (ed.), *Trade Union Century* (Dublin, 1994), p. 433.   143 Ibid.   144 O'Connor, *Derry labour*, see comments by Thomas Johnson, p. 103.   145 Ibid., p. 125.

to an uncertain central fund hardly inspired financial confidence. It also indicated the national executive's timidity about committing themselves to candidates.

Committing themselves to strike funds, on the other hand, generated substantial income, and this is where the Labour Party had the most power and expertise. The 1919 balance sheets reported that £1,729 was collected for the Limerick Strike Fund, with the bulk of donations coming from the ITGWU and the Mansion House conference who subscribed £1,000 and £500, respectively.[146] A directive to raise money for elections may have had equal success and allowed them more confidence to contest in 1918. Earlier in 1918, during the anti-conscription campaign, the Labour Party rallied its members to strike action on 23 April 1918, and the twenty-fourth annual conference recommended that all unions collect a strike levy of 3*d.* a week per member for the purpose of raising funds for the Labour Party in this fight. The total collected for the anti-conscription fund across Ireland was £207,000 and the collective active campaigning certainly motivated contributions.

Labour, it seems, were more comfortable in local elections, and in August 1919 plans were afoot for contesting the city, county, rural district and poor law guardians elections due to take place in January and June 1920. The aim was to 'put forward as many delegates as possible' because these were bodies 'upon which Labour should have adequate representation'.[147] The programme for local government mirrored that of the 1918 general election, with the main one being the recovery 'for the nation complete possession of all the natural physical sources of wealth in this country'.[148] By the end of June 1919 the balance sheet showed an income of £2,039, garnered from £1,446 carried over from 1918, plus delegates and affiliation fees totalling £294; the Labour Party had also made £30 from the sales of reports, £39 from the sale of pamphlets and £230 from the special appeal and stamp sales. When donations and the Limerick Strike Fund (plus interest) are added, Labour had a total income of £3,846. Expenses, including meetings and donations to strike funds, amounted to £2,847 and included printing at £281, postage and sundry at £39, pamphlets at £5 and funding an international delegation at £175.[149] The surplus was not enough to fund contests across all constituencies for local elections, so again the directive was that those who nominated candidates paid for their expenses.

The Labour Party did not fail to fundraise, which is evident in the monies garnered from affiliation fees and other funding initiatives. The Labour Party as a whole in Ireland had many fundraising activities in motion as the various elections approached, so targeting election donations from the same unions and members who were already contributing to strike funds was stretching resources too tight, despite substantially increased trade-union membership. Labour's skilled fundraising efforts reinforced trade-union movements rather than electoral candidates, so it was a lack of organization that sent them off course in 1918 and 1921. Failure

146 Twenty-Fifth Annual Report of the ILP&TUC, pp 114–17.　147 Ibid., p. 49.　148 Ibid., p. 65.　149 Ibid.

to fundraise for the general elections was by no means the only reason for Labour's withdrawal from the contests, and perhaps it was not even the strongest influencing factor, but it was certainly a contributing cause. The escalation of Sinn Féin support after the Easter Rising, and their 1917 by-election successes in particular, ignited a fundraising mission that was unmatched by any other party.

CONCLUSION

The finances outlined in this chapter do not account for the total expenditure of the various parties. There were other variables at play such as the methods and means of propaganda that were used by individual parties and the finances attributed to them. A further examination of costs will be conducted in later chapters, particularly in the examination of the methods used for disseminating propaganda in the next chapter.

4

Methods of propaganda

Political messages can be received and interpreted by different people in different ways, and the method of propaganda often determines the audience that is reached.[1] This chapter examines the type of media used and the reasons behind party or candidate media selection. An investigation into whether political parties and candidates were influenced by contemporary analysis on propaganda techniques will be carried out to see if they implemented this knowledge or if they were already implementing practices that later formed the core of modern skills. It will discuss why specific methods of propaganda were favoured over others, and query whether parties were restricted by existing media or if they advanced new methods.

Thematic content and propaganda stimuli are investigated in chapter 5. However, examples are provided here to demonstrate the effectiveness of methods. Through a study of the various types of propaganda used by individual parties and their candidates a theory emerges. This chapter begins with oratory or speech-making, a propaganda method utilized extensively by all parties in this era, which could be considered cost-free, although travel and accommodation expenses were accrued; for example to convey speakers to voters Sinn Féin faced a rather large bill of £103 19s. 4d. to cover petrol and transport in one constituency.[2]

ELECTORAL ELOQUENCE

The aim of discourse is to persuade and influence political ideology through propaganda, and rhetoric is the relationship between language and persuasion.[3] Discourse is the language or words used and the context of a communication, and takes into account the situation of the propaganda conveyance and the supports, such as images, that alter or add to the communication meaning. Therefore, discourse is both text and context together, and in public or private speeches it lies at the heart of message delivery.[4] There is a relational connection between speakers and audiences and while masterful oratorical skills are advantageous, a successful delivery requires the audience to listen to content and to believe in appearance as well as words. It is audience perception that endorses charismatic authority, and charisma is founded in the creation of a mutual bond between a leader and his or

---

1 K. Newton, 'Making news: the mass media in Britain', *Social Studies Review*, 6:1 (1990). 2 SFSCM, 13 Feb. 1919. 3 William M. Keith and Christian O. Lundberg, *The essential guide to rhetoric* (Boston, 2008), pp 3–4. 4 Cook, *The discourse of advertising*, p. 4.

her followers.[5] The larger the crowd in the era under study the more difficult it was to establish that connection, but mood or tone could be transferred in body language and pitch, and confidence by using a strong stance and projected speech delivery. Redmond, Dillon, Carson and de Valera became the spokespersons or message controllers of their respective parties. Delving into the personalities of politicians by examining how they delivered propaganda speeches is important, as is gauging audience responses.

Redmond has been, perhaps unfairly, described as a conservative or conciliatory politician. The tone of his later speeches lends to this observation as he maintained that Irishmen, once they had home rule, would be content with their Irish parliament and happy within the empire. But the IPP had united under Redmond, he had negotiated a home rule settlement with Britain, and he had gained both the party's and the majority of the population's support, at least up until the mid-war years. However, by the end of 1917 Redmond's charisma had waned. After his death in 1918 he was succeeded by Dillon, who became the main spokesperson during the election campaigns. Dillon was once described by T.P. O'Connor as 'tall, thin, fragile, his physique was that of a man who has periodically to seek flight from death in change of scene and air'.[6] He was, according to Frank Callanan, in many respects temperamentally miscast as a politician.[7] Dillon's opinions, when formed, became entrenched – although his integrity of political belief was unquestionable, particularly in the need to establish a highly disciplined nationalist movement; and his predilection was towards the agrarian left. These two beliefs form central messages in Dillon's election speeches. A heavy involvement in land agitation had enhanced a more inflammatory style of oratory, which was particularly evident in a speech in Kildare on 10 August 1880, when he advocated a general strike against rent. In contrast to the more appeasing style of Redmond, Dillon's rhetoric was determined and often provocative.

His election speech in Straide, Co. Mayo in December 1918 is a good example of how he obliquely championed the constitutional position by emphasizing the menace of physical force to associate Sinn Féin with a policy of failure. He asserted that all of Ireland's past struggles had resulted in 'suffering, sorrow and ruin'. To elaborate on the disparity between the two nationalist movements he drew attention to the value of the Land Acts, which had been implemented during the IPP's reign, by asking the audience to 'compare the condition of East Mayo today with what it was 33 years ago'. While he did not elucidate on the local gains, he posed a second question: 'What have they [Sinn Féin] ever done?' This time the audience verbally replied with 'Nothing'. Dillon had succeeded in engaging his audience by prompting them to participate actively.[8]

5 R. Neustadt, *Presidential power: the politics of leadership* (NY, 1962).   6 T.P. O'Connor, 'Review of the Parnell movement', *Dublin Journal*, 1:13 (Aug. 1887), p. 342, NLI, Ir 8205 d3.   7 James McGuire and James Quinn (eds), *Dictionary of Irish biography* (Cambridge, 2009), Frank Callanan on John Dillon.   8 *II*, 18 Dec. 1917

The unionist leader Edward Carson's angular and austere appearance was, according to William O'Brien 'as inexpressive as a jagged hatchet'. Yet his sombre and sober countenance assumed near charismatic proportions for unionists in Ireland.[9] He had assertively piloted unionists through the home rule crisis from 1912 to 1914 and, according to George Peel in *The reign of Edward Carson*, 'the power which he exercised in that quarter was scarcely otherwise than royal and the allegiance according to him might have been envied by kings'.[10] Cartoonists in this era satirized the monarchical tendencies asserted by Carson's political opponents, who sometimes disdainfully referred to him as 'King Carson'.[11] Nonetheless, this indomitable personality created an authority that continued to bear down heavily on opponents in election campaigns in 1918, and drew crowds of supporters to public meetings.

Carson's speeches reduced complexities to a series of points that culminated with the key issue upon which action was needed. The plight of the Protestant community in Ulster in the face of the home rule threat formed the opening or backdrop, which was regularly followed by the claim that there should be 'no coercion of Ulster'. Arguments were made in the form of a question, with a one-word answer that inspired an audience to react. For instance, in his address to the annual meeting of the UUC in November 1918 in Belfast he theatrically unpicked the idea of 'self-determination' by asking should there be 'self determination by the South and West of Ireland of the destinies of Ulster?' and answering 'Never!', to which there was an instantaneous response in 'cheers' by the audience.[12] The proof of loyalty to the United Kingdom by the enlistment of Ulstermen for the Great War was espoused, along with the 'lofty ideals' behind war support that inspired 'a great awakening' which had invoked a duty in Ulster 'to see that full advantage is taken of these ideals'. Carson closed this speech, as he did others, by championing the advantages of the union, claiming that 'the people of this country' were 'the spoiled children of the United Kingdom' and that they (unionists) had made the mistake of not taking their share in government. He did not need to use the words 'vote unionist', it was already there in the closing argument.[13]

Carson's rhetoric often comprised urgent directness of action where unionists were persuaded into collusion in his planned schemes both against home rule and in attaining votes through his regular use of the first person plural 'we' or 'ourselves'. This provided logic and collective motivation but the disadvantage was that its

---

9 Cruise O'Brien (ed.), *The shaping of modern Ireland* (London, 1960), p. 87. See also Steve Bruce, *God save Ulster* (Oxford, 1986), pp 199–200; Ann Ruth Willner, *The spellbinders: charismatic political leadership* (London, 1984). 10 Bruce, *God save Ulster*, pp 211–13; James H. Allister and Peter Robinson, *Sir Edward Carson, man of action* (Belfast, 1985), p. 15; George Peel, *The reign of Sir Edward Carson* (London, 1914), pp 3 and 9. 11 Joseph P. Finnan, 'Punch's portrayal of Redmond, Carson and the Irish question, 1910–1918', *Irish Historical Studies*, 33:132 (2003), 424–51; Andrew Gailey, 'King Carson: an essay on the invention of leadership', *Irish Historical Studies*, 30:117 (May 1996). 12 *AC*, 23 Nov. 1918. 13 *IT*, 16 Nov. 1918; *AC*, 23 Nov. 1918. See also H. Montgomery Hyde, *Carson* (London, 1987), p. 23.

power to alter perspectives and perceptions was limited. For example, in his speech to the UUC Carson told his audience that 'we cannot afford to wait in a great community like this' for government answers, and stated 'let us ... have the legislation that is suited to us'.[14] There was no need to change opinion among the disciples of unionism, but this form of rhetoric to swing borderline votes was weak and entirely impractical for those outside the collective 'we'. Carson, however, appealed mainly to those who adhered to unionist beliefs and sense of identity, so by drawing on the collective he attempted to orchestrate feelings of inclusivity and devotedness to a common cause. By 1921 he was succeeded by Sir James Craig, who up until this point had been the orchestrator of the major unionist anti-home rule propaganda rallies. Craig did not possess the same oratorical skills as Carson, but his steady business and military acumen continued to steer unionism towards maintaining the Act of Union, particularly in the bitterly fought 'partition election'.

Separatist nationalist Éamon de Valera was a new and unknown politician, and he had to speedily build reputation and draw public focus to Sinn Féin's ideals. His most powerful technique was the use of myth, interspersed with allusions to history.[15] He also regularly referred to his personal participation in the Easter Rising, although mainly directing attention to other rebels, who by this stage had become mythologized and etched into the Irish mindset as martyrs. Mary C. Bromage's fawning description of de Valera's return to Ireland after imprisonment in June 1917 observed 'a new rigidity about his mouth and a different thrust of the chin, though he still looked the teacher and scholar'. She described him as the embodiment of 'the legends of 1916', the man the 'surging crowds wanted to see, to touch, to sing about.' At the time of the Clare East by-election Robert Brennan claimed that voters saw de Valera as a 'leader'; 'Clare and all Ireland had found a champion worthy of the race. The people of Clare gave this young man, hitherto unknown to them, five thousand votes and only two thousand for his opponent ...'.[16] Farrell stated that 'under de Valera' Sinn Féin 'presented itself as a cohesive national party, united ... regimented ... and monolithic ... [T]here was neither dissent nor resignation. The party discipline appeared magical.'[17]

Throughout all elections de Valera's message was Sinn Féin's message, even when replaced by other speakers while he was interned. The ideals of republic, unity, Irish language and culture, abstention from Westminster (in a similar vein to Arthur Griffith, although outside the domain of empire) and economic self-sufficiency were consistently championed. The teacher had turned statesman physically, but oratorically there were mixed opinions. De Valera often became sidetracked in speeches in a manner that was akin to a meandering journey of thoughts on a series of ideals and issues. Darrell Figgis phrased it well when he observed that de Valera's mind was full of incomplete sentences: '[H]e never looked

14 *AC*, 23 Nov. 1918.   15 J.P. O'Carroll, 'Eamon de Valera: charisma and political development' in J.P. O'Carroll and John Murphy (eds), *De Valera and his times* (Cork, 1986), p. 24.   16 Mary C. Bromage, *De Valera* (London, 1967), p. 31; Robert Brennan, *Ireland standing firm: my wartime mission in Washington, and Eamon de Valera: a memoir*, ed. Richard H. Rupp (Dublin, 2002), p. 108.

to the end of what he wished to say – or, for that matter, of what he willed to do – but turned to follow a new thought before he, or any one else, had caught the first.' This mild criticism was enigmatically righted by adding: '[H]e did this so imperiously and impatiently, however, that he lent an air of tremendous decision to his own indecision.'[18] Fitzpatrick remarks that 'the elements of de Valera's strategy were expressed plainly enough in his inelegant speeches'.[19]

His strategy against unionists was regularly insolent and, unlike the IPP, who were more placatory, de Valera perceived unionism as a movement of the Protestant ascendancy class. His rhetoric advocated Irish unification where the majority rule should be applied and Ulster 'should not be petted and the interest of the majority sacrificed to her'. His bold resolution to the polarized political views was that if Ulster unionists failed to recognize the Sinn Féin position – which 'had behind it justice and right' – they should be condemned to collapse … 'they would have to go under'. De Valera elevated the rhetoric of nationalism to an art form in his speeches and projected a uniform ideal, which was that of a nation aspiring to a 'republic'. Nonconformity meant expulsion and repudiation, and the court of appeal was to be the Paris peace conference not the imperial parliament.[20]

Differing political opinions and oftentimes similar styles of oratory had a common goal – to secure votes on election day. Politicians aimed to provide basic facts or at least facts that provided a façade for truth. But, the truth was (and is) often elusive in political speeches, and people's perception of the truth is often anchored in their own political persuasion. Richard Mulcahy, in a 1922 staff notice, maintained that Sinn Féin 'facts must be the truth, the whole truth and nothing but the truth' and that the 'other side will … throw doubt on your real truths'.[21] Unionist truth was loyalty to the empire for the benefit of Ireland, particularly Ulster; the IPP's truth was home rule; and Sinn Féin's was an Irish republic. Deciphering the actual 'truth' was the preserve of the voting public, and propagandistic speeches along with other methods were the materials from which the truth was to be constructed.

The linguist Norman Fairclough states that discourse involves social conditions that shape the way in which individuals interact and, thereby, their production and interpretation of texts are framed.[22] This was important in election meetings as the conditions were often an impending election, and awareness of the speaker's intent was evident. The audience knew they were present at a meeting (private or public) to be persuaded or to have their decisions confirmed. An Irish audience often had to wade through a myriad of sensory material before a speech began as party platforms or indoor gatherings flaunted symbols and iconography of identity

---

17 Brian Farrell, 'De Valera: unique dictator or charismatic chairman?' in O'Carroll and Murphy, *De Valera and his times*, p. 35.   18 UCDA, Richard Mulcahy Papers, P7/B/341: article written by Darrell Figgis, 15 Sept. 1923, 'De Valera's Oratory'.   19 Fitzpatrick, 'De Valera in 1917: the undoing of the Easter Rising' in O'Carroll and Murphy, *De Valera and his times*, p. 103.   20 *II*, 20 Mar. 1918 and *IT*, 6 July 1917.   21 UCDA, Richard Mulcahy Papers, P7/A/42: staff notice 1922.   22 Norman Fairclough, *Language and power* (Harlow, 2001), pp 19–21.

such as flags, banners and shamrocks (discussed later in this chapter). An audience at public meetings might have been affected by the threat of violence or heckling (encouraging or obstructive), becoming distracted from content and more concerned with self-preservation. During the general election in the constituency of Tyrone East, Frank Gallagher admitted that during an IPP speech after eleven o'clock mass to rally support for Thomas Harbison, he waited until there was a lull in the speaker's comments and interrupted with contradictions 'in a voice that travelled nearly to Dungannon'. This he called 'first class sport'.[23] The atmosphere at crowded meetings also made herd persuasion possible, which proved beneficial if it was biased in the speaker's favour.

Outdoor public meetings where the political theatre of the open-air platform added a sense of drama were a regular occurrence during election campaigns in this era. Speeches were often held during organized fairs and markets, or in peopled areas of towns and cities, at crossroads or main centres to boost audience numbers. As the *Irish Times* reported on 28 January 1918 during the Armagh South by-election, 'meetings were held in the vicinity of almost all the churches in order that the congregations might be captured'. Large crowd numbers were perceived as a sign of party support or public interest in a candidate. Reports by newspapers of meetings whereby 'so dense was the crowd' that the speech had been 'attended by a large assemblage of electors' lent subsequent weight to the candidate and the message.[24] Indoor meetings were more intimate affairs and were useful for introducing and making a candidate personally known to existing party supporters. They were also useful for encouraging volunteer canvassers, and providing instruction and education on promoting specific party policies.

THE CLERGY

Attendance by the clergy on the platforms at public speeches offered credence and provided weight and authority. Clerical involvement in politics had been a matter of support and organization in the early to mid-1800s, but with the rise of Catholic affluence their influence and participation became more intense.[25] The clergy provided a pulpit information conduit during church services for disseminating a party policy that reached a large and captive target audience. In Roscommon North the *Roscommon Herald* reported that as soon as Sinn Féin's Fr O'Flanagan began his campaign he was joined by several young curates. He became a strong advocate for the party and toured the country during election campaigns addressing monster meetings.[26] Frank Gallagher described O'Flanagan as possessing a 'wonderfully resonant voice and a fine appearance' and maintained that his oratorical skills were 'politically pontifical'. In the Cavan East by-election Gallagher's

23 TCD, Frank Gallagher Papers, MSS 10050/40: Frank Gallagher to Cecilia Saunders, 30 Mar. 1918. 24 *IT*, 7 Dec. 1918. 25 K. Theodore Hoppen, *Ireland since 1800: conflict and conformity* (London, 1989), pp 77–9. 26 BMH WS 707: Michael Noyk.

incongruous remark was that O'Flanagan's 'appalling eloquence moves the great crowd'. He praised an address by O'Flanagan to Arthur Griffith, as if he were there in person (he was at that time in prison) because 'the thrill of it sent cold shivers of uncontrollable enthusiasm passing up and down my spine like the buckets in a mud boat'.[27]

Intervention by the Catholic hierarchy directly or indirectly influenced the outcome of the by-elections. The bishop of Limerick, Edward Thomas O'Dwyer, wrote a scathing letter just before the Longford South by-election in protest against the mistreatment of Irish prisoners (see plate 2). By questioning the British government on whether they had 'any intention' to give Ireland home rule in 'any shape or form' or if it was 'all humbug', he caused grave difficulties for the IPP. Redmond was already concerned that support for prisoners and Sinn Féin had become indistinguishable in the public mind. He petitioned Asquith and Henry Duke, the chief secretary for Ireland, for a swift amnesty to 'strengthen the position of the constitutional party'.[28]

The archbishop of Dublin, William Walsh, also published a letter in the newspapers condemning home rule, with signatures from three of the four Catholic archbishops, eighteen Catholic bishops, three Protestant bishops and several chairmen of the county councils (Dr John Healy, archbishop of Tuam did not sign the letter due – according to Monsignor Curran – to serious illness).[29] He stated that home rule would not 'contribute in the slightest degree to the pacification of our country'. The letter was reprinted in full in all the national dailies and many provincial newspapers, and the *Irish Times* referred to the letter as 'unique' because it combined Catholics and Protestants in common cause.[30] Sinn Féin seized the moment and drafted a handbill claiming that 'Archbishop Walsh writes Ireland has been sold', and they called for 'Votes for Joe McGuinness'.[31] The IPP immediately attacked the archbishop across columns of the *Freeman's Journal*, but they could not reverse the damage. Some within Sinn Féin believed that the letter secured the very narrow victory in Longford South. Others such as Dan McCarthy claimed the letter was of 'very little value coming so late' because he was only able to put the propaganda handbill 'in the hands of the people on their way to the poll'.[32] It did perhaps change the mind of wavering voters.

The IPP had their supporting clerics too, who preached publicly and canvassed on their behalf. In Longford South the local curate claimed that voters need not go outside their own parish to find a worthy successor to the incumbent John Phillips (the deceased IPP MP).[33] Canon Charles Quin, the parish priest of Camlough in south Armagh, contrasted the approaches of the two nationalist parties, asserting

27 TCD, Frank Gallagher Papers, MSS 10050/45, 2 June 1918 and MSS 10050/46: 16 June 1918. 28 HC, PD, vol. 86, cc 581–94, 18 Oct. 1916; Bodleian Library Oxford, Asquith Papers, MS 37, ff 132, 134, Redmond to Asquith, 14 and 30 Nov. 1916. 29 BMH WS 687(i); NLI Ephemera Collection, EPH C178. 30 For example see *IT*, 9 May 1917. 31 Elaine Callinan Collection: bishop of Limerick handbill; NLI, Ephemera Collection, EPH C88: *Archbishop Walsh writes Ireland has been sold*. 32 BMH WS 722: Dan McCarthy 33 *LL*, 14 Apr. 1917.

the insanity of the Sinn Féin movement and the sanity of the IPP. He passionately condemned 'the republican party', declaring that their triumph would result in 'Easter week propagated through all Ireland – that awful catastrophe, which meant rebellion, which meant blood, which meant disunion'.[34]

There is little evidence of Protestant clerical proselytization of unionist ideals during the election-campaign speeches. However, they did nominate unionist candidates, and therefore imparted an air of authentication. For the University of Dublin seats William Morgan Jellett was proposed by the bishop of Derry and two of his assenting electors were the dean of Derry and the Reverend John Wilson MacQuaid; and Arthur Warren Samuels had the Reverend A.A. Luce as an assenting nominator. In the Dublin constituency of Rathmines, Maurice Dockrell received outspoken support from Samuels, and fellow politicians such as Henry Hanna, along with Lady Arnott, who appealed to the women of that parliamentary division.[35] But, no clerical representative of Protestantism was present. Carson was supported on platforms by well-known unionists such as the duke of Abercorn, the marquis of Londonderry and Lieutenant-Colonel Sir James Craig, but there was never a Protestant reverend mentioned. One can only speculate as to the reason. The main one was the divergent denominations of Protestantism that existed in Ireland, which meant having no clerical representation was better than appearing biased in favour of one of these. Carson regularly condemned Catholic clerical interference in electoral politics, particularly that of Cardinal Logue in creating the nationalist pact for Ulster in 1918. 'I do not think that we would tolerate that kind of interference on our side,' he claimed, and he accused Cardinal Logue of 'compromising with folly', which earned Carson 'laughter' from his audience.

With the support of clerics or people of influence politicians used public speaking across all constituencies to appeal for votes, often at large gatherings. Those in attendance at these large public meetings were able to experience the ambiance, but it was difficult to hear the speaker (this was a time before microphones). Messages were often passed back by attendees, but many had to wait for the printed version in the local or national newspapers. Obtaining subsequent editorial in a local newspaper was crucial for political parties and candidates to ensure the dissemination of accurate speech content.

NEWSPAPERS

Two distinct ways of utilizing newspapers emerged after reports of political news systematically began in the 1760s: reports of party speeches or meetings and paid-for advertisements.[36] Newspapers were the main forum for disseminating political information and messages during all election campaigns. The importance

---

34 *IT*, 21 Jan. 1918; BMH WS 634: Jack McElhaw. 35 Ibid., 3 Dec. 1918 36 L.M. Cullen, 'Establishing a communications system: news, post and transport' in Farrell, *Communication and community*, p. 21.

of newspapers in the early 1900s for building awareness and influencing opinion cannot be understated, mainly because there was negligible competition from other media. Furthermore, during this period, the attention paid to political matters, particularly during elections, was unrivalled by any other news item (with the possible exception of war news in the early days of the Great War).

During this era censorship of seditious newspapers or editorial existed in Ireland and had been enforced under the Defence of the Realm Act (DORA) at the start, and for the duration of, the Great War. DORA 'forbade printing of seditious speeches, articles or other matters which might cause disaffection … or alarm among any of His Majesty's forces or among the civilian population'. Censorship was extended to press statements and information 'calculated to assist the enemy or to lead to a breach of the peace, but not to legitimate criticism'.[37] After the Great War's end, DORA was replaced by the Restoration of Order in Ireland Act (ROIA) because of continuing hostility as the War of Independence played out.

The mosquito press[38] were particularly adept at getting around the censor, often by issuing suppressed material in pamphlet form. This method of turning suppressed speeches into pamphlets or handbills was regularly adopted by Sinn Féin. For instance, Fr O'Flanagan's suppressed speech in Roscommon North was reprinted in the *Catholic Bulletin* in March 1917, and was turned into a pamphlet and circulated; and, as already mentioned, so was Bishop Walsh's claim that the IPP had sold Ireland by agreeing to partition.[39] Sometimes newspapers were closed and printing was confiscated, but this was usually only carried out as a last resort.[40] When closures occurred, they had significant negative impacts on a number of provincial newspapers – an example being the dismantling of the *Kilkenny People* by British troops during the Kilkenny by-election of 1918.[41]

During the Great War years newspapers were unusually thin, comprising only around eight to twelve pages, depending on the news of the day. Paper shortages during the war accounted for this, and subsequent internal conflicts prolonged modest productions. In the early twentieth century the front page was dedicated to advertisements, unlike the modern newspaper that captivates audiences with front-page headlines and images. The national dailies broke away from this practice quickly, but many provincial newspapers continued for some time afterwards, although there were exceptions, such as the *Roscommon Herald*.

It is impossible to assess with any certainty the real political influence of the provincial press as there were advantages and disadvantages. The political constituency message reached a local target audience speedily, but a strongly biased newspaper could lead to disaffection among non-party readers. Modern research

37 Virginia Glandon, *Arthur Griffith and the advanced nationalist press, 1900–1922* (NY, 1985), pp 147–52, 159; *London Gazette*, 1 Sept. 1914.   38 A term used to refer to the alternative press – they were small but had a stinging bite.   39 UCDA, de Valera Papers, P150/625: Fr O'Flanagan's suppressed speech in the *Catholic Bulletin*, Mar. 1917; BMH WS 722: Dan McCarthy.   40 Benjamin Z. Novick, 'DORA, suppression, and nationalist propaganda in Ireland, 1914–1915', *New Hibernia Review / Iris Éireannach Nua*, 1:4 (Winter 1997), 41–57.   41 BMH WS 907: Laurence Nugent.

suggests that newspapers with a known political prejudice were probably only partially successful as they did more to reinforce readers' existing opinions and failed to convert non-believers.[42] Richard Mulcahy pointed out in a later staff notice that pamphlets and books had a similar difficulty in that they betrayed their origin, and so were read only by the already convinced. Newspapers, however, inspired 'talk', and when details were good and convincing 'unbelievers' could be swayed.[43]

Provincial newspapers in this era were notoriously biased. For example, the *Connacht Tribune* began life as a paper to 'support the Constitutional Party of the Irish people' but became more separatist in tone after the Easter Rising. The *Galway Express* had been non-political until 1917 but it changed hands and subsequently became one of the strongest Sinn Féin papers; and the *Longford Leader*, owned by J.P. Farrell MP, clearly favoured the IPP. The provincial press reached target audiences in their thousands and were typically sold for 1½d. The *Galway Express* had a circulation of about 2,700 copies weekly by 1920, and the *Cork Examiner* reached 30,000 daily.[44] While provincial newspapers – every county had at least one – honed in on local happenings, they also frequently reproduced reports and commentary from national newspapers. Provincial newspapers also became feeders of local news to the larger national dailies, thus disseminating county news to a wider audience. The influence of the provincial press in shaping and reflecting local opinion cannot be underestimated and while some stalwart regional newspapers continued to support the IPP – including the *Longford Leader, Westmeath Examiner* (owned by John P. Hayden) and *Sligo Champion* (owned by P.A. McHugh MP) – their electoral losses in 1918 indicate that many others had shifted allegiance to Sinn Féin.

There were three main national dailies in Ireland, which also produced weekly editions – the *Irish Times, Irish Independent* and *Freeman's Journal* (and their *Evening Telegraph*). The *Irish Times* was originally the preserve of unionist opinion and had been formed as a Protestant newspaper. It is difficult to ascertain exact newspaper circulation figures for this period because the Audit Bureau of Circulation had not yet been founded (by the Society of British Advertisers in 14 October 1931), and other sources refer to figures from 1930 onwards. However, these later figures provide an indication of the newspaper market in Ireland and a pamphlet titled *An Irish daily newspaper*, which was created to raise money for the *Irish Press* in the late 1920s, stated that the *Irish Times* had a circulation figure then of 30,000.[45] Alongside the speeches of the main leaders, like Carson and Craig, the

42 Michael Dawson, 'Twentieth-century England: the case of the south-west', *Twentieth-Century British History*, 9:2 (1998), 201–18.   **43** UCDA, Richard Mulcahy Papers, P7/A/42: notes on the general principles of propaganda [1922].   **44** NA, CO 904, boxes 92–122 and 148–56A, Irish government police reports, 1914–21, Jan.–Feb. 1920 CO 904/111, inspector general's monthly report for Galway, Jan. 1920; NLI, Frank Gallagher Papers, *Irish Press*, MS 18361. See also Marie-Louise Legg, *Newspapers and nationalism: the Irish provincial press, 1850–1892* (Dublin, 1999) and Oram, *The newspapers book*.   **45** NLI, Frank Gallagher Papers, MS 18361: *An Irish daily newspaper; Irish Press*, 28 Apr. 1933.

speeches and advertisements of southern unionist candidates appeared regularly in the *Irish Times*. This was the forum through which southern unionists could appeal to supporters for votes throughout all the elections.

In Ulster, unionists expressed opinion through the pages of the *Belfast News-Letter* (founded in 1737 as a bi-weekly radical Presbyterian newspaper, in 1855 it became a daily), which advocated the economic, social and cultural benefits of maintaining the link with Britain. The price of 4*d.* for thirty-two pages reveals that the target audience was the more prosperous unionist businessman. Unionists regularly contributed to and received editorial in the *Dublin Daily Express*, the *Morning Mail*, the *Daily Irish Telegraph*, the *Belfast Telegraph*, the *Irish Post*, *Carlow Sentinel*, *Kilkenny Moderator* and the *Waterford Standard*, to name a few. They also issued a publication called *Notes from Ireland*, which was launched in 1886 by the Irish Unionist Association (IUA). Although not a newspaper in the classic sense, its influence in unionist circles was equal to that of the traditional newspapers that supported the union. It was produced by Irish unionists from their offices in Grafton Street, and while it was circulated in Ireland, its target audience was mainly people living outside Ireland – primarily in Britain – whose support was deemed vital for propagating unionist policies. *Notes from Ireland* was created because 'it is to be noted that the authorities quoted for these constantly recurring crimes and disorders are mainly Nationalist newspapers'.[46]

The *Irish Independent*, owned by William Martin Murphy, had set out to be politically neutral, but when readership increased it began to challenge IPP policy (although an anti-republican stance had been taken during the 1916 Rising, which Sinn Féin supporters found objectionable).[47] A difference of opinion on home rule finances during the Irish Convention debates in 1917 had outraged Murphy.[48] During the by-elections Dillon complained vehemently that the *Irish Independent* had 'opened a more villainous campaign against us' and 'from the … venom of its attack I gather that Murphy and Co. must be nervous as to our chances of reviving the movement'.[49] Circulation averaged at around 40,000 per day (before the war), and the *Irish Weekly Independent* sold an average of 50,000–72,000 copies per week in 1914–15, and 50,000–60,000 per week in 1915–16.[50] Stephen J. Browne, in *The press in Ireland: a survey and guide*, states that circulation of the daily edition in 1937 was 143,000–152,000.[51] Rotary presses, mechanized typesetting and a range of printing machines created a variety of printing fonts, and the price of newspapers fell to a penny or even a halfpenny after 1905, boosting circulation. The halfpenny cost and better quality printing

46 PRONI, Unionist Party, General Council Minutes Book, D 989 C/3/38: report for 1907–8; Graham Walker, *Notes from Ireland, 1888–1938*, Queen's University Belfast Library, n.d.. 47 Gwynn, *Redmond's last years*, pp 315–16. 48 Ibid. 49 TCD, JD, MSS 6842(522), John Dillon to T.P. O'Connor, n.d.; NLI, MS 12,082, Irish Parliamentary Party minute books, 16 May 1917. 50 *Irish Weekly Independent*, 30 Oct. 1916, p. 4 in Novick, *Conceiving revolution*, p. 48 51 Oram, *The newspapers book*, p. 106; Stephen J. Brown, *The press in Ireland: a survey and a guide* (NY, 1937; 1971), p. 171, TCD Library, Early Printed Books.

improved advertising revenue as the *Irish Independent* used five different type-faces (fonts) to enhance presentation.[52]

The main opponent of the *Independent*, the *Freeman's Journal*, began life as an IPP organ. The newspaper had been subsidized by the IPP since 1912 and continued to be so through 1918 and for a short time afterwards, until financial difficulties eventually prompted its sale in 1919, despite gallant efforts by Dillon to hold onto the paper. In an attempt to save the paper and expound constitutional policies, frustrated IPP supporters had asked 'why in the name of goodness does not the *Freeman* market a paper at a halfpenny?' The higher 1*d*. price was leading to heavy trading losses and aiding *Irish Independent* success. A suggestion was made that 'the people must have a halfpenny paper with wholesome political news not poisoned arrows directed at Redmond and his followers'.[53] Wholesome political news resided, like truth, in the realm of interpretation by the propagandist and recipient.

In 1919, the new owners, Dublin businessman Martin Fitzgerald and UK journalist R. Hamilton Edwards – with journalists on staff like Desmond Ryan and Sean Lester who leaned towards republicanism – began to openly express support of Sinn Féin.[54] By 1920 the newspaper had drifted entirely towards republicanism, so much so that Desmond FitzGerald stated that Sinn Féin was allowed to use their private wire for the daily transmission of 300 words to foreign correspondents.[55] The IPP in Ulster still had the UIL's *Irish News*, which was circulated among nationalists, and it continued to remain a party newspaper even after the 1918 defeat.[56]

In 1918 most newspapers were unsympathetic towards Sinn Féin policy or ideology. However widespread public support for Sinn Féin after the general election initiated change, and aversion gave way to an initial begrudging support – perhaps to maintain or increase circulation figures. For instance, the *Cork Examiner* altered its editorial to convey similar ideologies to that of Sinn Féin. Sinn Féin also had their own specialist newspapers where content sought to inculcate a sense of pride in being Irish. History and legend, language and literature featured heavily and they were priced to encourage readership from the lower classes. Griffith's *Sinn Féin* was published weekly. *Nationality* had a circulation of 4,500 and *The Nation* distributed about 2,700 copies weekly.[57] After the Easter Rising, separatist newspapers resurfaced and – with the exception of *An t-Oglach* – were sold openly in newsagents and news stands around Ireland. At party headquarters Sinn Féin also drafted 'Sinn Féin Notes' (usually created by Brennan or Griffith), which were sent to and published in provincial newspapers across Ireland. This idea was appropriated from the UIL and Hibernians, which had been distributing similar 'notes' for many years.

52 L.M. Cullen, 'Making news: the mass media in Britain', *Social Studies Review*, 6:1 (1900), 35. 53 TCD, JD, MSS 6753/357: letter to W. Doris MP, 9 May 1917. 54 UCDA P80/14(7), Desmond FitzGerald Papers, report on propaganda department, June 1920. 55 Ibid. 56 Inoue, 'Sinn Féin propaganda', 47–61. 57 Laffan, *The resurrection*, p. 33; NA, CO 904, boxes 92–122 and 148–56A, Irish government police reports, 1914–21, Galway, Jan. 1920.

As the 1920 local elections loomed Louis Walsh, a candidate for Derry South in 1918, remarked that

> the only paper that circulates amongst the country people in these places [Ulster] is Devlin's 'Irish News' and 'Irish Weekly'. We shall never be in a good position in Ulster until we have a decent weekly at least in Belfast ...[58]

The importance of an effective Sinn Féin newspaper in Ulster was stressed repeatedly and aside from some provincial newspapers that were sympathetic to the party, and sold approximately 140,000 copies a day, there was none.[59] The absence of a dedicated newspaper for the 1921 campaign was an electioneering shortcoming that may have cost votes. To outwit unionists in 1921, a spurious paper calculatedly named the *Unionist* – printed and published in Glasgow four times during May and receiving financial support from nationalists residing there – was launched and edited by Seán MacEntee. There were 20,000 copies posted into unionist strongholds in Belfast city and counties Antrim and Down, and the aim was to sell Sinn Féin's nationalism and disparage unionist electoral claims. A letter to the editor of the *Northern Whig* stated that 'practically all the unionist voters in all parts of County Antrim have had this paper sent them'. The *Belfast News-Letter* warned readers that the publication was on the enemy's side and that unionist electors were being deceived.[60] Sinn Féin also distributed through the *comhairlí ceantair* 20,000 copies of the *Irish buyer's guide*, 30,000 copies of the *Belfast trade boycott black list* and 225,000 copies of the *English trade boycott* (Leaflet) to impress on all Irishmen and women the importance of supporting Irish-made goods and the absolute boycott of English-made goods. There was also a call made for *cumainn* members to supply notices of Sinn Féin activities to their local press to generate editorial.[61] Sinn Féin's propagandizing was crafty and clever, but it did not win them the support they hoped for on election day in 1921.

All newspapers regularly printed the speeches of politicians and candidates, lending affirmative opinion and adverse commentary according to their bias. They were also useful for disseminating ideas, critiquing political opponents and giving voice to the ordinary voter in the 'Letters to the Editor' section. For example, in a letter to the *Freeman's Journal*, high praise was afforded to Patrick Lynch in Clare East, who was hailed as 'a patriotic, high-minded, and an absolutely honourable man'. Sinn Féin orators and organizers, on the other hand, were disparaged as 'disruptors of every hue, who are out for the destruction of the constitutional movement'. This letter tells us that the 'electioneering tactics of Sinn Féiners are to rush and hustle'. IPP methods were obviously less frenetic because 'the intelligent

58 NLI, Count Plunkett Papers, MS 11,405: Louis Walsh to Harry Boland, 4 Jan. 1919.   59 Kennedy, *The widening gulf*, pp 11–17.   60 *BNL*, 10 May; *NW*, 29 May 1921; Inoue, 'Sinn Féin propaganda', p. 52.   61 NLI, PB, MS 33,912/9: Sinn Féin Ard Fheis, honourary secretary's report, and MS 33/912/11: instructions to Sinn Féin *cumainn*.   62 UCDA, de Valera Papers, P150/550: letter to the editor of the *Freeman's Journal*.

electors', it was maintained, 'will not allow themselves to be rushed and stampeded by visionaries and crazy boys and girls'.[62]

While the focus of this work is on the domestic propaganda and electioneering of political parties and foreign fundraising, it is worth briefly mentioning that Sinn Féin was the most professional in reaching out to the foreign press. They launched a targeted campaign to stimulate international endorsement for their mandate to establish a republic and secure funds. The 'spot' news being supplied by English news agencies, such as the Exchange Telegraph, Central News and the Press Association, which obtained information directly from Dublin Castle, was a driving force in the determination to win favour with foreign journalists. In November 1919 the decision was taken to issue a daily newspaper with special articles on Ireland – the *Irish Bulletin*. The aim of the *Irish Bulletin* was similar to that of the unionist *Notes from Ireland*, but the main difference was that Sinn Féin's target audience was all foreign journalists and not just those in Britain. A telegraphic news service was also initiated on 16 June 1920 to 'correct and amplify the news received through other sources' and to 'combat the English Telegraphic News Agencies'.[63]

By advocating for the rights of small nations, as espoused in Great War propaganda, to seek a republic, and adding ongoing messages of atrocity in foreign media, Sinn Féin gained prestige and recognition. This was recognized by Sir Hamar Greenwood, who, on his arrival in Dublin to take up the position of commander-in-chief of Irish operations on 14 April 1920, remarked that officers and troops of the crown forces were exasperated by misrepresentation in the press. He acknowledged 'the total absence of counter propaganda on the part of the Government in reply to the very efficient circulation of systematic falsehoods' by Sinn Féin 'and their friends in England and America'.[64] The very use of the word 'efficient' demonstrated Sinn Féin's media propaganda success at home and abroad. Credence was given to Sinn Féin's efficiency by the attempt to counteract it with a government propaganda machine. Before the appointment of Basil Clarke as head of the Department of Publicity and Public Information in 1920 a Press Section of the army general staff was created to examine 'the papers and contradict untrue statements about the troops', to issue 'communiqués about actions in which the troops were involved, to report on attacks on military property and results of Courts-Martial on civilians' and to manage 'all other military matters affecting the press and publicity'.[65] By 1921 Greenwood, in the Commons, requested £900 to be granted to the Department of Publicity and stated that the appointment of Clarke, 'who was a trained journalist', was to 'take charge of the department in Dublin Castle, and to receive every journalist of every country in the world to supply him and the public with official information'.[66]

63 Ibid., Desmond FitzGerald Papers, P80/14(6): report of propaganda department, June 1920. **64** Gen. Sir Nevil Macready, *Annals of an active life* (London, 1924), ii, p. 454. **65** See Peter Hart (ed.), *British intelligence in Ireland, 1920–21* (Cork, 2002). **66** *FJ*, 21 Mar. 1921; Gary S. Messinger, *British propaganda and the state in the First World War* (Manchester, 1992), pp 145–61.

Newspapers were a crucial medium as educational standards had improved in Ireland since the Education Act of 1831 and the introduction of government financing.[67] The expansion of primary education had stimulated literacy, but this growth was fraught with religious, social and political difficulties. A large number deserted education after the age of 11, leaving many only barely literate.[68] The lower socio-economic group could read a cheap penny newspaper, but were ill-equipped to read anything of substance. However, news and political propaganda was received by a circuit wider than those who purchased newspapers because readers purveyed information to a larger audience. Rising affluence among the middle classes provided customers for printed material, and these customers were voters. Political news influenced how ordinary people thought and consumed political ideas, and it encouraged the political elite to appeal to people through this medium.

The Labour Party did not contest the two main general elections of this era, but they had established the *Irish Worker and People's Advocate* as a pro-labour alternative to Murphy's *Irish Independent*. Labour's paper was only four pages long and written by one or two people, and was funded from a small list of classified advertisers. In contrast, Murphy's newspaper was twenty-four pages long and was designed and produced by a large team. It was also liberally illustrated, and garnered huge revenue from its pages of sizeable advertisements.[69]

Newspapers were the principal conveyance for propaganda but they needed to be supplemented by party circulars, pamphlets, handbills, and advertisements. Even though all parties successfully attained free propaganda in newspapers, journalistic editing and censorship reduced a political candidate's control over reprinted speeches and editorial. To surmount this and to entice voters it was necessary to purchase advertising column inches in newspapers. Releasing short, targeted messages in this way guaranteed that the correct ideas were conveyed.

ADVERTISING

The term 'advertising' covers a broad spectrum of propaganda material that deliberately and specifically aims to promote the policies or manifestos of parties and candidates in the political arena. According to Paul Neystrom, a contemporary author, advertising aims to 'attract attention' in the hope of developing a genuine 'interest', which would change to desire and culminate with a 'decision to purchase'.[70] A later 1948 definition by the American Marketing Association saw advertising as 'any paid form of non-personal presentation and promotion of goods

67 Donald H. Akenson, *The Irish education experiment: the national system of education in the nineteenth century* (Abingdon, 2012), pp 143–6, 136 and 325. **68** *Irish School Weekly*, 19 May 1923 which cites figures for 1912 and 1913. **69** Christopher Morash, *A history of the media in Ireland* (Cambridge, 2010), pp 123–4. **70** Paul H. Neystrom, *Retail selling and store management* (London, 1914), pp 60–1; Philip Kotler, Gary Armstrong, John Saunders and Veronica Wong, *Principles of marketing* (London, 2002), p. 661.

and services by an identified sponsor', and they added the 'promotion of ideas' in 1963.[71]

During the election campaigns classified advertisements in newspapers were primarily used by all political parties to appeal for votes, and each party had their preferred medium. The high price of column inches was prohibitive for minimal budgets so larger consumer adverts were not used. The scale of charges for small prepaid advertisements in the *Irish Times* in 1920 was £1 for twelve words or under, with every additional word costing 3½d. A discount of 10 per cent was offered if a series of twelve or more insertions was prepaid. Advertisements not prepaid were charged at a minimum of £3 per insertion and publication of these advertisements was not guaranteed on any particular day, which could be problematic during election campaigns if a series of advertisements needed to run before election day.[72] Provincial newspapers were usually cheaper. The *Anglo-Celt*, for example, claimed the 'largest circulation of any provincial paper in Ireland' and sold for a price of 2d. Costs for advertisements were rendered according to subject. For legal notices there was a charge of 6d. per line, parliamentary notices were £1 per line, government advertisements were £1 per line; parliamentary election addresses were £1 per line; and local councils received a reduced rate at 6d. per line. A commercial-advertising sliding scale was also offered on a per-inch (single column), per-insertion basis, where one insertion cost 3s., three insertions 2s. 6d., thirteen insertions 1s. 6d. and on up to fifty-two insertions at 1s. 3d.[73]

At the outset of election campaigns the agents of contesting and selected candidates regularly ran promotional classified advertisements in national and local newspapers. For instance, in an *Irish Independent* advertisement, James Magee, the election agent for Denis Cogan, IPP candidate for Wicklow East in 1918, announced Cogan's selection, provided a biography to list the accomplishments of Cogan's public career and detailed the policies being advocated. This was one of twelve advertisements that ran on 30 November 1918 promoting unionist, IPP, Sinn Féin and National University of Ireland candidates.

Classified advertisements delivered short, pertinent and effective messages, and many candidates used their local newspapers. In order to reduce costs these advertisements usually contained a very simple message that could be conveyed using the fewest words and smallest amount of space. For instance, the unionist candidate John Good purchased a one-column, one-inch classified advertisement that appealed to voters in Dublin's Pembroke Division during the 1918 general election, stating: 'Our Empire needs your help. Do your Duty. Support Law and Order, and vote for Good.'[74] As already stated, most provincial newspapers dedicated the entire front page to classified advertisements but advertisements also appeared inside, and political candidates favoured these pages because the paid-for space

71 Ralph S. Alexander (ed.), *Marketing definitions: a glossary of marketing terms* (Chicago, 1964), p. 9. See also Reed H. Blake and Edwin O. Haroldsen, *A taxonomy of concepts in communication* (NY, 1975), p. 47; Neystrom, pp 60–1.   **72** *IT*, 30 Dec. 1920.   **73** *AC*, 31 Jan. 1920.   **74** Ibid., 14 Dec. 1918.

there appeared more like editorial. These one-column by four-to-six-inch advertisements covered an assortment of political guarantees. Sinn Féin candidates were
often more candid in their approach, and the 1920 elections provide a good example. In a three-column by three-and-a-half-inch advertisement for the Rathmines
constituency, Sinn Féin confronted voters by asking 'who betrayed Rathmines in
1918 and gave RATHMINES to UNIONISM and ORANGE ASCENDANCY?'.
The electoral results were provided to demonstrate their defeat by 1,405 votes. The
tone then lightened to point out that it had not been the Sinn Féin faithful who
betrayed Rathmines.[75]

All parties and candidates ran similar paid-for newspaper advertisements
throughout this era, and no one party surpassed the other in mainstream media in
terms of quality or quantity. Most contained short text and none carried images,
drawings or photographs, even though one of the impressive transformations in
newspaper printing was the availability of detailed illustrations – which were liberally used by clothing, fashion and health businesses.

EXTERNAL INFLUENCES ON ELECTORAL PROPAGANDA

During the battle against home rule in the years 1912 to 1914 unionists had devised
complex methods of persuasion in an attempt to maintain the union. Alongside
winning favourable editorial from Thomas Moles, the leading correspondent of
the *Belfast Evening Telegraph* and R.M. Sibbett of the *Belfast News-Letter*, an array
of propaganda pamphlets, posters, postcards and advertisements supplemented
other public propaganda exercises such as mass meetings, Ulster Day and the signing of the Solemn League and Covenant in 1912, and the Larne gun-running of
1914.[76] Other newspapers such as the *Irish Times*, *Northern Whig*, *Dublin Daily
Express* and *Derry People* carried editorial and publicity to support the unionist
cause. Behind this propaganda machine was Sir James Craig, who had gleaned
marketing techniques from the family Dunville Whiskey business. He was the one
who instigated a propaganda campaign that mobilized Ulster unionists to action
by strengthening their existing beliefs in the righteousness of the union by highlighting the potential disastrous consequences of a home rule government, evident
in the droll but clever postcard in plate 3. In 1918, 1920 and in 1921 the lessons
learned in rallying the anti-home rule cause came into force again to win votes.[77]

A new phenomenon during and after the Great War was the mass impact of
propaganda, which 'began to emerge as the principal instrument of control over
public opinion'.[78] Propaganda activities assumed a role of greater significance than

75 *II*, 12 Jan. 1920.   **76** Parkinson, *Friends in high places*, pp 91–102; Michael Foy, 'Ulster unionist
propaganda against home rule, 1912–14', *History Ireland*, 4:1 (Spring 1996), 49–53.   **77** Gustave le
Bon, *The crowd: a study of the popular mind* (London, 1896), p. 32; and Sigmund Freud, *Group psychology
and the analysis of the ego* (London, 1959), pp 13–14. R.A. Nye, *The origins of crowd psychology* (London,
1975); and Jaap Van Ginneken, *Crowds, psychology and politics, 1871–1899* (NY, 1992).   **78** David
Welch, *Germany, propaganda and total war, 1914–1918: the sins of omission* (London, 2000), p. 1.

ever before. Harold Lasswell, a leading American political scientist, stated that 'there is little exaggeration in saying that the World War led to the discovery of propaganda by both the man in the street and the man in the study'.[79] Propaganda had existed before the war, evidenced in the plethora of literature during and after the electoral campaigns of 1885 and 1886. The IPP and unionists produced editorial, pamphlets and handbills to promote interest in these elections, but these offered one-sided and unreliable views of policies. On the IPP side, for example, John Joseph Clancy, the home rule MP for Dublin North, issued a pamphlet titled 'Tracts on the Irish Question – no. 2 – the elections of 1885', in which he presented the party's election success of 1885 as proof of the nation's desire for self-government, stating that 'every Irish candidate who addressed a constituency last November, declared in favour of a Native Parliament'.[80] On the unionist side, the ILPU fought Parnell and the IPP in the southern provinces on the single issue of defence of the union. According to the *Irish Times*, 9 January 1886, 'the Union published and circulated 286,000 leaflets and pamphlets during the elections irrespective of those put in circulation by the candidates themselves'. These leaflets and pamphlets were circulated to draw attention to the supposedly malevolent devices and tactics of the Parnellites. Great War propaganda, however, inspired a call to action. Credible persuasive election propaganda with short and pertinent messages (rather than lengthy pamphlets) for mass appeal imitated the highly successful wartime enlistment campaigns.[81] Other propaganda activities were also emulated, but the variety and sheer volume of Great War propaganda makes it difficult to cover every aspect, so an examination of some areas where political parties mimicked or modified methods will be provided.[82]

The Sinn Féin standing committee announced in May 1919 that 'in future all pamphlets and circular letters are to be submitted to the standing committee before being passed for publication',[83] emulating how the War Office controlled the distribution of propaganda messages. Unlike other parties, Sinn Féin created their own election propaganda department with a paid and dedicated staff.[84] Another tactic applied by the War Office was the use of iconic figures to reinforce particular points and inspire sentiments such as patriotism. National heroes were used in Ireland to encourage enlistment, such as the text-heavy poster *Why Mr. Wm Redmond M.P. joined the army*.[85] A poster depicting James Craig announced that 'character counts in Ulster's political life', and asserted that it was 'absolutely necessary' to have 'a Government whose members are perfectly honest ... and men whom the lust of office does not kill, men whom the spoils of office cannot buy'. The 'strong, wise, calm, unshaken' character of Craig was espoused by the Church

79 Harold D. Lasswell, *Propaganda technique in the world war* (NY, 1938), p. v. **80** NLI, P 1214: J.J. Clancy, *Tracts on the Irish question* [pamphlet] (Dublin, 1886). **81** See ch. 5 re: Great War propaganda. **82** See Hoppen, *Elections, politics and society* and Walker, 'Parliamentary representation in Ulster, 1868–86', for more on elections in the 1800s. **83** SFSCM, 21 Feb. 1918, 1 May 1919 and 22 May 1919. **84** Ibid., 20 May 1919. **85** TCD, Digital Collections, World War I Recruiting Collection, EPB Papyrus Case 54b.

of Ireland archbishop of Armagh and primate of all Ireland, with support from others such as the Most Revd C.F. D'Arcy and the grand master of the Orangemen of Belfast, Sir Joseph Davison.[86]

War posters were more colourful and were printed on better quality paper as opposed to the later flimsy political sheets. Using imagery or pictures was more expensive than text, so font size or style was often used in election campaigns to lay emphasis on more salient messages. A good example is the anti-conscription poster in chapter 5 (see plate 15), where the leading arguments are emphasized in bold print or capital letters. 'Will you vote for conscription?' is headlined, and the call to action is also large and clear: 'Vote for McCartan and kill conscription!'.

While the Great War (and the Russian Revolutions) found expression in political propaganda, and some techniques and theories were appropriated by political parties, they do not provide a full view of the existing knowledge in Ireland on propaganda methods. Consumerism in Ireland had accelerated from about 1850 with the advent of the department store. Its display and mass selling to the more affluent middle-classes, who were driven by product acquisition and accumulation, influenced all advertisers including political candidates. These new-style retail outlets created a more manipulative propaganda approach and the business of advertising was born. The USA may have been the leader in the field, but Europe and Ireland quickly caught on. The idea of an agency that aimed to manage and develop strategies to promote products spread to Ireland, despite its scant industrial sector. As early as 1819 Johnston's Newspaper and Advertising Office opened at Eden Quay in Dublin; the Wilson Hartnell (Advertising) Agency was founded in 1879 in Dublin; the Kevin J. Kenny agency also existed during this era; and McConnell's was established in 1916.[87] Charles McConnell, in writing his ten-year-old agency's brochure in 1926, provided evidence of the variety of the agency's services in Ireland, stating:

> [W]e have a complete organization to carry out commercial research, copywriting, all classes of art-work, designing booklets and catalogues, printing and bill posting, writing and distribution from letters and folders, inserting of advertisements in newspapers, retail trade, word preparation, display of advertising and film to production of advertising novelties, etc.[88]

It has been generally assumed that all political parties in the early 1900s relied on their own propaganda departments or leaders or even local candidates to create advertising messages. While this was largely the case, particularly for constitutional nationalists, the concept of engaging with an external expert emerged in

86 PRONI, UUC Papers, D1327/20/4/142: *Men you can trust* poster. 87 J. Strachan and C. Nally, *Advertising, literature and print culture in Ireland, 1891–1922* (Basingstoke, 2012), pp 19–25; Hugh Oram, *The advertising book: the history of advertising in Ireland* (Dublin, 1986), pp 13, 31 and 52. 88 McConnells Advertising, promotional brochure (Dublin, 1926). See also John Fanning, 'Irish advertising – Bhfuil Sé or Won't Sé', *Irish Marketing Review*, 16:2 (2003), 3–13.

1910. A separatist article titled 'The advertising problem', published in *Leabhar na hÉireann* by the National Council of Sinn Féin, encouraged a study of advertising methods in the USA and promoted the idea that 'good advertising pays and bad advertising oftentimes does not'. The advantage of a 'good advertisement', the article maintained, is that it 'attracts attention, pleases the reader, and induces a desire to know more of the goods so advertised'. The main theme was that American advertising 'should be studied for the good that is in it', and that it should be modified for Irish needs. Good advertising 'included all recognized forms such as press advertising, catalogues, booklets, circulars, handbills, samples, electric signs, billboard window displays, show cards, novelties, etc.'.[89] The full content of the article covered the means by which all these methods should be used, particularly by their own party to promote policies and ideas.

The marketing methods employed by the FOIF during de Valera and Boland's tour of the USA in 1919 influenced later Sinn Féin propaganda methods. The importance of newspapers and a coherent publicity campaign were heralded in May 1919 in a detailed letter by the advertising agent Thomas Shipp to Daniel Colahan. Shipp specified that, 'I will organize for your Committee [the FOIF] a publicity campaign which will cover every class of newspaper in the United States', and he remarked that 'one of the most valuable things we have achieved is interesting the press in the movement and having them instruct Paris and Dublin correspondents to watch out for news on the Irish question'.[90] Regular requests were also made for 'pictures of prominent Irishmen in this country and in Ireland. Irish scenes, groups, official bodies, etc.'.[91] This instigated appeals to Ireland for these images and made clear the value of adding images to text in propaganda, which was adopted in handbills. The letter went on to provide intricate details of the campaign, which involved news dispatches, feature articles, pictures with captions, public meetings and interviews; it also noted that 'the motion pictures will be employed to further the publicity campaign'. Motion pictures were a relatively new phenomenon and though not used in election propaganda in Ireland (mainly because films were silent until 1927), they were used successfully in the promotion of the dáil loans.[92]

In a letter to solicit business the Tucker Advertising Agency highlighted the benefits of advertising in order to raise substantial funds, stating that 'advertising serves as a foundation for the United States Government's various Liberty Bond drives ... It made good in the United War Work campaign which raised $150,000,000, [and] in the Knights of Columbus drive for $2,500,000 in New York City (in 1918)', as 'it produced double the amount originally asked for'.[93] This inspired emulation of these advertising methods to raise funds, of which a minimal

89 Sinn Féin, *Leabhar na hÉireann*, pp 309–17.   90 AIHS, Shipp to Lynch, 19 Apr. 1919.   91 Ibid., 6 May 1919.   92 Ciara Chambers, *Ireland in the newsreels* (Dublin, 2012); Kevin Rockett, Luke Gibbons and John Hill, *Cinema and Ireland* (Syracuse, 1988); Irish Film Institute Archive, *The Dáil Bonds* (1919). This film was lost until 1965 until it was discovered in St Enda's, Rathfarnham, Dublin   93 AIHS, FOIF Papers, Tucker Agency letter dated 10 May 1919.

amount went to electoral campaigns and a substantial amount to establish Dáil Éireann and the Free State. De Valera and Boland may not have been aware of the specific content of these letters, but they were regularly in contact with the FOIF and no doubt learned about the propaganda strategies.[94] These methods were later absorbed by Sinn Féin in Ireland, so knowledge was gleaned directly in the USA, and from articles like 'The advertising problem', and from progressive domestic commercial propaganda. There was also personal contact with advertising professionals. In August 1917 Frank Gallagher remarked on a collegial meeting with 'the manager of Kevin Kenny's Advertising Agency'.[95] 'The advertising problem' article had instructed readers to 'place the matter [advertising] in the hands of a competent agency', and said that 'Ireland possessed more than one such agency, ready and willing to place its fund of experience at the service of every advertiser'.

Edward L. Bernays, in *Propaganda*, maintained in 1928 that there was a scientific rationale to propaganda, pointing out that 'a thing may be desired not for its intrinsic worth or usefulness, but because he [the consumer] has unconsciously come to see in it a symbol of something else, the desire for which he is ashamed to admit to himself'.[96] 'The advertising problem' article mirrors this thinking by directing the advertiser to 'dress his announcements in accordance with the particular public he desires to reach, and where various classes of people have to be appealed to'. Modern and contemporary advertising theories, although they relate to consumer advertising, were easily transferred to political advertising. A vote, unlike a product, as D.M. Reid states, is a 'psychological purchase'.[97] Attaining psychological intelligence enabled advertisers to gain an understanding of association, recall, perception and emotion to target and connect with customers or voters.[98] In 1895 Harlow Gale began researching advertising practices in an attempt to detect the mental process and relationships in people's minds to find out how font size, design and colour affected decision-making in product purchase.[99] Walter Dill Scott in the early 1900s focused on the idea of suggestion to influence consumer behaviour and he created the idea of personal association between a customer's own life and a product.[100] John B. Watson expanded on Ivan Pavlov's classical conditioning by attempting to predict and control behaviour, particularly outside the laboratory. This led to an understanding of how to control the behaviour of consumers, and how to elicit emotions such as fear, rage and love to

---

94 Ibid., letter from Diarmuid Lynch to Edward McSweeney, 4 Nov. 1920. **95** TCD, Frank Gallagher Papers, 10050/23: Frank Gallagher to Cecilia Saunders, 4 Aug. 1917. **96** Bernays, *Propaganda*, pp 28 and 100. **97** D.M. Reid, 'Marketing the political product', *European Journal of Marketing*, 22:9 (1988), 34–47. **98** Walter Dill Scott, *The psychology of advertising* (Boston, 1908); W.A. Friedman, *Birth of a salesman: the transformation of selling America* (Cambridge, 2004). **99** J. Eighmey and S. Sar, 'Harlow Gale and the origins of the psychology of advertising', *Journal of Advertising*, 36:4 (2007), 147–58; L.T. Benjamin, 'Science for sale: psychology's earliest adventures in American advertising' in J.D. Williams, W.N. Lee and C.P. Haugtvedt, *Diversity in advertising: broadening the scope of research directions* (Mahwah, NJ, 2004), pp 22–39. **100** Walter Dill Scott, *The theory of advertising* (Boston, 1903) and idem, *The psychology of advertising*.

activate purchase.[101] Taking a brief example from election propaganda in 1918 we see unionists attempt to elicit an emotional response by issuing a poster titled *The two Irelands. Facts. Not fiction!* where the impassioned question posed is: '[W]ill the British Public stand by Ulster, whose sons stood by them, or will they support Sinn Féin Ireland, which stabbed Britain in the back, and has such a ghastly record of disloyalty and crime?' (see plate 4).[102] War sentiments and grief were still raw and the intent behind this appeal was to stir those feelings and elicit a sense of conscience and tribute towards those who supported or died in the war effort to garner support and loyalty to the unionist cause.

POLITICAL POSTERS

Sinn Féin political leaders, had they read the aforementioned *Leabhar na hÉireann* article, would have learned that 'as one rarely stops to examine a poster ... only a very few words, boldly displayed, should be used'. They should be 'striking and original in design ... [B]right gaudy colours should be avoided' because this provides a better chance 'of securing intelligent appreciation.'[103] While modern theories might disagree with the advice on the use of colour, the notion of instant appeal remains. A Sinn Féin poster that aimed to draw distinct comparisons between Patrick Lynch and Éamon de Valera in the Clare East by-election outlines clear policy differences. Simple imagery of street signage is used – rather than heavy body copy – with only a few lines to draw the distinctions and the means to obtain political goals. De Valera points towards the peace conference as the road to freedom, whereas Lynch, who is presented as a crown prosecutor, points the way to 'Famine', 'Emigration' and 'Jail' to highlight the constitutional nationalist reliance on the imperial parliament for freedom (see plate 1). Very little prior knowledge, intellect or even astuteness was needed to interpret this image, and construing the differences between the two nationalist approaches was easy and immediate.[104] Similarly, a poster issued by the IPP candidate Patrick McKenna during the Longford South by-election in 1917 depicted a political dustbin crammed full of opposition politicians with protruding labels attached. The message 'Rubbish may be shot here' encouraged constitutional nationalists to act harshly to non-adherents (see plate 5).[105]

The most successful campaign during this era of elections was the *Put him in to get him out* poster created by Sinn Féin (see plate 6).[106] The importance of selecting an Easter Rising rebel as a candidate was affirmed by this very simple

101 R.E. Fancher, *Pioneers of psychology*, 2nd ed. (NY, 1990); D.P. Schultz and S.E. Schultz, *A history of modern psychology*, 9th ed. (Belmont, CA, 2008). 102 PRONI, UUC Papers, D1327/20/4/142: U.C.114: *Sinn Féin 'Guarantees' 'Safeguards' for Ulster*; D1327/20/4/142: U.C.132: *The two Irelands: facts not fiction*. 103 Sinn Féin, *Leabhar na hÉireann*, 'The advertising problem'. 104 BMH, Contemporary Documents, 227/7/B1[I]: *Vote for De Valera* poster (1917). 105 TCD, Samuels Collection, Early Printed Books, collection box 4 and OLS Samuels Box 4, 4SamuelsBox4_288. 106 NLI, Ephemera Collection, EPH E31: *Put him in to get him out*.

poster that spoke volumes.[107] The verification or acclaim of the prisoners' status was evident in the final line: 'The man in jail for Ireland'. The underlying message was that no crime had been committed by the candidate, because he was serving a prison sentence for the principles of freedom. The upright tight-lipped stance of the prisoner, arms folded in defiance of his internment, portrayed the proud sureness of the Sinn Féin message. This poster was first used to promote the candidate Joseph McGuiness in the Longford South by-election. The narrow win by only thirty-seven votes for McGuinness suggests that the poster may not have attained the expected conversion effect. So, why use it again and again for other candidates, subsequently? If propaganda opinion of the era is applied, the recommendation was that a poster 'should be bold in conception and striking in design and execution'. The function was 'to catch the eye of the passer-by and supply him with a sound suggestion'.[108] This poster met the criteria, and the prisoners, as William Murphy states, 'as survivors of the 1916 rising … did not make the ultimate "blood" sacrifice. Nonetheless, they became symbols of, and motors of, the profound political change that followed.'[109] To convince large numbers of people that there is only one valid point of view is an important goal of propaganda, as is eliminating all other options, and this poster sets out to achieve this.[110] According to the *Irish Independent*, this poster was 'displayed at every cross-road and village in the constituency'.[111] The passer-by obviously could not avoid it, interpretation was straightforward and did not require much decoding and it did not rely on a high level of literacy from a viewer. The uncomplicated image of a man dressed in prison attire with the large bold headline 'Put him in to get him out' holds no meaning without context. However, there was prior knowledge by viewers that elections were taking place and that rebels had been arrested and jailed so the headline did not need to fill in the blanks of 'put him in' government 'to get him out' of jail. Continued arrests and interments allowed for re-use, and the only change made by Sinn Féin was the name of the candidate on the poster. That this poster was reused many times introduced another major advantage. While the IPP and unionists also repeatedly advocated for their own causes, their posters did not repeat the same lines and the same image. In effect, Sinn Féin had mounted an aggressive repetitive poster campaign (that was more akin to modern advertising campaigns), and as elections progressed viewers quickly and readily associated the words and prisoner with a Sinn Féin candidate.

The introduction of proportional representation in 1919 altered election posters because candidates now needed to capture first-preference votes. Artistic and creative imagery did not disappear, but a dominant feature became the inclusion

---

107 See Laffan, 'The unification of Sinn Féin in 1917', p. 359 and Murphy, *Political imprisonment*, pp 77–9.   108 Sinn Féin, *Leabhar na hÉireann*, 'The advertising problem'. See also Henrik Dahl in *The pragmatics of persuasion* (Copenhagen, 1993).   109 Murphy, *Political imprisonment*, p. 79.   110 David Welch, 'Definitions of propaganda' in Nicholas J. Cull, David Culbert and David Welch (eds), *Propaganda and mass persuasion: a historical encyclopaedia 1500 to the present* (Santa Barbara, CA, 2003), p. 319.

of candidates' names, often presented in capital letters. The electorate now voted in numerical preference, numbered from one to the total number of candidates going forward in a constituency, so there was less space to promote policies or include creative imagery. Catchy headlines and memorable slogans became essential to capture voter attention. For instance, during the 1920 municipal elections, the Sinn Féin and Labour candidates of Dublin's Mountjoy Ward enticed voters by asking them to 'Strike a blow for Irish independence'. Candidates' names were listed in bold capitals, followed by a brief lowercase description of their occupation and home address. Only four numerical points at the end of the poster presented the key policies, and a final line requested voters to 'Vote early and solid for this republican ticket'.[112] An emphasis on personalities rather than issues was a shortcoming of these election posters by comparison to those prior to proportional representation.[113]

The production of posters incurred significant costs, depending on the quantities required, the range of colours used, and the cost of delivery. An example is the estimate for the printing of a very large poster campaign titled *The statement to the president of the USA*, printed by Maunsel & Co. Ltd of Baggot Street for Sinn Féin on 17 July 1918. The cost for 20,000 copies was £70 and for 50,000 copies £169.[114] The cost of printing advertisements, posting them, and all the clerical work in connection with the rural local elections in the towns of Bawnboy and Swanlinbar, Co. Cavan, comprising fourteen electoral divisions, according to the clerk, was a 'very satisfactory' £26.[115]

Posters could not work in isolation as they held minimal details. Supplementing them were handbills, booklets and pamphlets, which were crucial for disseminating comprehensive information on party policies and philosophies. The handbill or booklet provided scope for instruction from the top down to party members, canvassers and supporters. By 1921 the UUC demonstrated their awareness of successful propaganda by publishing a booklet titled *The Unionist Central Office parliamentary election manual*. Advice to unionist candidates and election agents on direct marketing (placards and advertisements) stressed the importance of bringing the 'name and the claims of the candidate forcibly to the attention of indifferent or ignorant electors'. To sway sympathies and gain electoral favour, 'a striking phrase or alliterative sentence' was recommended. An emphasis on 'reaching directly and personally [to] the various classes of electors' by distributing 'leaflets of special interest to them' displayed an understanding of the demographic range of potential unionist voters.[116]

The costs involved in producing pamphlets/handbills can be seen in the following examples. The Sinn Féin press bureau in September 1918 was granted a

111 *II*, 1 May 1917. 112 NLI, Ephemera Collection, EPH C75a–e: *Strike a blow for Irish independence.* 113 Seidman, *Posters, propaganda and persuasion*, p. 243. 114 NLI, William O'Brien Papers, MS 15,653(3). 115 *AC*, 19 June 1920. 116 PRONI, UUC Papers, D1327/20/4/148: *Unionist Central Office parliamentary election manual*, pp 49–52.

sum of £50 for the printing of pamphlets 'and other work in connection with the general election'.[117] Robert Brennan requested sanction for the publication of some pamphlets in June 1919, stating that the publication of one small leaflet cost about £11 [£320] for 10,000 copies. For the 1920 local elections the election subcommittee received a grant of £300 to cover the cost of printing 250,000 Sinn Féin programmes.[118] Unionists also set aside and paid funds for the printing and dissemination of propaganda. A statement of accounts in March 1920 detailed expenses totalling £225 for 'salaries and wages, travelling expenses, insurance, printing and advertising, &c' (unfortunately all these expenses were grouped).[119]

CANVASSING

The door-to-door canvass was an essential component for checking the register of electors, for face-to-face contact by a candidate or a candidate's representative and to ensure that a voter could be relied upon to attend the poll. Unionists believed that an early effective canvass 'by means of earnest and intelligent voluntary workers is by far the most powerful aid to success'.[120] The IUA in southern Ireland applied for canvassers in the several divisions where they ran candidates and urged that 'no time be lost in offering and undertaking this valuable voluntary service'. They appealed to the 'large number of women electors' whose assistance 'can help in canvassing and on the polling day'.[121] Lock and Harris argue that many voters vote for the same party as they have in the past because a voter's views on what parties stand for remain remarkably stable.[122] Therefore the personal canvass offered opportunity to suggest a viable alternative to fixed opinions, particularly in the case of Sinn Féin, which was fielding many unknown candidates in 1918. The Sinn Féin volunteer Michael Healy stated that 'there was a general canvass of the whole area [Loughrea, Co. Galway] as some of the elderly people had not yet learned the Sinn Féin gospel'.[123] Another advantage of the canvass was that some voters might have been unable or unwilling to attend public meetings (particularly if violence threatened), so this was another means to reach out.

Canvassing was free because most of the work was conducted by volunteers (although they were often supplied with literature, which did accrue costs). Strong local canvassing by one party often encouraged an opponent to step up their activities, and where a vacuum existed there was a desire to fill it. Nationalists in Omagh declared that they held the council in the 1920 municipal elections despite 'all the forces of well-organized Unionism and Orangeism' being 'arrayed against the Nationalists'. They triumphantly claimed that the unionist voters 'were canvassed

117 SFSCM, 6 Sept. 1918. 118 Ibid., 17 Dec. 1919. 119 PRONI, UUC Papers, D1327/14/5/9: Ulster Unionist Council, receipts and payments account, year ended 31 Dec. 1920. 120 Ibid., D1327/20/4/148: *Unionist Central Office parliamentary election manual*, p. 67; *IT*, 6 Dec. 1918. 121 BMH WS 1,765: Sean T. O'Kelly. 122 A. Lock and P. Harris, 'Machiavellian network marketing: corporate political lobby and industrial marketing in the UK', *Journal of Marketing Management*, 12:4 (1996), 313–28. 123 BMH WS 1064: Michael Healy.

and re-canvassed, and specially instructed ... but despite all these efforts the Nationalists have again obtained control of the Urban Council'.[124]

Organizations and movements that supported specific political philosophies supplied visible assistance to parties in election campaigns.[125] The IPP had support from the AOH, a movement which began in Ulster to oppose the Orange Order, and originated from Catholic agrarian movements like the Defenders and Ribbonmen of the eighteenth and nineteenth centuries. The founder of the AOH was Devlin, and he became grand master in 1905. The Orange Order was a Protestant fraternal organization that was based in Ulster and founded in 1796 in Co. Armagh, and it was instrumental in the formation of the Ulster Unionist Party. It too originated from an eighteenth-century agrarian movement, this one known as the Peep o' Day Boys. Both opposing organizations had aided electoral canvasses throughout the 1800s. Sinn Féin was new to canvassing but had support from the Irish Volunteers after the split from the main body of the National Volunteer movement. With the final release of interned Volunteers in 1917 Sinn Féin's membership increased again, providing support for election duties and fresh candidates for Sinn Féin. Released internees reorganized the Irish Volunteer movement and this unnerved the British government. A ban was placed on the wearing of military uniforms and on holding public meetings and drilling, but there was little yield to this ban by the Volunteers and the authorities were lax in enforcement. During the conscription crisis of 1918 numbers swelled in the Irish Volunteers, but once the crisis ended numbers fell away. The by-elections and general elections campaigns provided the rank and file with something constructive to do and Volunteers took an active part in conducting the house-to-house canvass for votes.[126]

Since the 1898 Local Government Act gave propertied women the right to vote in local elections and to run for urban and rural district councils, and particularly after the 1918 Representation of the People Act gave them the right to vote in parliamentary elections, they became an essential component of the propaganda war to secure votes, particularly on the canvass. The suffrage movement in Ireland, which largely consisted of educated, upper-middle-class women (ergo those most likely to be able to vote in 1918) not only encouraged women to run for local offices, they also urged them to vote and become politically active.[127] As Myrtle Hill points out, 'while women had participated in public campaigns, both political and social, in previous periods, their activities during the years 1880–1920 were particularly noteworthy'.[128] And, by 1918 women's movements were affiliated to volunteer

124 *Fermanagh Herald*, 24 Jan. 1920. **125** BMH WS 1,101: Martin Cassidy; WS 479: Commandant Michael Murphy; WS 1,006: Martin Kealy. **126** For examples see: BMH WS 1,101: Martin Cassidy; WS 479: Commandant Michael Murphy; WS 1,006: Martin Kealy. **127** M. Clancy, 'Shaping the nation: women in the Free State parliament' in Y. Galligan, E. Ward and R. Wilford (eds), *Contesting politics: women in Ireland, north and south* (Oxford, 1999), pp 201–18; M.E. Daly, 'The "women element in politics": Irish women and the vote, 1918–2008' in Esther Breitenbach and Pat Thane (eds), *Women and citizenship in Britain and Ireland in the twentieth century: what difference did the vote make?* (London, 2010), pp 81–94. **128** Myrtle Hill, *Women in Ireland: a century of change* (Belfast, 2003), p. 51.

movements and, congruently, to political parties, so they assisted prominently in election campaigns. They were often ancillary forces to the main organizations; for example, a distinct female organization reinforced the Orange Order, known as the Association of Loyal Orangewomen of Ireland, and Cumann na mBan buttressed the Irish Volunteers.[129] These women proved crucial in mobilizing the female vote and this aided victory for unionists and Sinn Féin in the 1918 general election.[130] Vigorous canvassing formed a core duty for young women (and men) as 'young girls were mobilized and worked on the register and on the canvass of the voters enthusiastically'.[131] Unionist women were also encouraged to canvass for their candidates and were reminded that it was the 'duty of every working woman at the present time to speak out her views with no uncertain voice'. The chairman of the Victoria Parliamentary Association, David E. Lowry, reminded women in this constituency in Belfast that they 'ought to be inspired to help in the cause'.[132] In 1921 Carson praised women for their past election work and called on 'every woman' to 'do her duty' again to 'return a strong Unionist Government for Ulster'.[133]

Volunteers and party-supporting organizations – such as Sinn Féin clubs, unionist clubs and associations, and the UIL and AOH for the IPP – were very effective canvassers and proved efficient for the most part in this duty, honing skills as the by-elections progressed. According to one Sinn Féin Volunteer in south Armagh, Volunteers conducted 'practically all the electioneering work: canvassing voters, marking the register, providing transport, getting voters out to the polling booths and taking charge at the polling booths'.[134] The IPP were less successful, as many in the AOH began to defect to the Irish Volunteer movement, mainly during the conscription crisis. Unfortunately for unionists and constitutional nationalists, men (and women) who might previously have campaigned on their behalf in the 1918 election were either still at the front line or making their way home. Many would not return in time to cast their votes on 14 December 1918, and, as discussed in chapter 1, in many cases the absentee voting papers did not reach them.

Party candidates were conveyed to their platform speeches in towns and villages throughout a constituency by Volunteers, and on election day voters were transported to polling booths. Cars and petrol became paramount for this activity but the latter was hard to come by because during the Great War and in its immediate aftermath car permits were needed and petrol was rationed. Acquiring petrol often required an element of sleuthing and ingenuity, and at times transgression of the law. Kitty O'Donnell of Cumann na mBan described a scenario where her husband procured nine tins of petrol from a bicycle shop. This was used in various cars that went from Dublin to the Roscommon North by-election. A petrol depot was raided in Dungannon, Co. Tyrone, for the Armagh South by-election, and a 'small quantity'

129 Garvin, *The evolution*, pp 107–10; Urquhart, *Women in Ulster politics*; Ward, *Women, unionism and loyalism in Northern Ireland*; McCarthy, *Cumann na mBan*; and Ward, *Unmanageable revolutionaries* (1983), ch. 4.   130 See ch. 1 on results.   131 BMH WS 492: John McCoy.   132 *BNL*, 10 Dec. 1918.   133 Ibid., 20 May 1921.   134 BMH WS 658: John Grant.

of petrol was taken.[135] Sinn Féin maintained that the AOH/IPP and unionists all had 'the advantage of ample funds' to corner all means of transport 'for the voters travelling to record their votes'. This inspired Sinn Féin to follow suit, and by the time the general election came there were plenty of cars for use and for sharing. Laurence Nugent, director of transport for the Pembroke District, stated that he engaged twelve cars from a southern garage and because polling in Sandyford and Ballyboden in Co. Dublin was over by noon he passed the cars to Gavan Duffy in South County Dublin and P.J. Little in Rathmines.[136] By 1921 rationing had ceased and the *Irish Independent* reported that unionist candidates in the north were 'liberally supplied with vehicles, including a fleet of splendidly equipped motor cars and chars-a-bane'. The anti-partition side, on the other hand, had few cars, but they decorated those they had with flags and emblems. This often provoked violent attacks and cars and/ or their bunting 'were wrecked when they made their appearance'.[137]

ELECTORAL VIOLENCE

Drilling, marching and parading by all nationalist Volunteer forces functioned as another free propaganda exercise. Volunteer canvassing and patrolling often led to electoral violence, but this was not unusual in Ireland. In *Elections, politics and society*, Hoppen provides extensive details on the ribbon groups in the 1800s that were involved in electioneering, where rioting often broke out. Electoral violence was largely linked to agrarian disputes and was a feature of rural elections throughout the century.[138] In late 1918, the general laxness of suppressing public military marching allowed Sinn Féin's Irish Volunteers the freedom to act as guards or 'peace patrols' at public meetings, election rooms and polling booths. There is little evidence of the UVF offering similar support to Ulster unionists in 1918, but there was a call for a general mobilization of unionist supporters. For example, in the Duncairn District of Belfast, the unionist workers 'turned up their machinery to the highest pitch' and 'toiled unceasingly … to the close of the poll'.[139]

The Hibernians' attitude to violence was similar to Sinn Féin volunteers' in that they believed the realization of legitimate political goals through the use of force was necessary. As Jackson states, 'it was perhaps not desirable or practicable, but violence was not out of the question'.[140] Hibernians launched an attack on Countess Markievicz at Lislea, throwing a huge paving stone that 'only missed her by inches', and, frustrated at their failure, they subsequently 'pelted her with sods and mud'.[141] In the Armagh South by-election, De Valera also came under attack, when a 'Hibernian attempted to drive a pike' through him.[142]

135 Ibid.;WS 355: Kitty O'Donnell; WS 353: James McGuill.   136 *IT*, 2 Feb. 1918; for examples see: BMH WS 676: Liam A. Brady; WS 782: Thomas McSea; WS 907: Laurence Nugent.   137 *II*, 25 May 1921.   138 Hoppen, *Elections, politics and society*, pp 378–408.   139 *BNL*, 16 Dec. 1918; *IT*, 6 Dec. 1918.   140 Jackson, *Ireland, 1798–1998*, p. 243.   141 BMH WS 755 (ii): Sean Prendergast.   142 Ibid.; WS 1764: Dr Vincent White; and WS 1,104: Thomas Brennan.

Outside polling booths and among audiences at campaign speeches, rival detachments of Volunteers – often carrying hurleys – readied for defence or combat. A sense of audacious presence and crowd enlargement were positive outcomes, but the negative impact was the occasional spill-over into violence or conflict. The latter often occasioned press reports about these hostile or aggressive actions, and depending on either the outcome or public perception there could be propaganda benefits or losses.[143] IPP supporters quickly learned to counter Sinn Féin with Sinn Féin tactics and imported their own peace patrols, usually members of the AOH. Wherever a Sinn Féin patrol was stationed, there was also an IPP patrol to be found.

Dillon's hometown of Ballaghadereen, Co. Mayo and the Redmondite stronghold of Waterford city were particularly violent during the 1917 by-elections and 1918 general election. Irish Volunteers were physically attacked by the Ballybricken Pig Buyers in Waterford, and they retaliated in kind. The Ballybricken Pig Buyers were central to the commercial activity of Waterford, and also played a major role in the city's social and political life. They were influential in the formation of local opinion. Dan McCarthy reported that he was armed with a gun, and fired on the 'Ballybricken crowd' when they closed in on him and the other Volunteers bearing 'ashplants'. He initially fired a warning shot in the air, but then fired again, hitting a man in the knee, believing him to be armed and ready to fire. Bottles and stones were hurled by each side at the other.[144] Ex-servicemen and Pig Buyers assembled in large groups to advance on Sinn Féin meetings and election rooms. In turn, Sinn Féin Volunteers charged at the Pig Buyers using heavy walking sticks or 'good stout ash plants', sending them to flight. During the 1918 general election the Sinn Féin candidate, Dr Vincent White, was hit and wounded by a large brick. William Archer Redmond was violently attacked by Paddy Murphy, a volunteer in Waterford, who was stopped only by an order from a commanding officer, who then proceeded to issue a 'lecture on good citizenship', perhaps indicating that violence was not always sought by either side.[145]

In Mayo, during Dillon's campaign, the RIC had to intervene when Irish Volunteers and IPP supporters clashed. Weapons were discharged, but no one was injured. Other campaign meetings around Ballaghadereen saw many 'clashes with the Redmondites'. Sinn Féin mobilized their Volunteers from one county/constituency into another to swell numbers for canvassing and protection, and again this created hostility. 'Outsiders' irritated the local IPP supporters, inciting violence on both sides. Thomas Brennan described a verbal confrontation between IPP and Sinn Féin supporters and believed it would have turned to physical violence but for the fact that only local men were involved on this occasion.[146] Disorderly

143 *FJ*, 2 Dec. 1918.   144 Thomas P. Dooley, *Irishmen or English soldiers? The times and world of a southern Catholic Irish man, 1876–1916: enlisting in the British army during the First World War* (Liverpool, 1995), p. 31; O'Connor, 'Trades councils in Waterford city' in William Nolan and Thomas Power (eds), *Waterford: history and society* (Dublin, 1992).   145 BMH WS 722: Dan McCarthy; WS 972: Tomas O'Cleirigh; WS 1,006: Martin Kealy.   146 Ibid., WS 1,104: Thomas Brennan.

I   *Vote for De Valera*. BMH, contemporary documents 227/7/B/I (1).
Courtesy of Military Archives (Ireland).

The Bishop of Limerick speaks :
How the Irish Prisoners are treated.

Sir,—The letter, signed Niam ni Pluingcead and Maire ni Riain, on the treatment of Irish prisoners in Lewes Jail, is very painful reading, and will unquestionably excite bitter and angry feelings in everyone who is not dead to all humanity.

As I read it, the first thought that came to my mind was one of regret that these poor victims of British rule had not been shot out of hand like their brethren in the rebellion. Surely Maxwell's summary method of dealing with Irish rebels was less cruel than the slow torture and degradation of Penal Servitude.

Then it occurred to me to consider whether the people of the United States will be allowed to know the facts of this case, and collate them with the suggestions, sincere or hollow, as the case may be, that are being offered for the political emancipation of Ireland. Is it all humbug? Is there any intention to give us Home Rule in any shape or form, or are all the discussions that are being carried on about it merely the latest shape which British perfidy assumes for its own purposes?

I rather think they are. But whether they are or not we are a mean nation if we take the benefit of the sacrifices of our fellow-countrymen, and allow themselves to linger and rot in English jails without at least a protest which the world will hear.

What has brought Home Rule to the front and given it the chance which it has at present of becoming law? Is it the droning of the English "friendlies" that they call the Irish Party? They are the "patriots" that allowed the wretched measure which has been passed by Parliament to be hung up during the war, and having suspended the liberties of their country turned to recruiting in Ireland for the British Government. They were "the one bright spot," and, whether it was stupidity or knavery, the distinction of it will attach to them for ever.

These are not the seed of the men by whom salvation is wrought in Israel. They are British Parliamentarians; and when they lost touch with their own country, and were absorbed in their dealings with the Liberal Whips, a new Ireland was growing up, reviving the language of their fathers, reading the history of their country, and breathing a spirit of manhood and independence. If we had a leader, who was an Irishman, they would have followed him to the death, but they never would be content with the servility to England and English parties that has been called Nationality. That is the explanation of the rebellion of 1916. It was a reaction against weakness and stupidity and corruption.

But, hopeless as it was, it has not been fruitless. It has galvanised the dead bones in Ireland, and breathed into them the spirit with which England has now to reckon. That is the trouble in the United States, and the treatment of our brave young countrymen in Lewes Jail will not do much to lessen it.

And if the Government of England thinks that such methods will subdue us in Ireland, or can be hidden from the civilised world, it will probably find out its mistake. But whatever be the purpose of this savagery, one would think that astute politicians, as the English unquestionably are, would see the transparent inconsistency of promising us a measure of self-government, and, at the same time, of imprisoning and deporting the very men who have convinced them of the righteousness, and the necessity of it.

I am, sir, etc.,

EDWARD THOMAS,

Limerick, 30th April, 1917.   Bishop of Limerick.

Electors of Longford Vote for the Man in Jail for Ireland.

Vote for McGuinness !

2   *The bishop of Limerick speaks: how the Irish prisoners are treated.*
    Elaine Callinan, private collection.

3   *Donegall Place, Belfast, under home rule.* Elaine Callinan, private collection.

THE TWO IRELANDS.

FACTS, NOT FICTION!

Ulster's Record.

75,000 Ulstermen voluntarily enlisted. In addition many thousands were prevented from enlisting owing to being on urgent War work.

Ulster gained **8** Victoria Crosses and **2410** other honours.

It had **42** Battalions of Infantry as against **37** Battalions for the rest of Ireland.

It had a full Division in the Firing Line with six reserve Battalions.

Contributed over **£1,000,000** to War Charities.

Equipped and maintained the largest Voluntary War Hospital in Ireland.

Equipped and maintained the finest Soldiers' and Sailors' Club in the United Kingdom, outside London, at which over **200,000** men slept and over **1,000,000** meals were served.

Supplied **95** per cent. of all the Aeroplane Cloth used by the Allies.

Its invested capital in the Linen Trade amounts to over **£20,000,000**.

It has the largest Linen Manufacturing Concern in the world.

It has the largest Firm of Linen Thread, Twine, and Netting Manufacturers in the world.

It has the largest Rope and Cable Works in the world.

It has the largest Shipbuilding Firm in the world.

It has the largest single Tobacco works in the world.

THERE ARE IN ULSTER :—

The largest single Flax Spinning Industry in the world.

The largest Linen Export Trade of any area of equal extent in the world.

Sinn Fein's Record.

From January 1st, 1919 to May 7th, 1921.

Courthouses destroyed	...	...	75
R.I.C. vacated Barracks destroyed...	...		561
R.I.C. occupied Barracks destroyed		...	25
R.I.C. vacated Barracks damaged	...		120
R.I.C. occupied Barracks damaged		...	165
Raids on Mails	...	...	1,734
Raids on Coastguard Stations and Lighthouses	...		58
Raids on Offices of Rate Collectors and Petty Sessions Clerks	...	...	102
Raids for Arms	...	...	3,138

	Killed.	Wounded.
Policemen	309	491
Soldiers	102	238
*Civilians	124	159
	535	888

*These figures do not include casualities in Ulster riots during June-September, 1920. 20 Civilian deaths occurred in Londonderry riots and 62 in Belfast riots during that period all due to Sinn Fein.

REBELLION, 1916.

	Killed.	Wounded.
Military Officers	17	46
Military, other ranks	86	311
R.I.C Officers	2	—
R.I.C. other ranks	12	23
Dublin Metropolitan Police	3	3
	120	383

Major M'Bride, who was executed for taking an active part in the Rebellion, speaking of the prospect of a German Invasion, said: "Should they land in Ireland they will be received with willing hearts and hands."

"**Ireland was a real Peril during the war.** They were in touch with German Submarines. Ireland stood as the gateway of Britian, and during the war her Coasts were blackened with our Ships. Ireland is girded with British wrecks, yes, and British seamen are there too. **They were prepared within two months of a German offensive to raise a huge force in IRELAND to stab Britain in the back** when we were engaged in a life and death struggle for the freedom of the world."—(The Prime Minister, Oct. 9, 1920.)

Will the British Public stand by Ulster, whose sons stood by them, or will they support Sinn Fein Ireland, which stabbed Britain in the back, and has such a ghastly record of disloyalty and crime?

Published by the Ulster Unionist Council, Unionist Headquarters, Old Town Hall, Belfast; and printed by A. H. Walls, 7 & 9, Victoria Street, Belfast.

4   *The two Irelands. Facts. Not fiction!* PRONI, Ulster Unionist Council and the deputy keeper of the records, UUC Papers, D1327/20/4/142, UC 132.

5 *A chance for South Longford* (Political Dustbin). The Board of Trinity College Dublin, Samuels Collection, collection box.

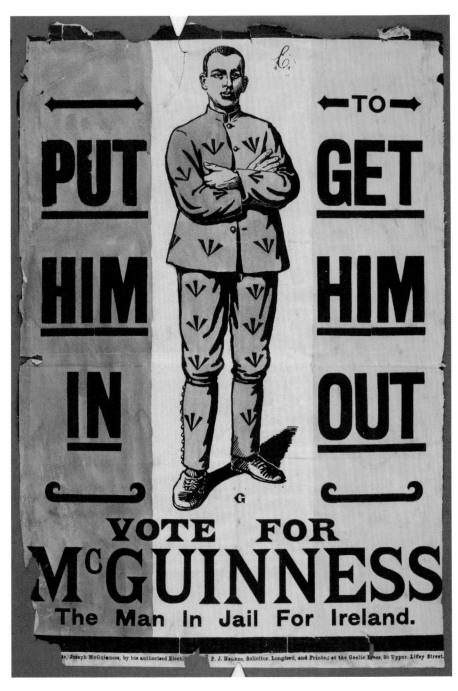

6 *Put him in to get him out.* The Board of Trinity College Dublin,
Samuels Collection, collection box.

7   *Union is strength* (pin badge). Elaine Callinan, private collection.

8   *Vote for Cosgrave* (shamrock pin badge). Elaine Callinan, private collection.

9   *Which?* The Board of Trinity College Dublin, digital collections,
Samuels Box 4/258.

DALCASSIANS !

Do You want a Hero to Represent you ?

— VOTE FOR —

DE VALERA.

Do you want a man who has given the greatest proof
of his love for his country that a man can give ?
Vote for De Valera !

What proof have have we that Mr Lynch will give the
best that is in him for the sake of his country, who has
spent so many years and exercised his brains so far—
well, not for Ireland ?

Mr Lynch being a lawyer, must know that England's
laws, inasmuch as being founded on the illegal Act of
Union, should not have legal or moral force in Ireland.
And he has been helping those laws. Why ? Was it
because of his burning love for Ireland ? Yet his supporters want you to elect him to fight for Ireland.
They say his policy is the policy of Parnell, of O'Connell, of Davitt. But you will see through all this, and
Vote for De Valera.

De Valera has given his head and his heart to Ireland.
He has studied her language which he speaks and
writes. He loves her literature—the literature of Saints
and Scholars. He is young and has not bent himself
in selfish aims. He has proved himself a hero. In
head and heart he is worthy to represent Clare.

VOTE FOR HIM !

Published for the Candidate by his authorised Election Agent,
H. O'B. Moran, Solicitor, Limerick, and Printed and Published
at the CHAMPION Works, Ennis.

10 *Dalcassians!* William O'Brien Papers, LOP 116/57.
Image courtesy of the NLI.

11 *Ulster's claim on Britain*. PRONI, Ulster Unionist Council and the deputy keeper of the records, UUC Papers, D1327/20/4/142.

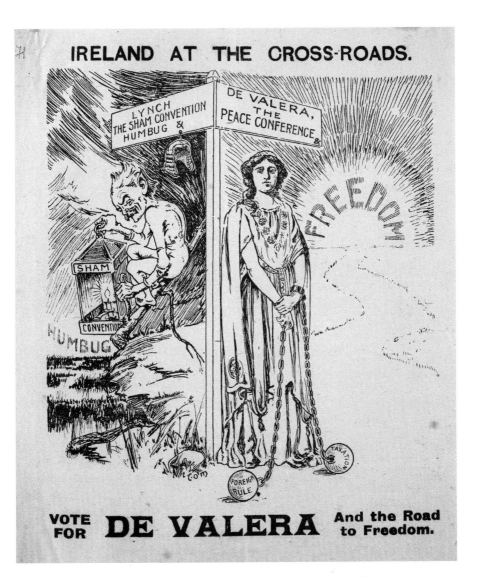

12   *Ireland at the crossroads.* William O'Brien Papers, LOP116/71.
Image courtesy of the NLI.

SINN FEIN "GUARANTEES."

"SAFEGUARDS" FOR ULSTER.

MR. DE VALERA'S THREATS.

Ulster has been assured that if she will only come into an all-Irish Republic she can have any "guarantees" and "safeguards" desired.

Mr. De Valera has been good enough to say that the "safeguards" he offers are: **"The safeguards of common sense."**

The official Nationalist party have charged and proved that the whole policy and practice of Sinn Fein—which now dominates Nationalist Ireland—is madness in its wildest and most violent form. Loyalists are asked to trust to the "common sense" of those guilty of the madness of Easter week, 1916, and the yet more imbecile folly of May, 1918, as revealed in the recent Government disclosures of the German plot.

At Killaloe, on July 5, 1917, Mr. De Valera said, "If Unionists do not come in on our side they will have to go under."

At Ballaghadareen, on 28th of the same month he declared, "Ulster must be coerced if she stands in the way."

At Cootehill, on September 2, 1917, he stated, "If you (Ulster) continue to be Britain's garrison we will have to do with you what we wish to do with the Power of which you are a garrison—and that is kick you out."

At Bessbrook, on January 27, 1918, he declared, "He recognised the Unionists as a rock on the road. They must, if necessary, blast it out of their path."

These are the real and undisguised sentiments of Mr. De Valera and his party towards those he asks to rely upon the safeguards of his common sense. What common sense or brotherliness has he exhibited for the last two years towards his own co-religionists of the Nationalist group? Let the orgy of violence and outrage from North Longford to East Tyrone answer.

Speaking at Castlebar, on January 20, 1918, Mr. De Valera said, "Their pro-Germanism was at the bottom anti-English. That was the psychology of their friendship for Germany and their hatred of England."

This is the sort of thing against which Irish Loyalists are arrayed and to which they will never yield.

Published by the Ulster Unionist Council, Unionist Headquarters, Old Town Hall, Belfast; and Printed by John Govan, 7 & 9, Victoria Street, Belfast.

13 *Sinn Féin 'Guarantees'. 'Safeguards' for Ulster.* PRONI, Ulster Unionist Council and the deputy keeper of the records, UUC Papers, D1327/20/4/142, UC 114.

SINN FEIN
Violence & Intimidation.

The Bishop's Appeal.

SINN FEIN has brought Violence and Terrorism into Irish Political Life.

Never before was it necessary for a Catholic Bishop to feel compelled to give such admirable advice.

Vote for REDMOND

And Defeat the Terrorising and Lying Tactics of the

PHYSICAL FARCE

AND

TAR AND CHALK PARTY.

Printed at " The Munster Express " Office, and published by P. A. Murphy, solicitor, Agent for the Candidate.

14 *Sinn Féin, violence & intimidation.* William O'Brien, LOP 116/100. Image courtesy of the NLI.

CONSCRIPTION!

Mr. Dillon, in the House of Commons, said on Dec. 21st, 1915 :

> "I feel it to be our duty to-day to warn the Government, and any Government that may succeed them, that Conscription we will not tolerate in Ireland.
>
> "It will be an ill day for England and for the Government that dare it, if they attempt to put Conscription in force in Ireland." . . .

Nothing but the strenuous opposition of the Irish Party has STOPPED Conscription in Ireland.

If Ireland is not represented in Parliament a Conscription Bill can be passed immediately WITHOUT OPPOSITION. The Irish Party is the one weapon to defeat Conscription. It is untrue to say the Rebellion prevented Conscription. The campaign of the Conscriptionists began in MAY, 1915, a year before the Rebellion. On the contrary, the Rebellion nearly brought Conscription by strengthening the hands of the militarists who demanded it.

VOTE FOR LYNCH

And Help to Keep Conscription Out of Ireland.

Printed and Published on behalf of the Nationalist Candidate, PATRICK LYNCH, by Chas. Nono, Printer, Ennis.

15   *Conscription!* UCDA, De Valera Papers, P150/550. Reproduced by kind permission of UCD–OFM Partnership.

Will You Vote for Conscription?

ENGLAND has been badly beaten in France.
ENGLAND wants more men to save her from utter rout.
THE WAR OFFICE is thinking of getting them in Ireland by Conscription.
THE ENGLISH PRESS is demanding Conscription for Ireland.
ON MARCH 26th, "The Morning Post" asked for it
ON MARCH 27th, "The London Times" asked for it.
ON MARCH 28th, "The London Globe," "The Daily Telegraph," "The Pall Mall Gazette," "The Evening Standard," asked for it.
ON FEBRUARY 22nd, a petition was presented in Parliament signed by 300,000 influential Englishmen demanding Conscription for Ireland

The Danger is Great !
England is Watching this Election !

After Waterford the Cabinet met and sat for several hours discussing, among other things, Conscription for Ireland.

The Irish Party, in December, 1915, **pledged themselves, through their spokesman, to accept Conscription whenever England thought it necessary** to win the war by imposing it.

Sinn Fein alone stands between you and the Death of your sons and brothers in France.

Every man between the ages of 18 and 45 will be taken if England has her way

Vote for M'Cartan
And Kill Conscription !

Printed by Margaret Powell, for the Candidate, at the MIDLAND TRIBUNE Printing Works, Birr, King's County.

16   *Will you vote for conscription?* William O'Brien Papers, LOP 116/94. Image courtesy of the NLI.

72

17 *Up Plunkett!* William O'Brien Papers, LOP 116/72.
Image courtesy of the NLI.

scenes erupted in many townlands, but IPP supporters were equally to blame. For instance, when Sinn Féin arrived into Ballaghadereen, led by a marching band, they were met by a 'fusillade of stones and bottles … poured into them from both sides of the road' with 'Sinn Féiners replying with revolver shots'.[147]

Serious violent disturbances also erupted in Cork. At the Shandon polling station ex-soldiers collided with Sinn Féin Volunteers and a 'fierce' exchange of stones and bottles ensued. A Volunteer 'peace patrol' charged and disbursed the rival crowds, but 'many were injured … others were knocked down and kicked'.[148] Two unionist canvassers, Major J.H. Phillips and Andrew Williams (brother of the unionist candidate Daniel Williams), encountered stone throwing and verbal abuse as they motored through the Cork suburb of Blackpool, but 'miraculously' they escaped injury.[149] The arrival of the police with fixed bayonets quelled the attacks but the result was that six soldiers home on leave and five Volunteers ended up in the infirmary. There were also other minor incidents such as window smashing.[150] Each side condemned the other for instigating violence.

The British government force charged with combatting violence during the 1918 election campaign was the RIC. This force was largely comprised of Irish Catholic men, and they were often accused by Sinn Féin of assisting the Redmondites (particularly in Waterford and Mayo). The RIC engaged in 'minor scenes' against armed Volunteers who had been sent into election areas by Sinn Féin. An incident in the Cavan East constituency saw Volunteers forming a cordon around the RIC, who had arrived because they believed they were there to enforce the law prohibiting drilling. The atmosphere was tense for a period, but it eventually cooled and there was no engagement between the two forces. In Waterford, however, after the close of polling, the Redmondite forces, armed with heavy sticks, rifles and revolvers violently attacked the Irish Volunteers' hall in Thomas Street. A party of British army forces in war kit, with fixed bayonets, appeared with a large contingent of RIC and they cordoned off the entrance to lower Thomas Street. According to Thomas Treacy, a Kilkenny Volunteer, the Irish Volunteers charged into the attacking Redmondites and after a vigorous encounter, including the discharging of firearms, the Redmondites broke and the RIC halted further attacks.[151] During Fr O'Flanagan's speech Redmond supporters 'came down on the Mall with bugles, blow horns, tin cans, drums and all kinds of noisy instruments' in an attempt to drown out his speech. In anger Sinn Féin Volunteers charged and attacked the Redmondites and eventually the RIC came between the two groups with fixed bayonets. Intervention by the RIC also fed into Sinn Féin propaganda and they used these violent attacks to create subversive literature. Yet, according to David Anderson, the RIC largely maintained its professional self-image as a civic institution.[152] These violent encounters did not happen in all constituencies. Most

---

147 *IT*, 16 Dec. 1918. **148** Ibid., 23 Dec. 1918. **149** Ibid. **150** Ibid. **151** BMH WS 755 (ii): Sean Prendercast; WS 1,093: Thomas Treacy; WS 972: Thomas Cleary. **152** David Anderson, *Policing and decolonisation: politics, nationalism, and the police, 1917–65* (Manchester, 1992), p. 25.

were like Wicklow East, which, according to the *Irish Times*, 'was fought in a spirit of friendly rivalry, and no incident occurred throughout the day that would mar the harmonious relations'.[153]

Where violence occurred or where there was even a threat of violence this may have intimidated electors and led to large numbers abstaining from voting.[154] This was an accusation levelled against unionists in 1921, particularly by nationalists and Catholics in Belfast. Early in the election campaign the *Freeman's Journal* reported on shots being fired by police outside a Catholic church during a police interrogation of 'girls' who were 'making a box collection for the Sinn Féin election fund outside St Patrick's Church' in Belfast. The congregation emerged from mass, and it was said that they became threatening when the police intervened to stop the collections. The crowd threw stones at the police, who fired their revolvers. This created panic and confusion and led to a policeman being wounded.[155] According to a report in the *Irish Independent*, 'it was evident that organized mobs had been set to work to intimidate the Catholic voters'. It was reported that 'Sinn Féin election workers are being pursued and arrested. Election literature is seized … the attitude of the 'Specials' themselves is partisan'.[156]

Catholics who had been expelled from the terrace streets of Ballymacarrett in the early 1920s after clashes with unionists made their way back from other parts of the city to vote. They were surrounded by hostile crowds and badly beaten, and three cars bearing voters were also 'smashed up'.[157] The *Manchester Guardian* declared that 'rarely has there been an election fought with such ruthlessness, such corruption and such unfairness' and added that 'the Unionists converted the election into a fair imitation of what one supposes the Silesian plebiscite to have been like'.[158] One aged nationalist voter, according to the *Freeman's Journal* on 25 May 1921, 'who was escorted to the polling station by an armoured car was set upon by the mob and was only rescued by the military after difficulty'. Evidence of similar attacks against unionists is difficult to find, but violence seems to have been confined to constituencies in Belfast as polling in Londonderry, for instance, was carried out without incident'.[159]

Sinn Féin's election campaign was hampered by violence and intimidation in 1921, but a lack of organization in Ulster constituencies also added to its difficulties. Of the nineteen Sinn Féin candidates, eight were in jail or interned and seven were 'on the run', which meant that they were not visible on election platforms and were represented by proxies. Sinn Féin also suffered from interruption in fund collections, ejection from polling stations, unionists impersonating nationalist voters, seizure of bicycles and restrictions on the use of vehicles. As the *Irish Independent* reported, 'harassing restrictions on the use of motor cars by nationalists and Sinn

---

153 *IT*, 17 Dec. 1918.   154 See ch. 1 on voter turnout.   155 *FJ*, 9 May 1921.   156 *II*, 20 May 1921.   157 Robert Lynch, 'The people's protectors? The Irish Republican Army and the "Belfast Pogrom", 1920–1922', *Journal of British Studies*, 47:2 (Apr. 2008), 375–91. *II*, 25 May 1921.   158 *FJ*, 26 May 1921.   159 *UH*, 28 May 1921.

Féin organizers are imposed, while unionist organizers get all the permits they ask for and a few more besides'.[160] However, to cast blame only on unionist aggression for nationalist difficulties neglects the fact that there was constant infighting. Constitutional nationalists made little effort to secure second-preference votes for Sinn Féin, much to the ire of de Valera. Devlin counter-argued that he had encouraged nationalists to work together to secure all votes. Sinn Féin activities were covered in Devlin's *Irish News*, but more pages were dedicated to nationalist candidates.[161]

Clashes between party-supporting movements and Volunteers were not always violent in 1917 and 1918. Some were conducted in good-humoured, affable competition, such as the ballad sing-off during the Armagh South by-election. Two large bonfires had been lit on opposite ends of a street, about sixty yards apart, by IPP and Sinn Féin supporters. Sinn Féin's Clare volunteers began singing republican songs and IPP supporters responded with ballads such as 'A nation once again', 'Deep in the Canadian woods' and 'God save Ireland'. According to the Volunteer John McCoy, 'if a really good effort was produced from either party it was applauded by both parties'.[162] Canvassing by volunteers and public oratory by candidates was bolstered by party symbols and balladeering. Over time voters came to recognize and associate colours or songs with particular political movements.

SYMBOLS AND BALLADS

Nationalist iconography during election campaigns included harps, shamrocks, round towers, wolfhounds, sunbursts, Celtic crosses, green and tricolour flags (depending on the particular brand of nationalism). Unionism exploited some of these images also, such as the harp, alongside the union flag and images of King William III. In *Our own devices*, Morris outlines the controversy about national symbols and provides a detailed explanation of a selection of official symbols.[163] This work intends an investigation into how and where symbols were used to encourage voter support and whether their use helped to transform opinion. The focus will be on the by-elections and the 1918 general election because use was minimal during the local-government elections of 1920, although symbols were used again in 1921 and in similar fashion to 1918.

Flags and banners were the most potent symbols and were used extensively as bunting that lined the streets and decorated crossroads and the platforms of public speeches. The IPP flag comprised a gold harp centred on a field of green, and they claimed that the 'old green flag' represented the flag of Ireland. The selection of the colour green represented Ireland and the harp her official symbol. During the election campaigns this flag appeared on motor cars that brought speakers and canvassers to voters and also decorated polling booths, particularly in constituencies

160 *II*, 20 May 1921. 161 Inoue, 'Sinn Féin propaganda', p. 55. 162 BMH WS 492: John McCoy. 163 Morris, *Our own devices* on national symbols and emblems.

where the IPP was strongest.[164] The importance of the flag can be seen in an IPP handbill that posed the confrontational question 'What is Wrong with the Green Flag?' The content associated their green flag with Irish national tradition, order and sturdy progress towards home rule, whereas the tricolour was married to revolution, anarchy and repudiation of the national tradition. The real question voters had to consider was why it was necessary to 'invent an absurd new-fangled flag for Ireland'. Voters did not have to rely on their own wit as the answer was provided in the condemnation of Sinn Féin: 'a fake flag is the right flag for a fake policy'. Sinn Féin's tricolour was consistently referred to as the 'rainbow' flag and IPP followers were regularly reminded to, as Nationalist candidate for Monaghan South Thomas Campbell stated, 'stand by the old green flag under which their fathers fought'. He criticized the 'yellow streak in their [Sinn Féin] flag' and highlighted that there were 'no white feathers on their flag – their flag was a flag of no surrender, and it was green all the time, and green all the way'.[165]

Unionist identity and convictions were embodied in the union flag (or Union Jack), which was evident in many references to this flag in election speeches.[166] During Dockrell's nomination in Rathmines, one of his supporters reminded the audience that 'the Union Jack was the flag for which Sir Maurice Dockrell sent three sons to fight [in the Great War], and it was for that flag that Mr Samuels sacrificed his only son'.[167] Union Jack bunting bedecked streets to welcome unionist leaders, such as Carson in Belfast in November 1918, when 'from every window along the route flags and streamers floated'.[168] Union colours were represented on pin badges (see plate 7). The reverse side marked this as a series of 'no surrender' badges that could be obtained from 'all newsagents or direct, post free' from the printers.[169] Ronald MacNeill maintained in *Ulster stands for union* that 'if there is a profuse display of the Union Jack', it is because it is in Ulster not merely 'bunting' for decorative purposes as in England, but 'the symbol of a cherished faith'.[170]

At the first anniversary of the Easter Rising, displaying the green, white and orange tricolour became a gesture of defiance among separatist nationalists. During the by-elections it became a symbol of Sinn Féin aspirations. *Nationality* reported that the tricolour was 'the flag of the Young Irelanders, adopted 70 years ago by them avowedly as a symbol of the union of Ireland against enforced union with England'.[171] In this way the history of the tricolour summoned a link with past battles for Irish freedom.

Sinn Féin's practice of decorating the streets with tricolour bunting began during the Longford South by-election campaign, when 'glittering and dancing in the brilliant sunlight were hundreds of tricolours, the Sinn Féin flag, waving from end to end of the procession'. This procession filled with marching men 'stretching

164 G.A. Hayes McCoy, *A history of Irish flags from earliest times* (Dublin, 1979), pp 22–3, 43–7. **165** BMH WS 707: Michael Noyk; *AC*, 7 Dec. 1918. **166** Hayes McCoy, pp 36–41. **167** *IT*, 3 Dec. 1918. **168** Ibid., 15 Nov. 1918. **169** Elaine Callinan Collection, *No surrender* badge by Wm Strain and Sons Ltd, Belfast. **170** McNeill, *Ulster stands for union*, ch. 1. **171** *Nationality*, 26 May 1917.

from Market Square almost to the Eattery at the opposite end of the town' was led (as was often the case) by young Sinn Féin supporters such as 'two charming, well dressed girls, carrying Republican flags'. During the campaign it was reported that the Sinn Féin colours could be seen everywhere, with 'thousands' of people bearing the 'well-known colours of the green, gold and white'.[172] During de Valera's Clare East by-election campaign a supporter on a train to Clare stated that there were 'so many republic flags displayed in the procession from Ennis station to the Old Ground Hotel that it appeared ... as if the road was one great blaze with the failing sunshine on the orange of the banners'.[173] The tricolour quickly became associated with the party and candidates, as evidenced by the *Roscommon Herald* report that 'many voters when asked their opinion on the election merely nodded to the flag in an approving manner'.[174]

The gravity and depth of passion regarding flags and colours and their associations with political parties was borne out in repeated sneers and insults by one party against another in an attempt to stress disparities. De Valera claimed that he stood for the tricolour (pointing to the flag on display) and not for the Union Jack, maintaining that Patrick Lynch 'was fighting under the Union Jack'. Supporters of Sinn Féin sometimes accused the IPP and unionists of colluding, including in the Armagh South by-election. John Cosgrove claimed he saw the 'unusual spectacle of Hibernians and Orangemen travelling together in the same public conveyance with the green Hibernian flag and the Orange Union Jack flying side by side'. This he termed an 'unholy alliance between Orange and Green' because the Hibernian slogan of 'Up Donnelly' was echoed by the Orange cry of 'To hell with the Pope'.[175]

Symbols can function to signify dissent, to establish legitimacy for a particular cause, or to protest against the legitimacy of a nation's ideology or actions.[176] Social scientists have long argued that symbols of a nation increase people's sense of psychological identification with their nation, or even identification with an imagined nation.[177] In Longford town the Sinn Féin colours, according to the *Roscommon Herald*, were

> seen everywhere through the district. Never in Longford has there been such a display of flags ... There were thousands of people present, and most of them carried the well-known colours of the green, gold and white. Every vehicle sported a flag, and some of them, especially motor cars, had several floating to the breeze.[178]

172 *RH*, 5 May 1917. **173** BMH WS 908: Laurence Nugent. **174** *RH*, 14 Apr. 1917. **175** Ibid., 30 June 1917; BMH WS 549: Robert Kelly; WS 605: John Cosgrave. **176** R. Firth, *Symbols: public and private* (NY, 1973); see also David A. Butz, 'National symbols as agents of psychological and social change', *Political Philosophy*, 30:5 (Oct. 2009), 779–804. **177** S. Feshbach and N. Sakano, 'The structure and correlates of attitudes toward one's nation in samples of United States and Japanese college students: a comparative study' in D. Bar-Tal and E. Staub (eds), *Patriotism in the lives of individuals and nations* (Chicago, 1997), pp 91–107. **178** *RH*, 5 May 1917.

And, in Clare East it was reported that 'demonstrative crowds ... with Republican colours and Irish flags, gathered'.[179] De Valera had a landslide victory in Clare East, with 2,975 votes over the IPP candidate. Similar examples can be taken from the 1918 general election, when flags and colours decorated all contested constituencies. Particularly evident were Sinn Féin colours, and in Ulster unionist colours adorned constituences that promoted unionist candidates. Baumeister and Leary maintain that people are 'empowered by the use of symbols to feel a strong sense of unity and belongingness, particularly in the wake of a threat'.[180] The flag, as a strong symbol of identity, visually characterized disparaties between parties and reinforced a political stance. They generated a strong sense of presence and showcased a party's enthusiasm to win votes. They also had an intimidatory impact that may have discouraged opponents' voters from presenting at the polls. Flags and colours helped build recognition of a candidate, but once the candidate and their policies became known, often old partisanships took over. During 1917 and 1918, however, the tricolour created brand recognition for the neophyte Sinn Féin party.

Another strong symbol during election campaigns was the shamrock, and nationalists of all hues used the shamrock as a symbol of Irish identity. Sinn Féin favoured shamrock-shaped button badges with printed messages and candidate images, which were worn by canvassers and party supporters (see plate 8).[181] What is striking is the use of the slogan 'A felon of our land!' (see plates 8 and 9). This demonstrates that Sinn Féin interconnected badges, banners and posters – all with similar or related messages. The poster *Which?* (see plate 9) depicts an imagined court scene, or perhaps mimics an Easter Rising court martial. De Valera stands resplendent in his Irish Volunteer uniform. Crown prosecutor Patrick Lynch, the IPP candidate, points to him as a felon, and the British judge, enveloped in the Union Jack, writes out the sentence. The poster and badge link together and they also relate to other propaganda that condemns Lynch's profession and promotes Irish freedom; and this poster connects with the *Put him in to get him out* poster because all suggest unjust imprisonment for Irish rebels.[182]

Unionist propaganda on the other hand identified with Britishness and Protestantism, although not always to the exclusion of a sense of Irishness.[183] The image of King William at the Battle of the Boyne astride a white horse became

179 *CC*, 12 May 1917   180 R.F. Baumesiter and M.R. Leary, 'The need to belong: desire for interpersonal attachments as a fundamental human motivation', *Psychological Bulletin*, 117 (1995), 497–529; and P.G. Davies, C.M. Steele and H.R. Markus, 'A nation challenged: the impact of foreign threat on America's tolerance for diversity', *Journal of Personality and Social Psychology*, 95 (2008), 308–18.   181 Alban Butler, *Butler's lives of the saints*, ed. Herbert J. Thurston (Notre Dame, 1956), i, p. 615; E. Charles Nelson, *Shamrock: botany and history of an Irish myth* (Kilkenny, 1991), pp 115–20.   182 Elaine Callinan Collection: vote for Cosgrave badge; TCD, Digital Collections, Samuels Box 4/258: *A felon of our land*. TCD, Early Printed Books, Samuels Collection, EPB OLS Samuels Collection Box 4 (Digital No. SamuelsBox4_258): *Which?*   183 Walker, *A history of the Ulster Unionist Party*, p. 1. See also Bew, *Ideology and the Irish question*, p. 64; Fitzpatrick, *The two Irelands*, particularly part 1.

popular on posters and banners (and in the modern era in murals on the gable end of houses in Protestant areas of Northern Ireland). Unionists also used the Red Hand of Ulster, which had its roots as a Gaelic Irish symbol.[184] During the Armagh South by-election the spectacle of the Red Hand emblazoned on a large flag being carried by unionists during a speaking rally infuriated de Valera. He pointed to the flag as it arrived, led by a band of unionist pipers, and proclaimed, '[T]here's the flag of Ulster.' Carson was then accused of being 'the man who would sell Ulster if it was convenient', and unionists generally were denounced as being 'a rock in the road' that 'must be stormed'. 'They [separatists] must', stated de Valera, 'if neces-sary blast it out of their path'.[185] Symbols had the power to evince strong, emotive reactions.

The clever location or shrewd placement of symbols and flags carried an elec-toral message to wider audiences. Automobiles and other vehicles were creatively used by all during election campaigns, adorned with flags and party colours. According to the *Roscommon Herald* on 14 April 1917 a Sinn Féin motor car with a mounted tricolour 'drew many a cheer along the way'. Dillon commented that Sinn Féin 'motor cars passed through the streets with new flags fluttering over them'; and one enthusiastic Volunteer claimed he sang 'The soldier's song' from the top of an outside car.[186]

Sinn Féin devised the imaginative idea of re-registering cars in order to evade arrest and recognition by authorities, as there were restrictions on the use of cars on polling day without a permit. The Irish Volunteers changed the registration on their cars to 'I.R. 1916'. This afforded recognition to Sinn Féin supporters and the electorate, because Volunteers collected and delivered speakers and voters; and the registration differentiated their vehicles from those of the opposition. They were, of course, held up by the RIC, and when questioned, the drivers 'referred the Constabulary to the Sinn Féin headquarters'. In a further act of defiance to British law, drivers' licences were issued by the Sinn Féin organization and were signed 'E. de Valera'.[187]

Sinn Féin's foremost anthem during the election campaigns was 'The soldier's song' and it was regularly used in tandem with Volunteer and Cumann na mBan marches, sung in both English and Irish.[188] Unionists sang the British national anthem 'God save the king'. These party anthems provided insight into the 'deep-est political aspirations, experiences, goals and values' of political movements.[189]

---

184 Belinda Loftus, *Mirrors: orange and green* (Dundrum, Co. Down, 1994), p. 38; Alvin Jackson, 'Irish unionist imagery' in E. Patton (ed.), *Returning to ourselves* (Belfast, 1995), pp 354–6.   **185** *Ulster Gazette*, 2 Feb. 1918.   **186** *LL*, 12 May 1917; BMH WS 397: Thomas Pugh.   **187** *Weekly IT*, 9 Feb. 1918. BMH WS 353: James McGuill; WS 907: Laurence Nugent; and WS 633: Michael Joseph Ryan.   **188** Ewan Morris, '"God save the king" versus "The soldier's song": the 1929 Trinity College national anthem dispute and the politics of the Irish Free State', *Irish Historical Studies*, 31:121 (May 1998), 72–90; Ruth Sherry, 'The story of the national anthem', *History Ireland*, 4:1 (Spring 1996), 39–43.   **189** Joseph Zikmund II, 'National anthems as political symbols', *Australian Journal of Politics and History*, 15:3 (1969), 73–4.

The British national anthem promoted profound unionist beliefs in song, such as the appeal for the king to be 'happy and glorious/ Long to rein over us', and to 'defend our laws'. Loyalty to the anthem and to the Union Jack was, according to Morris, useful when it came to distinguishing unionists from nationalists.[190] The substance of the distinctive characteristics, particularly between Sinn Féin and unionists, was in the lyrics, as they held the ingredients of the principles of those who performed them.

Unionists had their favoured ballads, and their themes often referred to the 1641 rebellion (in the ballad 'Portadown', for example), the Glorious Revolution or earlier battles between popular secret societies of the nineteenth century. For instance, 'Dolly's Brae' was a ballad about Orangemen and Ribbonmen fighting on Dolly's Bray, Co. Down in 1849. Ballads on Protestantism were also popular such as 'A fine true-hearted Protestant', which was sung to their air of 'A fine old English gentleman'.[191]

During the election campaigns ballads or poems were created to extol the virtues of candidates or condemn opponents. In Roscommon North the ballad 'Hurrah! Hurrah! for Plunkett' was performed to the air of 'The boys of Wexford', with electors told 'for Éire's right in freedom's fight./ Your manhood strong with Plunkett throng/ To win her liberty'.[192] In the Cavan East campaign a Sinn Féin election agent, Joseph Stanley, entertained the crowd at a public meeting by singing a newly composed ballad, 'Britannia to East Cavan'. The repetition throughout of the line 'Says the grand old Dame Britannia' (which appears three times in each verse and twelve times in total) allowed the crowd to swiftly absorb both lyric and tune to join in. The content of this ballad ridiculed the hold Britain had on the IPP by, for instance, satirizing the £400 annual salary received by their MPs – 'Four hundred quid on a fishing hook' – and mocking the fact that home rule lay dormant on the statute books.[193] Ballads could rouse a crowd at public meetings but they were also outward expressions of cultural or national identity, and they relied on familiar tunes to encourage audience participation. The symbols and ballads or anthems of all parties in the elections during 1917 and 1918 functioned as tools of psychological, social and political persuasion. Their persuasive influence was apparent in their incessant use. This is still evident today even in commercial and modern propaganda such as the international promotion of Ireland on St Patrick's Day by the use of the colour green, the presentation of shamrock to the President of the USA, the presence of the harp on the pint of Guinness, and the display of tricolours and union flags in Northern Ireland. Signifying the power of symbols was the visible anger by the authorities towards Sinn Féin's public displays of colours, which was evident in Co. Clare when the police were 'kept busy hauling down

---

190 Morris, *Our own devices*, p. 118.   **191** NLI, Ephemera Collection, EPH C287: *Songs for Protestants* (Dublin, *c.*1850).   **192** Ibid., William O'Brien Papers, LOP 116(76).   **193** TCD, Digital Collections, 679 (5/111: *Britannia to east Cavan*); BMH WS 755 (ii): Sean Prendergast; and NLI, William O'Brien Papers, LOP 116(37), (38), (40) and (41).

Republican flags', and in 1921 when their use sparked violence.[194] The presentation of symbols as gifts to honour leaders demonstrates their profound meaning. In Co. Clare 'young ladies' representing the local Cumann na mBan branch sang 'The soldier's song' as they presented Sinn Féin colours and a banner bearing the candidate's motto 'Justice for Ireland' to de Valera after he completed his tour of the constituency.[195]

Flags, banners, badges, belts and ballads were extolled as the weapons with which the nation's freedom might be won. The desire for music and pageantry filled townlands with colour and led to a demand by nearly every political candidate to have a pipers' band. More importantly, the symbols of nationalism and unionism expressed a visual identity.

NOVEL AND COST-FREE PROPAGANDA

In Roscommon North in 1917 a blanket of snow and drifts up to ten feet deep resulted in the election being dubbed 'the White Election'. Plunkett's campaign cleverly exploited the poor weather conditions by writing 'Up Plunkett' in the snow, using it as an advertising medium.[196] The *Roscommon Herald* of 17 March 1917 reported that O'Flanagan had found lines from an unknown poet written in the snow satirizing the independent candidate running against Plunkett and Devine, which 'put rather well the thought that was uppermost in the hearts of the people':

> Don't vote for Tully
> Or you will sully,
> The name and fame of the men who died,
> But true men
> Like you men
> Will honour them with pride.
>
> Tully's mixture
> Is not a fixture,
> It's just like margarine.
> Count Plunkett's pure,
> And it's secure,
> Don't mind poor Tom Devine.

Novel and cost-free propaganda techniques pervaded towns and cities to encourage donations during the dáil loan fundraising campaign. According to county inspectors, loan slogans were painted on walls, and stencilled on footpaths, lampposts and letterboxes. Handbills were distributed after masses and door-to-door

194 *CC*, 5 May 1917.   195 Ibid., 7 July 1917.   196 *II*, 29 Jan. 1917.

canvasses were conducted.[197] The paid-for and free loan propaganda methods indirectly strengthened election campaigning by augmenting voter support in the later elections through party recognition. Sourcing free propaganda opportunities was not unusual, and many forms were also used during elections. An irate solicitor from Dublin wrote to the *Irish Times* in January 1920 during the urban elections appealing for political parties to 'abstain from disfiguring the walls and wood-work in the city with ... paint'. He pointed out that in past elections the Dublin walls were 'painted and posters affixed without regard to public or private rights'.[198] Novel techniques were again used in 1921. A handbill titled *Revised scheme for elections* instructed 'that all the dead walls in the constituency are [to be] painted with Election Mottoes' and 'Telegraph poles should be covered with Election Literature'.[199]

CONCLUSION

A hypothesis emerges that the greater the array of propaganda, the higher the impact. Parties that placed propaganda at the fore in campaigning encouraged persuasion and altered voter opinion to attain a favourable electoral outcome. In Longford South, the *Roscommon Herald* reported that Sinn Féin 'posters and leaflets are scattered in every corner'.[200] The ubiquity and cacophony of election literature generally in Armagh South was expressed by the *Irish Times*, which reported that:

> Judging by the amount of election literature distributed in all parts of the constituency there is no shortage of paper in South Armagh. Leaflets, intended for distribution to stimulate the ardour of voters, were scattered broadcast, and the unfortunate voter had to pass through a regular barrage of fire from the literature guns as he went to his polling booth.[201]

However, it is problematic to argue in favour of any particular method of propaganda or even a selection of methods, without first investigating the content and themes of propaganda for elections. Chapter 5 throws more light on how voters were persuaded to cast in favour of a particular party or candidate.

197 *IT*, 8 Nov. 1919; NA, Dublin Castle Papers CO 904/110: RIC Reports Sept.–Dec. 1919, CO 904/111 Jan.–Feb. 1919; NAI, DE 1/1: Cabinet minutes, 19 Sept. 1919: minutes of Dáil Éireann ministry and cabinet, 26 Apr. to 19 Sept. 1919. 198 *IT*, 6 Jan. 1920. 199 Inoue, 'Sinn Féin propaganda', pp 50–1 200 *RH*, 5 May 1917. 201 *IT*, 2 Feb. 1918.

Propaganda themes and content

Identifying the central themes of political propaganda allows for a thorough investigation into how content may have influenced voters. Lasswell regarded 'content' as a set of 'messages' aimed at 'recipients' rather than as 'texts' to be interpreted by 'readers'. The underlying theory was that media generally produced powerful, direct and uniform effects on people. This remained the prevailing perception and propaganda approach throughout the early twentieth century.[1] The effectiveness of a theme can be measured in terms of uniqueness or prevalence, its application and relevance within the society in which voters lived, and the aspirations for an altered future. Throughout the election campaigns from 1917 to 1921 future reforms based on physical, moral and ethical standards were offered which aimed to transform Ireland or preserve the status quo.

Dominant political actors introduced diametrically opposed opinions on common themes (for instance the Great War) to uphold, condemn or highlight discordant stances. To gain credence, politicians endorsed the militant actions of supporting movements or condemned the perceived atrocities of opponents. Fundamental lofty ideals were espoused to unveil or fortify political ideologies that led to the development of new strategies to secure those aims. Sinn Féin, for example, backed abstention from Westminster and pursued sanction from an international forum for the recognition of Ireland's right to independence.

The contentious and incessant political wrangling that played out in election propaganda highlight the themes used to convert voters. Content tells us how the electorate interpreted political messages to decide to cast a vote in favour of a political party or candidate. It also offers insights into voters' interests – was the choice between a home rule government, rule from Westminster or a republic central to those casting votes, or were everyday concerns about farming, taxation and pensions greater influences? It is interesting to examine whether content altered as election dates loomed, and whether there were variances in message content for the general election as against local-government elections. This chapter intends to investigate electoral propaganda across all parties in a thematic manner to query why political parties and candidates believed the issues they focused on were central to winning votes.

---

1 Lasswell, *Propaganda techniques*. See also Mark O'Brien and Donnacha Ó Beacháin (eds), *Political communication in the Republic of Ireland* (Liverpool, 2014), pp 18–20, 201–16.

POLITICS OF THE PAST

The struggle to secure ideological dominance presented divergent interpretations of history and contrary claims on past political leaders. Association with a perceived glorious bygone era, or the creation of continuity with admired political predecessors was used by political leaders to provide unanimity and confidence in contemporary tactics. History, according to Reicher and Hopkins, was mobilized as a symbolic resource to define a group in a way consistent with the political agenda of its elites. According to Liu and Hilton, 'a central part of a group's representation of its history is thus its charter', to give an 'account of its origin and historical mission'. They also contend that the great advantage of history for politicians is 'that most of the participants in it are dead, and while immortal as symbols, can speak only through the tongues of present-day interpreters'.[2] High ideals were the fundamental motif for all political parties, and were transmitted to create and persuade acquiescence to a common wisdom in order to attain hegemonic domination. For instance, IPP candidates regularly provided an account of the history of home rule prior to promoting other electoral policies, and drew on past known political figures to reinforce party integrity.

Both nationalist parties laid claim to Parnell, Davitt, O'Connell, Wolfe Tone and Robert Emmet, and all parties advocated allegiance to or rejection of the 1798 rebellion and Grattan's parliament, depending on their political standpoint. For instance, Devlin stated in Longford South that 'we stand for the same principles and stand by the same leaders since everyone knows what our principles are. They were declared by Parnell and Davitt ... Those principles were: The land of the Irish for the people of Ireland, and Ireland for the Irish.'[3] The central tenet of this approach was to appeal to different political leanings: the Catholic Church and moderates could be kept on board, land issues dominated the concerns of the small farmers of rural Ireland (although not as much by 1917–18), the middle classes of the towns and cities could also be comforted in the knowledge that they would be the masters of their own island. 'Ireland for the Irish' suggested a self-governing nation that could in the future manage its own taxation and employment affairs. Most importantly, by linking with the idea of Parnell's Old Brigade, a combination of separatist aspirations with a constitutional strategy could be upheld.

Dillon's election speech in the village of Straide, Co. Mayo in December 1918 (mentioned in chapter 4) opened with the simple statement that 'this parish of Straide is an historic parish'. An immediate connection was made with Michael Davitt – the agrarian agitator and founder of the Land League – who hailed from the town. An automatic kinship between Davitt's conviction of 'the land for the people' and agrarian reform with the IPP's constitutional efforts was drawn, to

---

2 S.D. Reicher and N. Hopkins, *Self and nation* (London, 2001); J.H. Liu and D.J. Hilton, 'How the past weighs on the present: social representations of history and their impact on identity politics', *British Journal of Social Psychology*, 44:4 (Dec. 2005), 537–56.   3 *LL*, 12 May 1918.

focus attention on the Land Acts attained under IPP governance. No specifics on the historic personality or Land Acts were mentioned, but that was unnecessary. The audience made the connection and cheered the speaker on.

To demonstrate the current programme of inclusivity within the unionist agenda and to dispute IPP claims for a reconstitution of Grattan's parliament, Carson and Craig maintained that Grattan's parliament was a 'so-called Irish Parliament [that] was a gathering of representatives of the aristocracy and the Anglican ascendancy', where 'the Irish people were not represented at all'. They argued that this parliament passed thirty-two Coercion Acts which ultimately led to the 1798 rebellion, and what saved Ireland was the Act of Union.[4] Unionists, in Aristotelian fashion, presented a number of arguments or proofs to defend the union, one being the 'argument of history'. Here they claimed that Ireland had never been a whole and undivided nation, not even during the 'Druidic' or the 'Christian' periods. They asserted that Ireland 'has had many kings and rulers at one time' and that it was only under British rule that 'Ireland ever approached unity'.[5]

Sinn Féin, in similar tone to the IPP, laid historic claims to past icons of Irish politics. De Valera in Ennis, Co. Clare, said that 'if there was any party who were the logical followers of Parnell it was the Sinn Féin party ... Parnell acted out to kill the grip of landlordism as a preliminary to greater changes which were to be accomplished.'[6] Count Plunkett acknowledged that the IPP were the plausible descendants of Parnellism, because they had been 'brought together by one of the best patriots of Ireland, Charles Stewart Parnell'. However, the IPP did not live up to the principles taught by Parnell, and 'it was time they were thrust out of public life' (cheers).[7] The correct interpretation of Parnell, he argued, was Sinn Féin policy because

> Parnell had said in 1881 that 'it is no use relying on the Government, it is no use relying on the Irish members, it is no use relying on the House of Commons. You must rely on your own determination, and if you are determined, I tell you you have the game in your own hands.'

De Valera declared that Parnell had spoken 'about these things to prepare them for a campaign of misrepresentation, which he expected was about to be started by the Irish party'.[8] The IPP vehemently opposed such claims. For instance, Thomas O'Donoghue, MP for Meath South in 1918, criticized Sinn Féin's abstentionist policies by arguing that Parnell had said, 'I will never so long as there is breath in my body abandon the weapon that attendance at Parliament places in my hands.' And, O'Donoghue further argued that Davitt regarded abstention from parliament as 'a suicidal political programme'.[9]

4 PRONI, D1327/20/4/142: unionist handbill U.C. 101, *Some facts about the union and the Irish Parliament.*   5 Ibid., U.C. 121, *America and Ireland: what American Protestants say.*   6 *CC*, 30 June 1917.   7 *RH*, 12 May 1917.   8 *CC*, 7 July 1917.   9 *IT*, 14 Dec. 1918.

Sinn Féin also associated themselves with a more golden age in the nation's history by appealing to ancient Irish clans or tribes, as is evident in de Valera's handbill titled *Dalcassians!* (plate 10). The headline held no meaning unless the reader had prior knowledge that the 'Dalcassians' were a tenth-century Gaelic tribe known as the Dál gCais. The most famous leader, Brian Ború, became legendary after defeating the Viking Norse at the Battle of Clontarf in 1014.[10] The story goes that the country 'by degrees' supported Brian and he 'won their votes' and ultimately forced his brother to 'throw off the yoke and adopt the Cause of Independence'. That de Valera was a notional link to a mythical hero, as well as a tangible warrior of 1916, demonstrates his highly gendered propaganda themes, which hint at his vision for a future independent Ireland. In the final paragraph de Valera's devotion to and proficiency in the Irish language and his dedication to Irish literature reinforces the analogy with the past. All is linked back to the main point through the line saying that de Valera is the 'hero to represent you'.[11]

Sinn Féin, as Laffan points out, 'concerned themselves with abstractions rather than with material questions'.[12] If the 1918 Sinn Féin election manifesto is examined there is only a blithe reference to the development of 'Ireland's social, political and industrial life, for the welfare of the whole people of Ireland', in point three of a four-point plan. The rest of the document is based on nationalist theoretical principles that were all subject to using 'any and every means available to render impotent the power of England to hold Ireland in subjection'.[13]

Labour attempted to combine both the Easter Rising and labour working-class concerns. In his address to members at the 1918 annual meeting, William O'Brien passionately stated that Connolly 'had laid down his life for the working class in all countries (not just Ireland) … to spur them to resistance to the powers of imperialism and capitalism'. The ideals and principles of Connolly were the inspiration for Labour in Ireland; his were 'the plans and methods upon which we organize … and our place [is] in the forefront of the fighting army of Labour and in the battle for freedom and justice in this and all other lands'. O'Brien maintained that Connolly had 'fought the good fight' and that he fell in 'the battle for the right against the wrong'.[14]

Despite the association with 1916 through Connolly and pledges to 'carry on' and 'battle on' until the 'Workers' Republic for which you [Connolly] worked and fought and died' was realized, Labour withdrew from the contest in 1918 (and again in 1921).[15] They had veered towards republicanism before the 1916 Rising,

---

10 Roger Chatterton Newman, *Brian Boru, king of Ireland* (Dublin, 1997); John Francis Byrne, *Irish kings and high kings*, 2nd ed. (Dublin, 2001); Donnchadh Ó Corráin, *Ireland before the Normans* (Dublin, 1972). **11** NLI, LOP 116(52), William O'Brien Papers: *A bit of Dalcassian history*; LOP 116/57: *Dalcassians!* **12** Michael Laffan, 'Labour must wait: Ireland's conservative revolution' in Patrick J. Corish (ed.), *Radicals, rebels and establishments* (Belfast, 1985), p. 203. **13** *The manifesto of Sinn Féin as prepared for circulation for the general election of December, 1918* by the Sinn Féin Standing Committee in Macardle, *The Irish republic*, pp 919–20. **14** Report of the Twenty-Fourth Annual Meeting of the ITUC&LP, Aug. 1918: Wm O'Brien, chairman's address, pp 8–10. **15** Ibid.

but, as Laffan states, Labour was restrained by a number of fears, such as 'alienating not only the northern unionist workers, but also the Catholic majority of the population'.[16] Labour's supporters were trade-union workers, so their concerns were economic rather than political. There was also the problem of the Great War, as many who had enlisted hailed from working-class backgrounds. This difficulty was highlighted in Labour's support for and commemoration of those who died in both the Great War and the Easter Rising.

Labour also protested 'strongly' against the government, which refused 'to recognise the large demands on Irish Trades Unions' because of unemployment due to the destruction of businesses and premises during the Easter Rising, and a lack of compensation to 'capitalists for losses arising out of the same crisis'. This appealed to the working class rather than to separatist ideology, and it was no less of a complaint than that which might have been made by industrial unionists.[17] Sinn Féin, on the other hand, laid claim to the Easter Rising, petitioned for prisoner political status and endorsed rebel prisoners as candidates (see p. 80). The 1920 local-government elections energized Labour Party candidates and past doubts about Sinn Féin's rebel agenda were erased largely because of their 1918 election win.

Politics of the past were used in electoral propaganda to afford authenticity, lend credence to arguments, or proffer examples of failure in order to suggest that new methods were more viable. All parties relied on historic arguments and allied themselves with historic figures to makes these points. Political oratory was the main forum for engendering these associations. Speeches were made in front of crowds, and crowd reaction could be instantly measured. Therefore, if historical content was ineffective or drew a weak reaction, it would have been swiftly abandoned.

THE GREAT WAR

The content of Great War propaganda has been intricately researched by other scholars and therefore requires no great interpretation in this work.[18] However, as was seen in the previous chapter in the use of methods of propaganda, the influence of Great War propaganda on electoral propaganda was immense and therefore analysis is essential. The by-elections played out in the final years of the Great War, and the war's end instigated the general election. One of the main themes was Ireland's place within the British empire. Propaganda by the IPP and the Unionist Party during the Great War to encourage enlistment constantly appealed on the grounds of loyalty to the empire. Redmond had made imperial arguments

---

16 Laffan, 'Labour must wait', p. 207. **17** Report of the Twenty-Third Annual Meeting of the ITUC&LP, Aug. 1917, p. 54. **18** For a more in-depth analysis of Great War propaganda see, for example, P.M. Taylor, *Munitions of the mind: war propaganda from the ancient world to the nuclear age* (Manchester, 1990), pp 176–97; Lasswell, *Propaganda techniques*; Welch, *Propaganda and total war*. See also Mark Tierney, Paul Bowen and David Fitzpatrick, 'Recruiting posters' in David Fitzpatrick (ed.), *Ireland and the First World War* (Dublin, 1986), pp 47–8; and Novick, *Conceiving revolutions*.

for home rule for many years and he sustained this view throughout the war years, particularly during the home rule crisis. On the eve of Britain's entry into the war Redmond argued that because of Volunteer support the outcome would 'be good not merely for the Empire, but good for the future welfare and integrity of the Irish nation'.[19] Like Parnell, he believed that Irish nationhood was compatible with the link with Britain.[20] The prolongation of the war resulted in the continued suspension of home rule. News of war casualties and high death tolls, the fallout from the Easter Rising and the failure of the Irish Convention ultimately negated any attempt to promote a good relationship between Ireland and the empire.

Imperial rhetoric was entrenched in unionist propaganda during the war and continued throughout both general-election campaigns. Arguments insisted that the British empire embodied civilization and therefore 'in all future legislation the democracy of Ulster is to march on hand in hand with the democracy of Great Britain'. During the 1918 general election unionist voters were reminded that 'they took up arms to retain their citizenship in a United Kingdom and an Empire which had proved itself in the war the greatest asset of civilization and freedom that the world had ever seen', and that when war broke out 'their duty was to march their men into the camp of the empire'.[21] In rousing warlike passions for electoral purposes Carson urged voters to remember that 'wherever we met our enemies we could beat them'. The moral justification for winning at the polls was to remember the 'work and sacrifice' of the 'brave men' and 'those at home who mourned because they would never again look upon the faces of the brave men who had done so much for us'.[22] To reinforce Ulster's rightful position within the empire comparisons were made between Ulster's contributions to the war effort and the southern provinces' by assertions that out of a population of 386,947 in Belfast, over 46,000 volunteers enlisted in 'the fighting forces of the Crown during the war'. The 'proud record' of the '80,000 Ulstermen' who enlisted demonstrated allegiance to the empire, and voters were urged to 'keep Ulster in the empire by voting unionist' (plate 11).[23]

This appeal to imperial union was tempered by southern unionists during the 1920 local-government elections. The 1918 general election had resulted in a Sinn Féin majority, and the few unionist candidates in the south became more concerned with holding seats on urban and rural councils. Issues like housing and taxation became the focal arguments. Nationalists (Sinn Féin and constitutional) also honed in on these issues, as did other smaller parties, such as Municipal Reform. The war and empire slipped into the shade, but anti-home rule sentiment remained to the fore and the unionist William Jellett referred to it as 'worse than a farce'.[24]

19 HC, PD, vol. 65, cc 1828–9; Thomas Hennessy, *Dividing Ireland: World War I and partition* (London, 1998), pp 46–7.   **20** Pauric Travers, 'Reading between the lines: the political speeches of Charles Stewart Parnell', *Studia Hibernica*, 31 (2000/1), 243–56.   **21** *AC*, 23 Nov. 1918.   **22** *IT*, 15 Nov. 1918.   **23** PRONI, UUC Papers, D1327/20/4/142: *Ulster's claim on Britain: a proud record*.   **24** *IT*, 22 May 1920. .

Election propaganda began to emulate war propaganda by providing arguments on rights and wrongs to create a sense of justice or injustice for or against a political entity. While Sinn Féin busily accused the IPP of misguiding the youth of Ireland into war enlistment, the IPP (and unionist) counter-accusation was that Sinn Féin were 'friends of Germany'.[25] During the Longford South by-election they were charged with receiving £5,000 for their election campaigns from Germany, along with slurs of obtaining 'German gold'.[26] The *Longford Leader* scathingly remarked that they were 'entitled to ask who is paying the large sums they [Sinn Féin elections] will cost'.[27] The aim was to connect Sinn Féin with a widely perceived undesirable other (Germany) to dissuade voters. Substance for this form of propaganda was provided by comments like those of Griffith, who claimed 'I am not pro-German. But Germany is the enemy of England and England is my enemy. You may draw your own conclusions.' De Valera asserted that 'England and Ireland are in a state of war. While we are in a state of war, England's enemies must be Ireland's friends.'[28] Similarly, during the Clare East by-election, when de Valera stated that if Germany offered help to Ireland he would tell them 'it is to your advantage as well as to our interest, and certainly we'll combine'.[29] Yet, he denied accusations that Sinn Féin were 'the friends of Germany', and argued that the IPP had 'thrown themselves over to the English to be completely devoured'.[30] Blame by association sustained ethical denunciations for all parties.

Atrocity stories were, as Philip M. Taylor notes, a 'time-honoured technique of war propagandists'. Depicting Germany as a bloated 'Prussian Ogre' or 'Beastly Hun' brought home to civilians and potential recruits alike the terrifying consequences of defeat.[31] Germany was portrayed as the instigator, letting loose the dogs of war upon peace-loving nations, so moral condemnation was stacked against it. Sinn Féin emulated this in election propaganda to cast Britain as offender and place it in the role of the enemy that had to be demonized. They used IPP pro-war discourse and substituted 'Germany' for 'Britain' to fortify this opinion. In a poster for the Tipperary East candidate Pierce McCann, 'Irishmen!' were asked if they were going to elect a representative that 'murdered Padraig Pearse', 'that kidnapped hundreds of your brothers', that 'batoned and bayonetted 10,000 men and women of your own flesh and blood' and 'which has reviled your race in the four corners of the world'.[32]

Allied countries portrayed the German kaiser as a devil in spiked helmet, and depicted German soldiers as murderers and rapists (particularly of nurses and nuns). Sinn Féin did not go quite so far in their criticism of IPP members in election literature. However, in a poster for the Clare East by-election Patrick Lynch was portrayed as a pixie/elf-like creature with pointed ears (plate 12). In Victorian literature elves or pixies usually appeared in illustrations as tiny men with pointed

25 Novick, *Conceiving revolution*, p. 58. **26** *RH*, 5 May 1917. **27** *LL*, 28 Apr. 1917. **28** TCD, JD, MS 6741/446: *Liberty Digest*, 2 Feb. 1918. **29** *CC*, 30 June 1917. **30** *IT*, 29 Jan. 1917. **31** Taylor, *Munitions of the mind*, pp 179–80. **32** NLI, William O'Brien Papers, LOP 116/83: *Irishmen!*

ears. Their origin dates back earlier, but in the late 1800s people would have understood them as a mischievous or malicious diminutive woodland humanoid.[33] They
were sinister characters and were often described as ill-clothed or naked. In the
Sinn Féin poster, Lynch sits naked atop a tree branch in a woodland setting, and
hooked to a sign overhead is his lawyer's wig. He holds a candle enclosed in a glass
case with the words 'sham convention' (in reference to the Irish Convention proposed by Lloyd George). To the right of Lynch is the image of the maiden Erin,
but she is shackled by 'taxation' and 'foreign rule'. Within the beams of a sunburst
radiating out from a central disk is the word 'freedom'. In terms of imagery the
sunburst was a symbol of revolutionary ideology, and was often depicted either
emerging from behind a cloud or from just below the horizon. Freedom was portrayed as being almost achievable, and in visual propaganda the accompanying
words provided the clues as to its attainment. In this poster voting for de Valera
and his idea of appealing to the peace conference was the way to bring Ireland
along the 'road to freedom'.

Atrocity stories attracted attention in election propaganda, and unionists were
equally aware of their impact in creating alarm. The purpose was to stimulate voters into a desired action. To dismiss promises made by the IPP on home rule,
and particularly on Sinn Féin's republican aspirations, a text-laden unionist poster
titled *Sinn Fein 'Guarantees'. 'Safeguards' for Ulster* in fact repudiated any beliefs
in 'guarantees' or 'safeguards' (plate 13). It repeated the past IPP condemnation
that 'the whole policy and practice of Sinn Féin … is madness in its wildest and
most violent form', forewarning unionist readers of the potential dangers of a Sinn
Féin-led government in Ulster. The 'madness of Easter week, 1916' was emphasized, and a list of acts of atrocity and violent language perpetuated by Sinn Féin,
and de Valera particularly, was used to sway voters to turn away from the 'orgy
of violence and outrage from North Longford to East Tyrone'. For example, this
poster highlighted de Valera's comments against unionists at Ballaghadareen 28
July 1917, which maintained that 'Ulster must be coerced if she stands in the way';
and at Cootehill (Cavan) on 2 September 1917, when he stated that 'If you (Ulster)
continue to be Britain's garrison we will … kick you out'; and his previously mentioned South Armagh comments, deciding that they 'must, if necessary, blast it
[unionists] out of their path'.

The IPP employed aggressive attacks during election campaigns against Sinn
Féin acts of atrocity. Broadside posters with large black type that claimed clerical endorsement condemned Easter week. One such poster refers to Sinn Féin
as the 'physical farce' party or the party of 'violence & intimidation' (see plate
14). A subtitle refers to them as the 'tar and chalk' party to condemn Sinn Féin

---

33 Andrew Lang's *The Princess Nobody: a tale of Fairyland* (London, 1884) based on an existing
series of illustrations by Richard Doyle in *Fairyland* (London, 1869); Anne E. Duggan, Donald Haase
and Helen Callow (eds), *Folktales and fairy tales: traditions and texts from around the world*, 2nd ed.
(Westport, CT, 2016), p. 1082.

supporters for lighting tar barrels to celebrate the release of prisoners or election victories. (The *Kerry News* reported that after the release of prisoners 'hundreds of the inhabitants … singing rebel songs' lit several 'tar barrels and bonfires'.) The reference to chalk may have referred to its use in marking enemy targets, although this was not reported on until 1921, when constables Kelly and Hetherington were killed at Ballisodare after they were followed on the train from the midlands. When the train reached Sligo it was noticed that the carriage in which they travelled bore a peculiar chalk mark.[34]

There was an assumption that 'black propaganda' or 'hate propaganda' was nearly all deliberate lies devised by political parties to foster support and endorse ideologies (or by journalists or the state in the case of Great War propaganda).[35] Good atrocity propaganda, however, held either a modicum of truth or was based on truth and designed to motivate a fighting spirit, to instil a sense of fear of defeat, and to halt cruel or brutal acts by encouraging the selection of an alternative. In this Sinn Féin excelled. They began circulating atrocity stories or 'acts of aggression' during the by-elections and continued to publish these throughout the election campaigns. In June 1920 pamphlets were disseminated to journalists at home and abroad to 'influence public opinion'.[36] Large quantities were distributed through the Sinn Féin organization in Ireland, and 'large quantities' were sent to 'our friends in America' and to Sean T. O'Kelly and George Gavan Duffy in Paris.[37]

Atrocity stories, however, were merely one element of a much broader narrative of war propaganda. Another was the effect on Ireland by the threat of conscription.

CONSCRIPTION

Ireland was exempt from conscription when the Military Service Act was passed in Britain in 1916, but rumours of it being extended to Ireland abounded, creating concern that fed into nationalist election propaganda in 1917 and 1918. The *Roscommon Herald* remarked in early 1917 that 'young men who feared conscription were abroad night and day in noisy gangs'.[38] Alarmed by the possibility that conscription might be extended to Ireland, IPP supporters and candidates began to emphasize voluntary enlistment and condemned any form of a draft throughout the by-elections. For instance, in a speech in Boyle, Councillor Doherty (a potentenial IPP candidate for Roscommon North) stated 'his denunciations of conscription', which were loudly cheered.[39]

Count Plunkett and the independent candidate Jasper Tully vocally and emphatically condemned conscription during the Roscommon North by-election. Tully

---

34 *II*, 19 June 1917 and 23 Apr. 1921; *SCh*, 23 June 1917 or *Kerry News*, 22 June 1917.   35 John Horne and Alan Kramer, *German atrocities, 1914: a history of denial* (New Haven, CT, 2001); Jowett and O'Donnell, *Propaganda and persuasion*, pp 16–22.   36 UCDA, Desmond FitzGerald, P80/14(6): report of propaganda department, June 1920.   37 Ibid., P80/14(7).   38 *RH*, 10 Feb. 1917.   39 Ibid., 6 Jan. 1917.

accused Redmond of supporting conscription because of his statement that the IPP 'would vote for Conscription in Ireland if it was proved necessary'. Redmond had made this remark in the Commons in December 1915, but had added the caveat that he was 'not convinced that the compulsion of any class of people in this country is necessary to the ending of the war'.[40] Regardless of Redmond's caveat, his statement was used in election literature to promote Sinn Féin's Joseph McGuinness: 'Redmond pledged himself to the English Government to enforce Conscription in Ireland if the English Government "proved" to him it was necessary. Will you vote for Redmond's candidate or for Joseph McGuinness – the man in Jail for Ireland?'[41]

Battle lines were drawn to attract voter recognition for being the party that prevented conscription. The IPP claimed it was their 'strenuous opposition' that 'STOPPED Conscription in Ireland' (see plate 15). Sinn Féin argued that it had been the actions of Easter week. Laurence Ginnell contended that it was the 'Volunteers who prevented Conscription … and it was the events of Easter Week which made it impossible for the English to ever hope to enforce conscription in Ireland now'.[42] In a spirited rebuttal of Sinn Féin's claim, James Farrell declared:

> The fire-eating rebels tells us only for Easter Week they'd all be conscripted … and if you are mad enough to swallow this harum scarum indigestible mess of pottage called Sinn Féin you're bound soon after to have a very sick stomach and jolly well serve you right.[43]

The IPP's attempted hardline stance on conscription became utterly undermined when Lloyd George extended the military service bill in 1918 and introduced conscription for Ireland. This he did to raise a further 555,000 men for the war effort, of which 150,000 were expected to come from Ireland, to counteract the German spring offensive, which was launched on 21 March 1918 at the Battle of St Quentin. The IPP sought to limit political damage by withdrawing in protest from parliament and combining with Sinn Féin, the Roman Catholic bishops and priests, trade unions and some Protestant groups to oppose conscription. Their outrage was largely due to the fact that the implementation of home rule had been linked in a 'dual policy' of enacting the military service bill.[44] Dillon, keenly aware of the potential injury to the IPP if conscription was extended, had stated to O'Connor that 'if conscription comes on in October or November, there will be no room for the Constitutional Movement in this country'.[45] However, by walking out of the commons, IPP MPs emulated abstentionism and placed themselves on a parallel path to separatism, so voter uncertainty and confusion increased. Dillon forfeited command and turned public attention towards Sinn Féin.

40 HC, PD, vol. 77, cc 223–4, 21 Dec. 1915: John Redmond.   **41** *RH*, 14 Apr. 1917.   **42** *CC*, 30 June 1917.   **43** *LL*, 5 May 1917.   **44** Ward, 'Lloyd George and the 1918 Irish conscription crisis', 107–29.   **45** TCD, JD, 6742/516: John Dillon to T.P. O'Connor, 22 Aug. 1918.

With the combination of Redmond's death in March 1918 and the failure of the Irish Convention a month later voter confidence in the IPP plummeted.[46] Conscription now placed the party, which had been in the vanguard of wartime recruitment and the war effort, in condmenation of government policy. Yet recruitment posters and advertisements with IPP candidates' names still bedecked towns, villages, railway stations, shopfront windows and newspapers. As Fitzpatrick stated, recruits rushed to enlist, but not to the army – to Sinn Féin and the Irish Volunteers. However, as mentioned, once the threat of conscription passed, many ceased to be members.[47]

Sinn Féin propaganda in the Tullamore, King's County (Offaly) by-election exploited the conscription crisis to convert voters. Furthermore, their candidate, Patrick McCartan, ran unopposed because, according to Dan McCarthy

> we made the question of conscription one of the chief issues in our election speeches. We spoke rather strongly on the matter and advised the people at large that for every conscript that would be taken three policemen should be shot; that it was better to die at home than fight for a country that had kept us in subjection. In this way we worked up great enthusiasm. The people flocked to our side and the result was that our opponents failed to put up a candidate.[48]

The effective influence of the ubiquitous and persistent Sinn Féin anti-conscription propaganda was emphasized by Dillon, who remarked to O'Connor in September 1918 that 'with conscription in force and a general election in November – I do not think we could win ten seats'; and, he added, 'we have no adequate machinery to meet and deal with this devilish propaganda. I am doing my best to construct some machinery but it is very uphill work.'[49]

Sinn Féin won the anti-conscription propaganda battle with their strident claims that they alone stood between 'you and the death of your sons and brothers in France'. A vote for Sinn Féin, they claimed, would 'Kill Conscription!' (see plate 16). The IPP were accused of being 'recruiting sergeants' for the British army, an accusation that lingered in the war's aftermath.[50] As McConnel points out, it became incorporated as one of the dominant narratives of the Irish Revolution after 1922.[51] The arrival of IPP candidates at election meetings, whose last appearance was on recruiting platforms, was compared against Sinn Féin enthusiasts who had been only recently released from British internment camps. Public support for the IPP eroded.

46 Alan O'Day, *Irish home rule, 1862–1921: attempt to implement home rule, 1914–1918* (Manchester, 1998), pp 283–5; Joseph P. Finnan, *John Redmond and Irish unity, 1912–1918* (Syracuse, NY, 2004), p. 224; and Hennessey, *Dividing Ireland*, p. 220. **47** Fitzpatrick, *Politics and Irish life*, p. 127. **48** BMH WS 722: Dan McCarthy. **49** TCD, JD, 6742/536: letter from Dillon to O'Connor, 25 Sept. 1918. **50** John S. Ellis, 'The degenerate and the martyr: nationalist propaganda and the contestation of Irishness, 1914–1918', *Eire-Ireland*, 25 (2000–1), 26. **51** McConnel, p. 297.

In contrast to nationalist media, unconditional support for conscription was upheld by unionist publications and leaders. The *Irish Times* stated that 'the whole Unionist population of Ireland will accept conscription'. Protestant archbishops felt that 'Ireland's sons' had been 'omitted from the call' when conscription had been applied to England and Scotland, and that this 'would have been readily obeyed two years ago'.[52] Carson maintained that conscription shared the burden evenly, and that it was the only way to make every man take his fair share in the elementary duties and privileges of British citizenship. In a general election speech he referred to his efforts to include Ireland in conscription in 1916, and said that Ulster had been 'besmirched because they had allowed themselves to be dragged at the heels of the Nationalist Party in the South and West'.[53]

Unionist election propaganda regularly referred to Ireland's contribution to the war effort, and particularly Ulster's contribution. An election poster highlighted that the Ulster Unionist Party had urged the government 'to apply the Military Service Act impartially to all parts of Ireland', and claimed that 'the Protestant Churches in Ulster; the Corporation of Belfast; the Ulster County, Rural, and District Councils; the Loyal Orange Institution; and the other various Unionist Parliamentary bodies' had passed resolutions 'calling upon the Government to apply the Military Service Act to the whole of Ireland'. Constitutional national-ists were accused of blocking the way, while the Belfast workers' war record was 'unique in several respects', with the 'shipbuilding yards' holding 'three world's records made during the war'.[54] A handbill (see plate 11) listed Ulster's contri-butions to the war effort. For instance, Ulster had gained twenty-three Victoria Crosses, it had forty-two battalions of infantry (as against thirty-seven battalions for the rest of Ireland), it had contributed over £1,000,000 to war charities and it had supplied 95 per cent of all aeroplane cloth.[55]

During the 1920 local-government elections, a small number of unionist candi-dates also ran as ex-soldiers, and their key issues were the provision of housing and employment (see pp 191–6). Ex-soldiers had their concerns diminished under the weight of aspirations for an impending change in the governance of Ireland, and party principles. Promises were made that their bravery would be remembered, such as that made by Major Bryan Cooper, who proclaimed that Ireland would 'not easily forget [their] deeds'; but, ultimately they became lost in the complexi-ties of domestic war and partition.[56] In reality only unionists gave recognition to the practical concerns and interests of ex-soldiers in election pledges. The opin-ions and influence of ex-servicemen should have reverberated louder in post-war politics because more Irishmen fought in the Great War than in 1916, the War of Independence and the Civil War combined. On the eve of the creation of the Free State and the cessation of British rule in southern Ireland, historical representation

52 *IT*, 18 Apr. 1918.   **53** *AC*, 23 Nov. 1918.   **54** PRONI, UUC Papers, D1327/20/4/142, U.C. 107: *Ulster and Great Britain*.   **55** Ibid., *Ulster's claim on Britain*.   **56** Bryan Cooper, *The 10th (Irish) Division in Gallipoli* (Dublin, 1993), p. 139.

and memory there discriminated in favour of revolutionary expression.[57] The armistice in November 1918 ended the threat of conscription, but the after-effects continued into the general election, and through to the local elections, albeit with reduced import and mention.

WOMEN ELECTORS

During the Great War, commercial propaganda targeted women and utilized women to persuade men. For example, commercial interests used the image of the Irish peasant female to encourage the purchase of hygiene or luxury products among the working classes, and the 'colleen' became an icon to create brand personality. The message was that using soap or shampoo would lead to 'a purified working class cleansed of polluting labour'.[58] Great War propaganda in Ireland portrayed the nation as female to encourage enlistment across the political divides. A case in point is the poster *Will you answer the call?*, where Ireland as a female was in the foreground with long auburn hair and arm resting upon a harp.[59] Her white dress and blue mantle was similar to that of Mary, and the crown represented either Mary's role in the kingdom of heaven or Ireland's position within the empire. Through the strings of the harp a gallant, bugle-playing Irish soldier was visible, and the musical notes at the top were the opening bars of 'The last post'; to the side was a small village beside a lake, with a group of houses and a church spire, depicting the threat to Belgium and perhaps to any Irish village if the Germans were not defeated. Mother Erin pointed upward to employ what Pauline Codd calls the 'pull' factors, such as patriotism or compassion for 'poor little Belgium'.[60] Throughout the years of the Great War, women in propaganda encouraged men to enlist. Mothers, wives and daughters endorsed the departure of men to defend their honour, as in the poster *Will you go or must I?*, which showed a peasant Irish woman wielding a rifle and needling her husband or male relative to war as she pointed towards a smouldering Belgium.[61] These consumer and wartime propaganda ideas of using women to coax or convince were appropriated by political parties to inspire voters to conceive of alternatives.

---

57 Jane Leonard, 'Lest we Forget' in Fitzpatrick (ed.), *Ireland and the First World War*, pp 59–67; and '"Facing the Finger of Scorn": veterans' memories of Ireland and the Great War' in M. Evans and K. Lunn (eds), *War and memory in the twentieth century* (Oxford, 1997), pp 59–72; John Horne and Edward Madigan (eds), *Towards commemoration: Ireland in war and revolution, 1912–1923* (Dublin, 2013); Dolan, *Commemorating the Irish Civil War.* 58 A. McClintock, *Imperial leather: race, gender and sexuality in the colonial contest* (NY, 1994), p. 211; PRONI, MiC 604/1, diary of Robert Brown; John Philip O'Connor, '"For a Colleen's complexion": soap and the politization of a brand personality, 1888–1916', *Journal of Historical Research in Marketing*, 6:1 (2014), 29–55. 59 TCD, Digital Collections, Digital No: PapyrusCase 55_011: 60 Pauline Codd, 'Recruiting and responses to the war in Wexford' in Fitzpatrick (ed.), *Ireland and the First World War*, pp 25–6. 61 TCD, Early Printed Books, Digital Collection, EPB Papyrus Case 55c (Digital No. 55_094): *Will you go or must I*; and EPB Papyrus Case 55c (Digital No. 55_096): *Have you any women folk worth defending*.

Sinn Féin appealed to women within their own movement, and skilfully seized upon the new franchise qualifications. Many of the Great War themes that exemplified the role of women as supporters of the war effort who encouraged enlistment and promoted freedom for the allied side were absorbed into the themes of Irish freedom in election campaigns. For instance, the pamphlet *An appeal to the women of Ireland* claimed that Ireland had been personified as female because 'in woman the ancient Gael saw the great glory of his race'. A chronicle of the 'valiant champions of the dispossessed race' such as Patrick Sarsfield, Wolfe Tone, Robert Emmet, John Mitchel, Charles Stewart Parnell and Padraig Pearse, 'the grateful voices of the dead', now cried out to the women of Ireland to 'stand by their tortured sister Rosaleen'. It was pointed out that women could 'save Ireland' if they voted in similar fashion to 'Mrs Pearse' in order that the 'ancient ideal' could be realized. This use of history and Gaelic culture was meant to entice women to 'vote with Sinn Féin' and encourage others to do so. If the lure of the ancient did not satisfy, then the politics of fear was applied, as 'the physical safety of the race depends upon our immediate freedom'. The promise of a dynamic future in politics in the line the 'womenfolk of the Gael shall have a high place in the Councils of a freed Gaelic nation' was the final attempt to attract women to the Sinn Féin side.[62]

However, where women candidates ran for Sinn Féin, much of the campaigning was conducted for women by women, while the men propped up male candidates. Hanna Sheehy Skeffington described Markievicz's constituency as 'the worst managed constituency in Dublin', and the activist Meg Connery remarked that 'the one woman they have thrown as a sop to the women of the country has her interest neglected'. Winifred Carney complained that 'the organization in Belfast could have been better – much better'.[63] Laffan points out that there appeared to have been a disconnect between the Sinn Féin leaders and the rank and file on the role of women members, with the latter being 'more conservative in this respect'.[64]

Unionists also emulated Great War themes and, like Sinn Féin, created propaganda directly aimed at women. Encouragements went out to women 'to endeavour to interest other women … to see that their votes are registered in the constituency in which they live'.[65] Failure to cast a vote was warned against because 'a very great responsibility will soon be placed upon us in the exercising of our vote'. To increase anxiety and alarm, a handbill cautioned unionist women to be wary of IPP and Sinn Féin candidates who were posing as unionists, because they 'are prepared to promise anything to catch our vote, and to support many schemes that are quite impracticable of fulfilment'.[66]

Urquhart maintains that a communication network had been formed among unionist women during wartime fundraising initiatives, and that this had important

62 NLI, Sinn Féin, IR 94109: *An appeal to the women of Ireland*; John Hutchinson, *The dynamics of cultural nationalism: the Gaelic Revival and the creation of the Irish nation state* (London, 1987).   **63** Marie Mullholland, *The politics and relationships of Kathleen Lynn* (Dublin, 2002), p. 63.   **64** Laffan, *The resurrection*, p. 202.   **65** Ibid.; UUC Papers, D1327/20/4/142U.C. 155: Poster, *Women electors – consider!*   **66** Ibid.

political implications in strengthening unionist solidarity.[67] Kinghan points out that female Orange Lodges became useful networking arenas, particularly when they were given representation on the UWUC in 1920.[68] Meetings to petition unionist women collectively were enabled by the formation of these organizations, and it was advised that female unionists' meetings 'should be addressed by the candidate and women speakers whenever possible'.[69]

Unionists, like Sinn Féin, encouraged women to become active politically as canvassers, lobbyists, and supervisors of electoral registers. Propaganda was specifically targeted at women, outlining their role and responsibilities not only as wives and mothers, but also in relation to church, home, country and empire. Hanna Sheehy Skeffington and Dockrell placed small advertisements in the *Irish Independent* that addressed 'Ladies and Gentlemen'. As mentioned in chapter 4, Carson again in 1921 called on unionist women to do their duty and return candidates in Ulster.

The Labour Party became attentive not only to the voting potential of women but also to the assistance that could be given by 'the great hosts of the new voters who have come upon the new register'. They acknowledged that 'our sisters' became enfranchised 'only as the result of many generations of great efforts, as noble sacrifices, as gallant battles as any in the history of these people'. Linking with past Irish freedom crusades, O'Brien endeavoured to elevate the revolutionary struggle to attain the vote for women with that of the 1916 Rising. O'Brien also called for room to be made for women voters 'in our political as well as in our industrial work, and in the new constitution of the [Trade Unions] Congress and Party'. The militant strategies of some of the suffrage movements that 'had compelled the extension to our women comrades the right to vote' mirrored those of the 'fighting elements' of the Labour Party, and it was claimed that 'the lesson' would 'not be lost'. P.T. Daly, in a letter to the trades councils that represented unions at local/regional level, was more practical, wanting to know how 'women voters can be organized and associated with our work as a Labour Party?'[70]

No attempt was made by the IPP to overturn its unyielding opposition to women's suffrage in propaganda for the 1918 general election. As already discussed in chapter 1, the turnout of women was high in 1918 and again in 1920. The *Freeman's Journal* in January 1920 claimed that in Londonderry '40 per cent' of the municipal voters were women 'who are even more enthusiastic in the fight than are the men'.[71] In Galway almost half of the poll was 'composed of women voters', and in Dublin, 'in some wards women greatly outnumbered the men'.[72] Devlin attempted to make amends by addressing both the 'Ladies and Gentlemen' of the Falls Division of Belfast, and by emphasizing his record of reform, particularly

67 Urquhart, *Women in Ulster politics*, pp 65–6. 68 Nancy Kinghan, *United we stood: the official history of the Ulster Women's Unionist Council, 1911–1974* (Belfast, 1975), p. 41. 69 PRONI, D1327/20/4/148: *Unionist Central Office parliamentary election manual*, 5th ed., Aug. 1921. 70 Report of Twenty-Fourth ITUC&LP annual conference, Aug. 1918. 71 *FJ*, 15 Jan. 1920. 72 Ibid., 19 Jan. 1920.

in the old-age pension, which was created to support Irishmen and Irishwomen 'in frugal comfort in their own homes'. Outstanding issues such as housing, he argued, could be settled 'for themselves quickly and satisfactorily' if Irishmen and Irishwomen had home rule.[73]

Sinn Féin had been the most successful in mobilizing women in 1918. Such was the industry of the female separatist supporter that one nationalist agent complained that he had got nothing to eat all day, while his wife and daughter had been busily carrying food to Sinn Féin agents.[74] By targeting propaganda at women voters, unionists and Sinn Féin may have gained the advantage on polling day. As previously pointed out, it is unknown exactly how women voted, but turnout suggests that the female vote contributed to the success of Sinn Féin and unionists (and Labour in 1920 and 1921) and led to IPP losses.

THE EASTER RISING

Built into the rhetoric of the 1917 Roscommon North by-election that influenced Sinn Féin's policies in future elections (as discussed in chapter 2) was the vivid connection between Count Plunkett and the Easter Rising. Plunkett's election literature drew an analogy between the Rising and the by-election, particularly in a poster *The west's awake*. This title echoed that of a Thomas Davis ballad, so viewers were reminded of the rebellious days of the Young Ireland movement, and an antique font and ochre-toned background reinforced connections with the past. Phrases such as 'strike a blow for our small nationality' and 'will North Roscommon loosen their bonds or get us gaolers over Irishmen' served as a reminder that Irishmen remained in British prisons because they had struck out for freedom.[75] While Sinn Féin received no mention in any of Plunkett's election literature, the testimonial that he was the 'father of the young patriot who gave is life' formed a bond with the Rising for which Sinn Féin had received blame.[76] An *Irish Times* correspondent claimed that Plunkett won Roscommon North because of his anti-conscription stand 'plus the appeal to the people's sentiments in connection with the rebellion of Easter Week'.[77] Plunkett himself maintained that the reason was that 'his son died a martyr for Ireland'.[78] Plunkett's success in the election demonstrated what could be achieved, and, as already discussed, this led to reorganization within Sinn Féin and a drive to contest many of the future by-elections of 1917–18.[79] Plunkett's abstentionist policy upheld the more moderate ideals of Griffith's Sinn Féin, but new and more radical characters began to broaden separatist ideologies which included an appeal to the Paris peace conference to attain recognition of an Irish republic. Plunkett's literature called on voters to cast

73 Ibid., 30 Nov. 1918.   74 *IT*, 23 Dec. 1918.   75 NLI, Ephemera Collection, EPH E239: *The west's awake*.   76 Ibid., William O'Brien, MS LOP 116/74–8: *Ireland over all* and *Why you should support Count Plunkett*.   77 *IT*, 8 Feb. 1917.   78 *RH*, 10 Feb. 1917.   79 Laffan, 'The unification of Sinn Féin in 1917', p. 359.

in his favour to guarantee a 'seat for Ireland at the peace conference'. By sending Irish representatives to the peace conference Éire could fill the vacant chair amid the leaders of major countries, who are attired in recognizable costume, and seated at the peace conference table (see plate 17).[80]

The Easter Rising prisoner candidate who became most successful in this era was de Valera, who had been nominated for Clare East in 1917 while still interned. He provides a good case study to illustrate the impact of the Rising on election propaganda, mainly because, as Frank Gallagher points out, his choice as Sinn Féin candidate was dictated by one thing only: '[T]he brother of the leader of the old movement was dead ... De Valera had a status nobody else had – he was the last surviving commandant of the Rising.'[81] Robert Brennan claimed that his reputation immediately soared based on the military prowess he displayed during the Rising.[82] Townshend accepts that de Valera's battalion in Boland's Mill during the Rising did not encounter 'much of a fight', but maintains that his experience was similar to that of all the Volunteer leaders, who were indecisive as they 'tried to grasp the real nature of the battle they had so often fought in their imaginations'.[83] To encourage voter support in the Clare East by-election, Ginnell in speeches at Ogonnelloe and Killaloe, Co. Clare had stated that 'Eamon de Valera represented Ireland; Mr Lynch represented England. Ed de Valera fought under the flag of Easter Week of which the present election contest was a continuation ...'[84]

Two days after being selected as candidate de Valera began campaigning and he immediately sought to sway opinion from 'blood sacrifice' in the pursuit of independence to success at the ballot box, stating that 'every vote you give now is as good as the crack of a rifle in proclaiming your desire for freedom'.[85] Just a few months earlier he had stated privately in a letter to Simon Donnelly, commander of C Company in Boland's Mill during the Rising, that 'nobody should think however that contesting elections is the policy which the men here would advocate if they had a say in the matter'.[86] Clearly de Valera was aware that a political avenue was not desired by all and that many were unsure at this early stage whether contesting elections was the best course of action. He now had to appease the more militant advocates of republicanism and sway them towards politics.

Having the devoutly Catholic Eoin MacNeill at his side in order not to alienate 'the all-important support of the clergy', de Valera opened his speech in Tulla, Co. Clare, stating that, 'he had only to ask those brave boys in Dublin to face danger, and they did not fail ... [O]ne hundred and twenty boys stood out against 40,000 British soldiers ... with courage in their hearts knowing they were fighting for Ireland'.[87] In Limerick he argued that Ireland 'did not want to be a subject nation, but to be as free as England, France or Germany'. In a letter to the editor of

---

80 *RH*, 13 Jan. 1917 and 28 Apr. 1917; NLI, William O'Brien Papers, LOP 116/74 and 72. 81 Gallagher, *The four glorious years*, p. 12. 82 Brennan, *Ireland standing firm*, p. 98. 83 Townshend, *Easter 1916*, pp 175 and 261. 84 Ibid. 85 *CC*, 14 July 1917. 86 UCDA, de Valera Papers, P150/529: de Valera to Simon Donnelly, 23 Apr. 1917. 87 *CC*, 30 June 1917.

the *Irish Independent*, David Dolger, the parish priest of Piercetown, Co. Wexford, quoted de Valera as saying that 'the people of this country must make every preparation to secure their independence, and be ready to strike at the critical moment and bide their own time'. This suggests violent undertones to de Valera's speeches, yet earlier that year in Scarriff, Co. Clare he had promoted the idea of appealing to the peace conference, although he also remarked that he did not rely solely on it, stating 'as sensible men they would do everything that sensible men should do to get it [independence] ... If they went before the peace conference it would be for complete and absolute separation from England ... They would be slaves if they asked for less than sovereign independence ...' He regularly maintained that he 'stood by the proclamation of the Irish republic in 1916'.[88] This synthesis of peaceful (appeal to the peace conference) and truculent (Easter week) rhetoric in de Valera's speeches continued throughout the by-election campaign, and the result was a landslide victory.

Easter week became the exemplar for Sinn Féin candidates and their supporters to award legitimacy to the bloodshed of the Rising, but they walked a tightrope of praising it and ennobling its rebels while seeking an electoral mandate to pursue political ends and international recognition of their claim for a republic.[89] De Valera gradually transformed the Rising rebels from belligerents into political martyrs. While interned in Lincoln Jail in 1918 he drafted a letter for the Sinn Féin Mansion House meeting, which was subsequently reported on in many newspapers, in which he praised the 'glorious dead' and contended that 'it is not a slave's status that Irish heroes have fought and died for', but rather 'the securing for their beloved country her rightful place in the family of nations.'[90] The salient points within de Valera's letter were espoused by Sinn Féin speakers during 1918; and the underlying message was not a resort to violence but to negotiation and representation at the peace conference.

The conclusion can be definitively drawn that the Easter Rising rebels who died in 1916 were held up as the intrepid instigators of the Sinn Féin resolve to attain a republic. The survivors, many of them now candidates, were not only the guardians of the physical fight for freedom but the political expression of 1916 and all historic battles in the pursuit of that freedom from British rule. It cannot be overstated that the connection with the Rising was a mainstay of Sinn Féin electoral propaganda throughout 1917 and 1918.

The same cannot be said of the 1920 local elections. The rebels of 1916 and the Rising itself received occasional mention, but the issues that affected townlands and rural areas became paramount and parochial issues came to the fore, such as housing, pensions and farming. What is unusual about 1920 electoral propaganda was the utter absence of any mention to or condemnation of the ongoing War

88 *II*, 3 and 26 Nov. 1917; *FJ*, 2 July 1917 and 19 Jan. 1919. 89 Diarmaid Ferriter, *Judging Dev: a reassessment of the life and legacy of Eamon de Valera* (Dublin, 2007), p. 13. 90 *Killarney Echo* and *South Kerry Chronicle* and *SCh*, 16 Nov. 1918.

of Independence by any party, or even any correlation between it and the Easter Rising by Sinn Féin. Violence and intimidation were mainstays of 1921 electoral propaganda but in 1920 only random reports of the occasional spill-over into violence attained some attention – and this violence did not involve clashes between nationalists and the British military.

During all the by-elections and the 1918 general election campaign the IPP continuously vilified Sinn Féin's Easter Rising rhetoric. Voters were asked if they favoured a party of 'physical violence' over a constitutional settlement. For instance, the IPP's Hugh Garrahan in Longford South asked voters at a meeting in Ardagh if they were going to 'support a party whose only policy was what would lead to violence and destruction' and asserted that the policy of Sinn Féin was 'physical violence'.[91] Monsignor O'Farrell in Longford argued that Sinn Féin's policy was 'fantastic and absurd' and that it only 'ended in a cul-de-sac – a blind alley, a new political museum of skeletons and specimens of past ages'.[92]

Ulster unionists, according to Buckland, viewed the Rising with a modicum of complacency. Others wrought humour from the nationalist attempt to physically overthrow the British. Adam Duffin, the old liberal unionist, likened the Rising to a 'comic opera founded on the Wolf [*sic*] Tone fiasco a hundred years ago' and acerbically hoped that the rebels had captured Birrell, the chief secretary.[93] Many saw the Rising as an act of predictable treachery and proof that nationalists were disloyal at heart, regardless of their wartime enlistment numbers. A unionist handbill demanded to know whether loyalists should trust to 'the "common sense" of those guilty of the madness of Easter Week 1916'.[94] Carson cried 'shame be upon them' as 'in the darkest days of our history the contribution of the South and West of Ireland to the Empire was a rebellion in which they shot our soldiers'.[95]

The rehabilitation of Sinn Féin as a respectable political entity, while still retaining its connection to the heroic martyrs of Easter week, was masterfully choreographed. Fine-tuning this message throughout 1918 by sharpening the abstentionist policy and wedding it to an appeal (whether attainable or not) for Ireland to be at the peace conference captured many voters. There were still hardliners within republicanism who were determined to remain vigilant and alert to continued revolt, but the electoral success in 1918 placed the balance in favour politics, albeit only for a short period of time.

HOME RULE, UNION AND ABSTENTION FROM WESTMINSTER

Building an argument for home rule years after it had been placed on the statute books was a hard task. Dillon's method was to fervidly denounce the alternative, asserting that 'it is in my opinion a sin and a crime to tell the Irish people that they

---

91 *LL*, 28 Apr. 1917. 92 Ibid., 5 May 1917. 93 PRONI, MIC 127/17: A. Duffin to D. Duffin, 25 Apr. 1916. Patrick Buckland, *Ulster unionism*, p. 105. 94 PRONI, D1327/20/4/142, U.C. 114: *Sinn Féin 'Guarantees' 'Safeguards' for Ulster*. 95 Ibid., 15 Nov. 1918.

can win an Irish republic ... [T]hey will bring bloodshed and ruin and disaster upon the people ...' His pugnacious condemnation of violence as against constitutionalism supports this, and he reduced Sinn Féin policies to absurdity by using phrases such as 'their silly language' and 'silly actions'. IPP leaders and candidates regularly turned attention to their successes by asking if the voters wanted to undo 'the work that we have done for the last 35 years'.[96]

The IPP had nailed their flag to the Liberal Party mast on the home rule issue, so denouncing the actions of the British government in 1918 opened the debate on the kind of politics they really embraced. The persistent call was 'let us have home rule', but very little was said on what was to be done if home rule was obtained. Like Redmond before him, there was little future vision in Dillon's speeches. Dillon leaned on Parnell and Davitt to argue that 'unless you go to Parliament and face the English in the House of Commons you would be walked over'. He cited Poland, Bohemia and the 'Jugo Slavs' as examples, maintaining that despite the division of their countries, they 'attended Parliament until they attained liberation'. In contrast, Sinn Féin's antipathy to imperialism was strong, and they often referred to the IPP as 'Imperialist candidates'.[97] The obscurity of the home rule parliament, what abstention from Westminster actually meant and the internecine nationalist quarrels between a future home rule government and a republican government nourished unionist propaganda.

Carson called attention to the fact that he had never known 'a greater confusion in Irish politics' in the nationalist arena because 'there are Sinn Feiners and there are Nationalists'. He pointed his audience to Dillon's past claim that 'neither now nor at any time has there been any difference in the policy as [great as] between the Constitutional Nationalists and the Sinn Féiners'. This may have been untrue, but the aim was to depict disarray within the IPP after the death of Redmond, which he stated was 'tumbling down into the morass of Sinn Féinism'.[98]

Through the voice of Carson unionists habitually used aggressive rhetoric to take their audience to more dramatic places by employing the politics of fear. Unionists incessantly maintained that the home rule bill would result in the loss of Ulster's prosperity and that home rule would be 'Rome rule'. Belligerent irredentism formed a core content of Carson's speeches, and he persistently claimed that the 'democracy of Ulster is to march on hand in hand with the democracy of Great Britain'. His legal mind quickly tangled and untangled oft-used nationalist phrases to provide a definitive unionist solution. In 1918 Carson asked of home rule, 'Self determination of whom and of what? Self-determination by whom and of what? Self-determination by the South and West of Ireland of the destinies of Ulster? Never!' He received cheers of approval. He was also quick to mock Sinn Féin's slogans and turn them Ulster's advantage: 'England's difficulties', he claimed, 'were never Ulster's opportunities'.[99] In December 1918, he emphasized

---

96 *II*, 18 Dec. 1917.   **97** See *II*, 13 Mar. 1918 for example, Darrel Figgis speech at Waterford.   **98** For an example see *IT*, 16 Nov. 1918.   **99** Ibid.

unionist beliefs, stating that 'their whole future, and the future of those who came after them, was bound up in a closer connection with the United Kingdom', and that 'they must go on with an offensive policy, demanding that they receive exactly the same treatment in every respect as was given to their brothers and sisters in England and Scotland'.[100]

In contrast to the IPP and unionists, for Sinn Féin, abstention from Westminster and appealing to the peace conference were the means by which Easter week ideals and party policy could gain recognition and strength. The IPP continuously ridiculed Sinn Féin's plan to abstain, stating that it would damage industry and employment opportunities. Emmet Dalton, in a letter to the *Clare Champion*, retaliated by stating that

> the Redmondites are claiming that their policy of attendance at Westminster is constitutional, and that the Sinn Fein policy of abstention is unconstitutional ... By what right and by virtue of what Act does the Irish Parliamentary Party go to Westminster? By virtue of that Act which was passed by perjury, bribery and fraud – the Act of Union.[101]

Concerns over abstention from Westminster and Sinn Féin's declaration of a republic were widespread among unionists for ideological and pragmatic reasons. Major Robert Lyon Moore, a unionist from Donegal East, stated that 'complete separation from Great Britain' constituted 'a constant menace to the peace, happiness and prosperity of Ireland'.[102] Daniel Wilson, unionist candidate for Down West, remarked that 'Ulster claims to remain an integral part of the United Kingdom, and refuses to become part of a Sinn Féin pro-German republic.'[103] Others were concerned that Ireland would become a republic 'without any protection from the British Navy'.[104] At a meeting with Professor Eoin MacNeill, the Sinn Féin candidate for Londonderry city, questions were put to him by discharged and demobilized soldiers who were anxious that a republic would threaten 'pensions, employment, housing, income tax' and so on – demonstrating that local issues continued to concern voters even though the loftier ideals took precedence among political parties.[105] While MacNeill repudiated these concerns, they perhaps explain why the IPP was more successful in Ulster among nationalist voters because they were advocating for the retention of a nationalist political voice at Westminster.

The Labour Party had declared in favour of self-determination and abstention from Westminster at the end of September 1918 because of 'the proved futility of Irish members attending British parliament during the war', and they stood behind Connolly's goal of a socialist republic. Unlike Sinn Féin however, there was an exit clause on abstention which stated that it was not binding for the Labour

100 Ibid., 11 Dec. 1918. 101 *CC*, 7 July 1917. 102 *Derry Journal*, 11 Dec. 1918. 103 *BNL*, 4 Dec. 1918. 104 *SCh*, 7 Dec. 1918. 105 *BNL*, 14 Dec. 1918.

Party and could be overturned by a special congress of delegates.[106] These parallels between the Labour Party and Sinn Féin caused concern. Boland warned the standing committee that if enough trade-union candidates intervened in the campaign they could deprive Sinn Féin of up to twenty seats (which suggests that abstaining voters might very well have cast in favour of the Labour Party had they contested).[107]

Convinced they had received a mandate from the Irish electorate in 1918 and confident of continued support from the Irish people, Sinn Féin created Dáil Éireann in Dublin in 1919. This unicameral legislature was established because of their abstentionist policy and it made manifest their electoral promises of 1918, but no mention was made of establishing a republic. On 21 January in the Round Room of the Mansion House twenty-seven new members met for the first time to act as the government of a notional Irish state (many others were in gaol). Amid mounting violence in areas of Ireland as antipathy against the British government increased, the *Irish Independent* reported that the new assembly was 'conducted with order and dignity'.[108] An internationalist and lofty air prevailed as a declaration of independence for Ireland as a nation, and an address to the free nations of the world were read out and 'adopted with enthusiasm'.[109] The intended audience was France and the peace conference, and an awareness of the importance of securing international recognition was affirmed. Present also to record the momentous event were foreign journalists. Béaslaí later recalled that the public gallery of the Mansion House was 'packed with spectators' and many of them were foreign pressmen.[110] The salute to Irish-Ireland was that all other proceedings were conducted in the Irish language, with no speeches in English.[111]

Continuity with the available and familiar British model of Westminster was simply accepted by Dáil Éireann.[112] MPs became TDs, and the democratic programme gave a nod to socialism (because of the Labour Party's election withdrawal) through addressing ownership of property, the right to education, social welfare services and equality. Most of the twenty-seven present were not of a socialist disposition and one of them later doubted 'whether a majority of the members would have voted for it, without amendment, had there been any immediate prospect of putting it into force'.[113]

Establishing Dáil Éireann was a propaganda coup, as newspapers country-wide reported on the first day's proceedings. Farrell's work *The founding of Dáil Éireann* gives a comprehensive account and critique of the first dáil, so this work will focus briefly on the propaganda behind the funding of this counter-government. Most of the finances raised from the dáil loan, created and issued by Collins, funded

---

106 NLI, Thomas Johnson Papers, MS 17,249: national executive circular. 107 SFSCM, 19 Sept. 1918 and 7 Oct. 1918. 108 *II*, 22 Jan. 1919; Gallagher, *Political parties in the Republic of Ireland* (Dublin, 1985), p. 3. 109 *II*, 22 Jan. 1919. 110 Ibid., 24 Jan. 1962. 111 Ibid., 22 Jan. 1919. 112 Brian Farrell, *The founding of Dáil Éireann: parliament and nation-building* (Dublin, 1973), pp xviii, 83. 113 Béaslaí, *Michael Collins*, p. 259.

the creation of Dáil Éireann departments. Research into the monies raised has been covered in chapter 3 and in works such as Carroll's *Money for Ireland*, which shows how the dáil financed its activities and how funds were used; and Mitchell's *Revolutionary government in Ireland*, which explains dáil finances, how the loan was raised and how Dublin Castle attempted to suppress it. There are many works and biographies on Michael Collins but one worth mentioning is Hart's work *Mick: the real Michael Collins*, which highlights the frustration faced by Collins in trying to motivate constituencies to promote the bond drive.[114]

Influenced by the success of the Great War bonds and the USA's Liberty bonds (see chapter 3), and the aggressive advertising campaigns behind both (see chapter 4), Collins set about doing similar in Ireland. According to T.P. O'Connor, the second Liberty bond raised half a billion dollars for the US government by October 1917.[115] Printed copies of a dáil loan prospectus and an application form were issued to the media, and Sinn Féin clubs began collecting subscriptions.[116] Cult heroes pervaded press advertisements to persuade people to buy bonds. For instance, one advert asked, 'Pearse gave all. Won't you give a little? Buy Dáil Éireann bonds today'; and Michael Collins' dáil bonds film used a symbolic table to denote Robert Emmet's martyrdom.[117]

Many of these prospectuses were swiftly seized by the police, and, as mentioned in chapter 4, some provincial newspapers were suppressed for publishing information on the dáil loan. Collins informed local committees that he was compelled 'to adopt some other means of advertising' because of the actions 'of the English authorities in preventing newspapers from advertising'. He also stated that 5,000 handbills could be supplied, 'but it would be better if you could have them printed locally'.[118] A 'grave reflection' was cast on those who voted for independence but were not prepared to give 'proof of their faith' by lodging funds into the coffers of the Irish republic. To motivate purchases, Collins wrote to Sinn Féin constituencies and detailed those who had gifted monies in bold typeface.[119] By investing in the new state, support was provided for Sinn Féin's solution to the hardships suffered under British rule. The idea of amassing money from ordinary people was not a new one as the Roman Catholic Church had successfully done similar for new building projects in the 1800s.

EVERYDAY ISSUES

Gallagher points out that the Irish electorate has 'a desire for representatives who will perform a brokerage role between themselves and a state machinery' mainly

---

114 Peter Hart, *Mick: the real Michael Collins* (London, 2005), pp 186–99.   115 TCD, JD, MSS 6730/183: letter from T.P. O'Connor to Joseph Devlin, 11 Nov. 1917.   116 BMH WS 1413: Tadhg Kennedy; NLI, Ephemera Collection, EPH F243: Dáil Éireann loan.   117 The table in the film was said to be the block upon which Emmet was executed in 1803. NLI, IR 300, p. 47: advertisements for Dáil Éireann Loan; Irish Film Institute Archive, *The Dáil Bonds* (1919).   118 Ibid., IR 300, p. 47.   119 Ibid., PB Papers, MS 33,912/14: handbill; NLI, ILB 300, p. 2.

because the state or government 'is often seen as remote and hostile and is viewed with suspicion'.[120] In this era the key motivators were the elevated ideologies of home rule, republic or unionism. However, the ability of local candidates to look after the needs of the constituency was still an important criterion for voters in the local-government elections. While it was not the primary concern for the national elections in 1918 and 1921, as election day approached a growing anxiety loomed about how parties and candidates would manage the everyday issues under their favoured form of governance. Political parties and candidates realized that it was tactically wiser to alter their propaganda approaches to address these issues in the drive to win seats. The content of propaganda messages had to be sharpened to include a future vision for managing the routine affairs of a state, and solutions had to satisfy voters on the safety and security of the ordinary within the remit of the loftier ideals. The distinguishing precepts of political parties fuelled the initial thrust of political campaigning, but a disquiet obviously stirred within voters' minds on the future of old-age pensions, farming, access to education and more equitable taxation.

The 1908 Old Age Pension Act had not been framed with Ireland in mind but was rather the outcome of a long political debate in Britain to alleviate the miseries of old age among the industrial workers of England. It did, however, save thousands from the indignities of poor relief in Ireland. The IPP had not sought pensions for the aged, and nor were they consulted beforehand on the act's implications for Ireland, but they claimed credit during the by-elections and the general election campaign. They also attempted to inculcate a sense of fiscal fear by asking who would protect the government pensions.[121] To unsettle the electorate about voting for the unknown, IPP candidates alleged that the pensions could cease if Ireland cut ties with the British exchequer. For instance, Chas Laverty, a solicitor and IPP supporter in south Monaghan, emphasized that the British exchequer would, if they were not monitored in parliament, cut down the old-age pension because there would be 'no one to speak a word for this county unless the Carsonite gang'.[122] In the Falls Division of Belfast, Devlin reminded voters that 'under the Old Age Pension Acts up to the present £20,000,000 [had] been paid to Irish men and Irish women … whereas formerly they had no refuge in their old age'. He maintained that it was he who had 'laboured unceasingly and successfully' to have this pension increased from 5s. to 7s. 6d. per week, and that he would continue to campaign until the pension was increased 'to 10s. a week in view of the increased cost of living'.[123]

Creating confidence in Sinn Féin's abstentionist ideals was crucial in alleviating voter uneasiness about an Irish government managing its own fiscal affairs

120 Gallagher, 'Candidate selection in Ireland: the impact of localism and the electoral system', *British Journal of Political Science*, 10:4 (9180), 489–503.   121 Borgonovo, 'Throwing discretion to the wind: the 1918 general election in Cork city' in Caoimhe Nic Dháibhéid and Colin Reid (eds), *From Parnell to Paisley: constitutional and revolutionary politics in modern Ireland* (Dublin, 2010), p. 88.   122 *AC*, 7 Dec. 1918.   123 *FJ*, 30 Nov. 1918.

and protecting pensions. Sinn Féin's immediate reaction was to incessantly voice indignant outrage against the IPP for trying to quell the possibility of increasing pensions for Ireland's aged. O'Flanagan, during the Cavan East campaign, angrily condemned the IPP for attempting to create a state of anxiety. In Longford South it was pointed out that Redmond had stated that pensioners should be allowed to receive no more than half a crown a week (2s. 6d. [£7]). Ginnell argued that the old-age pension 'should no more be reduced than Redmond's salary of £400 a year to £300'.[124] To protect pensions Sinn Féin repeated their plan to appeal to the peace conference to guarantee Ireland's independence and management of tax affairs. By condemning exorbitant nationalist and unionist spend in towns and cities they endeavoured to reveal that pension affordability was attainable under republican administration. MacNeill announced that Londonderry contributed 'over and above' what it was compelled to pay to the British empire. He calculated that £700,000 was contributed annually and that most of the cost went to 'maintaining a British army of occupation'. Ireland was paying 'about thirty-five million pounds' because of the 'extravagant cost of Irish administration', and therefore taxation and payments made Ireland 'one of the most profitable of the so-called possessions of the British Empire'. Separating the exchequers could allow Ireland fund welfare payments and sever 'the trade monopoly which made the Irish people deal with her [Britain] for everything they wanted and everything they had to sell'.[125] A Sinn Féin supporter in Cavan West argued that England could not be trusted because 'Irish farmers could get £5 more per head for their cattle than the English were paying'.[126]

Unionists upheld the idea that with continued control by the British exchequer no change would be effected in state payments. Craig pledged reforms in housing for Ulster, but in all else he allied himself to British concerns because Ireland 'was likely to go on as an integral part of the United Kingdom for many years to come'.[127] Augustine Birrell, chief secretary during the home rule negotiations, had pointed out that Irishmen received over £1 million more in benefits, mainly for old-age pensions and land purchase, than they paid in taxes. Unionists repeatedly pointed this out. In contradiction, the IPP – since the outset of the third home rule bill – maintained that the idea that 'the introduction of old age pensions had made it impossible for Ireland to pay her own way has not real evidence to support it'.

Voter interest in the future of pension payments should have received more attention than it did, given that one-third of government expenditure in Ireland was on old-age pensions.[128] In 1918 the Irish voter, and in turn the political candidates, mentioned but did not dwell on the financial intricacies of the old-age pension to any great degree. Whether this was because it was a difficult subject that required sophisticated fiscal knowledge, or whether the additional arguments made by Sinn Féin on Ireland's possible net taxation gain under independence

124 Maume, p. 193; John Macnicol, *The politics of retirement in Britain, 1908–1948* (Cambridge, 1998), pp 157–8. **125** *FH*, 16 Dec. 1919. **126** *AC*, 7 Dec. 1918. **127** *IT*, 29 Nov. 1918.

were partially accurate is difficult to determine. There were also other more press-
ing concerns now that the Great War had ended. The farming boom brought about
because of wartime demand for food and agricultural supplies had ended, and
returning soldiers required housing and employment.

The interruption in house building during the war, particularly in Ulster,
had created serious shortages. The *Irish Times* reported that there were no vacant
houses in Belfast, and that at least 2,000 new homes needed to be built immediately.[129] Fiery exchanges followed between unionists and nationalists in Ulster on
housing. In the early months of canvassing for the 1918 general election Captain
Charles Craig, at a meeting of the South Antrim Unionist Association, emphasized
the necessity for 'a thorough-going housing reform'.[130] For unionists, the needs of
demobilized soldiers and industrial workers took priority, and as Carson declared,
they were not going to wait until the prime minister sorted out the problems of
nationalist Ireland, for housing reform for Ulster.[131] Devlin, in the Falls Division
of Belfast, claimed he had always considered it his 'special duty to champion the
cause of the working classes of this great city', particularly in relation to securing
'better housing of the workers'. He announced that if re-elected he would continue
to support housing reform and other measures at Westminster.[132]

Housing concerns unsettled southern politicians also and injected debate and
passion into the 1920 local elections, and to a much lesser degree in 1921. A letter
to the *Limerick Leader* condemned 'the wretched housing of the working classes,
and the "scourge of profiteering"'. High rates were killing the building trade and
paralysing the investor. The solution proffered was to 'be our own landlords by
purchasing our own houses' to have 'a direct interest in keeping down the rates'.[133]
P.C. Cowan's *Report on Dublin Housing* estimated that there was a need for improved
housing for at least 41 per cent of Dublin city's population (135,700 persons or
29,500 families), ergo 16,500 new houses were needed, along with a 're-model' of
13,000 tenements.[134] The Irish Convention committee on housing calculated that
the existing shortage of houses for Irish county boroughs was 28,950, with the
shortage in Dublin being 16,500 and in Belfast, 7,500. For all Irish urban areas,
the committee stated that a total of 67,500 houses were needed at a cost of £400
per house, amounting to £27,000,000 [£784,557,900] in total. However, it was
expected that 50 per cent of the loan charges for building were to be borne by the
central government, and that the work was to be conducted by local authorities.

---

128 NLI, JR, MS 15,252/2: John Redmond on home rule bill finances; Patricia Jalland, 'Irish home
rule finance: a neglected dimension of the Irish question, 1910–1914' in O'Day, *Reactions to Irish
nationalism*, p. 304. See also McConnel, p. 237. 129 *IT*, 3 Jan. 1919, 26 Feb. 1919; *NW*, 24 Jan.
1918, 19 Mar. 1918, 2 Oct. 1918, 3 Jan. 1919; *FJ*, 19 Nov. 1917, 27 Dec. 1917. 130 *IT*, 29 Nov.
1918. 131 *FJ*, 16 Nov. 1918. 132 Ibid., 30 Nov. 1918. 133 *LkL*, 16 Jan. 1920. 134 P.C.
Cowan, *Report on Dublin housing* (Dublin, 1918). For further information see: M. Daly, *Dublin the
deposed capital: a social and economic history* (Cork, 1985); Dublin Housing Inquiry, *Report of inquiry
into the housing conditions of the working classes in the city of Dublin* (London, 1914); Jacinta Prunty,
Dublin slums, 1800–1925: a study in urban geography (Dublin, 1998).

Devlin disagreed with the Belfast figures, believing them 'not very creditable'. However, he said he preferred to get the building work done rather than engage in controversy.[135] He stated that 400,000 houses at £400 per house were required in England and Ireland and this would cost the exchequer £160,000,000; and that the provision of adequate housing would reduce the spread of tuberculosis.[136] Labour candidates in 1920 pushed for the launch of a housing scheme without delay, and the application of a £2 10*s.* per hour minimum wage.[137] In the South Dublin Parliamentary Division, the unionist Thomas Robinson highlighted that 'there were other questions of great importance' and those were the 'housing of the working classes and of the poor'. Dockrell in Rathmines promised to ensure the 'betterment of the working classes'.[138]

Ireland differed from Britain in that there had been no physical destruction of property or infrastructure due to war (aside from the 1916 Rising), and therefore progress on forming a plan of reconstruction was slow. Poor housing was not just a city problem, yet little remedy was offered or debated by rural candidates across all parties during the 1918 elections. A correspondent from the *Irish Times* on 19 December 1918 provided vivid descriptions of the deprived conditions in an unnamed 'valley away from the lure of city, town and village' on general election day. He recalled cycling 'through three villages within a radius of nine miles', and described how his heart 'grew heavy' when he observed 'the streets of wretched dwellings, which were neither rain-proof nor wind-proof nor smoke-proof, nor smell-proof from the dung hills and stagnant cesspools.' There was 'not one word appear[ing] in the [election] addresses about this crying evil of habitation, fit only for swine, and not for human beings'.[139]

Whether unionist or nationalist, labour or independent the solution propagated was to amend taxation, particularly taxation on farming, because Ireland relied heavily on agricultural industry with three-fourths of the population living by farming. Most Irish farmers now owned their own land, with some eleven million acres having been purchased as a result of the Land Acts of the late nineteenth and early twentieth century. The IPP claimed it was they who had 'enabled the farmers to purchase their own holdings, secured decent cottages for the labourers to live in'.[140] Dillon, at a meeting in Adavoyle in Armagh South, stated that

> the Irish farmers were to-day the owners of their own land, and if they were to-day beginning to prosper, as compared with the position they occupied thirty years ago, who had they to thank? Not the baby politicians of to-day, but the men who had helped to take the yoke off their necks.[141]

Sinn Féin retaliated by criticizing the IPP for levying high taxes on farmers. 'Farmers! Your turn now' was the mantra. War taxation was the real future threat,

---

135 *FJ*, 30 Nov. 1918.   136 Ibid.; see NAI, 1911 census, B1 Form.   137 *KP*, 10 Jan. 1920.   138 *IT*, 23 Nov. 1918.   139 Ibid., 19 Dec. 1918.   140 *Dundalk Democrat*, 26 Jan. 1918.   141 *IT*, 28 Jan. 1918.

Sinn Féin argued, because 'very little of the colossal expenditure of this war has been recovered in taxation', and it was only a matter of time before 'crushing taxation' would be implemented.[142] Sinn Féin promised Irish farmers they would only pay £4 a year 'at the most' in taxation rather than the average of £10 an Irish farmer was paying at the time. Again, the Paris peace conference was to provide the answer because Sinn Féin was to 'have behind them England's claim that the "small nations" of the world should be free'. A claim before the 'Powers of Europe' could allow for a constitution to be drafted that would provide relief from a 'ruinous burden of taxation'.[143] They warned that after the war this burden of taxation on Ireland would increase from the IPP's agreed annual budget on taxation of £23,000,000 to £27,000,000 a year, and on top of that Ireland's contribution to the empire would not be less than £14,500,000, and the cost of government £12,500,000. They calculated that the tax per head of the population would be £6 7s., whereas an Irish Republic could reduce these taxes because the projected cost of government would not be more than £10,000,000 or £13,000,000 – even if a further small amount was imposed for internal development, encouragement of industries, farming operations, and subsiding export trade. This would bring the total to £3 per head of the population.[144]

Sinn Féin compared Ireland's taxation figures with a number of other small nations. Denmark, with a population of 2,464,770 and a revenue of £4,250,000, paid £1 13s. in tax per head. Greece, with a population of 2,133,806 and a revenue of £3,000,000, paid £1 3s. 6d. per head. Ireland, on the other hand, with a population of 4,376,600 and a revenue of 9,490,500, paid £2 3s. 3d. per head. Resolution, therefore, lay in complete withdrawal from Westminster and the creation of an Irish Council, which would use taxpayers' money to reform education through a National Education Fund, support industry and create co-operative banks.[145] It was pointed out that the IPP were ill-equipped to wage the battle against over-taxation because they collected a salary of £400 per year from the British exchequer. Those in receipt of government pay could not fight a land tax, as 'they must think of their own pockets first'.[146] No mention was made at this stage of future salaries for Sinn Féin ministers.

Sinn Féin's Cosgrave waged his propaganda war in Kilkenny on the issue of taxation. Now and again he alluded to the fact that Sinn Féin stood in the election in similar style to Owen Roe O'Neill and the old Irish during the days of the Confederation of Kilkenny, but he quickly moved on from these historic references

---

142 Britain in 1918 still had to finance the Allies to the sum of £405,000,000. HC, PD, vol. 105, cc 869–73, 23 Apr. 1918: Herbert Samuels; Victor Thuronyi, *Comparative tax law* (NY, 2003), pp 26–7. Further details on Irish taxation are available from Irish Statute Book, Finance Act 1918, 6 & 7 Geo. 5, c. 24; 16 & 17 Vict., c. 34; 32 & 33 Vict., c. 67 (Office of the Attorney General), http://www.irish-statutebook.ie/eli/1918/act/15.   **143** NLI, LOP 116, William O'Brien Papers: *Farmers! Your turn now.*   **144** TCD, Samuels Collection, Box 3 (Digital No. Samuels Box 3-040): *Hard facts.*   **145** Peter Brown, TCD, Personal Collection: pamphlet *Sinn Féin in tabloid form.*   **146** UCDA, P150/550, Eamon de Valera Papers: *Threatening a land tax.*

to hone in on Ireland's over-taxation, declining population and increases in 'lunacy' and 'pauperism'. Blame was squarely laid on weak IPP policies which had led to 'this degradation' and lack of industry in a city where previously a blanket industry had employed 4,000 hands when the population was 25,000. By voting Sinn Féin 'a soul' would 'come back to Ireland'.[147] The IPP's Magennis counter-campaigned to highlight that Cosgrave was an outsider and a Dublin Corporation man by releasing a poster titled *Kilkenny for a Kilkennyman*. Kilkenny city proved that it was not all high idealism that secured victory for Sinn Féin, and that localism still played a role in promoting candidates. This small city cast their votes for Cosgrave giving him a majority of 380.[148]

Unionists unreservedly slammed charges of over-taxation, and any notion that a separate legislature was the solution. According to a 1918 handbill they claimed that Ireland under the union had been permitted to have a separate exchequer until 1817 and during this time the national debt had risen from £28,000,000 to £147,000,000. An end to this insolvency only arrived when the exchequers were united and Great Britain accepted responsibility for that vast sum. They argued that the theory of over-taxation in Ireland had only been invented to justify financial proposals for the home rule bills, starting with Gladstone's bill in 1886.[149]

Ulster, it was pointed out, had invested in the linen trade, which amounted to over £20,000,000, and it now had the largest linen-manufacturing concern in the world. Ulster also had the largest firm of linen thread, twine and netting manufacturers, the largest rope and cable works, the largest shipbuilding firm and the largest single tobacco works in the world. Ulster had the largest single flax spinning industry in the world and the largest linen export trade too. Unionists, therefore, summoned the electorate to 'stand by Ulster' and not support nationalists.[150] Unionists warned that if Ireland separated from the British empire and obtained a republic then there would be 'no markets for cattle and produce'. In Cork city Daniel Williams argued that a vote for Sinn Féin would disfranchise Cork's important commercial and industrial centre, so the 'strong protecting arm of Great Britain' was necessary.[151]

These same arguments were made in the 1921 election in the north, but Sinn Féin could rely only on tax gains to be collected in Ireland free from the British exchequer because they had failed to gain entry to the peace conference talks. Using 'huge posters', they presented financial arguments against the establishment of the Belfast parliament – although an article reported that both Sinn Féin and nationalist parties disclaimed responsibility for the posters and rumours abounded that they had been erected by businessmen alarmed at the prospect of partition.[152] Unionists and nationalists pitched their campaigns from their stances on partition. Based on votes cast in Ulster in 1918 and again in 1921 these everyday issues

---

147 *II*, 20 July 1917. **148** *IT*, 8 Aug. 1917 and *II*, 13 Aug. 1917. **149** PRONI, UUC Papers, D1327/20/4/142, U.C. 111: *Has Ireland been robbed by England?* **150** Ibid., U.C. 132: *The two Irelands, facts not fiction!* **151** *IT*, 10 Dec. 1918. **152** *II*, 20 May 1921.

prompted voters to remain with parties that supported the link with the British exchequer.

PARTITION

A serious impediment to the home rule bill was propagated in the commons on 11 June 1912 when the Cornish Liberal MP Thomas Agar-Robartes proposed a motion for the exclusion of the four heavily Protestant counties of Antrim, Down, Armagh and Londonderry. His motion was defeated by sixty-nine votes, but it paved the way for a debate on exclusion and partition that continued until the formation of the Free State and beyond.[153] This section does not intend an analysis of exclusion or partition, but will briefly examine how political parties represented their views. The 1921 general election became known as the 'partition election' because this was the predominant and practically exclusive theme of electioneering propaganda by unionists and nationalists. No elections in this era altered standpoints on partition held since the introduction of home rule, and similar messages were regularly repeated, but in 1921 they became the focal point of practically all propaganda.

A few caveats at the outset on the position of unionists generally and southern unionists particularly are important. Unionist propaganda created the impression that Ulster was firmly Protestant and unionist. As Buckland states, this was not the case, as only the county borough of Belfast and the counties Antrim, Armagh, Down and Londonderry (including the city) had Protestant majorities.[154] Furthermore, unionism was not a homogenous entity across the island because the position and concerns of southern unionists differed. As O'Connor remarked in a letter to Dillon in 1916, there was a 'strong protest of the Southern Unionists against any form of partition' that made the solution of temporary exclusion 'more difficult than ever'.[155]

Letters to the editor in the *Irish Times* in 1918 divulge the variances in southern unionist opinion. For instance, one criticized the 'entire policy' of a speech delivered by Carson to the UUC in 1918 because it was 'limited to Ulster' with 'no thought of the southern Unionists'. Trepidation was voiced about whether 'Ulster, on the question of home rule, has definitely adopted the policy of "ourselves alone" or whether in the future ... Ulster Unionists will stand shoulder to shoulder with their Unionist brethren in the South'.[156] A week or so later another letter disputed that Carson had 'abandoned us'. The 'difficulty within southern unionism', it was claimed, was that they 'were scattered and unable to affect any real stand or return any member to represent them in parliament'. Carson's maxim,

153 HC, PD, vol. 39, c. 771–4; Stewart, *The Ulster crisis*, 58–9; O'Day, *Irish home rule*, p. 251; and *IT*, 19 June 1912 and 18 Oct. 1913; Denis Gwynn, *The history of Partition* (Dublin, 1950).   154 Buckland, *Ulster unionism*, p. 93.   155 TCD, JD, MS 6741/355: T.P. O'Connor to John Dillon, 31 Oct. 1916.   156 *IT*, 16 Nov. 1918.

it was argued, was to 'concentrate on Ulster, knowing that practical work for the Union' would be achieved and therefore 'Home Rule Ireland would never accept a division of the island'. Carson was likened to a bridge player holding an immensely strong hand, whereas southern unionists held weak and scattered cards. With the Sinn Féin opponent on one side and nationalists on the other, a strong hand was necessary to gain a 'grand slam' to culminate in 'closer connection with Great Britain and her Colonies'.[157]

Population counts and tax contribution comparisons between Ulster and the other three provinces were published in 1918 (and 1921) to highlight that Ulster paid more and that Ulster was 35 per cent more valuable than Munster and Connacht combined. Ulster unionists regarded partition as permanent because of the commercial, industrial and social position of Belfast and Ulster, compared with the rest of Ireland.[158] Carson in 1918 regularly maintained that 'we in Ulster will never give up our freedom and our liberty for any man'. This point was restated by southern unionists, who proclaimed (often in their *Irish Independent* advertisements) that the 'true interests of this country are best served by a steadfast maintenance for the whole of Ireland of the Legislative Union'. Hanna Sheehy Skeffington voiced opposition to partition, which 'would be disastrous to the interests of Southern Unionists'. Dockrell bound Ireland's interests with those of Great Britain and would 'oppose any measure involving the partition of Ireland'.[159] As the municipal elections played out in January 1920 rank-and-file unionists had been satisfied to wait for action and direction from Carson. They were now prepared to accept a parliament for the six counties in preference to the more dangerous nine counties because the loss of seats through local friction could have given the home rule party a majority.[160]

Unnerved and flustered by unionist intransigence, IPP leaders believed it 'fatal' if the government proposed or Ireland assented to 'any policy of partition'. County option had been favoured by the IPP in the hopes of retaining Fermanagh and Tyrone and a hope ('great hope') of holding 'some if not all of the other counties'.[161] A disconcerted O'Connor wrote to Redmond in 1917 wavering on his translation of Carson's opinion. First Carson 'blocks the way' to a home rule settlement and then Carson was 'anxious for settlement' but worried over 'losing all hold over his followers in Ulster'. O'Connor feared that home rule might amount to only 'separate treatment' by Britain rather that the ability 'to establish a unitary parliament' for all Ireland.[162] By May 1917 O'Connor had given up hope and claimed that 'all my efforts for county option had been futile'. Blame was cast on the state of Irish feeling and the bishop's manifesto.[163]

157 Ibid., 29 Nov. 1918: letter was signed 'A woman voter'. **158** PRONI, UUC Papers, D1327/20/4/142, U.C. 120: *Ulster and Ireland*. **159** *II*, 30 Nov. 1918. **160** PRONI, Carson Papers, D1507/A/32/1: letter to Carson, 3 Jan. 1920. **161** NLI, Redmond Papers, MS 15,215/2/B: O'Connor to Devlin, 16 Feb. 1917. **162** Ibid., O'Connor to Redmond, 29 Mar. 1917. **163** Ibid., 10 May 1917.

Conventional constitutional nationalists were not so forlorn in 1918, and without hesitation declared their opposition to the partition of Ireland. Denis J. Cogan, nationalist candidate for Wicklow East, affirmed that the answer for nationalists was 'an Irish Parliament with full powers of legislation in all Irish affairs, subject to the religious safeguards contained in the 1914 Act, and giving generous additional representation to our unionist fellow-countrymen'. Patrick Shorthall of Clontarf claimed similar, stating that he was 'convinced' that the principle of self-determination should apply, and he favoured an 'undivided Ireland by constitutional means'.[164] Special arrangements for unionist Ulster for these two candidates had not broadened beyond what had been on offer in 1914 – an offer that remained unacceptable to unionists, who perceived themselves as British, with, as Fitzpatrick points out, 'all the spiritual and material privileges that this conferred'.[165]

'No partition' and 'a united Ireland' were the two constants in Sinn Féin propaganda. In Sligo, Sinn Féin condemned the IPP record of consent to 'the dissection of Ireland'.[166] Yet the by-elections of 1918 brought two losses for Sinn Féin in Ulster constituencies (Armagh South and Tyrone East), demonstrating political impotence in this province. Only three seats were won by Sinn Féin in the 1918 general election in the area of Ulster that went on to become Northern Ireland. Ulster unionists were perceived as the enemy by Sinn Féin, as pawns of English conservatism, necessary only to maintain Britain's power base in Ireland. Only a few in Sinn Féin, such as Erskine Childers, grasped the obligation of providing unionists with a place of power in an independent Ireland.

The Labour Party similarly disparaged the 'claim of a minority government to pass [the] … partition of Ireland'. O'Brien asserted that organized labour in Ireland 'was absolutely agreed that there should be no such thing as partition. The trades unions of the north were determined they would not be separated from the trades unions of the south'.[167] Internally, to members at annual congress meetings, leaders reinforced the Labour Party position on partition by stating that 'Irish Trade Unionists would not have partition'.[168]

Initially all sides had held the opinion that Ireland must remain undivided. Sinn Féin believed abstention from Westminster was the 'only logical and long-called-for protest against the Union'. The IPP utterly rejected Sinn Féin policy and attempted to mollify both unionists and nationalists in Ulster by insisting on a policy of consent. By 1920, despite wars, uprisings, and conventions, the IPP had no fresh solutions to the Ulster problem.

Having attained 53 per cent of the seats in Ulster in the 1918 general election, and with the triumph of the coalition government in Britain, unionists were in a stronger position to demand their six counties. Nationalists were no longer able

---

164 *II*, 30 Nov. 1918.   **165** Fitzpatrick, *The two Irelands*, p. 25.   **166** TCD, JD, MS 6742: speech by Revd P.J. O'Grady addressing Sinn Féin meeting in Sligo in 1918.   **167** NLI, William O'Brien Papers, MS 8506/12: notebook and MS 15,653/3: *Dublin Evening Mail*, 19 Apr. 1917.   **168** ITUC&LP, Twenty-Third Annual Report.

to proclaim Ulster's homogeneity; Britain was utterly dependent on the votes of the Conservative and Unionist Party; and Sinn Féin retreated from Westminster, allowing unionist domination. Partition was now patently unavoidable – but its form was still unclear. By 1919 an Irish committee was appointed by the British government, headed by the Conservative MP Walter Long, which recommended two home rule parliaments, with a supervisory Council of Ireland to direct all sides eventually towards reunion of the whole island. In February 1920 Lloyd George ultimately reversed the committee's recommendations and appeased unionists by granting them their six-county Northern Ireland, which was ratified by the Government of Ireland Act.[169]

Sinn Féin's anti-partition message throughout the electoral campaigns was melded with demands for a united Ireland and abstention from Westminster. This unyielding approach was similar (but contrary to) the unionist partition demand and gave little leeway for compromise. The IPP protested against partition, but began to concede that temporary exclusion from home rule might be necessary. Nationalists on each side berated the other during 1918, with the result that the fight against partition was waged between them rather than by projecting a unified approach against unionist and British interests. John Cosgrove, a volunteer from South Armagh, remarked that after the election there, the feelings between Sinn Féin and the Hibernian organization became more antagonistic, and 'the intense hatred by Hibernians to everything republican did a lot of harm from 1918 up to the truce and it paved the way for the later partitioning of the country'.[170]

Voter interest in the topic can be deduced to some extent by the vehemence of the approach to partition by political candidates. Voters could also observe political and military attitudes and tactics in Ulster during riots and conflict, but much of the action – or lack of action – in the six counties of Ulster, particularly during the War of Independence, came after the 1918 election and had a greater impact in 1921. The coalition government had caved because of pressure from James Craig by September 1920, particularly in regard to supplementing reserve forces and establishing the Specials.[171] Voter confidence in the IPP's placatory approach swayed to favour Sinn Féin's doggedness on partition and other issues. For many Catholics in Ulster the IPP had wavered, which demonstrated incompetence in the face of the unionist challenge – but the fear of outright partition had convinced many to stand by Devlin in 1918.

Temporary solutions suggested by IPP candidates at least bought time, and may have protected Devlin's seat. It was the passionate counsel of the unionist leaders before, during and after the general election on the partitioning of Ulster from a southern home rule parliament that ensured victory in their stronghold constituencies in 1918. The local-government election results caused alarm for northern unionists, who believed that the PR-STV system hurt their efforts to

169 Hopkinson, *Irish War of Independence*, p. 153.   170 BMH WS 605: John Cosgrove.
171 Hopkinson, *Irish War of Independence*, pp 153–64.

attain majorities on county and rural district councils. As mentioned in chapter 1, this led unionists in Northern Ireland to abolish the PR-STV system in 1929 in favour of the previous first-past-the-post system.

The Government of Ireland Act 1920 had established parliaments in Dublin and Belfast with identical powers and limitations, and a Council of Ireland to consult on matters of common interest. When the bill was being debated at Westminster, the Ulster unionists – now led by Craig since Carson had become a lord of appeal – were not overly enthusiastic about a separate northern parliament for the six counties, but saw it as far preferable to any type of all-Ireland system.[172] Therefore, the 1921 election campaign opened and the electorate was encouraged to vote for all unionist candidates and to put questions of a controversial character into the background. Sinn Féin and nationalists were condemned because their candidates had to accept the principle of self-determination and, if elected, were to abstain from the northern parliament. Craig claimed that if the nationalist 'programme was anti-partition', he would 'go the whole way with them … if it meant that there was no partition between Great Britain and our own beloved country'.[173]

The IUA maintained that there was no 'practical half-way house between the policy of the Union, with equal partnership in the United Kingdom, and complete independence for Ireland'. They pointed out that any form of home rule was impossible without partition, and that as a permanent settlement this was disastrous to the best interests of the country as a whole. Southern unionists were called upon not to recede from this position because 'Ireland has now become the battleground of anti-Imperial activities'. Like their Ulster counterparts, they were called on to 'stand firm by their principles … in the interest of their country and the Empire'.[174] The Labour Party was condemned for allying with Sinn Féin and for aspiring to a 'Workers' Republic' that aimed 'at applying to Ireland the principles of Bolshevik Russia'. Concern was expressed that granting independence to Ireland, either openly or in the guise of dominion home rule, would lead to civil war between Ulster and the rest of Ireland. The decision taken was that it was 'futile' for unionists to take part in the elections in southern Ireland because 'the logic of events will demonstrate the impossibility of any form of government in southern Ireland short of either absolute independence or the Legislative Union'. Ultimately they upheld the policy of the union, being convinced that this was the only means for assuring good government 'and the highest interest of the country and of the Empire be promoted'.[175]

Published in the *Irish Times* in January 1921 was a proposal during a meeting of the members of the Allen, Larkin and O'Brien branch of the UIL in Great Britain that called for 'the recognized leaders of the League to take such action as they deem necessary to bring about the reconciliation of the forces of Sinn Féin and the UIL'. They called on leaders to take a 'bold step' and make a determined effort to bring about an amicable settlement of the Irish question. The letter suggested a

172 *IT*, 27 Jan. and 5 Feb. 1921.   173 Ibid., 4 May 1921.   174 Ibid.   175 Ibid., 18 Feb. 1921.

'fusion of the Irish Nationalist forces', and that a policy be proposed to the country because 'there is no longer any chance of Sinn Féin being able to fulfil their promise'.[176] Copies of this resolution were sent to Dillon, O'Connor, Devlin, F.L. Crilly (the UIL organizer for Scotland), J. O'Derrick and the members of the executive in Scotland. This resolution prompted an expressive reply from Dillon, which was published in the same newspaper, where he outlined his reasons for IPP inaction in the 1921 election.

Dillon maintained that he had not been able to discern any possibility of uniting those who still believed in the programme and policy of Parnell and the old party with the forces of Sinn Féin unless Sinn Féin's programme and methods were adopted. This he could 'not consent to do' and he outlined a number of reasons why the time was not yet ripe for the IPP to take any action. He maintained that the 1918 general election results had been accepted by the Irish race all over the world as giving a national mandate to the leaders of Sinn Féin to attempt to carry out their policy. Therefore, 'the most patriotic course' he could undertake was to 'maintain silence' and abstain from 'any attempt to interfere in public affairs' until he saw 'some substantial evidence of a change of mind on the part of the Irish people'. As yet, he acknowledged, this revolution had not yet come and there was 'no evidence of a change of feeling sufficiently widespread' for him to issue a policy on behalf of the IPP for the 1921 election.

Dillon's second reason for abstention was the 'policy pursued by the Government in Ireland during the last three years', which he saw as being 'carefully designed for the purpose of destroying the old Parnellite Party' and promoting 'disorder and strife'. This, he believed 'drove the nationalists in Ireland into the camp of the republicans'. With martial law in force and 'Tudor's men, the Black-and-Tans, and the Ulster Specials let loose on the country, civil rights, including freedom of meeting and freedom of the press, abrogated, and civil war in its worst form raging in Ireland', it was impossible to launch a policy. Any attempt by the IPP to contest the election could be perceived as supporting the government and interpreted by Sinn Féin as an attack that would lead to further conflict. The only option open to the IPP as far as he was concerned was to wait for 'both sides to draw their dogs and return to civilized methods'. His overarching belief was that 'the present phrensy ... will pass away' and at that point 'Ireland will realise that the only rational policy for them is that of the Parnellite Party'. Therefore, Dillon's plan was to wait for 'political sanity' to return and for new British statesmen who 'will arise' to realise that any settlement will need 'the acceptance and approval of the majority of the people of Ireland'.[177]

For entirely different reasons, both the IPP and the IUA decided not to contest the 1921 southern election, leaving Sinn Féin the scope to appoint candidates without contest. Despite some nationalist successes in the 1920 local elections, Dillon's wait-and-see attitude in 1921 sounded the death knell for the IPP. The

176 Ibid., 1 Feb. 1921. **177** Ibid.

only obstacle now in the way of Sinn Féin having complete control was the Labour Party, but they too chose to abstain from this election. Having considered whether they should nominate candidates, the Labour Party decided against taking part in the elections because of Lloyd George 'announcing war to the knife', an 'obvious design of the British Prime Minister to divide the democratic forces'. The Labour Party encouraged the electorate to vote 'only for those candidates who stand for the ownership and government of Ireland by the people of Ireland', which really was a command to support the Sinn Féin candidates and disregard any other nationalist opposition. This may also have influenced Dillon's decision not to field nationalist candidates. The key aim of the Labour Party was to discourage active participation in the election in order to 'keep its political party independent' and to reinforce this they discouraged members from aligning with other parties, 'no matter how friendly'.[178]

The Labour Party's vacillation and hesitancy to contest in 1918 and 1921, coupled with IPP despondency, and southern unionist inaction by 1921 resulted in there being no contest for parliamentary seats in southern Ireland. Partition – an issue that affected the whole island – could, therefore, only be fought in the northern constituencies between two stalwart, disparate rivals. Unionists were convinced that Sinn Féin posed a threat to peace because their hands were 'reeking with the blood of the innocent victims of their inhuman butcheries'. The southern War of Independence fuelled unionist propaganda about nationalist violence. Sinn Féin and the IRA's militant wing, preoccupied with war in the south, had failed to make a priority of Ulster and failed to protect Catholic minority interests, particularly in Belfast. Sinn Féin, however, was successful in some of the northern constituencies with Catholic majorities, so military activities affected voters, but other influences (intimidation and personation, for instance) also had an impact on electoral outcomes.[179]

Loyalists in Belfast's South Division maintained that securing an effective working majority in the new parliament was essential because 'it is your country, your home, your interests, and your liberties which are at stake'.[180] Craig called on nationalist Ireland to 'swallow the Partition Act', and cautioned that 'failure to secure an effective working majority would mean immediate submergement in a Dublin Parliament'. The fate of the six counties, he maintained, hung in the balance.[181] Unionists honed in on economic difficulties and the negative effects on industry without a unionist-led parliament in the north. Sinn Féin and nationalists generally were accused of inexperience, and unionists argued that if their opponents were elected to parliament the government would not function effectively. Their aim, the *Belfast Telegraph* claimed, was to get control of the north's wealth and industries.[182] Robert John McKeown, candidate for North Belfast, put forward

178 ILP&TUC, Twenty-Seventh Annual Meeting, 1, 2, 3, 4 Aug. 1921   179 NLI, PB, MS 33,912/9 Sinn Féin Ard Fheis, Nov. 1921.   180 *BNL*, 10 May 1921.   181 *II*, 10 May and *IT*, 26 Apr. 1921.   182 *Belfast Telegraph*, 18 May 1921.

the familiar unionist claim, asserting that nationalists hoped 'to bring about the fall of that great Empire on which the sun never sets. They in Ulster were holding the fort, as they had always held it, and would continue to hold it.'[183]

All nationalists contested seats on an anti-partition ticket and if elected agreed to abstain from the northern parliament. Sinn Féin invested considerable resources in their campaign, even though they suffered from government restrictions and their voters, from intimidation. Advertisements were placed in fifty northern newspapers to argue against partition, but their propaganda and message failed to impress voters and, as the results in chapter 1 show, the Ulster Unionist Party secured 40 seats and 68.5 per cent of the popular vote. The 1921 election was a battle between two divergent ideals – nationalism and unionism – with all sides seeking legitimacy for their identities. The end result demonstrated that there was no unity in the six counties and huge sections perceived their identity as remaining part of the United Kingdom. Despite nationalist opposition and Sinn Féin's claims for Ireland's unity, the polarizing views within the six counties could not be overcome, even when de Valera came to power in the Free State.

183 *NW*, 14 May 1921.

Conclusion

The concentrated campaign of Ulster unionists and the pervasive Sinn Féin propaganda and electioneering tactics brought victory. Influenced by the often wilful and sometimes witty print propaganda, widespread free editorial in newspapers and a plethora of electoral ephemera, many nationalist voters converted to separatism and steadfast loyalists were convinced to remain devoted to the union.

The sharp and crafty propaganda campaigns of 1917 and 1918 particularly, but not exclusively, introduced not only entrenched political ideals but earnest combat between two clearly opposing paradigms of nationalism, and between nationalism and deep-rooted unionist beliefs. Sinn Féin deposed the IPP in the 1918 general election in the three southern provinces of Ireland because it had converted the majority into believing in its abstentionist policy and assurance of an appeal to the post-war peace conference whether attainable or not. For a party with abstention and separatism as its central theme and posters that proclaimed 'Sinn Féin will have no English supremacy', Sinn Féin made the most effective use of British elections to promote its aims.[1]

The prolongation of the war, the failure of the 1916 home rule talks and the Irish Convention all contributed to the downfall of the IPP. However, in 1918 the party laboured under stale rhetoric that harked back to Land Acts, home rule crusades and Great War mobilization. The only novelty was spirited vilification of Sinn Féin ideals, but, in turning attention to the past, the IPP opened the way for critical opposition propaganda. This came in verbal assaults for collecting the £400 salary, and for corruption and jobbery.

Unionists reaffirmed their 1912 opposition to home rule and in 1918 and 1921 the same messages were reassigned to electoral campaigns that became augmented and energized by Great War rhetoric. Sinn Féin and Ulster unionists funded and managed numerous propaganda methods to persuade voters, convincing the electorate to support their brand of politics. By inducing followers to empower elite decision-making or acquiesce to peer pressure, both political entities presented systems that were credible to supporters. Unlike the tightly controlled system of Parnell's IPP that heavily influenced the choice of parliamentary candidates and propaganda, Redmond and Dillon's decentralized approach failed them in many constituencies in 1917 and 1918, and some constituencies reverted to the localism of the 1800s. The only system available for candidate selection and electioneering was through the local organizations, but disorganized and unsupportive leadership left UIL branches adrift.

Within Sinn Féin, disparate energies fused in 1917 to give voice to a separatist ideology, and as the by-elections played out Sinn Féin became a political party. In the following months, this party became the 'inheritors of the spirit of the leaders

---

1 PRONI, MIC14111: Sinn Féin election poster titled *Who owns Ireland?* See ch. 5.

of Easter week ... with the proclamation as their political guide', or the medium through which the message was interpreted practically.[2] By receiving the blame from newspapers and the government for initiating the Easter Rising, Sinn Féin gained recognition as a minor movement. The leaders set out to create a political order where the Rising formed the backdrop for change, but the way forward was the formation of a new state that removed the Rising's ruins.[3]

Participation in the Rising provided a rationale for political perpetuation, and its electoral appeal had been learned through success in Roscommon North in February 1917. Going forward, Rising conspirators were appointed as candidates under the guise of local selection. Rebels were transformed into politicians, but managing and in control at all levels was the standing committee, and ultimately de Valera. Separatists had started out disorganized and leaderless – and this had not changed after the Rising as several groups still operated which were often mutually antagonistic – but the appointment of de Valera as president and the subsequent organization of the party meant centralized control fostered a disciplined approach to electioneering and propaganda. Sinn Féin transformed into a professional and robust organization with roots at the local level.[4] Its shamelessly centralized control facilitated authority over the selection of specific candidates for each constituency, funding and the propaganda methods and messages; and, in an era of change it is bizarre they got away with it. The appointment of a standing committee and the localized *cumainn* allowed for the claim that the party was embodying the will of the people, so it could justify the process.

The Labour Party in the southern provinces had to employ more flexibility to allow an array of trade unions to voice opinions and submit candidates, and in 1918 their brand of politics was dimmed by the light of Sinn Féin's success. While elements of their policies were embodied in the first dáil's democratic programme, this was, as Laffan points out, mostly a 'thank you' gesture by Sinn Féin.[5] The *Irish Times* reported that the programme's 'astonishing vagueness allowed it to be associated with any one of a hundred brands of modern Socialism, or with them all'.[6] Unskilled and factory workers made political progress in 1920 but they were not nominated in sufficient numbers to effect dramatic change. Ulster labour, on the other hand, was more organized, and official Labour Unionist and the Belfast Labour Party, which was predominantly unionist, gained thirteen of the sixty Belfast Corporation seats in January 1920.[7]

The fundraising methods of unionists, the IPP, Sinn Féin and the Labour Party differed considerably. Unionists generated substantial finance from home-grown benefactors by targeting allies in Ulster's industrial sector. Funding was also sensibly generated through their associations and clubs, and prudently dispersed by offering tactically wise advice to avoid overspending. They had learned from

2 BMH WS 492: John McCoy. **3** John Coakley, 'The foundations of statehood' in Coakley and Gallagher, *Politics in the Republic of Ireland*, pp 21–3. **4** Laffan, 'The unification of Sinn Féin in 1917', 353–79. **5** Ibid., 'In the shadow', p. 38. **6** *IT*, 22 Jan. 1919. **7** See ch. 1, table 1.7.

past anti-home rule propaganda campaigns to target finances towards functional
propaganda methods, even in the generation of those funds. Sinn Féin and the
IPP also collected from their own clubs and leagues, and from Irish contributors
in general (and the Labour Party from trade unions), but for the IPP the donations arrived piecemeal and in low amounts, and by 1921 they were practically
non-existent. With only a very limited industrial sector in the southern provinces
to pursue, both nationalist parties were compelled to influence more affluent Irish
supporters abroad, mainly in the USA. The IPP's connections in America had
fallen by the wayside, forcing O'Connor to travel far and wide for success. The
rehashing of a hackneyed home rule narrative versus the fresh, focused and more
radical Sinn Féin programme turned his tour into a difficult battle for favour and
funds.[8] The IPP's privation reduced its control over propaganda spend and diminished its electoral influence. Dillon, like Redmond before him, viewed propaganda
as a poor relation to statecraft and he had lost touch with provincial organizations.
The disorganized treatment of propaganda funding and the decline of the party's
localized structures were strong causes of electoral defeat in 1918. Sinn Féin, on
the other hand, applied itself vigorously to fundraising campaigns and utilized its
Volunteer supporters to the maximum (particularly during the by-elections). The
development of a rational and reasonably controlled fiscal agenda, and the internal regulation of the dispersal of funds, played a pivotal role in securing election
success.

    While no particular method of propaganda guaranteed success, most political
parties and candidates in this era favoured public speeches at open-air meetings.
Along with the canvass, this afforded personal contact with electors. In speeches
and in print, Sinn Féin and unionists excelled in using a consistent messages, slogans, themes and images, such as 'Vote for de Valera, a felon of our land' and 'Keep
Ulster in the empire by voting unionist'. Those who could supplement speeches
with newspaper editorial and advertisements (to reach wider audiences, and those
distanced from speakers at open-air meetings), canvassing and clever displays of
symbols and colour created presence. Novel approaches to propaganda, such as the
re-registering of cars to 'I.R. 1916' by Sinn Féin, furthered electoral success, as did
using vehicles decorated with party colours.[9]

    The creation of unique identities by Sinn Féin and unionists, propagated
through the use of symbols, iconography and ballads, reinforced a constant stream
of propaganda messages. Ulster unionists generated public awareness with their
union flags and banners of red, white and blue. In similar style, but with contrary
messages and symbols, tricolour banners and flags abundantly decorated towns
and villages to promote Sinn Féin during election campaigns. Scant use of IPP
symbols in many constituencies reduced that party's visual presence, and so rein-
forcing the home rule argument with imagery was neglected.

8 See ch. 2; Doherty, 'The party hack', 345–7. 9 *II*, 1 May 1917; BMH WS 722: Dan
McCarthy.

The emulation of American and European marketing methods in Ireland in the early 1900s and the growth of advertising agencies was proof of an increasing realization that the tools of commercial and political marketing were essential to success. As discussed in chapter 4, the 1910 article 'The advertising problem' astutely remarked that 'no new industry can hope to be even moderately successful without enlisting to its aid at least a moderate degree of business-making publicity'.[10] This advice is equally applicable to political parties, and the prodigious, and often radical and zealous, propaganda efforts of unionists and Sinn Féin paid dividends at the ballot box. The temperate approach of the IPP, combined with a haphazard candidate-selection process, enervated fundraising and pedestrian leitmotifs doomed it to subordination in a post-war world where the skills of mass marketing and public relations had accustomed the public to new ideas.

Sinn Féin's formation of a funded and staffed department of propaganda ensured a coherent and targeted campaign. This department also raised and managed finances, and flooded the voting market with strong messages and unique identity symbols. After their 1917 Longford South success, election machinery was honed, core policy was tweaked and aggressive attack replaced conventional diplomatic oratory. Sinn Féin's narrow win in Longford South had been gained with the help of the *Put him in to get him out* poster campaign. From this, a party brand was unveiled and with constant repetition there was instant association.

Unionist skills lay in adapting and refreshing their sharp anti-home rule message to encourage political adherence to their philosophy, and they held fast to a time-honoured fidelity to the union. Ideological disparities between separatists and unionists were propagated across electoral propaganda efforts, highlighting the divergent views on the governance of Ireland. Unionist propagandistic strength was homogeneity of message, and an array of propaganda techniques conveyed their doctrine. Unionist voters adhered to the call for collective balloting that brought victory in Ulster in 1918 and 1921 and in a pocket of Dublin in 1918. In 1920 propaganda messages were supplemented by proposals to manage the everyday issues that were particular to local government. Unionists won control of many urban councils in Ulster, but competition from Sinn Féin and the PR-STV voting system reduced their domination, particularly in the rural elections. The strength of unionism during these election campaigns and its continuing endurance in Ulster was (and remains) its branding and sense of identity. This enabled instant recognition in posters, handbills and political ephemera, in the words of leaders, candidates and canvassers, which facilitated recall at the polling booth.

As Ulster unionists inched closer to partition, southern adherents grew frustrated and anxious, and began to vacillate between embracing and impairing home rule negotiations. Carson privately complained that southern unionists had not been 'prepared to run any risks ... [I]t is very difficult to ascertain what the South

---

10 Sinn Féin, *Leabhar na hÉireann*, 'The advertising problem', p. 309.

and West want us to do as they only talk in generalities.'[11] The gradual popularization and localization of the movement in the northern counties pulled apart a tentative all-Ireland unionism, and ultimately left southern unionists stranded in a nationalist dominated Free State.[12]

The *Irish Times* attributed the IPP's failure to 'two great mistakes': '[I]t agreed to the partition of Ireland as an alleged settlement of the Irish question', and, 'after the rebellion, it made itself a boxer of wood and a drawer of water to the people who gloried, and still glory, in the rebellion'.[13] Fanning maintains that it was the prolongation of the Great War that turned home rule into 'a cosmetic exercise that sowed the seeds for the downfall of the constitutional nationalists'.[14] Redmond had, as Finnan points out, seen the war as 'an extraordinary chance to break the impasse between nationalists and unionists in Ireland', and had the war ended quickly home rule would not have remained suspended for years.[15] However, by 1917 the wavering of IPP leaders on the Great War made it difficult for voters to interpret irresolute attitudes. War was a tangible and visual reality during the by-elections and remained a vivid memory in the immediate aftermath of the armistice and in 1921. As mentioned, whole nations had engaged in combat and this triggered concerns over who should govern and the best political structure that fit the interests in the minds of ordinary voters.

The extension of conscription to Ireland in March 1918 fuelled public anxiety and it dealt the IPP a severe blow. Sinn Féin, on the other hand, gained a valuable anti-conscription propaganda platform. Enforcing conscription on Ireland was always going to be difficult, particularly during the latter war years when high death tolls had weakened war support. Given that all major nationalist parties (and the Labour Party and the Roman Catholic church) had actively campaigned against conscription, voters were now challenged to distinguish the difference between the two forms of nationalism. The conscription crisis increased membership of Sinn Féin clubs (albeit briefly) and led to growing public support. This combined with the 'German Plot' arrests, which facilitated the reappearance of the *Put him in to get him out* campaign, weakened the IPP considerably.

Disorganization and lack of an efficient political machine also undermined Dillon's leadership. While the IPP still retained roots in provincial Ireland, it lacked the necessary supports and cohesion to contest against a fresh, ambitious rival. The depleted numbers of the AOH, which operated in a similar fashion to Sinn Féin's Irish Volunteers during elections, reduced the IPP's presence in many constituencies and contributed to their electoral defeat. A high degree of disaffection by IPP MPs and by voters who were now jaded with imperialism converted many to the idea of abstention from Westminster. Growing disgust at 'the humbug, muddling and treachery' of the party led many, according to the *Irish Independent*, to express their 'wrath' in the polling booths to wipe 'the discreditable and corrupt

---

11 Alvin Jackson, *Sir Edward Carson* (Dublin, 1993), p. 32. 12 Ibid., *Ireland*, p. 227. 13 *IT*, 7 Feb. 1917. 14 Fanning, *Fatal path*, p. 355. 15 Finnan, p. 230.

Party practically out of existence'. With its usual anti-IPP venom, this newspaper maintained that Dillon 'thoroughly deserves the fate which has overtaken him' because 'Ireland's interests were scandalously sacrificed'.[16]

Heavily influenced by Wilsonian commentary on self-determination Sinn Féin sought an appeal to the post-war peace conference to forge a domestic alternative to Westminster and create international recognition. Propaganda methods and themes, and wily electioneering tactics, had accustomed the electorate to their abstentionist policies and peace conference aspirations, so by the time voters went to the polls in 1918 Sinn Féin had established widespread voter awareness and many now championed the party's cause. The *Irish Independent* phrased it well when they remarked that 'if we do not know what Sinn Féin means to do there is no excuse for us, for we have been told plainly enough, in hundreds of speeches and in dozens of newspapers in Ireland for the last 18 months'.[17] The same could be said of Ulster unionists and their electoral propaganda. By establishing the notional counter-state in 1919 and acquiring pledges of allegiance at the local council level in 1920, a foundation was established that allowed Sinn Féin to shrewdly to seize control by 1921. However, voters who were nervous about partition gave their allegiance to the home rule ideals rather than the more revolutionary and radical aspirations of Sinn Féin.

Nationalists still fielded a large number of candidates in the 1920 municipal elections who continued to advocate a constitutional approach, and they attained 12.8 per cent of the vote (21.8 per cent if independent candidates are included as many were nationalists) under the proportional-representation system of voting. However, in the rural elections the following June, Sinn Féin's 74.7 per cent victory was a landslide in comparison to the nationalist 5.6 per cent and Labour's 4.6 per cent. The tone and mood of Ireland had altered by 1920. The creation of Dáil Éireann introduced radical change in the mindset of separatists, partition loomed, skirmishes had broken out in many areas of Ireland as a prelude of the war to come, the IPP centre had collapsed and the Labour Party had entered the field as the voice of trade unions and the working class. Aside from Ulster, where unionists remained in the majority, Sinn Féin and the Labour Party polled well above the IPP in the three southern provinces.[18]

The electorate in December 1918 voted in favour of Sinn Féin in Ireland's three southern provinces and enabled the claim that the results of the 'national plebiscite held under British law and British supervision' indicated the 'will of the Irish people' as to the 'government under which they live'.[19] But, if Ulster's results are added then the claim of a homogeneous desire for self-determination does not hold up. Unionists in Ulster followed instructions to vote solidly for their

---

16 *II*, 30 Dec. 1918. **17** Ibid. **18** See appendixes 2 and 3. **19** UCDA, de Valera Papers, P150/627: booklet by de Valera titled *The foundation of the Republic of Ireland*; P150/687: Speech or article titled 'The Irish people exercised the right of self-determination, and declared for an independent republic. The basis of Ireland's right.'

own candidates to maintain the union and establish a policy of material prosperity in 1918, 1920 and again in 1921. Furthermore, if the total votes for IPP candidates in 1918, the low turnout and the absent votes are calculated, and the method of the first-past-the-post voting system are taken into consideration Sinn Féin's 'landslide' victory is questionable. The proportion of votes attained in 1918 in an all-Ireland context gave Sinn Féin only 47.6 per cent of the total vote, unionists 25.8 per cent and the IPP 21.8 per cent (minus the uncontested seats).

The dominance of national and constitutional issues had inhibited the development of the Labour Party in 1918. The Labour Party's retreat was a relief to Sinn Féin, which could now avoid the battle for working-class votes. It was ill-fated for home rulers who had hoped to split the vote and retain some seats. Labour movements were more interested in trade-union militancy than politics, and even by 1920 they had yet to unite coherently under the banner of their political party – as evidenced in Cork, where a rival union contested against the Sinn Féin/Labour coalition in 1918, and in their coalition with Sinn Féin in 1920 in a number of constituencies. The Labour Party's political future was precarious and this has been well documented in works by Emmet O'Connor, Michael Laffan and Niamh Purséil.[20]

The success of Sinn Féin and unionists (and the Labour Party in 1920) was buoyed by the powerful influence of new voters, and particularly women voters. A considerable amount has been written about the pre-war suffrage movements, however more attention needs to be paid to post-suffrage women's politics. From 1918 to 1921, whether because of the novelty factor of attaining the vote, or a genuine interest in political affairs, women took their new electoral roles and franchise powers seriously, as evidenced by the many reports about their turnout on election day. It is likely that in similar fashion to men they cast their votes in favour of unionist candidates in Ulster and Sinn Féin in the three southern provinces, and marginalized the IPP, who had disregarded their past demands for suffrage. Yet, there was no real attempt by any party to develop a new feminist politics around women's issues. Women's reactions to this merits further attention, as does an analysis of women's attitudes and responses to the 1898 Local Government Act, which granted suffrage at the local level. The politicizing effects of war service on women and the anti-conscription campaign also merit more in-depth analysis. Sinn Féin, unionists and the Labour Party (and the women within them, although small in number) defined women as active participants within electoral propaganda and in the political process. The exclusion of women under 30 from the franchise reinforced the idea of women voters principally as wives and mothers, but that did not eliminate them as canvassers and voters. They were of equal

---

20 Emmet O'Connor, *A labour history of Ireland, 1824–2000* (Dublin, 2011); Laffan, 'In the shadow'; Niamh Purséil, *The Irish Labour Party, 1922–73* (Dublin, 2007); Lane, *Essays in Irish labour history* (Dublin, 2008); and for a later history Michael Gallagher, *The Irish Labour Party in transition 1957–82* (Manchester, 1982).

importance as the young men in securing votes, as is evidenced in the personal classified advertisements in the print media where appeals for votes were made to 'Ladies and Gentlemen' and 'Irish men and women' by separatists and unionists, and Devlin in Belfast. The Labour Party was in the difficult position of trying to merge the dominance of the masculine in its trade-union movements with that of working women, but it too attempted to encourage active participation by women in electioneering. Strategic targeting of women voters and the empowerment of the youth enabled Sinn Féin, unionists and the Labour Party to successfully staff their propaganda war.[21] The industry of female separatist supporters, alongside male Volunteers, brought victory to Sinn Féin in 1918 and again in 1920.

Sinn Féin's electoral gains were in part the result of successfully incorporating and tailoring new propaganda techniques. However, as Townshend points out, 'whether they [voters] really knew what the party [Sinn Féin] stood for is another issue'.[22] Sinn Féin voters were not sanctioning the future physical war against Britain that began in 1919, nor were they approving its continuation in the local elections of 1920. Nationalist voters endorsed an innovative and fresh approach for freedom from Westminster, even if there was some vagueness on its future. The IPP had success in the urban council elections, but gloom at leadership level and the decision to postpone challenges for an interval in expectation of a changing Irish mindset left the party bereft of candidates in 1921 to contest for the southern parliament, allowing all 124 candidates appointed by Sinn Féin to be returned. This is, no doubt, the point at which there was no return for the IPP because the outcome presented Sinn Féin with a mandate to negotiate the Anglo-Irish treaty and set the wheels in motion for establishing its control over the Free State.

The 1918 results indicate at a cursory glance that Sinn Féin converted voters in the three southern provinces and in parts of Catholic Ulster, and unionists held the support of their adherents in Ulster and areas of Dublin. Yet some of Sinn Féin's wins (Louth and Wexford South being examples) were very narrow, indicating a bewildered nationalist electorate with limited choice. However, ultimately the IPP failed to impress with their unaltered home rule arguments. In Ulster in 1921 Sinn Féin and nationalists lost out heavily to unionists who gained the largest number of votes in all ten constituencies and received more than 50 per cent of the votes in all but one – Fermanagh-Tyrone. The six counties had returned in favour of partition and the nationalist vote had lost out.

Political transformation in Ireland was influenced by the election campaigns which inculcated the policies and beliefs of Sinn Féin and unionists (and labour movements in 1920) into the minds of the people by propagandizing ideas. The votes cast by unionists and separatists in 1918 provide evidence that strident propaganda campaigns altered public opinion, and the 1920 local-government elections embedded a deepening resolve to remain steadfast to those beliefs. However, as previously stated in chapter 1, intimidation and violence, absent voters, a much

21 See ch. 4. 22 Townshend, *The republic*, p. 62.

reduced number of emigrants and the weakness of a credible alternative political programme resulted in high voter disaffection in 1918, 1920 and 1921.

The dichotomy of separatism and unionism was evident in the themes that were rooted in their propaganda. They were the pillars upon which the impetus for change was formed. The leaders of that change were the new political elite and their voluntary supporters, through the vigorous electioneering activities and propaganda messages that instigated a political upheaval in Ireland. Although partition divided the island in 1921 and opinions collided in a civil war from 1922 to 1923, the elections of 1917 to 1921 established Irish party systems and policymakers that influenced the political landscape for decades. The propaganda techniques and practices developed by revolutionary electioneers continued to influence the propaganda and marketing techniques of all major parties after partition.

Appendix 1

1918 general election results, candidates elected opposed

(Names in bold are the winners)

Candidate	Political affiliation	Constituency	Electorate	Votes received	% of valid votes	Age (where known)
Robert McCalmont	U	Antrim East	24,798	**15,206**	**94.6**	37
Daniel Dumigan	SF			861	5.4	
Robert O'Neill	U	Antrim Mid	18,032	**10,711**	**79.3**	35
Joseph Connolly	SF			2,791	20.7	33
Peter Smiley	U	Antrim North	19,110	**9,621**	**78.3**	39
Patrick McCarry	SF			2,673	21.7	
Charles Craig	U	Antrim South	23,235	**13,270**	**85.1**	49
Kevin O'Sheil	SF			2,318	14.9	
James Lonsdale	U	Armagh Mid	17,339	**8,431**	**59.7**	53
Liam O'Brien	SF			5,689	40.3	30
William Allen	U	Armagh North	19,529	**10,239**	**78.2**	52
Ernest Blythe	SF			2,860	21.8	29
Patrick Donnelly	IPP	Armagh South	15,905	**4,345**	**98.2**	40
Dr James McKee	SF			79	1.8	
William Lindsay	U	Belfast (Cromac)	21,637	**11,459**	**76.6**	52
James Freeland	Labour			2,508	16.8	
Archibald Savage	SF			997	6.7	
Sir Edward Carson	U	Belfast (Duncairn)	19,085	**11,637**	**81.0**	64
Maj. William Davey	IPP			2,449	17.1	38
Dr Russell McNabb	SF			271	1.9	
Joseph Devlin	IPP	Belfast (Falls)	15,756	**8,488**	**72.3**	47
Éamon de Valera	SF			3,245	27.7	36
Thomas Moles	U	Belfast (Ormeau)	16,343	**7,460**	**59.1**	47
William Stewart	Independent unionist			4,833	38.3	
James Dobbyn	SF			338	2.7	

Candidate	Political affiliation	Constituency	Electorate	Votes received	% of valid votes	Age (where known)
Capt. Herbert Dixon	U	Belfast (Pottinger)	17,084	**8,574**	**70.6**	38
Samuel Porter	Labour			2,513	20.7	43
James Bennett	Labour			659	5.4	
Bernard Campbell	SF			393	3.2	
Thomas Burn	U	Belfast (St Anne's)	18,693	**9,155**	**74.7**	43
William Alexander	Independent			1,752	14.3	
Dermot Barnes	SF			1,341	11.0	
Samuel McGuffin	Labour Unionist	Belfast (Shankill)	22,971	**11,840**	**73.8**	55
Samuel Kyle	Labour			3,674	22.9	34
Michael Carolan	Independent			534	3.3	43
Thompson Donald	Labour Unionist	Belfast (Victoria)	19,494	**9,309**	**69.9**	42
Robert Waugh	Labour			3,469	26.0	
Winifred Carney	SF			539	4.0	31
Robert Lynn	U	Belfast (Woodvale)	19,802	**12,232**	**90.7**	45
Robert Haskin	SF			1,247	9.3	
James Walsh	SF	Cork (city) (2 seat constituency)	45,017[1]	**20,801**	**34.3**	38
Liam de Roiste	SF			**20,506**	**33.8**	36
Maurice Talbot Crosbie	IPP			7,480	12.3	
Richard L. O'Sullivan	IPP			7,162	11.8	
Daniel Williams	U			2,519	4.1	
Thomas Farrington	U			2,254	3.7	
Edward Kelly	IPP	Donegal East	16,015	**7,596**	**61.1**	35
Robert Moore	U			4,797	38.6	
Sean O'Flaherty (Withdrawn)	SF			40	0.3	
Joseph O'Doherty	SF	Donegal North	17,538	**7,003**	**69.5**	27
Philip O'Doherty	IPP			3,075	30.5	
Peter Ward	SF	Donegal South	16,894	**5,787**	**54.9**	27
John Donovan	IPP			4,752	45.1	
Joseph Sweeney	SF	Donegal West	19,296	**6,712**	**62.0**	21
Daniel McMenamin	IPP			4,116	38.0	36

1 Micheál Martin, *Freedom to choose: Cork and party politics in Ireland, 1918–1932* (Cork, 2009) claims that the Cork city electorate increased from 12,000 to 50,000 with the passing of the Franchise Act.

Candidate	Political affiliation	Constituency	Electorate	Votes received	% of valid votes	Age (where known)
David Reid	U	Down East	17,846	**6,007**	**42.3**	46
Michael J. Johnson	IPP			4,312	30.4	
Dr Russell McNabb	SF			3,876	27.3	
James Craig	U	Down Mid	17,195	**10,639**	**93.8**	47
Joseph Robinson	SF			707	6.2	30
Thomas Brown	U	Down North	18,399	**9,200**	**81.0**	39
John Davidson	Ind.			2,153	19.0	
Jeremiah McVeigh	IPP	Down South	18,708	**8,756**	**59.2**	48
Capt. John Johnson	U			5,573	37.7	44
Alexander Fisher	Independent			436	2.9	
Éamon de Valera	SF			33	0.2	36
Daniel Wilson	U	Down West	17,997	**10,559**	**86.0**	53
Bernard Campbell	SF			1,725	14.0	
Richard Mulcahy	SF	Dublin (Clontarf)	14,588	**5,974**	**64.9**	36
Sir Patrick Shortall	IPP			3,228	35.1	46
Sean T. O'Kelly	SF	Dublin (College Green)	21,414	**9,662**	**77.2**	36
Joseph Briscow	Independent Nationalist			2,853	22.8	
Philip Shanahan	SF	Dublin (Harbour)	19,520	**7,708**	**58.9**	42
Alfie Byrne	IPP			5,386	41.1	36
Desmond Fitzgerald	SF	Dublin (Pembroke)	17,698	**6,114**	**47.5**	30
John P. Good	U			4,138	32.1	
Charles O'Neill	IPP			2,629	20.4	
Sir Maurice Dockrell	U	Dublin (Rathmines)	18,841	**7,400**	**50.2**	68
Patrick Little	SF			5,566	37.7	34
George Moonan	IPP			1,780	12.1	46
Joseph McGrath	SF	Dublin (St. James's)	13,121	**6,256**	**80.1**	31
John Kelly	IPP			1,556	19.9	
Michael Staines	SF	Dublin (St. Michan's)	17,642	**7,553**	**65.4**	33
John Nugent	IPP			3,996	34.6	49
Countess Constance Markievicz	SF	Dublin (St. Patrick's)	18,785	**7,835**	**65.8**	50
William Field	IPP			3,752	31.5	75
James Kelly	Independent Nationalist			312	2.6	45

Candidate	Political affiliation	Constituency	Electorate	Votes received	% of valid votes	Age (where known)
Thomas Kelly	SF	Dublin (St. Stephen's Green)	19,759	8,461	59.9	50
Patrick Brady	IPP			2,902	20.6	50
Henry Hanna	U			2,755	19.5	
Frank J. Lawless	SF	Dublin County	19,799	9,138	67.4	48
John Clancy	IPP	North		4,428	32.6	71
George Duffy	SF	Dublin County	17,829	5,133	38.6	36
Sir Thomas Robinson	U	South		4,354	32.7	
Thomas Clarke	IPP			3,819	28.7	
Arthur Samuels	U	Dublin	4,541	1,273	43.1	66
Sir Robert Woods	Independent	University		793	26.8	53
William Jellett	U	(Trinity		631	21.4	61
Stephen Gwynn	IPP	College)		257	8.7	54
Edward Archdale	U	Fermanagh	14,496	6,768	52.0	65
Kevin O'Sheil	SF	North		6,236	48.0	27
John Séan O'Mahoney	SF	Fermanagh	13,962	6,673	58.9	54
James Cooper	U	South		4,524	39.9	36
Patrick Crumley	IPP			132	1.2	58
Pádraic Ó Maille	SF	Galway	24,956	11,754	77.2	40
William O'Malley	IPP	Connemara		3,482	22.8	65
Bryan Cusack	SF	Galway North	21,036	8,896	69.0	36
Thomas Sloyan	IPP			3,999	31.0	
Frank Fahy	SF	Galway South	18,507	10,621	85.9	38
William Duffy	IPP			1,744	14.1	53
Donal Buckley	SF	Kildare North	13,274	5,979	68.7	52
John O'Connor	IPP			2,722	31.3	68
Art O'Connor	SF	Kildare South	13,925	7,104	82.4	30
Denis Kilbride	IPP			1,515	17.6	70
James O'Mara	SF	Kilkenny South	16,410	8,685	82.4	45
Matthew Keating	IPP			1,855	17.6	49
James Dolan	SF	Leitrim	30,079	17,711	85.1	36
Gerald Farrell	IPP			3,096	14.9	
Richard Hayes	SF	Limerick East	21,095	12,750	77.9	40
Thomas Lundon	IPP			3,608	22.1	
Prof. Eoin MacNeill	SF	Londonderry	16,736	7,335	50.7	51
Sir Robert Anderson	U	(city)		7,020	48.5	47
Maj. William Davey	IPP			120	0.8	38
Hugh Anderson	U	Londonderry	21,306	10,530	72.7	51
Patrick J. McGilligan	SF	North		3,951	27.3	29

Candidate	Political affiliation	Constituency	Electorate	Votes received	% of valid votes	Age (where known)
Denis Henry	U	Londonderry	21,199	**8,942**	**54.7**	54
Prof. Arthur Conway	IPP	South		3,981	24.3	43
Louis Joseph Walsh	SF			3,425	20.9	38
Joseph McGuinness	SF	Longford	20,449	**11,122**	**72.7**	43
James Patrick Farrell	IPP			4,173	27.3	53
John Joseph O'Kelly	SF	Louth	29,176	**10,770**	**50.6**	46
Richard Hazleton	IPP			10,515	49.4	38
Éamon de Valera	SF	Mayo East	21,635	**8,975**	**66.5**	36
John Dillon	IPP			4,514	33.5	67
John Crowley	SF	Mayo North	21,212	**7,429**	**80.8**	48
Daniel Boyle	IPP			1,761	19.2	59
Joseph McBride	SF	Mayo West	21,667	**10,195**	**88.7**	
William Doris	IPP			1,568	13.3	58
Liam Mellows	SF	Meath North	14,716	**6,982**	**65.0**	26
Patrick Cusack	IPP			3,758	35.0	
Edmund Duggan	SF	Meath South	14,716	**6,371**	**70.4**	44
Thomas P. O'Donoghue	IPP			2,680	29.6	
Ernest Blythe	SF	Monaghan	16,175	**6,842**	**48.7**	29
Michael Knight	U	North		4,497	32.0	
John Joseph Turley	IPP			2,709	19.3	
Seán MacEntee	SF	Monaghan	16,164	**7,524**	**63.0**	29
Thomas Campbell	IPP	South		4,413	34.0	47
Prof. Eoin MacNeill	SF	NUI	3,819	**1,644**	**66.9**	
Prof. Arthur Conway	IPP			813	33.1	
Kevin O'Higgins	SF	Queen's	26,063	**13,452**	**67.5**	26
Patrick Joseph Meehan	IPP	County		6,480	32.5	41
Sir William Whitla	U	Queen's	2,039	**1,487**	**92.6**	67
John Blake Dolan	SF	University		118	7.4	
Harry Boland	SF	Roscommon	22,093	**10,685**	**71.6**	31
John Patrick Hayden	IPP	South		4,233	28.4	55
John Joseph Clancy	SF	Sligo North	18,448	**9,030**	**68.0**	28
Thomas Scanlon	IPP			4,242	32.0	44
Alexander McCabe	SF	Sligo South	18,013	**9,113**	**82.1**	32
John O'Dowd	IPP			1,988	17.9	62
Pierce McCann	SF	Tipperary East	16,232	**7,487**	**61.0**	36
Thomas J. Condon	IPP			4,794	39.0	
Patrick J. Moloney	SF	Tipperary	14,716	**8,744**	**76.4**	49
John Cullinan	IPP	South		2,701	23.6	60?

Candidate	Political affiliation	Constituency	Electorate	Votes received	% of valid votes	Age (where known)
Thomas Harbison	**IPP**	Tyrone	23,023	**11,605**	63.3	54
King Houston	U	North-east		6,681	36.4	
Seán Milroy	SF			56	0.3	41
Arthur Griffith	**SF**	Tyrone	22,182	**10,442**	57.6	46
William Thomas Miller	U	North-west		7,696	42.4	53
William Coote	**U**	Tyrone South	22,465	**10,616**	56.9	55
Denis McCullough	SF			5,437	29.1	35
John Skeffington	Independent Nationalist			2,602	13.9	
Capt. William Archer Redmond	**IPP**	Waterford (city)	12,063	**4,915**	52.6	32
Dr. Vincent White	SF			4,431	47.4	33
Cathal Brugha	**SF**	Waterford	24,439	**12,890**	75.4	44
John James O'Shea	IPP	County		4,217	24.6	
Laurence Ginnell	**SF**	Westmeath	24,014	**12,435**	75.4	66 [from baptism date]
Patrick H. Weymes	IPP			3,458	21.0	77
Sir Walter Nugent	Independent Nationalist			603	3.7	53
Roger Sweetman	**SF**	Wexford North	23,022	**10,162**	58.6	44
Sir Thomas Esmonde	IPP			7,189	41.4	56
James Ryan	**SF**	Wexford South	23,168	**8,729**	51.5	27
Peter Ffrench	IPP			8,211	48.5	74
Seán Etchingham	**SF**	Wicklow East	15,241	**5,916**	53.9	48
Alexander Keene	U			2,600	23.7	
Denis Cogan	IPP			2,466	22.4	
Robert Childers Barton	**SF**	Wicklow West	11,673	**6,239**	82.0	37
The O'Mahony [Pierce O'Mahony]	IPP			1,370	18.0	68

Sources: Walker, *Parliamentary election results, 1918-92*, pp 4-9; *Weekly IT, 14* Dec. 1918; *II*, 30 Dec. 1918; *CE*, 30 Dec. 1918.

Appendix 2

1920 urban election results

County	Total elected	Unionist	Sinn Féin	Labour Party	Nationalist	Reform/ Ratepayer	Independent
Ulster							
Antrim	120	68	1	31	11	0	9
Armagh	66	24	12	14	16	0	0
Belfast	60	37	5	13	5	0	0
Cavan	27	2	10	8	0	0	7
Donegal	45	5	23	4	5	5	3
Down	117	81	5	15	12	0	4
Fermanagh	21	10	2	2	6	0	1
Londonderry	27	17	0	4	4	0	2
Londonderry city	40	19	10	0	11	0	0
Monaghan	48	9	23	7	5	0	4
Tyrone	75	30	12	11	19	0	3
Total	**646**	**302**	**103**	**109**	**94**	**5**	**33**
Leinster							
Carlow	24	3	9	6	4	0	2
Dublin	141	35	43	28	14	16	5
Dublin city	80	1	41	16	9	11	2
Kildare	33	2	7	15	9	0	0
Kilkenny	24	1	10	5	6	0	2
King's	42	9	10	10	2	11	0
Longford	24	1	9	4	2	4	4
Louth	51	2	21	9	11	6	2
Meath	39	1	14	9	4	1	10
Queen's	9	0	3	3	2	0	1
Westmeath	24	0	1	12	0	0	11
Wexford	63	1	21	22	2	13	4
Wicklow	36	1	17	12	4	0	2
Total	**590**	**57**	**206**	**151**	**69**	**62**	**45**

County	Total elected	Unionist	Sinn Féin	Labour Party	Nationalist	Reform/ Ratepayer	Independent
Munster							
Clare	24	0	13	5	4	0	2
Cork	135	4	42	41	11	15	22
Cork city	50	0	24*	4	14	2	6
Kerry	45	2	24	9	9	0	1
Limerick	15	0	8	7	0	0	0
Limerick city	40	0	26	5	0	5	4
Tipperary	93	0	31	25	5	8	24
Waterford	39	1	13	12	1	6	6
Waterford city	40	0	20	3	14	0	3
Total	**481**	**7**	**201**	**111**	**58**	**36**	**68**
Connacht							
Galway	66	1	28	14	15	0	8
Mayo	31	1	12	5	0	4	9
Roscommon	9	0	4	5	0	0	0
Sligo (1919)†	24	0	7	5	0	8‡	4
Total	**130**	**2**	**51**	**29**	**15**	**12**	**21**
All-Ireland Total	**1,847**	**368**	**561**	**400**	**236**	**115**	**167**

Sources: Local Government Board Ireland, Annual Report for the year ended 31 Mar. 1920; *IT*, 20 Jan. 1920 (PR Society of Ireland Abstract of Results); *II*, Jan. 1920; *CE*, Jan. 1920; and *FJ*, Jan. 1920 and *FJ*, 18 Jan. 1919 (Sligo). * Cork City: Sinn Féin and Labour coalition. † Sligo election was held under the Sligo Corporation Act of 1918. ‡ 8 Ratepayers.

Appendix 3

1920 rural district council election results, in seats[1]

County	SF	SF and Labour	Labour	Nationalist	Unionist	Farmer's Union	Ind.	Total
Leinster								
Carlow	13		7					20
Dublin	12	2			3		2	19
Kildare	15		5				1*	21
Kilkenny	16		2	1				19
King's	19		2					21
Longford	20							20
Louth	18		1	8			1	28
Meath	20					1		21
Queen's	18	3			1			22
Westmeath	15		5	3				23
Wexford	12		7					19
Wicklow	13	3		3				19
Total	**191**	**8**	**29**	**15**	**4**	**1**	**4**	**252**
Munster								
Clare	20							20
Cork	32							32
Kerry	20							20
Limerick	20							20
Tipperary North	19		1					20
Tipperary South	23							23
Waterford	17	3						20
Total	**151**	**3**	**1**					**155**

---

1 Results were taken from the *Freeman's Journal*, 12 June 1920 and crossed checked against the *Irish Times* and regional newspapers where results were published.

County	SF	SF and Labour	Labour	Nationalist	Unionist	Farmer's Union	Ind.	Total
Connacht								
Galway	20							20
Leitrim	19							19
Mayo	24							24
Roscommon	20							20
Sligo	19	1						20
Total	102	1						103
Ulster								
Antrim	1				17		3†	21
Armagh	5			3	14		1	23
Cavan	20			1				21
Donegal	15			3	2			20
Down	4		2	1	13			20
Fermanagh	6			5	9			20
Londonderry	4			4	11			19
Monaghan	16				4			20
Tyrone	8			7	11			26
Total	79		2	24	81		4	190
All-Ireland Total	523	12	32	39	85	1	8	700

* 1 nationalist. † 1 unionist, 2 nationalist.

Note: In calculating the urban and rural election results, a number of newspapers were used and there were conflicting results at times. A best estimate, based on reported figures, was used.

Appendix 4

1921 Northern Ireland election results

Constituency	Seats	Electorate	Quota	Candidates	Political affiliation	First preferences
Antrim	7	93,566	9,994	John Milne Barbour	U	17,735
				Maj. Robert O'Neill	U	16,681
				George Boyle Hanna	U	12,584
				Robert Crawford	U	5,976
				Robert Dick Megaw	U	8,326
				John Fawcett Gordon	U	2,967
				Joseph Devlin	N	9,448
				Louis Walsh	SF	4,951
				Joseph Connolly	SF	1,281
Armagh	4	53,977	9,307	Richard Best	U	15,988
				Michael Collins	SF	12,656
				Maj. David Shillington	U	9,730
				John Dillon Nugent	N	6,857
				Frank Aiken	SF	1,301
Belfast East	4	40,198	7,182	Richard Dawson Bates	U	10,026
				Capt. Herbert Dixon	U	8,849
				Thompson Donald	U	6,856
				James Augustine Duff	U	3,585
				Archibald Savage	SF	3,573
				Thomas Joseph Campbell	N	2,373
				Harry Cassidy Midgley	Ind. Lab.	645
Belfast North	4	43,194	7,971	Lloyd Campbell	U	12,875
				Samuel McGuffin	U	11,596
				William Grant	U	6,148
				Robert John Mckeown	U	3,562
				Michael Carolan	SF	3,235
				Francis Patrick Harkin	N	1,509
				Revd John Bruce Wallace	Ind.	926
Belfast South	4	40,566	7,261	Thomas Moles	U	17,248
				Hugh MacDowell Pollock	U	6,334
				Sir Crawford McCullagh	U	5,068
				Julia McMordie	U	2,372
				Dermot Barnes	SF	2,719
				Bernard McCoy	N	1,688
				James Baird	Ind. Lab.	875

Constituency	Seats	Electorate	Quota	Candidates	Political affiliation	First preferences
Belfast West	4	57,914	10,691	Thomas Henry Burn	U	13,298
				Robert John Lynn	U	9,315
				William John Twaddell	U	10,316
				Joseph Devlin	N	10,621
				Denis McCullough	SF	6,270
				Seán MacEntee	SF	2,954
				John Alexander Hanna	Ind. Lab.	367
				Richard Byrne	N	311
Down	8	93,138	9,021	Sir James Craig	U	29,829
				Éamon de Valera	SF	16,269
				John Miller Andrews	U	12,584
				Thomas Robert Lavery	U	2,863
				Capt. Harry Hill Mulholland	U	4,665
				Robert McBride	U	3,297
				Thomas Wallace McMullan	U	2,692
				Patrick O'Neill	N	7,317
				Alexander Adams	Ind. Lab.	1,188
				Patrick Lavery	SF	327
				Patrick M. Moore	SF	149
Fermanagh and Tyrone	8	95,272	9,306	Arthur Griffith	SF	21,677
				Edward Mervyn Archdale	U	10,336
				William Coote	U	9,672
				Seán Milroy	SF	1,846
				William Thomas Miller	U	9,165
				James Cooper	U	8,754
				John (Seán) O'Mahoney	SF	4,979
				Thomas Harbison	N	7,090
				Joseph P. Gillen	N	5,591
				Kevin Roantree O'Sheil	SF	4,464
				Seán MacEntee	SF	179
Londonderry	5			Sir Robert Newton Anderson	U	13,466
				Eoin MacNeill	SF	11,866
				Dehra Chichester	U	8,709
				John Martin Mark	U	8,155
				George Leeke	N	6,298
				John Walsh	SF	4,020
				Hugh Wilson Shields	N	1,474
Queens University, Belfast	4	2,528		Dr John Campbell	U	835
				John Hanna Robb	U	368
				Prof. Robert James Johnstone	U	279
				Dr Hugh Smith Morrison	U	243
				John (Seán) Blake Dolan	SF	201

Bibliography

PRIMARY SOURCES

Great Britain

Bodleian Library Oxford

Asquith Papers

Houses of commons and lords, parliamentary debates

tcd.ie/library/collections/databases

Imperial War Museum

Aftermath of the Easter Rising (film newsreel by Topical Budget)

National Archives, Kew, London

Dublin Castle Records, TCD/library/collections/databases
Government spending on propaganda publications
Home publicity during the 1914–18 war, INF 1/317 (1939)
National War Aims Committee minutes and reports, 1917–18

UK Parliamentary Archives

Representation of the People Act 1918

Ireland

County Archives

Cork City and County Archives: IE CCCA/RDC163, 1899–1925
Dublin City Archives
Limerick City: L/FR/FE/2/1–13: Electoral Registers Post-1898 Local Government Act (1912)

Dáil Éireann Debates

Oireachtas.ie

Irish Film Archives
The Dáil Bonds (1919)

Military Archives
Bureau of Military History, Contemporary Documents
Bureau of Military History, Witness Statements

National Archives of Ireland
1901 and 1911 censuses, http://www.census.nationalarchives.ie
Cabinet Minutes
Central Statistics Office, 'Census Results 1911 and 1926: Distribution and Changes in the Population'
Chief Secretary's Office Papers
Irish Labour Party and Trade Union Congress Annual Reports
RIC, 'Demonstrations on the release of Sinn Féin prisoners and deportees in June, 1917'

National Library of Ireland
Art Ó Briain Papers
Charles Gavin Duffy Papers
Count Plunkett Papers
Department of Local Government Papers, 1920–1
Diarmuid Lynch, 'History of the FOIF'
Ephemera Collection
Frank Gallagher Papers
Harrington Papers
Irish Large Books
Irish National Aid Association Papers
Irish Parliamentary Party Minute Books
J.F.X. O'Brien Papers
John Redmond Papers
McGarrity Papers
Michael Hayes Papers
Peter Golden Papers
Piaras Béaslaí Papers
Robert Barton Papers
Sinn Féin
Sinn Féin Standing Committee Minutes
Spálpin, Sinn Féin and the Labour Movement (Dublin, *c.*1917)

Thomas Johnson Papers
UIL National Directory
William O'Brien Papers

Private Collections

Elaine Callinan Collection
Peter Brown Collection, TCD (kindly shared)

Trinity College Dublin Manuscripts and Archives Research Library

Frank Gallagher Papers
John Dillon Papers
Samuels Collection, Early Printed Books

University College Dublin Archives

De Valera Papers
Desmond FitzGerald Papers
Ernie O'Malley Papers
Gavan Duffy Papers
Michael Hayes Papers
Records of the Fianna Fáil Party
Richard Mulcahy Papers

Northern Ireland

Public Record Office of Northern Ireland

Armstrong Papers
Carson Papers
Papers relating to Tyrone and Fermanagh Political Elections
Sinn Féin election posters and ephemera
Ulster Unionist Council Records
Unionist Party, General Council Minutes Book

United States of America

American Irish Historical Society, New York
Friends of Irish Freedom Papers

Library of Congress

Congressional Records

NEWSPAPERS AND PERIODICALS

National dailies/weeklies
Irish Independent
Irish Times
Freeman's Journal

Regional newspapers
Anglo-Celt
Armagh Standard
Belfast Evening Telegraph
Belfast News-Letter
Belfast Weekly Telegraph
Clare Champion
Connacht Tribune
Cork Constitution
Cork Examiner
Daily Dublin Chronicle
Daily Graphic
Donegal News
Drogheda Independent
Dundalk Democrat
Evening Star
Fermanagh Herald
Frontier Sentinel
Kerry News
Kilkenny Moderator
Kilkenny People
Killarney Echo
Leitrim Gazette/Advertiser
Leitrim Guardian
Limerick Leader
Longford Leader
Midland Reporter
Nationalist and Leinster Times
Nenagh Guardian
New Ireland Echo
Northern Whig
Reynolds's Newspaper
Roscommon Herald
Roscommon Journal
Saturday Record
Sligo Champion

South Kerry Chronicle
Southern Star
Strabane Chronicle
Ulster Gazette
Ulster Guardian
Ulster Herald
Waterford News
Westmeath Independent
Westmeath Nationalist

Special Interest
Advertising Age
Church of Ireland Gazette
Factionist
Irish School Weekly
Irishman
Nationality
Sinn Féin
Voice of Labour
Workers' Republic

Foreign (including Britain)
Irish World
Liberty Digest
London Gazette
Manchester Guardian
New York Times
Pall Mall Gazette
Punch
The Times
Westminster Gazette

CONTEMPORARY PUBLICATIONS, MEMOIRS, BOOKS, PAMPHLETS AND REPORTS

Béaslaí, Piaras, *Michael Collins and the making of a new Ireland*, vol. 1 (London, 1926).

Clarke, Kathleen, *Revolutionary woman: Kathleen Clarke, 1978–1972*, ed. H. Litton (Dublin, 1991).

Cowan, P.C., *Report on Dublin housing* (Dublin, 1918).

Devoy, John, *Recollections of an Irish rebel* (NY, 1929).

Dublin Housing Inquiry, *Report of inquiry into ed. the housing conditions of the working classes in the city of Dublin* (London, 1914).

Gallagher, Frank, *The four glorious years*, 2nd ed. (Dublin, 2005).

Griffith, Arthur, *The resurrection of Hungary: a parallel for Ireland* (Dublin, 2003).

Gwynn, Stephen, *John Redmond's last years* (London, 1919).

Healy, T.M., *Letters and leaders of my day*, vol. 1 (London, 1928).

Macready, Sir Nevil, *Annals of an active life*, vol. 2 (London, 1924).

McCartan, Patrick, *With de Valera in America* (Dublin, 1932).

McNeill, Ronald, *Ulster stands for union* (London, 1922).

Notes from Ireland – microfilm edition, Queen's University Library, Belfast, n.d., and Boston College, PRONI.

O'Connor, T.P., 'Review of the Parnell movement', *Dublin Journal*, 1:13 (Aug. 1887).

——, *Memoirs of an old parliamentarian*, vol. 2 (London, 1929).

O'Hegarty, P.S., *The victory of Sinn Féin* (Dublin, 1925).

Sinn Féin, *Leabhar na hÉireann: the Irish year book* (Dublin, 1910): National Library of Ireland, Ir 94109/i/8.

Thom's Directory 1915, 1920 and 1921.

SECONDARY SOURCES

Abbott, Richard, *Police casualties in Ireland, 1919–1922* (Cork, 2000).

Adelman, Paul, *Gladstone, Disraeli and later Victorian policies* (NY, 2014).

Akenson, Donald H., *The Irish education experiment: the national system of education in the nineteenth century* (Abingdon, 2012).

Alexander, Ralph S. (ed.), *Marketing definitions: a glossary of marketing terms* (Chicago, 1964).

Allister, James H., and Peter Robinson, *Sir Edward Carson, man of action* (Belfast, 1985).

Anderson, David, *Policing and decolonisation: politics, nationalism, and the police, 1917–65* (Manchester, 1992).

Augusteijn, Joost (ed.), *The Irish Revolution, 1913–1923* (Basingstoke, 2002).

Baines, Paul R., *Political marketing: theories and concepts* (London, 2011).

Barberis, Peter, John McHugh, Mike Tyldesley, *Encyclopaedia of British and Irish political organisations: parties, groups and movements of the 20th century* (London, 2000),

Bardon, Jonathan, *A history of Ulster* (Belfast, 1992).

Barnouw, Erik (ed.), *International encyclopaedia of communications*, vol. 3 (NY, 1989).

Bar-Tal, D., and E. Staub (eds), *Patriotism in the lives of individuals and nations* (Chicago, 1997).

Bartlett, Thomas, and Keith Jeffery (eds) *A military history of Ireland* (Cambridge, 1996).

Baumesiter, R.F., and M.R. Leary, 'The need to belong: desire for interpersonal attachments as a fundamental human motivation', *Psychological Bulletin*, 117 (1995), 497–529.

Beatty, Aidan, *Masculinity and power in Irish nationalism, 1884–1938* (Canada, 2016).

Bernays, Edward L., *Propaganda* (NY, 1928).

Bew, Paul, *Ideology and the Irish question: Ulster unionism and Irish nationalism, 1912–1916* (Oxford, 1994).

——, *Ireland: the politics of enmity, 1789–2006* (Oxford, 2007).

——, *John Redmond: life and times* (Dundalk, 1996).

Blake, Reed H., and Edwin O. Haroldsen, *A taxonomy of concepts in communication* (NY, 1975).

Borgonovo, John, *Dynamics of war and revolution* (Cork, 2013).

Breitenbach, Esther, and Pat Thane (eds), *Women and citizenship in Britain and Ireland in the twentieth century: what difference did the vote make?* (London, 2010).

Brennan, Robert, *Ireland standing firm: my wartime mission in Washington, and Eamon de Valera: a memoir*, ed. by Richard H. Rupp (Dublin, 2002).

Bromage, Mary C., *De Valera: the rebel gunman who became president of Ireland* (London, 1967).

Brown, Stephen J., *The press in Ireland: a survey and a guide* (NY, 1937; 1971).

Bruce, Steve, *God save Ulster* (Oxford, 1986).

Buckland, Patrick, *Ulster unionism and the origins of Northern Ireland, 1886 to 1922*, vol. 2 (Dublin, 1973).

Butler, Alban, *Butler's lives of the saints*, vol. 1, ed. by Herbert J. Thurston (Notre Dame, 1956).

Butler, D., *British political facts* (Basingstoke, 2011).

Butler, D.E., *The electoral system in Britain since 1918* (Oxford, 1963).

Butz, David A., 'National symbols as agents of psychological and social change', *Political Philosophy*, 30:5 (Oct. 2009), 779–804.

Byrne, John Francis, *Irish kings and high kings*, 2nd ed. (Dublin, 2001).

Cahill, Liam, *Forgotten revolution: Limerick Soviet 1919: a threat to British power in Ireland* (Dublin, 1990).

Callan Tansill, Charles, *America and the fight for Irish freedom, 1866–1922: an old story based on new data* (NY, 1957).

Callanan, Frank, *The Parnell split, 1890–91* (Syracuse, NY, 1992).

Callanan, Mark, and Justin F. Keogan (eds), *Local government in Ireland, inside out* (Dublin, 2003).

Carroll, F.M., *American opinion and the Irish question, 1910–1923: a study in opinion and policy* (Dublin, 1978).

——, 'De Valera and the Americans: the early years, 1916–1923', *Canadian Journal of Irish Studies*, 8:1 (June 1982).

——, *Money for Ireland: finance, diplomacy, politics, and the First Dáil Éireann loans, 1919–1936* (Westport, CT, 2002).

Carroll, Michael P., *American Catholics in the Protestant imagination: rethinking the academic study of religion* (Baltimore, MD, 2007).

Carty, R.K., 'Social cleavages and party systems: a reconsideration of the Irish case', *Journal of Political Research*, 4 (1976), 195–203.

——, *Party and parish pump: electoral politics in Ireland* (Waterloo, ON, 1981).

Chambers, Ciara, *Ireland in the Newsreels* (Dublin, 2012).

Chatterton Newman, Roger, *Brian Boru: king of Ireland* (Dublin, 1997).

Chubb, Basil, *The government and politics of Ireland*, 3rd ed. (London, 1992).

Clarke, Kathleen, *Revolutionary woman: Kathleen Clarke, 1978–1972*, ed. by H. Litton (Dublin, 1991).

Coakley, John, 'The significance of names: the evolution of Irish party labels', *Études Irlandaises*, 5 (1980), 171–81.

Coakley, John, and Michael Gallagher (eds), *Politics in the Republic of Ireland*, 3rd ed. and 5th ed. (London, 1999, 2010).

Coleman, Marie, *County Longford and the Irish Revolution, 1910–1923* (Newbridge, Co. Kildare, 2003).

Cook, Guy, *The discourse of advertising* (NY, 2001).

Cooper, Bryan, *The 10th (Irish) Division in Gallipoli* (Dublin, 1993).

Corish, Patrick J. (ed.), *Radicals, rebels and establishments* (Belfast, 1985).

Craig, F.W.S., *British electoral facts, 1832–1987* (Aldershot, 1989).

——, *British electoral facts, 1885–1975*, 3rd ed. (London, 1976).

Crossman, Virginia, *Healthcare in Ireland and Britain from 1850: voluntary, regional and comparative perspectives* (London, 2015).

——, *Local government in nineteenth-century Ireland* (Belfast, 1994).

Cruise O'Brien, Conor (ed.), *The shaping of modern Ireland* (London, 1960).

——, *Parnell and his party 1880–90* (Oxford, 1957).

Cull, Nicholas J., David Culbert and David Welch (eds), *Propaganda and mass persuasion: a historical encyclopaedia, 1500 to the present* (Santa Barbara, CA, 2003).

Cullen Owens, Rosemary, *Smashing times: a history of the Irish women's suffrage movement, 1889–1922* (Cork, 1984).

Cullen, L.M., 'Making news: the mass media in Britain', *Social Studies Review*, 6:1 (1900).

D.G. Pringle, 'Electoral systems and political manipulation: a case study of Northern Ireland in the 1920s', *Economic and Social Review*, 11:3 (Apr. 1980), 187–205.

Dahl, Henrik, *The pragmatics of persuasion* (Copenhagen, 1993).

Daly, M.E., *County and town: 100 years of local government in Ireland* (Dublin, 2001).

——., *Dublin, the deposed capital: a social and economic history* (Cork, 1985).

Daly, M.E., and K. Theodore Hoppen (eds), *Gladstone, Ireland and beyond* (Dublin, 2011).

Daly, Paul, Rónán O'Brien and Paul Rouse, *Making the difference? The Irish Labour Party, 1912–2012* (Cork, 2012).

Davies, P.G., C.M. Steele and H.R. Markus, 'A nation challenged: the impact of foreign threat on America's tolerance for diversity', *Journal of Personality and Social Psychology*, 95 (2008), 308–18.

Dawson, Michael, 'Twentieth-century England: the case of the south-west', *Twentieth-Century British History*, 9:2 (1998), 201–18.

de Bromhead, Alan, Alan Fernihough and Enda Hargaden, 'The Sinn Féin election in Ireland, 1918', working paper 2018-08, Queen's University Centre for Economic History, June 2018 at http://www.quceh.org.uk/uploads/1/0/5/5/10558478/wp18-08.pdf.

Dill Scott, Walter, *The psychology of advertising* (Boston, 1908).

——, *The theory of advertising* (Boston, 1903).

Doherty, Erica, '"The party hack, and tool of the British government": T.P. O'Connor, America and Irish Party resilience at the February 1918 South Armagh by-election', *Parliamentary History*, 34:3 (2015), 339–64.

Dolan, Anne, *Commemorating the Irish Civil War: history and memory, 1923–2000* (Cambridge, 2006).

Dooley, Thomas P., *Irishmen or English soldiers? The times and world of a southern Catholic Irish man, 1876–1916: enlisting in the British army during the First World War* (Liverpool, 1995).

Doorley, Michael, *Irish-American diaspora nationalism: the Friends of Irish Freedom, 1916–1935* (Dublin, 2005).

Duggan, Anne E., Donald Haase and Helen Callow (eds), *Folktales and fairy tales, traditions and texts from around the world*, 2nd ed. (Westport, CT, 2016).

Eighmey, J., and S. Sar, 'Harlow Gale and the origins of the psychology of advertising', *Journal of Advertising*, 36:4 (2007), 147–58.

Ellis, John S., 'The degenerate and the martyr: nationalist propaganda and the contestation of Irishness, 1914–1918', *Éire-Ireland*, 25 (2000–1).

Ellul, Jacques, *Propaganda: the formation of men's attitudes* (NY, 1968).

Evans, Eric J., *Parliamentary reform in Britain, c.1770–1918* (London, 2013).

Evans, M., and K. Lunn (eds), *War and memory in the twentieth century* (Oxford, 1997).

Ewing, Keith, and Samuel Issacharoff (eds), *Party funding and campaign financing in international perspective* (Oxford, 2006).

Fairclough, Norman, *Language and power* (Harlow, 2001).

Fancher, R.E., *Pioneers of psychology*, 2nd ed. (NY, 1990).

Fanning, John, 'Irish advertising – Bhfuil Sé or Won't Sé', *Irish Marketing Review*, 16:2 (2003), 3–13.

Fanning, Ronan, *Fatal path: British government and Irish Revolution, 1910–1922* (London, 2013).

Farr, Martin, 'Waging democracy: the British general election of 1918 reconsidered', *Cercles*, 21 (2011), 65–94.

Farrell, Brian (ed.), *The creation of the Dáil* (Dublin, 1994).

——, 'Labour and the Irish political party system: a suggested approach to analysis', *Economic and Social Review*, 1:4 (1997), 477–92.

——, *Communications and community in Ireland* (Dublin, 1984).

——, *The founding of Dáil Éireann: parliament and nation-building* (Dublin, 1973).

Farrell, David M., *Electoral systems: a comparative introduction*, 2nd ed. (Hampshire, 2011).

Feingold, Mordechai, *History of universities*, vol. 23/1 (Oxford, 2008).

Ferriter, Diarmaid, *A nation and not a rabble: the Irish Revolution, 1913–23* (London, 2015).

——, *Judging Dev: a reassessment of the life and legacy of Eamon de Valera* (Dublin, 2007).

——, *The transformation of Ireland, 1900–2000* (London, 2004).

Finnan, Joseph P., 'Punch's portrayal of Redmond, Carson and the Irish question, 1910–1918', *Irish Historical Studies*, 33:132 (2003), pp 424–51.

——, *John Redmond and Irish unity, 1912–1918* (Syracuse, 2004).

Firth, R., *Symbols: public and private* (NY, 1973).

Fitzpatrick, David, 'The disappearance of the Irish agricultural labourer, 1883–1916', *Irish Economic and Social History*, 7 (1980).

——, *Descendancy: Irish Protestant histories since 1795* (Cambridge, 2014).

——, *Harry Boland's Irish Revolution* (Cork, 2003).

——, *Ireland and the First World War* (Dublin, 1986).

——, *Oceans of consolation: personal accounts of Irish migration to Australia* (NY, 1994).

——, *Politics and Irish life, 1913–1921: provincial experience of war and revolution* (Cork, 1998).

——, *The two Irelands 1912–1939* (Oxford, 1998).

Follis, Brian, *A state under siege: the establishment of Northern Ireland, 1920–1925* (Oxford, 1995).

Foster, Roy, *Modern Ireland, 1600–1972* (London, 1989).

Foy, Michael, 'Ulster unionist propaganda against home rule, 1912–14', *History Ireland*, 4:1 (Spring 1996), 49–53.

Freud, Sigmund, *Group psychology and the analysis of the ego* (London, 1959).

Friedman, W.A., *Birth of a salesman: the transformation of selling America* (Cambridge, 2004).

Gailey, Andrew, 'King Carson: an essay on the invention of leadership', *Irish Historical Studies*, 30:117 (May 1996).

Gallagher, Michael and Michael Marsh, *How Ireland voted in 2011: the full story of Ireland's earthquake election* (Basingstoke, 2011).

Gallagher, Michael, *Electoral support for Irish political parties* (London, 1976).

——, 'The pact general election of 1922', *Irish Historical Studies*, 22:84 (Sept. 1979), 404–21.

——, *Irish elections 1922–44: results and analysis* (Limerick, 1993).

——, *Political parties in the Republic of Ireland* (Dublin, 1985).

——, *The Irish Labour Party in transition, 1957–82* (Manchester, 1982).

——, 'Candidate selection in Ireland: the impact of localism and the electoral system', *British Journal of Political Science*, 10:4 (1980), 489–503.

Gallagher, Michael, and Paul Mitchell (eds), *The politics of electoral systems* (Oxford, 2008).

Galligan, Yvonne, Eilís Ward and Rick Wilford, *Contesting politics: women in Ireland, north and south* (Boulder, CO, 1999).

Garvin, Tom, 'Nationalist elites, Irish voters and Irish political development: a comparative perspective', *Economic and Social Review*, 8:3 (1977).

——, *The evolution of Irish nationalist politics* (Dublin, 2005).

Glandon, Virginia, *Arthur Griffith and the advanced nationalist press, 1900–1922* (NY, 1985).

Greaves, C.D., *The Irish Transport and General Workers' Union: the formative years, 1909–1923* (Dublin, 1982).

Gwynn, Denis R., *De Valera* (London, 1933).

——, *The history of partition* (Dublin, 1950).

Hamond, J.L., *Gladstone and the Irish nation* (London, 1928).

Harbinson, John F., *The Ulster Unionist Party, 1882–1973* (Belfast, 1973).

Hart, Peter, *Mick: the real Michael Collins* (London, 2005).

——, *The IRA at war, 1916–23* (Oxford, 2005).

——, *British intelligence in Ireland, 1920–21* (Cork, 2002).

Hayes McCoy, G.A., *A history of Irish flags from earliest times* (Dublin, 1979).

Hennessy, Thomas, *A history of Northern Ireland, 1920–1996* (Dublin, 1997).

——, *Dividing Ireland: World War I and partition* (London, 1998).

Hepburn, Anthony C., *A past apart: studies in the history of Catholic Belfast, 1850–1950* (Belfast, 1996).

——, *The conflict of nationality in modern Ireland: documents of modern history* (London, 1980).

Hill, Myrtle, *Women in Ireland: a century of change* (Belfast, 2003).

Holmes Janice, and Diane Urquhart (eds), *Coming into the light: the work, politics and religion of women in Ulster, 1840–1940* (Belfast, 1994).

Hopkinson, Michael, *The Irish War of Independence* (Dublin, 2004).

Hoppen, K. Theodore, *Elections, politics and society in Ireland, 1832–1885* (Oxford, 1984).

——, *Ireland since 1800: conflict and conformity* (London, 1989)

Hora, Kevin, *Propaganda and nation building: selling the Irish Free State* (London, 2017).

Horne, John (ed.), *Our war: Ireland and the Great War* (Dublin, 2008).

Horne, John, and Alan Kramer, *German atrocities, 1914: a history of denial* (New Haven, CT, 2001).

Horne, John, and Edward Madigan (eds), *Towards commemoration: Ireland in war and revolution, 1912–1923* (Dublin, 2013).

Hutchinson, John, *The dynamics of cultural nationalism: the Gaelic Revival and the creation of the Irish nation state* (London, 1987).

Inoue, Keiko, 'Propaganda of Dáil Éireann: from truce to treaty', *Éire-Ireland*, 32:2–3 (1997).

——, 'Sinn Féin propaganda and the "partition election", 1921', *Studia Hibernica*, 30 (1989–99).

Jackson, Alvin, 'Unionist politics and Protestant society in Edwardian Ireland, *Historical Journal*, 33:4 (Dec. 1990), 839–66.

——, *Ireland 1798–1998: war, peace and beyond* (Oxford, 1999).

——, *Sir Edward Carson* (Dublin, 1993).

——, *The Ulster party: Irish unionists in the house of commons, 1884–1911* (Oxford, 1989).

——, *Home rule: an Irish history, 1800–2000* (Oxford, 2003).

Jeffery, Keith, *Ireland and the Great War* (Cambridge, 2000).

Jowett, Garth S., and Victoria O'Donnell, *Propaganda and persuasion*, 5th edn (LA, 2012).

Keith, William M., and Christian O. Lundberg, *The essential guide to rhetoric* (Boston, 2008).

Kenneally, Ian, *The paper wall: newspapers and propaganda in Ireland, 1919–1921* (Cork, 2008).

Kennedy, Dennis, *The widening gulf: northern attitudes to the independent Irish state, 1919–1949* (Belfast, 1988).

Kennedy, Thomas C., 'War, patriotism and the Ulster Unionist Council, 1914–1918', *Éire-Ireland*, 40:3 (Fall/Winter 2005), 189–211.

Kenny, Kevin, *The American Irish: a history* (Abingdon, 2000).

Killen, John, *John Bull's famous circus: Ulster history through the postcard, 1905–1985* (Dublin, 1985).

Kinghan, Nancy, *United we stood: the official history of the Ulster Women's Unionist Council, 1911–1974* (Belfast, 1975).

Kissane, Bill, *Explaining Irish democracy* (Dublin, 2002).

Kotler, Philip, Gary Armstrong, John Saunders and Veronica Wong, *Principles of marketing* (London, 2002).

Laffan, Michael, 'The unification of Sinn Féin in 1917', *Irish Historical Studies*, 17:67 (Mar. 1971), 353–79.

——, *The resurrection of Ireland: the Sinn Féin Party, 1916–1923* (Cambridge, 2005).

Lalor, Brian (ed.), *The encyclopaedia of Ireland* (Dublin, 2003).

Lane, Fintan, and Donal Ó Drisceoil (eds), *Politics and the Irish working class, 1830–1945* (Basingstoke, 2005).

Lane, Fintan, *Essays in Irish labour history* (Dublin, 2008).

Lang, Andrew, *The Princess Nobody: a tale of Fairyland* (London, 1884).

Lasswell, Harold D., *Propaganda technique in the World War* (NY, 1938).

Laver, Michael, 'A new electoral system for Ireland?', *Studies in Public Policy*, 2: The Policy Institute, TCD (1998).

le Bon, Gustave, *The crowd: a study of the popular mind* (London, 1896).

Lee, J.J., and Marion R. Casey (eds), *Making the Irish American: history and heritage of the Irish in the United States* (NY, 2006).

Lee, J.J., *Ireland, 1912–1986* (Cambridge, 1989).

——, *The modernisation of Irish society, 1848–1918* (Dublin, 2008).

Legg, Marie-Louise, *Newspapers and nationalism: the Irish provincial press, 1850–1892* (Dublin, 1999).

Lipset, S.M., and S. Rokkan, *Party systems and voter alignments* (NY, 1967).

Liu, J.H., and D.J. Hilton, 'How the past weighs on the present: social representations of history and their impact on identity politics', *British Journal of Social Psychology*, 44:1 (Dec. 2005), 537–6.

Lock, A., and P. Harris, 'Machiavellian network marketing: corporate political lobby and industrial marketing in the UK', *Journal of Marketing Management*, 12:4 (1996), 313–28.

Loftus, Belinda, *Mirrors: orange and green* (Dundrum, Co. Down, 1994).

Lucey, Donnacha Seán, and Virginia Crossman, *Healthcare in Ireland and Britain from 1850: voluntary, regional and comparative perspectives* (London, 2015).

Lynch, Robert, 'The people's protectors? The Irish Republican Army and the "Belfast Pogrom", 1920–1922', *Journal of British Studies*, 47:2 (Apr. 2008), 375–91.

Lyons, F.S.L., 'The Irish Unionist Party and the devolution crisis', *Irish Historical Studies*, 6:21 (1948), 1–22.

——, 'The machinery of the Irish Parliamentary Party in the general election of 1895', *Irish Historical Studies*, 8:30 (Sept. 1952), 115–39.

——, *Ireland since the Famine* (London, 1973).

——, *John Dillon: a biography* (London, 1968).

——, *The Irish Parliamentary Party, 1890–1910* (Westport, CT, 1975).

Macardle, Dorothy, *The Irish Republic: a documented chronicle of the Anglo-Irish conflict and the partitioning of Ireland, with a detailed account of the period 1915–1923* (London, 1937; NY, 1968).

MacDonagh, Michael, *The life of William O'Brien, the Irish nationalist* (London, 1928).

Macnicol, John, *The politics of retirement in Britain, 1908–1948* (Cambridge, 1998).

Mair, Peter, 'The autonomy of the political: the development of the Irish party system', *Comparative Politics*, 11 (1979), 445–65.

Mair, Robert Henry (ed.), *Debrett's house of commons and the judicial bench* (London, 1886).

Manning, Maurice, *James Dillon: a biography* (Dublin, 1999).

Marsh, Michael, 'Localism, candidate selection and electoral preferences in Ireland: the general election of 1977', *Economic and Social Review*, 12:4 (1981), 267–86.

Martin, F.X., *The Irish Volunteers, 1913–1915: recollections and documents* (Newbridge, Co. Kildare, 1963).

Martin, Micheál, *Freedom to choose: Cork and party politics in Ireland, 1918–1932* (Cork, 2009).

Maume, Patrick, *The long gestation: Irish nationalist life, 1891–1918* (Dublin, 1999).

McCarthy, Cal, *Cumann na mBan and the Irish Revolution* (Cork, 2007).

McClintock, A., *Imperial leather: race, gender and sexuality in the colonial contest* (NY, 1994).

McConnel, James, *The Irish Parliamentary Party and the third home rule crisis* (Dublin, 2013).

McGarry, Fearghal, *The rising, Ireland: Easter 1916* (Oxford, 2010).

McGough, Eileen, *Diarmuid Lynch: a forgotten Irish patriot* (Cork, 2013).

McGuire, James, and James Quinn (eds), *Dictionary of Irish biography* (Cambridge, 2009).

Messinger, Gary S., *British propaganda and the state in the First World War* (Manchester, 1992).

Miller, David W., *Church, state and nation in Ireland, 1898–1921* (Pittsburgh, PA, 1973).

Miller, Kerby A., 'Emigrants and exiles: Irish cultures and Irish emigration to North America, 1790–1922', *Irish Historical Studies*, 22:86 (Sept. 1980), 97–125.

——, *Emigrants and exiles: Ireland and the Irish exodus to North America* (Oxford, 1988).

Mitchell, Arthur, *Labour in Irish politics* (Dublin, 1973).

——, *Revolutionary government in Ireland: Dáil Éireann 1919–22* (Dublin, 1995).

Moloney, Tadhg, *Limerick constitutional nationalism, 1898–1918: change and continuity* (Cambridge, 2010).

Montgomery Hyde, H., *Carson* (London, 1987).

Morash, Christopher, *A history of the media in Ireland* (Cambridge, 2010).

Morris, Ewan, '"God save the king" versus "The soldier's song": the 1929 Trinity College national anthem dispute and the politics of the Irish Free State', *Irish Historical Studies*, 31:121 (May 1998), 72–90.

——, *Our own devices: national symbols and political conflict in twentieth-century Ireland* (Dublin, 2005).

Morton, Grenfell, *Home rule and the Irish question*, ed. Patrick Richardson (London, 2014).

Moss, Warner, *Political parties in the Irish Free State* (NY, 1933).

Mullholland, Marie, *The politics and relationships of Kathleen Lynn* (Dublin, 2002).

Mulvagh, Conor, *The Irish Parliamentary Party at Westminster, 1900–1918* (Manchester, 2016).

Murphy, William, *Political imprisonment and the Irish, 1912–1921* (Oxford, 2014).

Nelson, E. Charles, *Shamrock: botany and history of an Irish myth* (Kilkenny, 1991).

Neustadt, R., *Presidential power: the politics of leadership* (NY, 1962).

Nevin, Donal (ed.), *Trade union century* (Dublin, 1994).

Newton, K., 'Making news: the mass media in Britain', *Social Studies Review*, 6:1 (1990).

Neystrom, Paul H., *Retail selling and store management* (London, 1914).

NicDháibhéid, Caoimhe, and Colin Reid (eds), *From Parnell to Paisley: constitutional and revolutionary politics in modern Ireland* (Dublin, 2010).

Nolan, William, and Thomas Power (eds), *Waterford: history and society* (Dublin, 1992).

Novick, Ben, 'DORA, suppression, and nationalist propaganda in Ireland, 1914–1915', *New Hibernia Review/Iris Éireannach Nua*, 1:4 (Winter 1997), 41–57.

——, *Conceiving revolution: Irish nationalist propaganda during the First World War* (Dublin, 2001).

Noyes, John E., 'William Howard Taft and the Taft arbitration treaties', *Villanova Law Review*, 56 (2011).

Nye, R.A., *The origins of crowd psychology* (London, 1975).

O'Brien, Joseph V., *William O'Brien and the course of Irish politics, 1881–1918* (Berkeley, CA, 1976).

O'Brien, Mark, and Donnacha Ó Beacháin (eds), *Political communication in the Republic of Ireland* (Liverpool, 2014).

O'Brien, William, *Forth the banners go* (Dublin, 1969).

Ó Broin, Eoin, *Sinn Féin and the politics of left republicanism* (London, 2009).

O'Carroll, J.P., and John Murphy (eds), *De Valera and his times* (Cork, 1986).

Ó Ciosáin, Niall, *Print and popular culture in Ireland, 1750–1850* (Dublin, 2010).

O'Connor Lysaght, D.R., 'Plunkett, George Noble, Count Plunkett in the papal nobility (1851–1948), *Oxford dictionary of national biography* (Oxford, 2004).

O'Connor, Emmet, *Derry labour in the age of agitation, 1889–1923*, ii: *Larkinism and syndicalism, 1907–23* (Dublin, 2016).

——, *A labour history of Ireland, 1824–2000* (Dublin, 2011).

——, *Reds and greens* (Dublin, 2004).

O'Connor, John Philip, 'For a colleen's complexion': soap and the politicization of a brand personality, 1888–1916', *Journal of Historical Research in Marketing*, 6:1 (2014), 29–55.

Ó Corráin, Donnchadh, *Ireland before the Normans* (Dublin, 1972).

O'Day, Alan, *Irish home rule, 1867–1921* (Manchester, 1998).

——, *Reactions to Irish nationalism, 1865–1914* (London, 1987).

——, *The English face of Irish nationalism: Parnellite involvement in British politics, 1880–86* (Dublin, 1979).

O'Doherty, Katherine, *Assignment America: de Valera's mission to the United States* (NY, 1957).

O'Donnell, James D., *How Ireland is governed* (Dublin, 1965).

O'Donovan, John, *Members and messengers: Carlow's 20th century parliamentarians* (Carlow, 2003).

O'Leary, Cornelius, *Irish elections, 1918–1977* (Dublin, 1979).

Oram, Hugh, *The newspaper book: a history of newspapers in Ireland, 1649–1983* (Dublin, 1983).

——, *The advertising book: the history of advertising in Ireland* (Dublin, 1986).

Parkinson, Alan F., *Friends in high places: Ulster's resistance to Irish home rule, 1912–14* (Belfast, 2012).

Pašeta, Senia, *Irish nationalist women, 1900–1918* (Cambridge, 2013).

Patton, E. (ed.), *Returning to ourselves* (Belfast, 1995).

Peel, George, *The reign of Sir Edward Carson* (London, 1914).

Phoenix, Eamon, *Northern nationalism: nationalist politics, partition and the Catholic minority in Northern Ireland, 1890–1940* (Belfast, 1994).

Pringle, D.G., 'Electoral systems and political manipulation: a case study of Northern Ireland in the 1920s', *Economic and Social Review*, 11:3 (Apr. 1980), 187–205.

Prunty, Jacinta, *Dublin slums, 1800–1925: a study in urban geography* (Dublin, 1998).

Purséil, Niamh, *The Irish Labour Party, 1922–73* (Dublin, 2007).

Reicher, S.D., and N. Hopkins, *Self and nation* (London, 2001).

Reid, D.M., 'Marketing the political product', *European Journal of Marketing*, 22:9 (1988), 34–47.

Roche, Desmond, *Local government in Ireland* (Dublin, 1982).

Rockett, Kevin, Luke Gibbons and John Hill, *Cinema and Ireland* (Syracuse, 1988).

Sartori, Giovanni, *Parties and party systems: a framework for analysis*, vol. 1 (Cambridge 1976).

Savage, Robert (ed.), *Ireland and the new century: politics and culture* (Dublin, 2003).

Schultz, D.P., and S.E. Schultz, *A history of modern psychology*, 9th ed. (Belmont, CA, 2008).

Seidman, Steven A., *Posters, propaganda and persuasion in election campaigns around the world and through history* (NY, 2008).

Shannon, Richard, 'Peel, Gladstone and party', *Parliamentary History*, 18:3 (1999), 317–52.

Sherry, Ruth, 'The story of the national anthem', *History Ireland*, 4:1 (Spring 1996), 39–43.

Sinnott, Richard, *Irish voters decide: voting behaviour in elections and referendums since 1918* (Manchester, 1995).

Stewart, A.T.Q., *The Ulster crisis: resistance to home rule, 1912–14* (London, 1967).

Strachan, J., and C. Nally, *Advertising, literature and print culture in Ireland, 1891–1922* (Basingstoke, 2012).

Taylor, P.M., *Munitions of the mind: war propaganda from the ancient world to the nuclear age* (Manchester, 1990).

Thuronyi, Victor, *Comparative tax law* (The Hague, 2003).

Townshend, Charles, *Easter 1916: the Irish rebellion* (London, 2005).

——, *The republic: the fight for Irish independence* (London, 2013).

Travers, Pauric, 'Reading between the lines: the political speeches of Charles Stewart Parnell', *Studia Hibernica*, 31 (2000/1), 243–56.

Urquhart, Diane, *The ladies of Londonderry: women and political patronage* (London, 2007).

——, *The minutes of the Ulster Women's Unionist Council and executive committee, 1911–40* (Dublin, 2001).

——, *Women in Ulster politics, 1890–1940* (Newbridge, Co. Kildare, 2000).

Van Ginneken, Jaap, *Crowds, psychology and politics 1871–1899* (NY, 1992).

Vaughan, W.E. (ed.), *A new history of Ireland: Ireland under the union 1870–1921* (Oxford, 1976; 1989).

Vaughan, W.E., and A.J. Fitzpatrick, *Irish historical statistics* (Dublin, 1978).

Walker, Brian, '"The lost tribes of Ireland": diversity, identity and loss among the Irish diaspora', *Irish Studies Review*, 15:3 (2007), 267–82.

——, *Irish parliamentary election results, 1800–1922* (Dublin, 1978).

——, *Parliamentary election results in Ireland, 1918–92* (Dublin, 1992).

——, *Ulster politics: the formative years, 1868–86* (Belfast, 1988).

Walker, Graham, *A history of the Ulster Unionist Party: protest, pragmatism and pessimism* (Manchester, 2004).

——, *Notes from Ireland* (1888–1938), Queen's University Library, Belfast, n.d.

Walsh, Maurice, *The news from Ireland: foreign correspondents and the Irish Revolution* (NY, 2001).

Ward, Alan J., 'America and the Irish problem, 1899–1921', *Irish Historical Studies*, 16:61 (Mar. 1968), 64–90.

——, 'Lloyd George and the 1918 Irish conscription crisis', *Historical Journal*, 17:1 (1974), 107–29.

——, *Ireland and Anglo-American relations 1899–1921* (London, 1969).

Ward, Margaret, *Hanna Sheehy Skeffington* (Cork, 1997).

——, *In their own voice: women and Irish nationalism* (Cork, 1995).

——, *Unmanageable revolutionaries: women and Irish nationalism* (London, 1983; 1995).

Ward, Rachel, *Women unionism and loyalism in Northern Ireland: from 'tea makers' to political actors* (Dublin, 2006).

Welch, David, *Germany, propaganda and total war, 1914–1918: the sins of omission* (London, 2000).

Wheatley, Michael, 'John Redmond and federalism in 1910', *Irish Historical Studies*, 32:127 (May 2001), 343–64.

——, *Nationalism and the Irish Party: provincial Ireland, 1910–1916* (Oxford, 2005).

Williams, J.D., W.N. Lee and C.P. Haugtvedt, *Diversity in advertising: broadening the scope of research directions* (Mahwah, NJ, 2004), 22–39.

Willner, Ann Ruth, *The spellbinders: charismatic political leadership* (London, 1984).

Zikmund II, Joseph, 'National anthems as political symbols', *Australian Journal of Politics and History*, 15:3 (1969), 73–4.

THESIS

Callinan, Elaine, 'Discourse and discord: the rhetoric and rationale of John Redmond in the pursuit of home rule for Ireland, 1910–1914 (TCD, MPhil, 2011).

Walker, Brian, 'Parliamentary representation in Ulster, 1868–86' (PhD, TCD, 1976).

Walsh, Fionnuala, 'The impact of the Great War on women in Ireland 1914 to 1919' (PhD, TCD, 2017).

Index

Numbers in bold refer to illustrations.